The Yankees
in the Early 1960s

The Yankees in the Early 1960s

WILLIAM J. RYCZEK

McFarland & Company, Inc., Publishers
Jefferson, North Carolina, and London

All photographs provided by the National Baseball
Hall of Fame Library, Cooperstown, New York

LIBRARY OF CONGRESS CATALOGUING-IN-PUBLICATION DATA

Ryczek, William J., 1953–
The Yankees in the early 1960s / William J. Ryczek.
p.   cm.
Includes bibliographical references and index.

ISBN-13: 978-0-7864-2996-7
softcover : 50# alkaline paper ∞

1. New York Yankees (Baseball team)—History—20th century.
I. Title.
GV875.N4R93   2008   796.357'64097471—dc22   2007027717

British Library cataloguing data are available

Cover photograph: Mel Stottlemyre, Yankee pitcher from 1964 to 1974

Manufactured in the United States of America

McFarland & Company, Inc., Publishers
Box 611, Jefferson, North Carolina 28640
www.mcfarlandpub.com

For my mother, Katherine Ryczek,
from whom I acquired
a love of reading and writing

Acknowledgments

First and foremost, I owe a huge debt to those who graciously agreed to be interviewed for this book. They include:

Craig Anderson
Ray Barker
Rich Beck
Dennis Bennett
John Blanchard
Gil Blanco
Len Boehmer
Don Bosch
Ed Bressoud
Hector Brown
Bill Bryan
Bill Burbach
Larry Burright
Don Cardwell
Duke Carmel
Joe Christopher
Galen Cisco
Tex Clevenger
Jim Coates
Billy Cowan
Jack Cullen
Bud Daley
Joe DeMaestri
John DeMerit
Bill Denehy
Jack DiLauro
Ryne Duren

Doc Edwards
Dave Eilers
John Ellis
Chuck Estrada
Jack Fisher
Bob Friend
Rob Gardner
Jake Gibbs
Joe Ginsberg
Jim Gosger
Eli Grba
Joe Grzenda
Kent Hadley
Bob Heise
Bob Hendley
Bill Hepler
Rick Herrscher
Jim Hickman
Joe Hicks
Chuck Hiller
Dave Hillman
Al Jackson
Johnny James
Ken Johnson
Bob Johnson
Fred Kipp
Bobby Klaus

Lou Klimchock
Gary Kroll
Clem Labine
Jack Lamabe
Phil Linz
Ron Locke
Hector Lopez
Al Luplow
Jim Lyttle
Felix Mantilla
J.C. Martin
Jim McAndrew
Lindy McDaniel
Danny McDevitt
Gil McDougald
Tom Metcalf
Bob Meyer
Pete Mikkelsen
John Miller
Larry Miller
Herb Moford
Bill Monbouquette
Archie Moore
Al Moran
Dennis Musgraves
Don Nottebart
Nate Oliver

Jim Pisoni
Jack Reed
Roger Repoz
Dennis Ribant
Gordon Richardson
Don Rowe
Dick Schofield
Ted Schreiber
Rollie Sheldon
Norm Sherry
Tom Shopay
Billy Short
Bobby Gene Smith
Tracy Stallard
Hal Stowe
John Sullivan
Hawk Taylor
Ron Taylor
Ralph Terry
Frank Thomas
Lee Thomas
Tom Tresh
Bill Wakefield
Steve Whitaker
Gordon White
Nick Willhite
Dooley Womack

I was amazed at my subjects' detailed recall of events that happened forty or more years ago, and thankful that they were kind enough to share them with me. In particular, I would like to thank Ralph Terry for relating his experiences in the 1960 and 1962 World Series; Phil

Linz, who was as lively, friendly and funny as he was in 1964; Steve Whitaker and Roger Repoz, who, after the many years that have passed, have some very interesting insights about having been expected to follow in the footsteps of Mickey Mantle; Johnny Blanchard and Rollie Sheldon, who shared the story of their exploits with the 1961 World Series champs; and Jack Reed, a bright, pleasant man, who, during a career of playing second fiddle, became the maestro one night in Detroit.

Others who provided particularly detailed and interesting interviews were Johnny James, Ryne Duren, Ray Barker, Dooley Womack, Tom Metcalf, Bob Meyer, and Tom Tresh. Womack's South Carolina humor and charm, his admiration for Mickey Mantle and his humility made him an entertaining as well as informative subject.

Gordon White, a New York sportswriter for many years, helped me immeasurably on my history of the New York Titans football team, and was again a terrific source of information. Many former players described Ralph Houk's personality and management style, but it was White who provided the definitive portrait of the Major's tobacco chewing exploits.

I spent a great deal of time looking through old newspapers and magazines, and I want to thank the research staffs of the Wallingford Public Library, the New York Public Library and the Central Connecticut State University Library, particularly an anonymous faculty member at the latter institution who smuggled me in to use the faculty copier when the public one had broken down.

With any project that involves years of work and little financial reward, some encouragement is needed along the way. I want to thank my fellow members of the Society for American Baseball Research, particularly Steve Krevisky, possibly the most knowledgeable Yankee fan on the planet, for always asking how the book was coming along, and urging me to finish. Another SABR author, Kerry Keene, provided a quote on the final game of the 1960 World Series.

My wife, Susan, was once again extremely helpful with her knowledge of grammar and, particularly, many obscure nuances of punctuation.

Finally, I want to thank my friend Fred Dauch, who read the entire manuscript, provided some very helpful advice on structure and greatly influenced the final form of the book.

Table of Contents

Introduction

This project began as a book to be called *Rags to Riches and Riches to Rags*, a story about the Yankees and Mets in the 1960s, a decade during which the Yankees went from World Champions to last place and the Mets from the basement to World Champions. Extensive research of periodicals and interviews with more than 140 former players produced a story that was illuminating, informative, and roughly twice the length of *War and Peace*. My publisher and I decided to divide the work into one book about the Yankees through 1966, and one on the Mets through 1969, with about 50,000 words left over for an undetermined future project.

What follows is the first volume: the story of the Yankees' triumphs from 1960 through 1964, and their subsequent descent into the basement in just two painful years. From 1921 through 1959, when the Yankees dominated baseball, three men, Miller Huggins, Joe McCarthy and Casey Stengel, held the managerial reins for 36 of the 39 years. During the next seven years, the Yanks had four different managers. Stengel won a pennant and was fired. Ralph Houk won three pennants and two World Series but wasn't a crowd pleaser. Yogi Berra won a pennant and was fired. Poor Johnny Keane didn't win anything at all.

The aura of invincibility that surrounded the Yankees for so many glorious seasons died hard, and the Yankee players and management, particularly Houk, refused to believe that the club had fallen so far and so fast. Surely, they insisted, another pennant was in store when the injured Yankee stalwarts returned to form.

By 1966, however, the Yankee stars of 1960 had retired, been traded, or fallen victim to injury, and there was no one in the wings to take their places. Fans who followed the Yankees when they were winning stopped coming to Yankee Stadium. Meanwhile, the Mets, who were losing even more games than the Yankees, were setting attendance records at Shea Stadium.

Given the number of New York baseball fans who grew up in the 1960s, writing about the Yankees seemed a natural. Yet, how could one write an original work about a team whose exploits have been more publicized than perhaps any sports franchise in the history of athletics? The humor of Yogi Berra and Casey Stengel, the home run heroics of Mickey Mantle and Roger Maris, and the exploits of Whitey Ford have been described by authors far more talented than I.

Fortunately, there is much more to the Yankee story. There were players like Ralph Terry, a sensitive, intelligent young pitcher who opened the decade by surrendering the fateful home run to Bill Mazeroski in the seventh game of the 1960 World Series, then came back to beat the Giants 1–0 in the final game of the 1962 Series. There were "the Bootstrappers," Luis Arroyo, Rollie Sheldon and Johnny Blanchard, who for one magical season in 1961, in the shadow of Mantle and Maris, performed feats they had never performed before and would never duplicate

1

again. There were promising youngsters like Roger Repoz and the superbly talented but tragically high-strung Steve Whitaker, whose careers were sidetracked by the high expectation of becoming the next Mickey Mantle. There were historic October games, and the recollections of many of the key players in those encounters combine to paint a fascinating and intricate picture of the final contests of the 1960 and 1962 World Series.

I interviewed a number of players who haven't been quoted in other works. Even those who had limited time in the big leagues had compelling tales about their experiences in professional baseball. They were witness to historic events, and many had insights into star players that added immensely to the story.

A few players declined to be interviewed. Bobby Shantz dropped me a note wishing me luck, but said he really didn't like talking about 1960, when he was on the losing end of a gut-wrenching World Series. "I'm living in the present," said another former Yankee reliever who shall remain unnamed, "and I'm sick of talking about the past." A few weeks later, an advertisement appeared in my local newspaper for an autograph show featuring several former Yankees and Mets. Prominently displayed was the name of the former pitcher, miraculously cured of his distaste for recalling the past. For the most part, however, interviewing players I'd idolized as a boy was a wonderful experience, an opportunity to add flesh and blood to heroic bones.

I hope these stories rekindle happy memories for old New York baseball fans. With its 162 game season, baseball is an entertainment to be absorbed in bits and pieces. Football games are tense, sixty minute dramas that command undivided attention. Much of our baseball spectating, however, is done in combination with other events in our lives—a few innings on the car radio listening to the banter of Phil Rizzuto and Joe Garagiola, or half-consciously hearing the voice of Red Barber as we drift off to sleep listening to the Yankees play the Angels on the coast. People of my generation remember where they were when President Kennedy was assassinated. In that same generation, most baseball fans remember where they were when Willie McCovey lined out to Bobby Richardson to end the 1962 Series. This book is for serious fans who remember much more. The mention of the name Tom Tresh, Jake Gibbs or Jack Reed may conjure up a memory of a Labor Day picnic with the family or a summer drive with a girlfriend. I hope this book evokes many such thoughts and that you experience half the pleasure reading it that I have gotten from writing it.

• 1 •

The World
Turned Upside Down

The fall of the Yankees during the 1960s is perhaps best illustrated by two quotes from the *New York Times*, ten years apart. While covering the Yankee contingent in the Florida Instructional League, veteran beat writer John Drebinger reported on November 22, 1959: "[T]he Yanks' chief interest is a young outfielder, Joe Pepitone, who hails from Brooklyn. Only 19, Joe, a left handed swinger, hit .285 with Fargo the past season and is looked upon as a very fine prospect."

Two years earlier, Pepitone had been a very big question mark. Joe grew up in the Park Slope section of Brooklyn in what would now be called a dysfunctional family, headed by a strong father who would now be called a violent psychopath. Willie Pepitone was a construction worker who beat up anyone who crossed him, beat up anyone he thought had crossed him, and repeatedly beat up his oldest son Joseph.

No matter how much Willie battered and abused his son, Joe, as is so often the case, idolized his father and tried desperately to gain his respect. The best way to do that, of course, was to beat people up. Like most boys in Park Slope, young Pepitone belonged to a gang, the Washington Avenue Boys, and spent much of his time on the Brooklyn streets. But Joe didn't like to fight. He was skinny, and fast, and the youngster's best weapon was usually his speed, which he used to run away from trouble. On the few occasions he stood and fought, Joe took the worst of it, which infuriated his father. For letting someone else beat him up, Joe often had to endure another pummeling at the hands of Willie.

At the age of seven, Pepitone's uncle introduced him to stickball, where he showed a remarkable ability to hit a Spaldeen great distances. He switched to baseball at fourteen, and caught the attention of a Yankee bird dog named John King. King became like a second father to Pepitone (a much kinder one) and attached himself to the Pepitone family. He followed Joe's progress as he played for Manual Arts Training School and the semipro Nathan's Famous Hot Dog team (a club which some Yankee teammates might have thought was named after him). Many of the players on the Nathan's team were nearly ten years older than Pepitone, and some had minor league experience, but the youngster held his own.

Willie Pepitone loved baseball and was delighted that Joe was playing. He attended nearly every game, and responded in his usual fashion, berating and hitting his son when he played poorly and attacking anyone who crossed Joe on the field. He once climbed out of the stands to assault a player who'd spiked Joe, and started so many fracases that King told him he was hurting Joe's chances of a professional career. Willie responded by saying he wouldn't let Joe play anymore, which precipitated a brawl in which Willie smashed an ashtray and sent shards of glass into his son's eye. Fortunately, there was no permanent damage, but the incident so frightened Willie that he never hit Joe again.

When Joe was a senior in high school, Willie Pepitone, just 39, suffered a heart attack. Two days later, Joe joined his father in the hospital. At the end of school one day, while Pepitone was at his locker, he was approached by a classmate named George O'Dell. O'Dell pointed a gun at him and said, "Stick 'em up." The gun went off. Later, Pepitone loved relating the story. "I felt the blood," he told his Yankee teammates. "Then my knees got weak. I started thinking to myself, 'This is it, you've got to be sorry for all the bad things you've done. Confess—before it's too late.'" The bullet had passed through Pepitone's body, and blood was seeping from a wound in his back. He was rushed to the hospital, where he received the last rites.

Fortunately, the wound wasn't fatal and there was no permanent injury. Joe and his father both went home to recuperate, but Willie was not a good patient. A physical man like Willie Pepitone couldn't lose himself in a book, or engage in quiet conversation. He began arguing constantly with Joe, who told his mother one night, "Mom, I wish he'd die." That night, Willie Pepitone died, and for years Joe carried a deep guilt with him. Despite his father's brutal treatment of him, Pepitone missed his father terribly, and went into a deep depression. He didn't leave the house for a month, and later said that when he recovered, he determined that he would never let anything bother him again. Joe Pepitone was going to have a good time.

The shooting and his father's death turned Pepitone's life upside down, but he returned to play ball before his senior season ended. Most major league teams were scared off, either by the possibility that his injury might have lasting effects, or the conclusion that Pepitone was prone to trouble. On August 13, 1958, the Yankees signed him for a $20,000 bonus, far less than the $50,000 the Indians had offered a year earlier. That was a Yankee trademark. They didn't pay big bonuses, but somehow they always seemed to get the best prospects at bargain prices.

Pepitone squandered virtually all of his bonus money on a new Thunderbird, a boat, and several $250 silk suits, and reported to the Yankees farm club in Auburn, New York. In Auburn, Pepitone established several firsts. On his first night, he and teammate Phil Linz were involved in a water fight at the team hotel, during which Pepitone accidently sprayed his manager with a fire extinguisher. He was docked $250, his first baseball fine. Later in the season, in the back seat of a car, he had his first sexual experience. Fines and sex were to become habits with Pepitone.

When Pepitone turned out to be fine physically, it appeared that the Yankees had won their gamble, just as they had when they bought Joe Dimaggio from the San Francisco Seals despite the fact that he had a knee injury of unknown severity. Scouting reports on Pepitone were terrific. He had all the tools: a lightning quick bat, good speed and great fielding skill both at first base and in the outfield.

"He was the type of guy all pitchers hate to see at the plate," said Yankee pitcher Tom Metcalf. "He had a quick bat and made contact with the ball. He had tremendous wrists. Joe could really snap the bat and get the barrel out over the front edge of the plate, and get it there quickly. He's a guy who could have been in the Hall of Fame. He had some of the greatest tools I've ever seen." "Pepitone had as much ability as anybody I've ever seen play," said pitcher Bill Monbouquette.

In November, 1959, when Drebinger wrote so glowingly of Pepitone's potential, Mickey Mantle was 28 years old, with several years of stardom ahead. Then it would be someone else's turn. As surely as Dimaggio had followed Ruth and Mantle had followed Dimaggio, the Yankees would develop a superstar to succeed Mantle and the New York dynasty would rumble on, as it had for decades. Pepitone seemed ideal for the role. A left-handed power hitter with incredibly fast hands, he was made for the short right field porch in Yankee Stadium. An Italian boy from Brooklyn, he would draw fans to the Stadium like Dimaggio had in the '30s and '40s.

The script was familiar. Just as Mantle was beginning to decline, Pepitone would arrive on the scene in time-tested Yankee fashion, pinch hitting and playing occasionally, honing his skills and learning to do things the Yankee way. Then, his apprenticeship served, he would become the next Yankee superstar.

Pepitone progressed steadily through the Yankee farm system, and in his fourth year batted .316 with 21 home runs and 87 RBI at Amarillo in 1961. The following spring, he reported to camp with the Yankees, where Dimaggio was an instructor. "Good wrists," Dimaggio observed. "Good looking hitter. A nice swing and good power. And in the outfield, he's got the knack of going back for a ball.... That's an instinctive thing, and this boy Pepitone looks as though he might have it." "I don't think he can miss with the goods he's got," said manager Ralph Houk. "It's all up to him."

Houk had noted a disturbing tendency, however, in the budding young superstar. When Pepitone concentrated on baseball, he was terrific, but he often lost his focus. After a laudatory profile in *The Sporting News*, correspondent Til Ferdenzi noted that "Pepitone's minor league career was pockmarked by 'personal problems.'" At Binghamton in 1960, after Pepitone's marriage became troubled, he went into a slump and the Yankees had to send former player Gerry Coleman and scout Bill Skiff to pass on some harsh words regarding Pepitone's attitude and lifestyle. Pepitone told Skiff he was tired of baseball and wanted to go home. "Fuck the Yankees," he said. To Skiff, a long-time Yankee employee, that was like saying to a priest, "Fuck the Pope." He lashed out at Pepitone, who began crying. Skiff took a softer tone, and managed to talk Pepitone into staying at Binghamton and putting more effort into his play.

In 1962, Pepitone made the Yankee roster and spent about half the season in New York, pinch hitting and learning to play first base. After the first pitch thrown to him in his first game, he got into an argument with the plate umpire. After a game-winning home run, Houk said, "If he pays attention to business and continues to bear down, he's going to hit a lot of home runs." Houk never used such qualifiers when talking about his other rookies, like Tom Tresh, Phil Linz and Jim Bouton.

When the Yankees visited Los Angeles, Mantle, who Pepitone idolized, took him to a Hollywood party featuring naked starlets and various sexual combinations in the swimming pool. Joe hooked up with a girl he thought was 19, but later found out was just 13. Night life was not unusual on the Yankee teams of the '50s and early '60s, but Pepitone seemed to elevate fun to a new level. Houk assigned veteran Moose Skowron to room with him, figuring that the Moose, who was notoriously good with young players, would be a steadying or, if necessary, terrifying, influence. On one occasion, Skowron locked Pepitone out of the room when he stayed out late, but even the Moose was no match for the flamboyant youngster. After catching Pepitone leaving for a night on the town at three in the morning, Houk and GM Roy Hamey sent him to the minor leagues.

Pepitone also acquired a reputation for two other unsavory habits, falling deeply into debt and hanging around with mobsters, a dangerous combination. The Copacabana was his hangout, and the older Italian wiseguys stroked his ego and told him what a great ballplayer he was going to be. Joey was going to make all the Italians proud of him. They even offered to break Skowron's legs so Pepitone could take his job. Pepitone ran up a $3,000 tab at the Copa during his rookie season, even though he spent part of the year in Richmond.

In December, 1962 the Yankees, confident that Pepitone was mature enough to play in the big leagues, traded veteran first baseman Skowron to the Dodgers for much-needed pitching. Moose received a telegram from his brash successor, who had taunted him throughout his rookie season, constantly telling Skowron he was going to take his job. The telegram read: DEAR MOOSE: TOLD YOU SO. JOE PEP.

This was a move the Yankees had made time and again, replacing an aging veteran with a talented youngster. They traded Hank Bauer for the younger Roger Maris, replaced Hall of Famer Phil Rizzuto with Tony Kubek and Yogi Berra with Elston Howard, winning pennants and World Series titles all along.

For two years, the elevation of Pepitone was a success, as the Yankees won pennants in '63 and '64. Joe made the All-Star team both years, hit a total of 55 home runs and drove in 189 runs. The Yankee dynasty, with youngsters like Pepitone, Tresh, Bouton and Al Downing replacing the old guard, was rolling right along. Young veterans like Kubek, Bobby Richardson, Clete Boyer, Ralph Terry and Bill Stafford appeared to have many productive seasons ahead of them.

By 1969, just five years later, the seemingly solid foundation had long since crumbled. Kubek retired due to a serious neck injury, Richardson left baseball to spend more time with his family, and Boyer was traded to the Braves. Bouton, plagued by several seasons of arm trouble, was learning to throw the knuckleball for the Seattle Pilots and taking copious notes on the activities of his teammates. Terry was a professional golfer. Stafford hurt his arm at the age of 23 and, at 30, was pitching for Phoenix of the Pacific Coast League. Tresh, often injured, struggled to hit .200, was traded in June, and retired at the end of the season. Virtually all the young talent was gone, and in its place were people like Gene Michael, Jake Gibbs and Mike Kekich.

By 1969, only Downing and Pepitone remained from the core of the pennant winning '63 club. Downing suffered from arm miseries and had incurred the club's wrath by holding out all spring. Pepitone had been a decade-long enigma and, finally, the Yankees lost their nearly infinite patience with the wayward first baseman. In August, more than ten years after Drebinger's hopeful report of 1959, came the second quote which encapsulated the Yankee decade. Gerald Eskenazi wrote: "[T]he Yankee management handed Joe Pepitone its first suspension in recent New York history.... The Bombers' long-haired first baseman, in the throes of domestic and financial difficulties, bolted the team before the game, minutes after learning that he had been fined $500 for leaving the bench during last Wednesday's game here against the Chicago White Sox."

Pepitone was the first Yankee to be slapped with such a heavy fine since the famed Copacabana incident in 1957, and the first suspended since catcher Buddy Rosar in 1942. The sequence of events began on August 12, when Pepitone failed to show up for a game. He spent the day at Coney Island and decided he didn't want to play that night. Joe, depressed, went on a friend's boat, smoked a little marijuana, and decided he was fed up with baseball. The next day, Pepitone reconsidered, called Houk and asked if he could return. Houk agreed, docked Pepitone two days' pay, and allowed him to rejoin the club on the 14th.

On August 26, Pepitone told Houk his shoulder was bothering him, and left the park without permission. That was when Houk fined and suspended him. Pepitone, whose financial situation was one of the causes of his distress, was furious and bolted the club. "You don't fine a guy $500," he said, "for leaving the ball park. There's more to it than this. Much more." Another thing that disturbed Pepitone was the fact that the last Yankee to be suspended was a non-entity named Buddy Rosar. He'd hoped it had been Babe Ruth.

Indeed there was more to the story. The Yankees issued a press release stating that Pepitone "was not yet psychologically prepared to rejoin the team." "He's confused," Yankee President Michael Burke said, "but I think most of the problem is money. We'll see what we can work out together." Burke said the Yankees had made substantial salary advances to Pepitone over the past three years.

On September 1, Pepitone met with Houk, then held a press conference to announce that he would return to the team. He was forthright and humble in discussing his many problems. "Everybody likes to give his mother something," said the mod-looking 28-year-old, wearing an orange and green bandana, "and I can't give my mother anything but trouble." Pepitone admitted to severe emotional problems caused by the breakup of his second marriage, but denied many of the outlandish rumors that were circulating. He didn't owe money to loan sharks. He was not buried under past due alimony and child support obligations, and said he owed less than $5,000. For the last three years, Pepitone disclosed, he had been living on $50 a week, which was all his lawyer gave him from his $38,000 annual salary.

The public airing of Pepitone's difficulties led many to reflect on the tragedy of a great talent gone to waste. "Joe Pepitone should have been a $100,000 ballplayer," said Ted Williams, then managing the Washington Senators. "All this was a theater for Joe," said Yankee pitcher Steve Hamilton, "but his attention span was so short. When he could bear down and play baseball, he was great, but then his mind wandered." Robert Lipsyte wrote, "[H]e never had the really great year he should have had. And in spring training each following year, he would announce that 'a new Joe Pepitone' had arrived, ready to bat .300, hit 40 home runs and make $100,000 a year ... but each new Pepitone inherited the problems of his predecessor."

"I know I didn't bear down all the time the way I should have last year," one new Pepitone said in the spring of 1965. "I thought I was bearing down, but I wasn't. That's what I've learned. And that's what I intend to do this year." But he didn't. He never did. Hal Stowe, who played with Pepitone in the minors, put it simply. "Pepi had all the ability of anybody in the world," Stowe said. "He just never did put that ten cent head of his together."

Joe had all the ability, but he could never grow up. "I'll never forget the first time I met Joe Pepitone," said outfielder Roger Repoz. "There were two young guys the Yankees had signed — Pepitone and Rich Barry. They were both crazy. Barry was a big, blond guy from Southern California. What a slugger this guy was! He hit them over light towers. Somehow, Joe and Rich got hooked up and were on their way to spring training in Florida and as a lark they pulled into a gas station and held it up with a water pistol — just to see if they could do it. The Yankees were pretty quick to put Barry in some other part of the country where he'd never get together up with Joe again, because Joe had star ability."*

"Joe was accused of a lot of things," said former Yankee Duke Carmel. "He was the kind of guy who was in the wrong place at the wrong time. I've always felt that way, even with the troubles he had afterwards. I grew up in Harlem. A few guys from I knew from Harlem started showing up and hanging around him. I said, 'Joe, what are you doing? These guys are no good. I grew up with these guys.' But he still hung around with them."

After the 1965 season, Houk told Pepitone, "Change your way of living or you're gone." Pepitone asked if he would be traded, and Houk said he couldn't get much for him anymore. "It makes me sick," Houk said, "the way you're throwing your life away. My god, what a future you have. You could almost be a Joe Dimaggio." Pepitone told Houk how his personal problems had impacted his play. "I know about your troubles, Joe," Houk replied. "I'm sorry. But that's all behind you now. You can't destroy your life. You have to think of yourself. You've got to start thinking about baseball as a business." Pepitone also had to think about his teammates, Houk added. He was letting them down with his sorry effort. Houk was a master motivator, but he was never able to change Joe Pepitone.

The next season, after some lackadaisical efforts, Houk tried a harsher approach and threatened to punch Pepitone if he didn't start putting out. "Houk took Pepitone in his office one day," recalled first baseman Ray Barker, "and gave him a royal ass-chewing. He left the door open and the clubhouse was quiet as could be, because everybody wanted to hear what he was saying. Houk said, 'Do you want to be a $30,000 ballplayer all your life? Goddamn it, with all the talent you've got!' Pepi came out and it was like, 'Ha, ha, I got my ass chewed out. So what.'

*Actually, Barry and Pepitone "held up" a car repair shop where they both hung out quite a bit. The police arrived while they were still at the scene, handcuffed the two players and were about to haul them off to jail while they protested that the whole thing was a gag. Manager Steve Souchock arrived and convinced the police to let his players go. "Souchock just shook his head," Pepitone wrote in his autobiography, "like he didn't know what to do with us."

It went in one ear and out the other." When Elston Howard was traded to the Red Sox in 1967, Pepitone jokingly said to him, "Get me traded." "You're doing a pretty good job of it yourself," Howard replied. "You don't need help."

In the 1950s, someone like Skowron or Hank Bauer might have sat Pepitone down and laid down the law. But there was no one on the Yankees of the mid–'60s to take on such a role. Mantle was supposed to be the team leader, but no one had a more active night life than the leader. For Pepitone, Mantle was what psychologists refer to as an enabler. "They used to have what they called a 'rat pack,'" said Tom Metcalf, "guys on the team that were kind of hell-raisers. We were on a flight leaving New York, when Mantle grabbed the microphone and said, 'We have a new king of the rat pack. We were on an eight day home stand and Joe Pepitone never slept at home one night we were here.' Joe loved it because he idolized Mickey."

By 1965, Yankee fans were booing the sensitive first baseman, although they weren't as brutal as they were to Roger Maris. The fans booed Maris's every move, but they had a love-hate relationship with Pepitone. They hooted when he stuck out in key situations, but cheered him when he got big hits, or when he jumped up on the dugout roof to do the Twist to the music of Paul Revere and the Raiders on Date Night. Pepitone was almost always booed on the road.

Pepitone was generally liked by his teammates, who recognized him as the immature, overgrown teenager that he was. He never hurt anyone, and his irresponsible actions were usually detrimental only to him. "He was a nice guy," recalled outfielder Tom Shopay, "and a funny guy. He had that shit-eating grin on his face a lot. He was always looking around with his head bobbing up and down...." "My son was a little guy," said Billy Cowan, who played with the Yankees in 1969, "about four or five, and he thought Pepitone was the greatest guy in the world. Pepi treated him just like he was his kid."

His teammates loved to tease him and Pepitone craved the attention, for it made him feel part of the team. One day in the Yankee clubhouse, the players were watching a football game on television, which led Pepitone to tell everyone what a great football player he had been. Bouton, referring to Pepitone's nose, said he would be ruled offside every time he lined up. Stafford said he'd need an extra large face mask to cover his nose. Whitey Ford said that he would have to stop after each touchdown to remove his helmet and comb his hair.

Pepi's hair was a particular concern. In his first years in the big leagues, he spent more time arranging his coiffure than he spent taking batting practice. By the mid–'60s, Joe's curly black locks had become quite sparse, and he took to wearing a toupee, which required just as much care as his departed natural hair. In 1969, New York beauty consultant Mark Traynor created women's hairstyles known as the Hawk and the Pepitone. The Hawk, named after Ken Harrelson, featured bangs, and the Pepitone was a sculpted style with swept bangs sprayed in place as tightly as Pepitone's toupee.

The story of Pepitone's tribulations was the only major Yankee news in September of 1969. The pennants of the early '60s were a dim memory, and in new, vibrant Shea Stadium the Mets were making all the headlines. They played to packed houses every night, while the Yankees, nearly 30 games out of first place, performed in an almost empty Yankee Stadium. The facility had deteriorated along with the team, and New York fans preferred winning baseball in a new stadium. On September 17, just 5,025 fans saw Yankee lefty Fritz Peterson win his 16th game. The next evening 6,020 saw Mel Stottlemyre win his 19th. The following night, the Yankees left for Baltimore and the Mets, leading the Eastern Division of the National League, returned to New York and drew 51,885 for a doubleheader against the Pirates. A total of 165,000 watched the weekend series between the two clubs.

Even the most embittered Yankee hater from the '50s and early '60s had to feel, in some deep, dark corner of their soul, compassion for the now meek pinstripers, who struggled to steal, bunt and scratch out an occasional victory. The Yankees hit bottom in 1966, finishing last in the American League. Their descent had been sudden, losing the 1964 Series in seven games, finishing a distant sixth in 1965 and in the basement the following year.

The Mets and Yankees didn't play a meaningful game against each other until the 2000 World Series, but off the field the Mets delivered a sound economic and public relations thrashing to New York's American League club, immediately establishing themselves as lovable symbols of ineptitude. Their success at the gate made the Yankees desperate to shed their image as cold, unloved winners. By mid-decade, they had succeeded. They became cold, unloved losers.

By the end of the decade, the Yankees, who had scorned the Mets as comical upstarts in 1962, had adopted virtually every Met tactic. They had birthday parties at the Stadium. They held art contests. They hosted contestants from the Miss Universe pageant. They had a day of contests, including egg-throwing and a wheelbarrow race. Pop singer Paul Simon threw out the first ball at one game. Eighty one year old poet Marianne Moore threw out the first ball on opening day. After viewing a lively Met crowd at Shea, Joe Durso wrote of the five bands roaming the stands and the lively atmosphere, "The joint was jumping like Yankee Stadium." On September 27, 1969, while the Mets basked in the glory of a division championship, the Yankees held a Fan Appreciation Day. Twenty one thousand, only thirteen thousand of whom paid, showed up. Not only had the Yankees lost their supremacy on the field, they had committed a number of public relations blunders that enabled the Mets to hire George Weiss, Yogi Berra, and most important of all, the man who created the Met image, Casey Stengel.

How did it happen? How was a team that won 14 pennants in 16 years reduced to an also ran? Some said it was the advent of the free agent draft in 1965, but by that time, the Yankees were already in their downward spiral. Others said that owners Del Webb and Dan Topping, once they had decided to sell the team, failed to invest in the farm system and develop young prospects. Stars like Mantle, Ford and Howard got old and there was no one to replace them. In the early '60s, however, the club had a number of young prospects like Pepitone, Tresh, Bouton and Stottlemyre.

Injuries played a key role in the Yankees' fall. In his final years, Mantle was a shadow of his old self. Maris and Kubek suffered premature eclipses, as did Bouton, Stafford, and Terry. Another reason the Yankees began to lose was that the other American League teams finally began to believe that the champions could be beaten. For years, the Yankees mystique had caused opposing fielders to fumble ground balls in the late innings, and opposing pitchers to yield key hits. By the middle of the decade, it was the Yankees who found unusual ways to lose games. The vaunted Yankee mystique was a mere memory of days past.

◆ 2 ◆

Casey's Last Hurrah
The 1960 Season

In 1959, for only the second time in eleven years, the New York Yankees did not win the American League pennant. Late in May, they found themselves in last place, and when the ledgers closed on September 29, the Yankees were third, 15 games behind the pennant-winning White Sox. Their 79–75 record represented the lowest win total since 1925. For a team that set an all-time record with a payroll of more than $700,000, the season was a terrible disappointment, due in part to a rash of injuries. Mickey Mantle hurt his shoulder. Pitchers Don Larsen and Tom Sturdivant had sore arms. Third baseman Andy Carey missed much of the season with hepatitis and first baseman Bill Skowron was limited to just 74 games by a broken wrist. Further, many of the players who had been instrumental in the championship seasons of the '50s were slowing down. Yogi Berra, 34, hit just 19 home runs and had but 69 RBI, a far cry from his MVP seasons of 1954 and 1955. Hank Bauer, 37, batted .238 with only nine home runs and Gil McDougald, 31, .251 with four homers. Bob Turley, the 1958 Cy Young winner, struggled with a sore arm and went from 21–7 to 8–11. Larsen, who had never fulfilled the promise of that splendid October afternoon in 1956, was 6–7.

The Yankee slump actually dated to the beginning of August, 1958, when the club was in first place by 17 games. They won just 27 of their last 55 games, but still finished ten games ahead of the White Sox. The Yanks rebounded from a 3–1 deficit to beat the Braves in the World Series, but three wins did not mean that the team was as strong as it had been earlier in the decade. After the poor 1959 campaign, it appeared that perhaps the era of Yankee dominance might be at an end.

Mantle had, for him, a subpar season in '59, batting .285 with 31 home runs and only 75 runs batted in, not bad, but not as good as the high standard he'd set by winning the Triple Crown in 1956. "Mantle can do anything," Stengel said late in the season, "but when he don't hit, he's just another guy that's fast going to first." During the winter, there were rumors that Mickey would be traded. "There was a time," reported *Sports Illustrated*, "when the Yankees were the greatest thing in baseball and Mickey was the greatest thing on the Yankees. A glance at last year suggests that this is no longer the case." General Manager George Weiss pointed out that Mantle's performance had declined ever since his Triple Crown season and sent him a contract calling for $55,000, $17,000 less than he had earned the previous year. Mantle sent it back unsigned, and remained at his Dallas home, while Weiss took the offensive. "We have been pampering this boy for nine years," Weiss said in early March, "and I think it's about time he acted like a man." "This is the year Mantle must learn the facts of life," he told reporters. "He must learn he can't bulldoze us into meeting his terms." Since Mantle's only options were to sign or sit out the season, it's not certain how he could "bulldoze" Weiss.

The press dutifully rallied behind the Yankees. Nearly every story mentioned Mantle's strikeouts, and minimized his accomplishments. "At 28," said the *New York Times*, "[Mantle] still has the potential. But the indisputable fact remains that ever since his big year in 1956 he has been receding steadily." *Sports Illustrated* wrote, "The fact that Mickey Mantle is now an official holdout for the first time in his career adds little to the luster of the Yankee legend or to Mickey's stature as a national hero."

"Whoever is advising Mickey Mantle these days," wrote Joe Trimble in *The Daily News*, "is doing a bad job. The Yankee star's continuing holdout and bitter remarks about the club have head man George Weiss madder at him than he ever has been at any ballplayer." "Mickey is a hillbilly in a velvet suit," Trimble added later. "He isn't grateful or even gracious ... out of false pride, he has become a sullen holdout and is guilty of a disgraceful exhibition of ill-conduct when he refuses to sit down, man-to-man, to discuss the contract with general manager George Weiss." "[Weiss is] sore," Dick Young quoted Assistant GM Roy Hamey as saying. "No other player, not even Dimaggio, has refused to come to camp to talk it over with him." "It is less a matter of money now than of attitude," Weiss said.

Yankee broadcaster Phil Rizzuto taped a segment in which he said, "Mickey is using the old ultimatum technique. Either meet my price, or I don't play.... That seems a bit silly, because without baseball Mantle would be a has-been instead of a right-now." The debate made for good press, but everyone knew the stalemate would be resolved shortly after spring training began.

Ryne Duren, the burly, bespectacled relief ace, was also holding out, but with Mantle making headlines, few noticed. In 1959, Duren earned $16,000 as perhaps the best relief pitcher in the American League, with 14 saves (only one behind the league leader) and a 1.88 ERA. For his efforts, Weiss sent him a 1960 contract, which Duren received on Christmas Eve, for $12,000, the maximum 25 percent cut allowed under baseball's rules. The Yankees had not won the pennant and Weiss was in no mood to give out raises. Everyone would have to bite the bullet. Everyone, that is, but Weiss, who supposedly received incentive compensation based upon the amount he could save in salary negotiations (10 percent of the difference between a budget established by the owners and the amount actually paid by Weiss).

"My God," Duren said recently, "I had my best year. I couldn't pitch any better than that." His record had been even better, he pointed out, until late in the season, when Stengel left him in a game until he tired and gave up a few runs, sending his ERA, as Duren said, "all the way up to 1.88." He felt, with the pennant out of reach, the club had intentionally tried to worsen his statistics and damage his negotiating position for the following year.

The public, of course, knew nothing about Duren's salary or the insulting offer. "In those days," he said, "it was your death if you mentioned numbers." There was good reason for that, since the clubs were trying to portray holdouts as greedy, while most fans would have been shocked to find that Duren, the Yankees' ace reliever, was being tendered the lowest amount Weiss could legally offer.

When spring training started, Duren was in Florida but still unsigned. After a few days, he told writer Til Ferdenzi he had made flight reservations and was going home. "I want to play ball," he told Ferdenzi, "but I can't play for this." Ferdenzi told him he shouldn't leave, and Duren said he would make a deal. If all of the writers wrote down the salary they thought Duren should earn, and gave it to Ferdenzi, Duren would agree to sign a contract for the average of the writers' recommendations. Ferdenzi agreed and presented the numbers to Weiss with Duren's pledge. The Yankee GM was furious, since the press had discovered how little he wanted to pay his ace reliever. With the reporters making Duren's case rather than supporting Weiss's, the GM drew up a contract for the average figure of $17,500 [a whopping $1,500 raise] and Duren signed it. "Weiss told me it was the dirtiest thing any player had ever done to him," Duren said.

Mantle's case had a much higher profile than Duren's, and Weiss wasn't about to be taken in by any tricks. This was not the first time he had done battle with the Yankee star. Mantle received $7,500 his rookie year and got a raise to $10,000 for his second season. He received $12,500 in 1953 and $17,000 the next year, each time after difficult negotiations. When he had his tremendous season in 1956, Mantle was earning $32,500. After batting .353, with 52 home runs and 130 RBI, Mickey wanted to double his salary. Weiss nearly had a stroke. If he doubled his salary after each good year, Weiss told his 25-year-old star, how much did he expect to make when he was 35? Then, as the clincher, Weiss pulled a manila file out of his desk drawer, a file filled with reports from detectives Weiss had hired. If those reports were made public, Weiss said, it could hurt Mantle's image and his marriage. Mantle decided to call Weiss's bluff, and said he still wanted $65,000. Finally, Yankee co-owner Del Webb met personally with Mantle, and agreed to the $65,000 figure. The reports stayed in the manila folder, for while Weiss might threaten, he knew it wasn't a wise thing to tarnish the reputation of his leading drawing card.

Weiss didn't forget, however. In 1957, Mantle was not as good as he had been in '56. His average went up to .365, and he hit 34 home runs, but he didn't win the Triple Crown, and his home runs and RBIs were down. Weiss sent him a contract calling for a $5,000 pay cut. After a 42 homer season in '58, Weiss tried to cut Mantle's salary by $10,000. Thus, by the time the 1960 negotiations rolled around, there was no love lost between Mantle and his general manager.

The 1960 battle ended as everyone knew it would. After many recriminations from both sides, Mantle, with no alternative but to sit out the season, came to St. Petersburg and capitulated on March 11th. He signed for $65,000, a mere $7,000 cut, and was back to where he had been in 1957.

A new Yankee outfielder had arrived in camp shortly before Mantle ended his holdout. For several years, New York's Triple A farm club had been based in Kansas City. When the latter city acquired a major league franchise in 1955, the Yankees seemed not to have noticed, and still used Kansas City as a source of young prospects. Athletics' owner Arnold Johnson was an old friend of Yankee co-owner Dan Topping and general manager Weiss. Topping made the franchise's move from Philadelphia to Kansas City possible by selling him the Yankee farm club. Weiss had been the one who suggested Johnson buy the Athletics from the Mack family. He also helped stock the team by trading Johnson players the Yankees didn't want. Another Yankee connection was Parke Carroll, the Athletics' general manager, who had been business manager of the Newark Bears when Newark was a Yankee farm club. Johnson even owned Yankee Stadium at one time, but was required to sell it when he acquired the Kansas City club. He still maintained a number of business connections with Topping.

Not surprisingly, trade activity between the Yankees and Athletics was brisk. Between late 1954, when the Athletics moved to Kansas City, and November, 1959, there had been 14 trades with the Yankees involving 53 players. Ralph Terry, Hector Lopez, and Duren had all come to New York via Kansas City. In 1957, the Yankees traded a pack of bodies to the Athletics for pitchers Art Ditmar and Bobby Shantz, and got Kansas City to throw in a teenaged bonus player named Clete Boyer. In 1960, nine former Yankees appeared on the Kansas City roster and nine former Athletics were on the Yankee squad. When Johnson died in 1960, a writer expressed surprise that he hadn't left Bud Daley, Kansas City's best pitcher, to the Yankees in his will.

"One scarcely can remember," said The New York Times, "when the Yanks last made a deal with a club other than their Kansas City pals, the Athletics." One reason the Yankees traded so frequently with Kansas City was that no other club in the American League wanted to give them anyone of value who might help them to another pennant, and interleague trading was allowed only for a brief period near the winter meetings. "I know we'll take a lot more ribbing," said Weiss after his fifteenth trade, "but it simply got down to where we couldn't close a deal with any other club."

The fifteenth trade would be the Yankees' best. During the 1959 season, manager Stengel and veteran infielder McDougald were sitting together in the dugout in Kansas City. "If we had to get one more ballplayer on our club," Stengel asked McDougald, "who would you get?" "I just pointed," said McDougald. "I said, 'There's the man out there.' It was Roger Maris."

The 25-year-old Maris, six feet tall and a sturdy 195 pounds, was the son of a railway worker, who had been a football, track and baseball star in Fargo, North Dakota.* It was too cold in North Dakota to play high school baseball, but Maris played summers on the American Legion team. He was better known, however, as a football star, and once returned four kickoffs for touchdowns in a single game. When he graduated, Maris was courted by a dozen colleges, and planned to accept a football scholarship to the University of Oklahoma to play for legendary coach Bud Wilkinson. It took just a week on campus to convince Maris he had made a mistake. "Hitting the books just wasn't for me," he said a few years later.

Roger tried out with the Cubs, who told him he was too small. He contacted the Cleveland Indians, who had offered him a $15,000 bonus the previous summer. Now, however, the Indians offered $5,000, plus an additional $10,000 if he made it to the major leagues. Maris waited until January, hoping Cleveland would sweeten its offer, but when they didn't, he accepted it.

In 1953, Maris went to Daytona Beach and attended his first professional camp, put on a professional uniform for the first time, and had his first argument with a professional baseball official. Indian farm director Mike McNally wanted to send the young rookie to Class D ball. Roger wanted to play for Fargo, his hometown team, which was in a Class C league. If he couldn't go home, Roger told McNally, he was going home.

Maris prevailed, went to Fargo, and had a good year. The following spring, he threatened to walk out of camp when coaches tried to tamper with his swing. He backed down, and tore up the Eastern League, batting .325 with 32 homers and 111 RBI. In 1955, he had his second run-in with a Cleveland official, this time manager Dutch Meyer of Tulsa. Meyer didn't like Maris and Maris didn't like Meyer, so Roger proposed a solution. He should be sent to Reading, to play for Jo Jo White, who he liked. Again, Cleveland gave in and Maris played very well at Reading, earning an invitation to train with the varsity in '56.

Most players in their first major league camp were just thrilled to be there. Not Roger Maris. He wanted to play, and when he didn't he asked manager Al Lopez why. Lopez told him why and then sent him to Indianapolis.

In 1957, Maris came to the big leagues to stay. On the second day of the season, he hit his first major league home run, an eleventh inning grand slam off Detroit's Jack Crimian. After getting off to a good start, Maris suffered from a pulled hamstring, a wrist injury and a pulled muscle in his rib cage and finished the season with a .235 average.

Indian manager Bobby Bragan platooned Maris with Rocky Colavito in 1958, and made it clear he didn't think Roger had the ability to be a major league regular. In the middle of the season, Maris was traded to the Athletics. The Athletics wanted Colavito (who they eventually got in 1964) but Cleveland GM Frank Lane convinced them to take Maris instead. Lane said Colavito was too popular to trade, and that Maris would eventually be just as good. Maris's combined average in 1958 was only .240, but he hit 28 home runs. "You could see he had the instincts to be a real good ballplayer," said Lou Klimchock, who played for Kansas City. "He had a great arm and hit the ball real hard for us. At the end of the season in 1959, Roger was in a slump. We were out of the race, playing in Chicago and behind by a run with two out in the

---

Maris was actually born Maras in Hibbing, but moved to Fargo at a young age and adopted it as his home town. He changed the spelling of his last name when people teased him by calling him Mar-ass.

ninth. He hit a popup to Nellie Fox and Fox, of all people, drops it. You know where Maris is? Standing on second base. He busted his tail. The next guy gets a hit, Roger scores and we eventually win the ballgame."

In 1959, Maris got off to a tremendous start, had an emergency appendectomy in late May, tried to come back too soon, and went into a tailspin. He bounced back and, at the end of July, was leading the league with a .344 average. For the rest of the season, Roger's average was .165, bringing his season mark down to .273, with 16 home runs. In the midst of his hot streak, the Kansas City fans decided that, later in the season, between games of a doubleheader, they would hold a day in his honor. When Maris's day dawned, he was mired in a 3 for 65 slump. "By the time the date arrived," he said, "I wasn't sure I'd have nerve enough to show up." Maris did appear, of course, and in the ninth inning of the first game, just prior to the ceremony, struck out with the bases loaded.

The slump was draining on Maris, but it was a blessing for the Yankees. "If he'd stayed healthy," speculated Ralph Terry, "I think they'd have had a hard time getting him out of Kansas City." During the winter meetings, the Pirates offered the Athletics shortstop Dick Groat, who would win the 1960 National League MVP award, for Maris. The deal was agreed upon, but when Pirate manager Danny Murtaugh and GM Joe Brown retreated to a hotel room to think about it, they changed their minds.

Maris didn't remain with the Athletics for long. On December 11, 1959, the Yankees acquired Maris, shortstop Joe DeMaestri and first baseman Kent Hadley for Bauer, Larsen, first baseman-outfielder Norm Siebern, and future Met icon Marvin Throneberry. Essentially, it was Maris for Siebern, whom Stengel had tired of. Siebern was quiet, unemotional and passive, and Stengel, who had a difficult time understanding silent ballplayers, thought he lacked passion and desire. Neither Hadley nor DeMaestri figured to get much playing time with the Yankees. Hadley wasn't much of a fielder, but he was a left handed hitter with power and could be a threat off the bench. DeMaestri was slated for a utility role.

"They gave up a lot to get Roger," said Terry, "but they didn't give up any stars. Most of the lesser teams just needed starters. They had half a dozen positions to fill." At the time, many thought the Athletics had finally gotten the better end of a deal with the Yankees. White Sox manager Al Lopez predicted that Siebern would hit more home runs than Maris. "I may be wrong," said Arnold Johnson, "but I have a strong feeling that our last trade with the Yankees will turn out to be the best we have made." Stengel thought the success of the deal would hinge on one question. Could Maris handle the pressure of playing in New York?

The acquisition of Maris filled the huge void in the Yankee outfield created by Bauer's decline, but it did not solve all of Stengel's problems. Mantle, now under contract, would play center, Maris would play either left or right, and Hector Lopez would probably be the third outfielder, but who would pitch? Whitey Ford, the ace of a weak staff, finished the 1959 season with a sore arm, and was bothered by gout. Art Ditmar (13–9) had a good year in '59, but the rest of the starting staff was so-so. Turley went from the Cy Young Award winner to 8–11. He was no longer "Bullet Bob," having lost the steam on his once-powerful fastball. Terry was a relatively unproven youngster whose best season was 11–13 with the Athletics in 1958. The bullpen was in disarray. Duren, its ace, was recovering from a broken wrist.

Many pitching coaches say, "The best pitch in the world is strike one." Ryne Duren's best pitch was his first warmup toss, which invariably hit the backstop on the fly. "The first time it happened," said Duren, "was at Yankee Stadium. They had changed the mound. Turley wanted it flat for some reason. He kind of came from the side and he didn't like that big drop. What I would do is throw the first pitch as hard as I could and adjust from there. One day in Yankee Stadium I threw the first warmup and I thought my knee was going to hit me in the chin. At that point, you've got to let the ball go. It went really high. That was no contrived thing at all.

But everybody got such a big kick out of it. The writers sort of laughed about it and [coach] Frank Crosetti said, 'God, that's a good idea, do that again.' Casey said, 'That'll make 'em think a little bit.'"

Bullpen coach Jim Hegan had an even more radical idea. "One time, when I was warming up in the bullpen," Duren said, "Hegan told me, 'When you get real loose, see if you can throw one in the dugout from out here.' It's 430 or 440 feet from the bullpen mound to the dugout. So every once in a while I'd throw one out of the bullpen and see if I could get it in the dugout. It would come bouncing in through the infield or bounce over by third base and into the dugout. They knew I was warming up."

Duren loved the idea. In 1964, when he was with the Phillies, Ryne was watching rookie Gary Kroll throw in the bullpen. Kroll was 6'6" and threw extremely hard, having struck out a record 306 batters one year in the California League. "When you get good and loose," Duren told Kroll, "throw a couple over the catcher's head into the tent." "You'd hit the tent," said Kroll, "and there would be a big clang. That noise would go around the whole ballpark. So I threw a couple into the tent." "When you get to the mound," Duren said, "The first ball — I want you to throw it up to the screen." "So I threw it to the screen," Kroll said. "The first batter was Willie Mays. He took three swings and left. He didn't want to hit against me."

"When Ryne would get up to throw," said pitcher Johnny James, "we'd all leave the bench because the catcher was right in front of us. We'd scatter. I used to walk all the way down to where the foul line met the fence. One time I was watching the game from there while Ryne warmed up. All of a sudden people were yelling at me. I looked up just in time to see a ball right in front of my face. You didn't want to be around when he was warming up."

While Duren's warmup antics were humorous, there was nothing funny about being in the batter's box when he was pitching. Duren worried that, throwing as hard as he did, he might maim or even kill someone. "I think it was 1960, in Chicago," he recalled. "They brought me in to pitch to one hitter, Jim Landis. I played winter ball with Jim and was a good friend of his. His wife and my wife were friends. My first pitch was right at his head and he went down. I thought, 'It would be terrible to hit him.' The next pitch was right at his head. He just did get out of the way. The third pitch was right at his head again. It was almost like he ducked out from under his helmet and it was suspended in midair. The ball hit the helmet and knocked it clear back to the screen. It was a terrible sound but it didn't hurt him at all. He went down to first base and Casey came out and took me out of the ballgame. They brought in Bobby Shantz, and Gene Freese hit into a double play and laughed all the way down to first base. He was so happy they'd taken me out."

One of the legends surrounding Duren was that he was wild because he couldn't see. "Without my glasses," he said, "I was 20/200 in my left eye and 20/70 in my right." His corrected vision was nearly normal (20/30) and he could see the plate well enough. What he couldn't see were balls hit back at him. "My depth perception was poor," Duren said, "and it was probably more dangerous for me to be on the mound than it was for batters to be at the plate. The guys used to laugh at me when I'd throw my hands up. They'd say, 'The ball was past second base when your hands went up.'"

His poor depth perception also made it difficult for Duren to bat. In ten big league seasons, he managed just seven hits. "He was a terrible hitter," wrote Ralph Houk. "He choked way up on the bat and it was like he was using a hammer to hit a nail." Once, with Duren at bat, Cleveland center fielder Jimmy Piersall stationed himself just a few feet behind second base.

One of Duren's seven hits, however, was one he would never forget. After the Yankees traded him to the Angels in 1961, Ryne started a number of games. One of them was against the Yankees in Los Angeles. His mound opponent was Turley, who had been struggling with a bad arm. On that night, however, Turley pitched better than he had all season. He struck out four Angels in a row in the early innings, and shut Los Angeles out for the first five frames. The Yankees had a 1–0 lead, and Turley had two Angels out in the sixth with Ted Kluszewski on third. He lost the plate and walked the next two batters, loading the bases. That didn't seem to present a problem, however, since Duren was the next batter. Turley threw two fastballs right past him, as Duren waved helplessly at the ball. "He shook his head," said Duren, "and I knew he was going to throw another fastball." Sure enough, the next pitch was a high fastball. "You never throw a high pitch to a guy with glasses," Duren said. He made contact and hit a weak ground ball up the middle. It dribbled through the infield into center field, the third hit of Duren's career, his first since 1958, and two runs scored. The next batter, Albie Pearson, hit a three run homer and Turley was gone. When the game was over, Duren had beaten the Yankees 5–3.

No one wanted to be in the bullpen when Duren was warming up. Not many wanted to be at the plate when he was pitching. Another place they wanted to avoid was anywhere in the vicinity of the big righthander when he'd been drinking, which was most of the time. No one in baseball had a worse reputation for alcohol abuse than Ryne Duren, who acquired the image of a mean, outrageous drunk. Reporters, who in those days never mentioned such issues directly, referred to his "low capacity for fuel consumption." "Ryne was very tough to be buddies with," said pitcher Eli Grba, who waged his own battle with alcohol. "If you talked to Ryne when he wasn't drinking, he sounded like an intellect. But he'd take two drinks and he was gone. You didn't want to be around him. He was a bad drunk." Duren was considered so hopeless that when one of his old teammates contacted him when he was entering alcohol rehab for his own problem, he told Duren, "If an SOB like you can get sober, anybody can."

During his career, Duren was involved in numerous alcohol-related incidents. In 1957, while playing for Ralph Houk in Denver, he made a scene at a night club, then went to a coffee shop and happened to run into the band leader, with whom he'd had words at the club. A wrestling match ensued, and a plain clothes policeman began beating Duren with a blackjack. Duren's teammate Siebern, one of the most quiet and mild-mannered of the Denver players, intervened and both he and Duren were arrested. Houk reprimanded Duren, but insisted alcohol wasn't involved, and did nothing more than strengthen his curfew regulations.

Johnny James recalled an incident shortly after the Yankees won the 1958 pennant. "We'd clinched in Kansas City and were on the train to Chicago," he recalled. "Casey had us all in the one car that was reserved for us. He was facing us and talking to us about not getting into any trouble, because the reporters would pick it up." At that point, Duren, obviously inebriated, entered the car behind Stengel, who couldn't see him come in. Houk, then a Yankee coach, saw Duren, sensed trouble and moved to intercept him before he could reach Casey. Duren had liked Houk when he played for him at Denver, but when Ryne was drunk, he didn't like anybody. Houk grabbed Duren and tried to quiet him, but the pitcher mashed Houk's cigar into his face and the battle was on. "Ralph and Ryne were wrestling around in the car," said James. "Casey, who couldn't see or hear the altercation going on behind him, was lecturing us about not getting into trouble and right behind him one of his coaches and one of his pitchers were rolling around in the aisle." It was not the first time the two had clashed, Houk said, for he had been forced to "tame Duren with his fists" when the two were at Denver. The morning after the incident, Duren and Houk had breakfast together and all was forgiven. When Duren was sober, he got along fine with Houk and just about everyone else.

After he retired from baseball, Duren hit bottom, sobered up and embarked on a career of lecturing and counseling on substance abuse with all the fervor of a reformed sinner. "I was very notorious as a drunk," he said, "so I might as well be that way sober." Duren, now in his 70s, is a soft-spoken, thoughtful and very complex man, who after many years of introspection and analysis, finally understands what happened to him nearly 50 years ago. He grew up in a small town in Wisconsin, and played in Kansas City with the Athletics, but in the '50s Kansas City was major league in name but minor league in many ways. Playing in New York was an almost surreal experience. "When I broke into pro ball," said Duren, "there were Mantle and Ford, just great ballplayers, and you didn't dream that you'd ever be playing with them. Then one day, here you are, with the greatest team, not only playing on it, but a bona fide member of it."

Duren was 29 before he made it to the big leagues to stay, but in 1958 and '59, he was the finest reliever in the American League, and the most intimidating. "The kid throws hard enough to suit me," said Stengel. "The ball makes a strange sound, like a small jet, as it travels toward the catcher and lodges, kerplunk, in Yogi's mitt. Duren is a splendid product of the Atomic Age." Duren made the All Star squad both years, led the league with 20 saves in 1958, posting a magnificent 2.02 ERA, and was named *The Sporting News* rookie pitcher of the year. From April 30th through July 16th, he pitched 36 innings without allowing an earned run. The following year, Duren was pitching even better when, running in from the bullpen after a game with the Red Sox, he tripped over a couple of fans, fell awkwardly, and broke his wrist in two places.

In 125 innings over the two year period, Duren struck out 163 batters. Although impressive in its own right, his ratio of 11.7 strikeouts per nine innings is even more staggering when one considers that strikeout totals were much lower in the '50s than in the current era. "Bullet Bob" Turley, in his Cy Young season of 1958, averaged just over six strikeouts per nine innings.

Everything is bigger in New York, and Duren's success did not go unnoticed. "In 1959," he recalled, "I was probably getting as much fan mail as anyone." Anyone included Mickey Mantle, Whitey Ford and Yogi Berra. "A cartoonist had me holding up the Yankees with one hand. You'd read one article after the other telling you how great you are, and your fan mail is piling up."

The respect and acceptance of his teammates was more important to Duren than fan mail. Most days, he rode to the ballpark with the great Mantle. After one game, in which Duren had been particularly overpowering, Mantle came into the locker room and stopped in front of him. "I'll never forget this," Duren said. "Mickey came by my locker and said, 'I don't believe what the fuck I just saw! I don't believe anybody can throw the ball that hard.' They'd just kind of shake their head in awe of me. In your very private moments, you'd have to say, 'I guess I am something special.'"

Despite the adulation of the fans and his teammates, Duren could never truly come to admire himself, and always suspected that he was not the real thing. One day, he feared, everything would suddenly collapse and he would be exposed as a fraud. "That's the insecurity of adolescence that I never got out of until I stopped drinking," he said. "I finally got out of adolescence when I was 40 years old." In the meantime, Duren used alcohol as an escape.

In the spring of 1960, Duren, emotionally, was still an adolescent of 31 and, physically, still suffering the aftereffects of his wrist injury. "I had the cast on for 12 weeks," he said, "because the bone was slow to heal. The doctor put a hell of a cast on it and my arm atrophied." When the season began, Duren was not at full strength, and the Yankee bullpen was without a stopper.

The best Yankee pitcher in the spring of 1960 was the diminutive right hander, Johnny James, who had been in the New York farm system since 1953. James was not a highly regarded prospect, and spent three years at the Double A level. "The Yankees always had a bunch of big, strong pitchers in their organization," said James, who was not one of them. He stood 5'10" ("5'10" was probably a stretch," he admitted.) and weighed just 150 pounds. "I was really skinny," James said. "When I was in high school, I always used to check the major league rosters, because I knew I wasn't going to be very big and I wanted to see if there was anyone my size in the majors."

Finally, after six minor league seasons, James was called up to the big leagues and made his Yankee debut in relief in September of 1958, in a nationally-televised Game of the Week

Ryne Duren was one of the hardest throwers and the most dominating relief pitcher of the late 1950s. Troubled by a lack of control both on the mound and in his personal life, he was traded to the Angels in 1961.

against the Washington Senators. The first batter he faced in the seventh inning was Albie Pearson, the shortest player in the majors at 5'5". James always had trouble with his control. "There was no way I was going to throw him a strike," he said. "I walked him on four pitches." Bob Nieman lined a sharp single to left field. Catcher Clint Courtney was the next batter. "I realized I was in trouble," said James, "so I threw a really good fastball. He ripped it right to Gil McDougald at second base." McDougald caught the ball in the air, threw to Tony Kubek to double Pearson off second and Kubek threw to first for a triple play. The inning, which had begun so inauspiciously, was suddenly over. James, stunned, walked off the mound. "Casey and the guys on the bench were waiting to congratulate me," he recalled. "There were four steps going down to the dugout. I tripped, fell headfirst and landed right on top of Casey." It was a fitting conclusion to one of the most unusual debuts in major league history.

Despite his late season heroics, James spent the 1959 season at Richmond, appearing in 70 games, posting a 9–6 record and an excellent 1.91 ERA. Richmond manager and former Yankee pitcher Eddie Lopat said James had one of the best sliders he'd ever seen. James reported to the Yankee camp the following spring, 26 years old and, despite his lengthy travails in the minor leagues, confident he would make the club. "Since I was seven years old," James said, "I'd always had the ambition to pitch for the Yankees and nothing or nobody could dissuade me from that thought. I was either too dumb to realize that I shouldn't have tried or I just had a very strong belief in myself." James was so confident he'd even held out for a higher salary. "I was pretty proud of that," he said. "I'd pitched only three innings in the big leagues and I was holding out already."

James was the sensation of the Yankee camp. He ripped off seven scoreless innings, then combined with fellow rookie Bill Bethel to no-hit the Philadelphia Phillies. It was a good time to pitch well, for if James was ever going to make the Yankee roster, 1960 was the year. The pitching staff was more unsettled than it had been in many seasons. James continued his strong pitching, racking up 17 shutout innings before finally surrendering a run. He received the James P. Dawson Award as the outstanding rookie in the Yankee camp, and *The Sporting News* picked him as the top rookie pitching prospect in the American League.

"One writer told me I forced Casey to keep me that year," James said. "Every article talked about my size. One time that spring, we got rained out, and I went over to Casey in the hotel lobby. I talked to him to see if he thought I'd ever make the team. He mentioned my height. They always did." Nonetheless, James' excellent spring won him a spot in the Yankee bullpen, where he would pitch middle relief and dodge the errant warmup throws of Ryne Duren.

Another diminutive Yankee rookie was the aptly-named lefthander, Billy Short, who stood just 5'9". Short had been 17–6 at Richmond in 1959, and was being compared to Whitey Ford. "We were the same size," Short said recently. "I think that was as far as it went. There was really no comparison other than size." In 1960, given the Yankee need for pitchers, and Short's great minor league record, there was great hope that the similarity extended beyond vertical measurement. "I was really young," Short recalled, "and a bit on the cocky side, so I expected to make the team." He was in the service during the off-season and didn't report from Fort Sam Houston until late March. "I'm ready to pitch tomorrow," he said when he arrived. In the three weeks of training camp that remained, Short pitched well and made the club.

Not every Yankee pitcher was short and wiry. One of the big, strong, hard-throwing youngsters in camp was Jim Coates, a raw-boned hillbilly from Farnham, a tiny Virginia town located between the Potomac and Rappahannock Rivers that was home to just 97 people.* Like James, Coates had control trouble in the minors. "I could throw the hell out of the ball," he said, "but I was wild."

---

*When he was a farmhand at Richmond, Coates was called the Pride of Northern Neck, for the Chesapeake section from which he hailed. Many of his teammates would have substituted "Red" for "Northern."

That was an understatement. In 1952, at the age of 19, Coates started a game for the Yankee farm club in Olean. He got through the first two innings without difficulty. In the third, he walked the first five batters on just twenty pitches, not one of which was anywhere near the plate. "The harder I threw," he said, "the wilder I got." After the fifth walk, Bunny Mick, the Olean playing manager, trotted in from his position in right field. "He said," Coates recalled, "'You son of a bitch, you're going to stay out there until you get them out.'" Mick trotted back to the outfield and watched as Coates walked the next two batters. He went back to the mound and again told Coates he was staying in there. Six more walks followed, a total of 13 in succession. "Some guys wouldn't even get into the batter's box, I was so wild," Coates said. Finally, a full sixty minutes after the inning had started, Coates retired the side, much to the relief of the opposing hitters and the remaining fans.

Recalling the incident recently, Coates said, "I've seen ballplayers that it would have affected pretty badly, but it didn't bother me. It just made me say, 'I'll get you next time.'" That statement was made with the perspective of fifty years. At the time, the ordeal shook Coates badly. He didn't sleep that night, and said in 1960 he had dreaded going back to the Olean ballpark. "The fans started calling me The Wild Boy from the Country," he said. "Everywhere I went I could hear them saying that."

In 1955, Coates caught the Yankees' eye by winning 15 games and leading the Eastern League with 182 strikeouts. He pitched two games for the Yankees in 1956, and had a great season at Richmond the next year, winning 14 games and again leading his league in strikeouts. The Richmond manager was former Yankee pitching star Lopat, who took Coates under his wing and helped him with his control, both of his pitches and his temper. In a poll of International League managers, Coates was rated the best pitching prospect in the league, the player most ready for the major leagues, and the pitcher with the best fast ball.

Coates didn't make the Yankee staff in 1958, due to a hairline fracture in his arm. He defied Lopat's instructions to take it easy when he returned, and injured the arm again. After missing nearly the entire year, Coates reached the big leagues to stay in 1959. He was out of options and, even though he hadn't pitched much in 1958, had too much talent to give away. Coates spent most of the season in New York and compiled a 5–1 record, winning his last four starts.

By the time he reached the big leagues, Coates had decent control — at least when he wanted to. Throughout his career, he had a reputation for throwing at hitters and was involved in a number of brushback battles. "He was the headhunter at that time," recalled pitcher Galen Cisco. "I didn't mind pitching inside," Coates said recently. "Some of the best pitchers in the world throw inside. Look at Roger Clemens. Casey told me that the plate had two sides to it and I could take whatever side I wanted. I'd brush you back, I'd move you out. You had to go. It's just that simple."

"One time," said Bud Daley, "Coates and I made a bet that every time we pitched against a certain hitter he would be knocked down at least one time each game. After I retired, I went to an old timer's game and this guy was there. He said, 'How come Coates used to knock me down all the time?' Coates was mean. He'd just as soon knock you down as not." Throughout his career, Coates was involved in a number of brawls that began when he sent a batter sprawling in the dust. In his first full year in the big leagues, he fired a pitch at the head of Early Wynn, himself a notorious brush back artist. "Some day I may get all nine of them," Wynn vowed after the game.

"Coates hated Jimmy Piersall and Piersall hated him," said James. "He used to throw at Piersall all the time." Coates once threw at Piersall when Jimmy was standing next to the plate watching him warm up.

Coates also had a running feud with Piersall's Cleveland teammate, Vic Power. In 1961, he hit Power with a pitch. Power went down to first base and started yelling at Coates, who began throwing repeatedly to first, even though Power was standing on the bag. It wasn't enough for Coates to hit Power once; he was going to drill him while he was running the bases.

Coates didn't mellow with age. In 1966, when he was 33 years old and pitching in the Pacific Coast League, he nailed Vancouver's Ricardo Joseph on the wrist with a fastball. In the ensuing melee, Santiago Rosario of Vancouver hit Seattle catcher Merritt Ranew on the head with a bat and inflicted a near career-ending injury. Ranew was carried off the field on a stretcher with a brain injury, and spent the next ten months recovering. The next day, Coates was assaulted in the hotel lobby by Joseph, and suffered a broken nose and four loosened teeth. The following year, Coates was back in the majors, pitching for the Angels, when he hit Cleveland's Tony Horton in the head and precipitated another brawl.

"One day we were on an airplane," said one of the Yankee pitchers. "The writers were asking the players about throwing at guys. They said, 'Can you look a guy in the eye and then

Jim Coates was a tough hillbilly from Virginia who was known as one of the premier brushback artists of his time. Coates also had another disconcerting habit. He slept with his eyes open.

throw at him?'" Duren said, no, he couldn't do it. It was bad enough to hit somebody, Duren said, let alone to do it intentionally. Bob Turley said he couldn't do it either. Art Ditmar said he could hit somebody, but not in the head. "They asked Coates, 'Could you look at a guy's head and then throw at it?' He said, 'You're goddamn right.' He was a mean hombre."

In addition to flattening opposing batters, Coates had one other disconcerting habit. "I roomed with him once and I'd never do it again," said Daley. "He used to sleep with his eyes open. We called him 'The Mummy.'" Coates isn't sure if he slept with his eyes open for, as he said, if he knew it, he would have been awake. "We were on a plane one time," he said, "and I was sitting by the window next to [trainer] Joe Soares. Casey's wife was walking from the back to the front of the plane. She goes up and tells Casey, 'You'd better go back there and look. I think one of your players is dead.'"

When the 1960 season began, Coates was part of a pitching staff that posed more questions than answers. Would Turley rebound from a poor season? Could Short and James pitch in the big leagues? Was Duren's wrist fully healed? Would Terry realize his potential? Before the season, *The Sporting News* set forth seven keys to a successful Yankee comeback. First, Turley would have to bounce back. When the season was over, Turley had won just one more game in 1960 than he had in '59 and 12 less than he had in '58. Second, the club needed to add one solid starting pitcher. They didn't. Third, Maris needed to adapt to playing left field. When the season started, Maris was in right. Fourth, the club needed an "emphatic rise" by Mantle. Mantle played better than in '59, but batted just .275. Fifth, Kubek needed to improve his fielding at short, which he did. Sixth, the third base problem needed to be solved, which it wasn't, and finally, Skowron had to have an injury-free, productive season, which he did. By the end of the season, only two of the questions had been answered in a positive manner, yet the Yankees managed to win the pennant.

The club certainly didn't look like pennant contenders in the spring, posting an 11–21 record in exhibition games. "This is the most baffling training season I have run into in my twelve seasons as manager of the Yankees," Stengel said. "The old Yankees are dead," proclaimed *Sports Illustrated*, "and their replacements are not in the same class. This is a sound team but it is far from being a great one and it will need lots of luck to rise above third place ... they are going to have a heck of a time winning the pennant ... New York has not only lost its physical edge over the other clubs but its psychological advantage, too. No one is in awe of the magical pin-striped uniform any more."

Major league baseball had an unusual schedule in 1960, as the National League began play one week before the American. In he Yankee opener, on April 19 in Boston, Coates pitched a complete game and Maris showed why the Yankees had been so eager to acquire him. He had a single, a double and two home runs, driving in four runs in an 8–4 win.

In the early weeks of the season, the club was erratic. At the end of May, they were in fourth place with an 18–17 record, four games behind the surprising Baltimore Orioles, who led not only the Yankees, but also the defending champion White Sox.

Not many expected Baltimore to maintain its early pace. Since moving from St. Louis, the Orioles had been fixtures in the second division, and had never had a winning record. In 1954, their first year in Baltimore, the club lost 100 games and finished 57 games out of first. In 1959, the Orioles finished sixth with a record of 74–80, twenty games behind the pennant-winning White Sox. They didn't have much success in between.

The continuous losses tore at Baltimore manager Paul Richards, an intense man who hated to lose. Yet, since taking over the Orioles in 1955, Richards had done little but lose, 417 times in five years. His best finish was 76–76 in 1958. Richards was a pitching guru, but his team had virtually no power, hitting only 54 home runs in his first season. In 1959, the Orioles hit 109 homers, which placed them next-to-last in the league.

A tall, thin, taciturn Texan from Waxahachie, Paul Rapier Richards was a former major league catcher of modest playing ability and soaring ambition. He had some unusual talents. In 1926, while in high school, Richards pitched and won a game right handed one day and won another pitching left handed the next day. He did a little ambidextrous relieving in the minors, but concentrated on catching, where he excelled defensively.

Richards signed with the Dodger organization as an infielder, but when he reported in the spring, he noticed an overabundance of infielders and a shortage of catchers. Richards therefore said he was a catcher, and it was behind the plate that he began his professional career.

Richards reached the big leagues with Brooklyn in 1932, and saw irregular duty with the Dodgers, Giants and Athletics through 1935. In 1936, he was sent to Atlanta of the Southern League, where he remained for seven years. As a veteran catcher, Richards was invaluable in working with both young and old pitchers. Dutch Leonard, a veteran knuckleballer, arrived in Atlanta in the mid–'30s, sent there mainly because no big leaguer could catch him. Richards learned to handle the knuckler, and helped Leonard work his way back to the major leagues, where he became a 20 game winner and pitched until the age of 45. For Richards, it was the beginning of a lifelong relationship with the knuckleball.

In 1938, at the age of 29, Richards was named player-manager, and led Atlanta to the league championship. The Crackers swept through the playoffs and the Dixie Series and Richards, in his first season at the helm, was honored as the minor league manager of the year.

In 1943, with major league rosters depleted by military call-ups, Richards returned to the major leagues as a player, catching for the Tigers through 1946. He worked with a young pitcher named Hal Newhouser, who had tremendous potential but had won only 34 games in four seasons. Richards alternately encouraged and berated Newhouser, and helped him win back-to-back MVP awards in 1944 and 1945.

When the regulars came back from the war, Richards returned to the minor leagues, serving as player-manager of the International League Buffalo Bisons for three years. In 1951, he assumed his first major league managing post, and led the long-suffering Chicago White Sox to four consecutive first division finishes. After moving to Baltimore as both field manager and GM in 1955, however, Richards' magic touch disappeared.

People who met Paul Richards generally respected him, often feared him, frequently disliked him, but they never forgot him. Although he had only a high school education, Richards was a voracious reader who once won a bet by reciting the entire Gettysburg Address without missing a line. A dynamic public speaker, he disliked small talk, and was somewhat of a mystery to his players and fellow managers. "Paul is the kind," said legendary baseball executive Frank Lane, "who would rather have your respect than your affection." Lane had the greatest admiration for Richards' ability in the dugout. "But I never liked him," he added. "Richards looked out for Richards, but nobody did his job any better. He was tough and aloof, and when he walked into a clubhouse it was like a cold, sharp wind sweeping through it."

Roy Terrell wrote in *Sports Illustrated*, "[Richards] seldom praises good performance, for in his code that is what a ballplayer is supposed to give. He discourages familiarity, having little or nothing to do with his team off the field." "He never made friends with any of the ballplayers," said Joe DeMaestri.

"He didn't really say a heck of a lot to anybody," recalled pitcher Chuck Estrada. "He was a very quiet man. I was 20 years old when I was called up to the big leagues. We were in Kansas City when one of the coaches said, 'Mr. Richards wants to talk to you.' I'm just a raw kid from the sticks and I'm saying, 'Oh, my god.' I walked into his office and he said, 'What nationality are you?' I said, 'Spanish and Italian.' He said, 'Well, you can go now.' That was it."

Richards believed he could win ballgames through the sheer strength of his intellect, and loved to make moves on the field, pinch-hitting and changing pitchers frequently. He was one of the first to play lefty-righty percentages to the hilt. "On the field," said longtime executive John McHale, "he is usually two or three moves ahead of anybody else." "He was probably the smartest manager I ever played for," said DeMaestri, "and one of the toughest."

Some of Richards' moves were unorthodox. When he first began playing night games in the minor leagues, he noticed that pitchers were having a difficult time reading his signs, so he bought four bicycle reflectors and fastened them to the bottom of his chest protector. When Richards wanted to signal for a fastball, he covered three reflectors. Two covered reflectors meant a curve.

As a manager, Richards sometimes took a pitcher off the mound for just one batter, moved him to another position and then back to the mound. He seized every advantage, no matter how small. In 1961, Tiger manager Bob Scheffing complained that the bases at Baltimore's Memorial Stadium were too low. That hurt Scheffing's club, which could run, but not Richards,' which could not.

Perhaps Richards' most famous innovation was the development of the oversized catcher's mitt for handling knuckleball pitchers. When the Orioles first acquired Hoyt Wilhelm, Richards cringed as he watched catcher Gus Triandos struggle to contain Wilhelm's darting knuckleball. In 1959, there were 38 passed balls with Wilhelm pitching, and by May of 1960, there were 11 more. Other managers had solved the problem by trading Wilhelm. Not Richards. He produced the big mitt, which measured 41 inches in diameter, and Oriole catchers missed only three more Wilhelm knucklers the rest of the year.

One of the shortcomings of the big glove was that it was very difficult for the catcher to handle throws from the outfield on tag plays at the plate. Richards had another idea. When the pitcher was running past the catcher to back up home plate, he flipped his fielding glove to the catcher, who tossed the big basket to the pitcher. The glove worked marvelously until 1967, when the American League passed a rule limiting the size of the catcher's mitt. In 1966, the White Sox had probably the best bullpen in the major leagues, featuring knuckleballers Wilhelm and Eddie Fisher, and had just acquired Wilbur Wood, a third flutterballer. Since there were virtually no other knuckeballers in the league, the rest of the clubs decided it would be a good idea to ban the big glove.

Richards was a difficult taskmaster. "I don't know whether today's players would go through with the work he put us through," said Oriole pitcher Jack Fisher. "It was tough. But it was what made us. He was one man that you'd better respect or you weren't going to be around. He put us through fundamental drills and we worked on fundamentals until they were coming out our ears. We hated it at the time, but look at some of the things that go on today. Pitchers don't cover first base, or they don't back up bases. That became second nature to us. It was that kind of work that made us what we were."

"Paul Richards was one of the smartest baseball men I ever knew as far as strategy and planning a game," said pitcher Hector "Skinny" Brown, who played with the Orioles from 1956–62. "But you had to do it his way." In spring training one year, Richards asked Brown to show the other pitchers how to get a lead off second base. "Paul," he asked, "do you want me to show them how to lead off your way?" "Brownie," Richards replied, "is there any other way but my way if you're going to play for me?"

During his early years at Baltimore, Richards moved a lot of pieces around his chess board, with a purpose but meager results. Between 1954 and 1957, 114 different players appeared on the Oriole roster. Richards traded pitchers Bob Turley and Don Larsen to the Yankees for an accumulation of bodies, and tried to develop youngsters to take their place.

As a former catcher, Richards' greatest skill was developing young pitchers and getting additional mileage out of fading veterans. Finally, by the spring of 1960, Richards' efforts bore fruit. Baltimore's young pitching staff, with four young righthanders and one flame-throwing lefty, was the envy of the American League. Twenty-one-year-old Jerry Walker made the 1959 All-Star squad with an 11–10 mark and 20-year-old Milt Pappas was 15–9. Fisher, also 20, arrived midway through the year. The following spring, Richards discovered 21-year-old Steve Barber, who had toiled in D ball the previous season, and Chuck Estrada, the eldest of the group at 22, who had won 46 games in his three previous minor league seasons.

The "Baby Birds" all threw very hard, and some were quite wild. In 1958, Estrada led the Sally League in strikeouts with 181 and walks with 153, while Barber walked 143 in 159 innings at Pensacola in 1959. He had an experience much like that of Coates at Orleans. His manager, Lou Fitzgerald, told Barber before a start that he didn't care if he walked 500 batters, he was going to pitch the entire nine innings. After three walks in the first inning, Fitzgerald went to the mound. "You've got 497 walks left," he said, and returned to the dugout. Barber pulled himself together and won the game.

Not only was Barber fresh from a D classification, he hadn't even been a winner at that level. In three seasons in the minors, he'd never had a record better than .500. Barber also had a reputation for a hot temper, and once, during a salary dispute, left spring training to work as an electrician. He was cantankerous and difficult to manage, but he could throw hard. In Miami, during spring training in 1960, a rudimentary timing device was used to clock of number of baseball's hardest throwers, including Duren, Sandy Koufax, Turley, and Barber. Barber, at 95.55 mph, was the fastest of them all.

In 1960, Richards put all of his youngsters in the rotation, and the results were remarkably good. The five Baby Birds, all under the age of 23, found the strike zone often enough to be effective and missed it enough to keep the hitters loose. By early June, Estrada and Barber each had records of 5–1, and Barber had a 1.55 ERA. "Oh, my god," said Fisher. "What stuff Barber had. He threw a ball that catchers absolutely hated to catch, because it was a real, real heavy sinker. The difference between catching Estrada and Barber was like night and day. Triandos used to say, 'I could go back there and catch Estrada with a pair of tweezers, even thought the speed of the ball might have been faster." Catching Barber was tough and hitting him was even tougher. "Unless you got it right on the good spot of the bat," Fisher continued, "it was like you were hitting a lead weight."

In addition to his fine pitching, Richards had two outstanding youngsters, Ron Hansen and Brooks Robinson, on the left side of the infield. Shortstop Hansen would win Rookie of the Year honors while Robinson, already in his sixth year at the age of 23, made the All Star team for the first of many times. Jim Gentile, a flashy 26-year-old rookie first baseman drafted from the Dodgers, also made the All Star squad, and finished with a .292 batting average, 21 home runs and 98 RBI. Gentle, Hansen and Estrada were named to the All-Rookie team. If the Baltimore youngsters could hold up through a complete season, the Orioles were going to surprise some people.

To win the pennant, the Orioles would need to outlast the White Sox, who returned their pennant-winning club virtually intact. Speedsters Luis Aparicio, Nelson Fox and Jim Landis got on base and waited for sluggers Ted Kluszewski, Minnie Minoso, Sherm Lollar and Roy Sievers to drive them home. Chicago's weakness was pitching, for Early Wynn and Billy Pierce were getting old. Wynn and Bob Shaw, who combined for 40 victories in the pennant winning '59 season, won just 26 in 1960. Could the White Sox's offense and speed carry them to a second straight title?

The Yankees were an enigma. Were they a powerhouse like the old championship teams, or were they more like the mediocre Yankees of 1959? Maris got off to a flying start, and appeared to be a threat to win the Triple Crown. For the first half of the season, he was among the leaders in batting average, and led in home runs and RBI. He hit 13 home runs in June, giving him 24 for the season. "[Y]ou might say," wrote Drebinger, "that Roger marks the difference between the stumbling Yanks of a year ago and the club that's fighting around the top right now."

Moose Skowron was almost as hot as Maris.* During his Yankee career, which began in 1954, the Moose had always hit well, topping the .300 mark in each of his first four seasons. He also hit homers and drove in runs. Whenever he was on the field, Skowron was a major contributor to the Yankee offense. The problem was that he was in the trainer's room too often and on the field too infrequently. "He seems to like the clang of the ambulance," Stengel once said. Doctors told Skowron his muscles lacked elasticity, making him prone to pulls, which had sidelined him a number of times during his career. In 1957, while lifting an air conditioner, Skowron suffered a back injury that caused him to miss most of the World Series and was to plague him for the rest of his career. In 1959, after missing time early in the season with his bad back, Skowron stretched for a bad throw from third baseman Hector Lopez, resulting in a collision and a broken wrist, which shelved him for the year. Through 1959, his frequent injuries limited Skowron to an average of less than 110 games a season. Only in 1956 had he played a full year.

While recovering from his wrist injury, Skowron started swimming, in order to elasticize the taut muscles which caused him so much trouble. He reported to spring training in 1960 claiming to be in great shape, and primed for his best year. Skowron was the most consistent Yankee, and played virtually every game. In early August, he was the American League's lead-

---

*Skowron got his nickname from his grandfather, who thought he looked like Italian dictator Benito Mussolini.

ing hitter, and wound up playing in 146 of the club's 154 games, batting .309, with 26 home runs and 91 RBI.

While Maris and Skowron started out hot, Mantle was in a woeful slump. He was late reporting to camp after his holdout, suffered a swollen knee almost immediately upon his arrival, and sat out several exhibition games. At the end of May, Mickey was hitting just .228, and was being booed regularly at the Stadium. On Memorial Day, Mantle caught a fly ball for the final out of the second game of a doubleheader and ran toward the dugout as fans poured onto the field. "They grabbed my cap and nearly put out my eye in the process," Mantle said. "They were grabbing and clawing at my glove. I finally put my head down and bulled through the pack like a fullback." While fighting his way through the crowd, Mantle was hit hard on the jaw.

Mantle went to Lenox Hill Hospital to have his jaw X-rayed, and the Yankees said they would use additional security to see that, in the future, Mantle could reach the dugout safely. That evening, several fans called the Yankee offices to claim that Mickey had struck them or their children. Mantle denied throwing punches at anyone. He wouldn't think of taking a swing at a kid, he said, for he had four of his own. "On the other hand," he added, "you have to protect yourself in a situation like that. Sure, I warded off people with my hands, but it was more like swimming breast-stroke than punching or even straight-arming." Nevertheless, Mantle's public image suffered another blow. Now he was more than just an ingrate who had held out for an outrageous salary. He was a bully who was beating up kids. Worse yet, he was a bully with a .228 batting average and only six home runs. Why couldn't he be more like Maris, whose sterling play was making him a fan favorite?

There were other problems. The infield, with the exception of Skowron, was unsettled all season. Kubek was the regular shortstop, but Stengel also used him in the outfield. McDougald shuttled between second and third, then to the bench, as Stengel played Boyer and Bobby Richardson. Richardson, who batted .301 in 1959, slumped to .252 and rode the bench during the second half of the year. Boyer played both third base and shortstop, but went into a batting slump late in the year and was replaced by McDougald. Gil was no longer the fielder he had been, but Boyer was not the hitter McDougald was. Richardson could field but wasn't hitting.

The Yankees, who had always seemed to be three deep at every position, were woefully thin. The bench, which in past years included Elston Howard, Enos Slaughter and Gene Woodling, now had Ken Hunt, Kent Hadley and 39-year-old Elmer Valo. Johnny Blanchard, who would become the best pinch hitter in the American League in 1961, rarely left the bench. He didn't get to the plate until May 29, and didn't get his first hit until mid–July. Valo, counted on to be one of the Yanks' top pinch swingers, was released early in the season. Hunt was sent to Richmond. Hadley hated pinch hitting and did poorly.

A powerful, left handed hitter who came to the Yankees in the Maris trade, Hadley was not about to move Skowron off first base, but a big lefty could make a good living as a role player in Yankee Stadium. Long after his regular playing days were over, Johnny Mize had been an integral part of several Yankee pennant winners. Slaughter did the same. But Hadley simply could not accept the role.

Hadley was an anthropology major at USC who had been signed by the Tigers in 1956 and traded to the Athletics the following year. He didn't hit for average in the minors, but led the Southern Association with 34 homers in 1958. After a so-so rookie year, he went to the Yankees without much enthusiasm. "I was apprehensive because of all the talent they had," he recalled. "I was not cut out to be a pinch hitter. I was cut out to be a starter, get my four turns at bat and get all my cuts. I'm an emotional person and I couldn't deal with it. I started to think, 'If I'm going to have to make my living as a pinch hitter, I was going to have a tough row to hoe.'" In August, Hadley finally got to play regularly —for the Richmond Virginians of the International League — and the Yankees obtained veteran Dale Long from the San Francisco Giants to take his place. Hadley's major league career was over.

Hadley left New York with bitter feelings. "I don't have good memories of the Yankees," he said recently. After he was told he was being sent to Richmond, Hadley had to ride back to New York on the train with the rest of the team. "Once you're released, you're kind of a leper," he said. "They needled me in the clubhouse. 'Are you still here, Hadley, because we heard Dale Long's coming to New York?' We got on the train and no one would go near me. I sat by myself until Mel Allen came and sat by me. He said, 'Kent, I'm sorry,' as if he was the only friend I had on the train."

The rest of the bench consisted of DeMaestri and Boyer, defensive specialists who were of little use offensively. Only Berra and Lopez, when they weren't starting, and Bob Cerv, who had been re-acquired from Kansas City (thank God for the Athletics) in May, were of any use off the bench.

The Yankees also lacked a strong defense. Lopez, in his first season in the outfield, made an adventure of nearly every fly ball. McDougald was slowing down, and lost a game for Ford in early June with two ninth inning errors. The two best defensive infielders, Boyer and Richardson, played irregularly.

After a sluggish start, the Yankees made a move in June. They won 13 of 14, and 20 of 25, to move into first place. Drebinger was ready to hand the pennant to New York, writing of "the gay dash of the Yankees which seems to be giving promise to an early liquidation of the American League." Drebinger was premature, however, for while the Yankees were not as bad as they appeared to be in April and May, they were not as good as they seemed in June. Furthermore, the White Sox and Orioles showed no signs of collapse. After holding first place for nearly a month, the Yanks dropped out of the lead in late July.

The pitching, which had Stengel so worried in the spring, justified his concerns. "It wasn't anywhere close to what we had in the early '50s," said McDougald. "Should the Yankees lose the pennant," Drebinger wrote in mid–September, "the pitchers will be blamed." Turley, one of the first to experiment with a no-windup delivery, tried going back to using a windup, then went back to the no windup. With either motion, he was not the Turley of 1958. His 9–3 record was deceptive, and his performance was erratic all season. Turley did not pitch a complete game until the middle of June. Then he went into a slump and was dispatched to the bullpen.

Coates got off to such a good start that he pitched in the first all star game.* Thanks to tremendous offensive support, he won his first nine decisions, despite having an ERA above four runs per game. On July 9, Coates suffered his first defeat since June 21, 1959, ending a string of 13 wins in a row. The end of Coates' winning streak was followed by a losing streak, which lasted for two months. He was taken out of the rotation but, shuttling between the bullpen and starting duties, still finished 13–3.

The rest of the staff was struggling. In late June, Ford was just 3–5. Short, billed as the next Ford, had suffered an elbow injury earlier in his minor league career. He'd rushed his conditioning when he got out of the Army in the spring of 1960, which put a further strain on his tender elbow. Short got off to a fast start, and by the first week in May had three wins under his belt. "I don't believe that any pitcher in my time here," said Stengel, "ever came up with more stuff, more ambition, more determination and better working habits." Then the elbow flared up again and Short lost his control. "In the fourth or fifth game," he recalled, "my elbow started bothering me a little. It would tighten up in maybe the sixth or seventh inning. The next time it would tighten up in the fourth or fifth, and then in the third and-boom-I was out of there." By the first week of June, Short was out of New York.

Ditmar, Coates, Turley, Ford and Terry did most of the starting, but none of them had as

---

From 1959 through 1962 two all star contests were played each year.

many as 30 starts. Ford had trouble finishing, and many wondered if he had become a six inning pitcher. When Short was sent to Richmond, Eli Grba, who wound up pitching one of the most important games of the Yankee season, was recalled and started a few games. "We've got to get some starting pitchers," Stengel said at the All Star break, "or we will be in bad shape."

The bullpen was as unsettled as the starting rotation. James, who Casey didn't even want on the team, won five of six decisions, but rarely pitched in clutch situations. Duren was wild and unreliable, walking 49 in 49 innings, and Stengel rarely used him in the latter stages of the season. Little lefty Bobby Shantz was 34 and had had arm trouble ever since winning the Cy Young Award in 1952. He'd missed the last six weeks of the 1959 season. Shantz was effective in spots, but couldn't handle a heavy relief load. Duke Maas, who won 14 games as a starter in 1959, suffered from a sore arm early in the season. He pitched decently in relief, but was not the stopper Stengel needed to replace Duren. The starters also did relief duty between turns, with mixed results.

The Yankee staff needed help if they were to hold off the Orioles and their talented young pitchers. In July, the Yanks sent scout Bill Skiff to Jersey City to check on 20-year-old Richmond right hander Bill Stafford. Stafford looked good, Skiff reported, and there was also a veteran left hander on the Jersey City squad who could help the Yankee bullpen immediately. On July 22, with the Yankees holding a lead of just three percentage points over the White Sox, they acquired veteran left-hander Luis Enrique Arroyo from Jersey City for cash and minor league pitcher Zack Monroe. On July 26, Arroyo made his Yankee debut with two hitless innings to preserve a win for Ditmar. "It's great to be a Yankee," he said. The veteran lefthander, 9–7 in 39 games with Jersey City, proved a great acquisition, appearing in 29 games and posting a 5–1 record, 7 saves and a 2.85 ERA.

In order to provide help for the starting staff, the Yanks brought up Stafford. In 1959, Stafford had a very disappointing season, posting a record of 1–8 at Richmond before he was sent down to the Eastern League. In 1960, however, he bounced back and was the Yankees' best young pitching prospect. At the time he was recalled, Stafford was 11–7 at Richmond and leading the International League with a 2.00 ERA.

Despite his youth, and being excitable by nature, Stafford was surprisingly poised under the pressure of a tight pennant race. In his first start, against the Red Sox, he faced Ted Williams in the first inning and got him out. Although he wasn't involved in the decision, Stafford pitched well, and in 11 games down the stretch, fashioned a 3–1 record and 2.25 ERA.

In late July, after the White Sox had beaten the Yankees three straight times at the Stadium, to build a two game lead, Grba hurled a complete game win in the series finale. Had they lost, the Yanks would have been three games back and sliding. Grba's win pulled them to within one length of the Sox. "Praise the Lord," Stengel said after the game, "from whom all blessings flow." "Tom Meany and Ralph Houk both wrote," recalled Grba with pride, "that I pitched the most important game of the year. Nobody was pitching complete games, and the bullpen was shattered and all screwed up. I'm rather proud of that year."

With Arroyo a Yankee, Stengel elected to send James, the sensation of training camp, to Richmond. Although he was 5–1, he had been hit hard lately, and his ERA had risen to 4.40. In his last appearance for the Yankees, James pitched three scoreless innings against the White Sox and was feeling pretty good. When he left the field that day, Mantle congratulated him and patted him on the backside. "I thought," said James, "I'm finally getting on the team. Mickey said something to me. I was getting ready to go into the shower when Pete Previte came up to me and told me Casey wanted to see me. There's only one reason the old man wants to see you, and that's to send you down. I knew he didn't want to say 'Nice game,' but I was hoping that's what it was. I went to his office and Casey was sitting there with his jock strap on. He started talking and I had no idea what he was saying. All of a sudden he leaped off the desk and said,

'When you get down to Richmond, make them give you a low target.' That's how I knew I was going back to Richmond." Stengel told James he needed another pitch, and that he should learn to throw a screwball or a forkball.

James refused to go. He was 27 and had pitched too long in the minor leagues, he said, to start over. James went back to his hotel and stayed there for several days. "Tony Kubek was my roommate," he said, "and every day Tony would come back and say, 'John, they told me to tell you to get down to Richmond.' One day he said, 'John, they told me to tell you to get down to Richmond or they're going to stop paying you.'" James decided to get down to Richmond.

On July 31, the White Sox were in first place, the Yankees were ½ game behind and the Orioles were third, 3½ games in back of Chicago. Cleveland was also in contention, just two games behind the Orioles. The fact that the Yankees, with their shaky pitching, were just ½ game out of first was due in large part to the hitting of Maris. On July 20th, Roger slugged his 31st home run, which put him 11 games ahead of Babe Ruth's 1927 pace. He was in the top ten in batting with a .314 mark and led the league with 76 RBI, twelve in front of Skowron, who was second.

In late July, Maris stopped hitting. After his 31st homer, he went into a slump. His batting average dropped below .300 and he had a home run drought. Maris had always been a streak hitter, prone to dreadful slumps. For the first half of the 1960 season, he batted .320, with 27 home runs and 69 RBI. For the second half, his marks were .239 with 12 homers and 43 RBI.

On August 14, the Yankees played a doubleheader against the Washington Senators. In the sixth inning of each game, a potential double play ball proved the undoing of a Yankee star. In the first game, Mantle grounded into a double play. He mistakenly thought there had been two outs, and stopped running half way down the first base line. The fans let loose with a torrent of catcalls and Stengel pulled him from the game. "I took him out because he didn't run," said Stengel, "and I'm tired of seeing him not run. If he can't run, he should tell me." Stengel's action had the desired effect on Mantle, who returned the next day and hit two home runs.

In the second game of the doubleheader, Maris slid hard into Senator second baseman Billy Gardner attempting to break up a double play. Gardner's elbow hit Maris in the ribs and inflicted a severe bruise. Roger's ribs were so sore he couldn't swing a bat, and his availability appeared at first to be a day-to-day proposition. Yet, day after day went by and he failed to appear in the lineup. Finally, on August 26, Maris appeared as a pinch hitter and singled in a run. Still, however, he was not well enough to start, and there was talk that he was coddling his injury just a little too much. Five days later, on the 31st, Maris finally re-entered the starting lineup, after missing two and a half weeks, but did not hit like he had early in the season. He'd lost his sharpness, and any chance he may have had to catch Ruth. The pursuit would have to wait a year.

When Maris returned, the Yankees were in first place, one game ahead of the Orioles, whose young pitching staff was holding up surprisingly well under the pressure of a tight pennant race. By the end of the year, rookie Estrada would win a league-leading 18 games, Pappas would be 15–11, Barber 10–7 and Fisher 12–11. The infielders kept hitting and Richards kept his club in the thick of the battle. When the Orioles returned from a road trip in mid–August, they were greeted at the airport by nearly 3,000 fans, who had pennant fever for the first time since the Orioles had moved to Baltimore. On the 3rd of September, the Orioles moved into first place when Fisher beat the Yankees in Baltimore. The following day, Estrada beat them again to boost the lead to two games. With the addition of Stafford and Arroyo and the resurgence of Ford, the Yankee pitching was better, but now they couldn't hit.

During the first two weeks of September, the Orioles and Yankees battled neck and neck, and when Baltimore arrived in New York on September 16 for a four game weekend series, they were one percentage point behind the Yankees.

On Friday night, Stengel sent Ford, pitching on just two days rest, to the mound against

21-year-old Barber. Barber was fast but wild, walking seven. Lopez and Maris reached him for home runs, while the Orioles got nothing off Ford. With two outs in the ninth, Whitey had allowed only five hits and no runs, extending his string of scoreless innings against the Orioles to 33. A Baltimore rally drove him from the mound in the final inning, but Shantz finished off the 4–2 victory, giving the Yankees a one game lead. Although Ford had just ten wins, it was his fifth triumph of the year against the Yankees' closest rival.

On Saturday, Turley pitched against 22-year-old Estrada. "It was wonderful," said Estrada. "I'm from a town of 300 people and here I am pitching in this gigantic ballpark with all that history. The place was packed and they were booing me and all that fun stuff. It was exciting. I was playing against the greatest players in the game. What have you got to lose? People talk about pressure, but my job was just to get ready to play and then whatever happens, happens."

Estrada pitched a terrific game. The teams were tied 2–2 in the bottom of the sixth, when Berra hit a fly ball to deep right field. "They had that low right field fence in those days," Estrada said. "Al Pilarcik was the right fielder and he jumped too soon. The ball landed about one row back." The Orioles, as they had all season, came back. Gentile's home run tied the score in the seventh. In the bottom of the eighth, the Yankees loaded the bases. Richardson hit a line drive back at Estrada. The ball hit off the tip of his glove and caromed into the outfield. Two runs scored and the Yankees had a 5–3 win. Mantle, as hot as Maris was cold, had homered. "He has been spectacular in the field," gushed Stengel, "a hustler, great with the bat and I want to tell the fans how I feel about him." After the Yankees clinched the pennant, Casey called Mantle the club's MVP.

On Sunday the Yankees finished off their youthful challengers with a doubleheader sweep. Terry pitched a two hit shutout in the final game of the series, giving the Yankees a four game lead over both Baltimore and Chicago, who were tied for second. The Yankees had played their closest challengers head-to-head and beaten them four straight times. "They were all great games," said Fisher, "but they just happened to beat us."

Although the Yanks had 11 more games to play, the race was over, for the Yankees never wilted in the stretch. "When I first came to the Yankees," said Bud Daley, "they had four or five guys that I'd played with in Kansas City. They said, 'Hey, Bud, wait until you see these guys in September. They look like a different club.'" In 1964, Roger Repoz came up to the Yankees during the pennant drive. "I remember going to the ballpark," Repoz said, "and Mickey and Whitey were playing dice games. Here we are in the middle of a pennant race where if you lose one game you're out and they're playing dice. They were used to the pressure. The other teams just folded when they saw them coming."

The Yankees won all 11 of their remaining games, finishing the season with a 15 game winning streak. Terry won the pennant clincher against the Red Sox in Fenway Park on September 25. Fittingly, Arroyo, who had steadied the shaky bullpen, saved it, throwing just one pitch to get the final out. On the final day of the season, Dale Long, who batted .366 and strengthened the weak Yankee bench, hit a ninth inning, game-winning two run home run into the Yankee bullpen.

It had been an uneven season in the Bronx. The Yankees were 6–4 in April, 13–13 in May, 21–8 in June, 13–14 in July, 22–11 in August, 20–7 in September and 2–0 in October. The pennant was the Yankees' 25th, and Stengel's 10th, surpassing Connie Mack's American League record. Casey, the oldest manager to win a flag, was tied with his mentor, John McGraw, for the most pennants by any manager in the long history of major league baseball. In a few days, he would attempt to win his eighth World Series. On the same day the Yankees clinched the pennant in Boston, the Pittsburgh Pirates secured their first National League championship since 1927. The upstart Pirates, who had finished fourth the previous season, were the only obstacle standing between Casey and another World Championship.

◆ 3 ◆

A Hanging, Harry
High School Slider
The 1960 World Series

Prior to the seventh game of the 2001 World Series, after the Arizona Diamondbacks had posted three one-sided wins and the Yankees had taken three heart-stopping cliffhangers, many drew a comparison to the 1960 Fall Classic. In 1960, the Yankees won three games by wide margins, while the Pirates took four nip-and-tuck affairs and the series. "There were so many runs scored by the Yankees," said Pirate reliever Clem Labine, who gave up seven of them in just four innings. "How did we ever beat them?" The common wisdom was that an immensely superior New York team had had victory snatched from their grasp by an overmatched Pirate club that got a few lucky breaks.

The Yankees may have outscored the Pirates, but the common wisdom was simply not true, for entering the Series there was little disparity between the two clubs. "The Pittsburgh Pirates," wrote Roy Terrell in *Sports Illustrated* after the seventh game, "playing the same kind of baseball they played all year, beat a New York Yankee team which was playing over its head."

Many called the 1960 Pirates, who finished fourth in 1959, Cinderellas. The aberration, however, was 1959, not 1960. In 1958, the Pirates' young team, which had struggled mightily in the early half of the decade, finally matured, and finished second. Danny Murtaugh was named Manager of the Year and GM Joe Brown was Executive of the Year. Although Pittsburgh dropped to fourth place in 1959, they were just nine games out of first, despite terrible seasons by nearly every one of their key players. Pitcher Bob Friend, who won 22 games in 1958, gained weight in the off-season, lost his first seven decisions of 1959 and finished 8–19. George Witt, 9–2 with a 1.61 ERA in 1958, had arm trouble and was 0–7 with a 6.88 ERA. Bob Skinner's average dropped from .321 to .280, Bill Mazeroski's from .275 to .241 and Dick Groat's from .300 to .275. Mazeroski's home run production dropped from 19 to 6. Roberto Clemente, the Pirates' best player, hurt his arm and played in only 105 games. Had even one or two of those key players duplicated their 1958 season, the Pirates might well have won the '59 pennant.

While the Pirates weren't David, the Yankees certainly weren't Goliath. "The Yankees are still not the Yankees, at least not the Yankees of old, and they haven't been for some time," wrote Terrell, picking the Pirates to win the Series in six games. "Today their pitching is shaky and their hitting erratic; only superior power and a weak league, which the Yankees were a long way from dominating, enabled them to sneak through." "They form a reasonably good ballclub," wrote Arthur Daley, "better than average, but that's all." The Yankees posted 97 victories and needed a late surge to hold off the Orioles. The Pirates won 95 games and beat second place Milwaukee by seven lengths, one less than the Yankee margin over Baltimore. The Pirates' main weakness was a lack of pitching depth, for the staff was thin after Vern Law, Friend and ace reliever Roy Face. In a post-season series, however, pitching depth rarely plays an important role.

In nearly all categories, the Pirates were at least the equal of the Yankees. They had a team batting average of .276 compared to New York's .260. Although the Yankees hit considerably more home runs (Maris, Mantle and Skowron had more homers than the entire Pittsburgh team), and outhomered the opposition by 70, the Pirates played in cavernous Forbes Field, where the left field foul pole was 365 feet from home plate and the distance to the left center field fence was 457 feet. Pittsburgh's team ERA was 3.49, while New York's was 3.52.

Further, the Pirates had compiled their record in the National League, generally considered to be stronger than the American. In 1963, *Sports Illustrated* compared the records of American Leaguers traded to the National League and vice versa, and concluded that the senior circuit was tougher. Pete Runnels, the AL batting champ in '60 and '62, batted just .253 for Houston in '63. Dick Stuart, a part time first baseman for the Pirates in '62, led the AL in RBI the next season. The National League, which had just begun its long run of domination in the All Star Game, had been much quicker than the American to sign African-Americans when the color line was broken. In 1960, 41 of the 57 black major leaguers, many of whom were stars, played in the National League.

While New York and Pittsburgh were roughly equal in ability, experience favored the Yankees, who were perpetual World Series contestants. The Pirates had not appeared since 1927, when they had been swept by one of the best Yankee teams of all time. Only four Pirates, Labine, Don Hoak, Rocky Nelson and Gino Cimoli, had ever appeared in a World Series game, while more than half of the Yankee roster had Series experience. Moreover, other than Labine, the Pirate players had made only cameo appearances, while many of the Yankees had been in numerous classics, with Mantle, Berra and Ford holding a plethora of records. In all, 14 Yankees had played in 245 postseason games, while the four Pirates had appeared in just 18.

The Yankees entered the Series in good health, while the Pirates were handicapped by the fact that Dick Groat, who would be named the National League's Most Valuable Player, had broken his wrist in early September. He said he was ready to play in the Series, and he did, but he wasn't the same player who won the MVP trophy.

Many believed the outcome of the Series was determined before it began, when Stengel announced that Art Ditmar, not Whitey Ford, would start the opening game. Casey was going to save Ford for the third game, which would take place in Yankee Stadium, due in part to the fact that Whitey had never won a World Series game on the road. During the last week of the season, while the Yankees prepared for the Series, everyone assumed Ford would start the opener. Stengel said he hadn't yet decided, and would give Whitey a two inning stint the last day of the season before making a choice. That was a strange statement, even for Casey Stengel. After nine years in the big leagues and 133 wins, did Ford need to prove himself in a two inning relief appearance?

"I figured I'd better pick Ditmar," Stengel said when announcing his choice, "because he sometimes won the first game of important series for me, especially against Chicago when I needed the first one." The oddsmakers apparently disagreed with Stengel for, once Ditmar was named the opening game starter, odds on the Yanks dropped from 13–10 to 6–5.

Creating an air of mystery was one of Stengel's favorite pastimes. He loved unorthodox moves, particularly with his mound staff, and his pitchers rarely had defined roles. "Stengel brought you in anytime," said Craig Anderson, who pitched for Casey with the Mets. After playing for a manager for a while, said Anderson, a pitcher could usually determine what his role was and how to prepare for it. Not with Casey. "I could never figure out what he was going to do," Anderson said. "That made it a little harder, because we didn't know whether to warm up, or how hard we should warm up, or whether we were going to start or relieve." "Once in 1959," Eli Grba recalled, "Gary Blaylock and I warmed up for 13 consecutive days and never got in a ballgame."

The 1960 Yankee staff went through the entire season without falling into a pattern. Ditmar, Ford and Turley were principally starters, but had 20 relief appearances among them. Coates and Terry shuttled back and forth between starting and relieving, and the others had little idea when or if they would pitch.

The decision to start Ditmar defied logic. After the Series, Stengel said, "Ditmar won 15 games for me in the regular season and Ford won 12." While Ditmar was indeed the leading New York winner, he had been inconsistent and was by no means the standout pitcher on the staff. Despite winning only 12 games, Ford was the Yankees' money pitcher. Whitey had been bothered by an elbow strain early in the year, and didn't win his first game until the middle of May, but throughout the late summer, as the Yankees battled the Orioles, he was superb. Ford shut Baltimore out three times, and beat them in the crucial game of the season on September 16. He had five Series wins while Ditmar had never started a World Series game.

Nearly every Yankee was shocked when the opening game pitchers were announced. "How can you not pitch Ford?" asked Grba recently. "He's your best pitcher." Ryne Duren agreed. "He should have started Ford in the first game because he was our best pitcher going away, at least late in the season when he got feeling good." Even the Pirates were surprised. "Everybody thought Ford would start," said Pittsburgh infielder Dick Schofield.

Nevertheless, it was Ditmar versus Vernon Law at Forbes Field on October 5 — at least for one-third of an inning. After yielding a walk, a double and two singles, which resulted in three Pittsburgh runs, Ditmar was gone in favor of Jim Coates. "I did what I was trying to do," Ditmar said after the game, "get them to hit the ball on the ground."

Center fielder Bill Virdon broke the back of a budding Yankee rally in the fourth inning with a running catch on Berra just short of the right center field wall. In the fifth, Coates gave up a home run to Mazeroski, the Pirate second baseman's first home run at Forbes Field since July 16, which gave the Pirates a 5–2 advantage. Law, struggling on a bad ankle, was no more than adequate, but Roy Face relieved and finished the 6–4 Pirate victory.

Face, a most unlikely-looking ballplayer, stood only 5'8" tall and weighed just 155 pounds. He looked more like the carpenter he was during the off-season than one of baseball's premier relief pitchers, which he was during the summer. Face was a journeyman pitcher until he learned the forkball from former star reliever Joe Page in the Pirate camp one spring. In 1959, Face was 18–1, and in 1960, he appeared in a league-high 68 games and had 24 saves.

In addition to starting Ditmar, Stengel made one other unusual move. In the second game of the 1922 Series, Stengel, playing for the Giants against the Yankees, had been humiliated when John McGraw removed him for a pinch runner in the second inning. In the first game of the '60 Series, Stengel inflicted a similar humiliation upon young Cletis Boyer. The Yankees trailed 3–1 in the top of the second and had two runners on with nobody out. Boyer, New York's 23-year-old third baseman playing his first World Series game, was due up. As he walked toward the plate, Stengel called him back to the dugout. "When Casey called me back," Boyer said after the game, "I thought it was to tell me something, maybe to ask me to try to hit to right or give me a hint on what kind of pitcher Vernon Law is." Stengel was calling Boyer over, however, because he was sending Dale Long up to bat for him.

Stengel's expression "Hold that gun" was dreaded by players such as Bobby Richardson and, later with the Mets, Chris Cannizzaro. When they heard those words, they knew they were out of the game. "One time we were in Cincinnati," former Met Billy Cowan said, "and we got something going in the first or second inning. Chris was batting seventh or eighth and Casey sent up a pinch hitter for him. Casey was yelling, 'Canzoneri!' Chris was kind of hot-headed, and he just hunched his shoulders up and didn't answer. Casey's yelling at him to come back, and finally he yelled, 'Canzoneri, get back here. What the hell do you think you're doing? You're not going to hit in this situation,' and he jerked him out of the game. Chris walked back like somebody stole his wallet. He never even got to bat once." "He'd send Jesse Gonder up to bat for Chris in the third inning," said Bobby Klaus. "Chris would be walking out of the dugout and he'd hear, 'Hold that gun.' Canzy'd get so pissed."

Boyer didn't get the 'Hold that gun' command. "He never said another word to me," Boyer related. "All he did was tell Dale Long to grab a bat ... I can't figure it out." "Of course I decided to make my move early," Stengel said after the game. "How was I gonna know we'd get any-body on base in the ninth." Long flied out, the rally died and Boyer did not start again until the sixth game. His confidence was badly damaged and he was furious with Stengel. Boyer never forgave him. Three years later, at a banquet, he said, "I don't like him and I don't know any player who does."

Ford and Boyer remained on the sidelines for Game Two, as Turley, who won only nine games during the regular season, struggled through 8⅓ innings, yielding 13 hits, but winning easily 16–3. Mantle hit two home runs (one a 478 foot shot) and drove in five runs, tying a record that would last for nearly 48 hours. The Series was tied at one game each as the two teams headed for New York.

Ford finally appeared in the third game, the first at Yankee Stadium, and pitched his first World Series shutout, a four hitter, as the Bronx Bombers bombed the Pirates for the second day in a row. The score was 10–0 and the game was over after the first inning. Pirate starter Vinegar Bend Mizell missed the team bus to the park, which was perhaps a message from a higher authority that he should have stayed in bed. Like Ditmar, Mizell didn't survive the first inning. After yielding three singles and a walk, he was gone, trailing 1–0 and leaving the bases loaded. Labine relieved and gave up a dribbler to Elston Howard which went for a base hit and the second run.

Bobby Richardson came up with the bases loaded. Richardson half expected to hear "hold that gun," but Stengel was not about to repeat his strategy of the first game. The Yankees were ahead, and he wanted Richardson to bunt and squeeze home a second run. When the count went to 3–2, the bunt went off. Richardson swung and hit the ball into the left field bleachers, the seventh World Series grand slam and Richardson's first home run since April 30th. Richardson hadn't even hit a grand slam in high school, let alone professional ball, and had just three home runs in his big league career.

"He couldn't have hit a grand slam off me in my day if he had to," said Labine, then 34, with his best days behind him. "But he did." Labine was no longer in his day and this day was all Richardson's. In the fourth inning, he singled in two more runs, giving him six RBI, break-ing the record Mantle had tied in Game Two. The six RBI were only one less than Richardson had driven in since the All Star break.

After three games, the Yankees seemed primed for a runaway. They had a .397 team bat-ting average versus Pittsburgh's .250 and had out-homered the Pirates six to one. The Pitts-burgh staff, which was quickly being chewed up, had a combined ERA of 8.31. In 154 National League games, Murtaugh had never used more than five pitchers in a single contest. In two games in a row he had employed six.

The Yankees hoped to finish off the Pirates in New York during the next two games. "The Yankees have removed the last remnant of suspense," wrote columnist Jimmy Powers. "If you have a sadistic streak, you probably are relishing this series. Know something? It could get worse."

The fourth game began in the same fashion as the previous two. Ralph Terry, making his first World Series start, looked as sharp as Ford, setting the Pirates down in order in the top of the first, striking out two. In the bottom half of the inning, Bob Cerv led off with a single and Kubek followed with a double. With two runners on, none out, and Maris, Mantle and Berra coming up, the Yankee Stadium crowd was roaring, anticipating another rout. Following their two crushing defeats, it appeared as though the Pirates were teetering on the brink. A first inning rally might finish them off.

Maris hit a pop fly to short right field. Cerv tagged up but retreated to third when he saw Clemente's strong throw headed for the plate. Murtaugh then ordered Mantle walked intentionally to load the bases for Berra. What followed was perhaps the key play of the entire Series. Law, the Pittsburgh starter, threw an inside slider to Berra, handcuffing him. Yogi hit the ball weakly to third base. Don Hoak, who was shading Berra over toward shortstop, dashed back toward the line, backhanded the ball and stepped on third to force Kubek. He then threw to first, where National League umpire Dusty Boggess ruled that the throw beat Berra for an inning-ending double play. "Yogi got out of the box fast," said Terry. "He was across the base and had already come down one stride beyond the bag. And that umpire called him out!" Berra and first base coach Ralph Houk jumped up and down in protest, but to no avail, and the rally was over. "We lost the series in the fourth game," Skowron said two months later. "Yogi was safe at first but they called him out on a double play."

Terry pitched superbly, not allowing a hit for the first four innings. The Yankees gave him a 1–0 lead on a home run by Skowron, but the Pirates rallied in the fifth. Gino Cimoli, playing because of a hand injury to Bob Skinner, blooped a single to left. The next batter, Smoky Burgess, topped an overhand curve and hit a high hopper to Skowron at first. Burgess, a rotund 5'8" 187 pounder, chugged out of the box as Skowron prepared to make the easy double play. When Moose reached for the ball, however, it stuck in his glove. That took care of the double play, but there was still plenty of time to get the force on Cimoli. Skowron didn't get it. His throw pulled Kubek off the bag and umpire John Stevens called Cimoli safe. "He was out by a yard," said Terry.

Terry settled down and retired the next two batters, which brought Vernon Law to the plate. Law, a good hitter, doubled into the left field corner to tie the game. Bill Virdon followed with a bloop single to center and the Pirates took a 3–1 lead. Three runs on two bloops and a fielding misplay should have given Terry an indication that this might not be his series.

There was one more key play in Game Four. In the bottom of the seventh, the Yankees rallied. One run was in, making the score 3–2, and there were runners on first and second with none out. Law was removed in favor of Face. Cerv, the first batter to face the little forkballer, hit a long drive to right center. "When that ball was hit," said Terry, "I said, 'Nobody's going to catch that.'" Cerv was also certain the ball was headed for the bleachers. About the only person who thought the ball would be caught was center fielder Virdon.

Before the Series started, Murtaugh had called Virdon the best defensive center fielder in the National League. Virdon had played with Cerv in the Yankee farm system, knew of his power to the opposite field, and was playing slightly toward right center. As the ball rose toward the 407 marker, he took off at full speed to intercept it. As he hit the warning track, Virdon leaped, caught the ball and crashed into the fence. The rally was ended and the Pirates held on to tie the Series at two games apiece.

The fifth and sixth games were a continuation of the pattern established during the first four. The Pirates won Game Five, as Ditmar was shelled again and didn't survive the second inning. Stengel was second-guessed mercilessly, for before the game he had vacillated between Ditmar and Stafford. When Stafford relieved and pitched five scoreless innings, the chorus of dissatisfaction grew louder. In two starts, Ditmar had thrown a total of 32 pitches and given up six hits and four runs in just one and two-thirds innings.

For 6⅓ innings, the Pirates' little left hander Harvey Haddix baffled the Yankees with his low curve. When Haddix tired, Mutaugh went to the mound and held out his right hand, palm down, about waist high, the signal that he wanted the little man, Roy Face. Face finished up the Pirates' win and Pittsburgh had a 3–2 lead.

In Game Six, Ford shut out the Pirates 12–0, setting up a seventh game at Forbes Field on October 13. The Pirates, who had been blanked just four times all year, had been shut out twice by Ford in the space of five days. After six games, the statistics were mind-boggling. The Yankees had outscored the Pirates 46–17, outhit them .341 to .241 and out-homered them eight to one. Richardson had already set a Series record by driving in 12 runs, after knocking home only 26 during the entire season.

Despite all their heroics, however, the Yanks were no better than even. "The last time I checked the rule book," Murtaugh said after the sixth game, "they still were settling the World Series on games won and lost, not on total runs." "Maybe the Yankees were the best team on paper," said Dick Schofield recently, "but in that particular year, I don't think anyone was going to beat us. All year long, we won games like you couldn't believe. It was magic. We were probably a little more excited than the Yankees because they'd been there so many times before. We hadn't."

"I think anyone on that team will tell you it's the most fun they ever had playing baseball." Schofield said. "I don't care who we were playing. I think they were going to wind up losing one more game than we did. We could have played 99 games and we still would have beat them by one."

The Pirates of 1960 were indeed a scrappy, feisty, determined bunch, even though their two biggest stars were decidedly low-key. Law, the team's best pitcher, was a quiet, reserved Mormon known as the Deacon. Clemente, their best hitter, was also quiet and kept to himself. The rest of the team was a little different. "Everybody had a nickname that was some kind of animal," Schofield said. "We had a dog, a quail, a whale and a tiger. It was just a great, great atmosphere. We had some nice guys on that team-really nice guys. I'm not sure you find those kind of people any more."

One of the Pirates was not so nice. The emotional leader of the club was the Tiger, third baseman Don Hoak. Four years earlier, at the age of 28, Hoak batted .215 for the Cubs and thought he might be finished. When he was traded to the Reds, he told Cincinnati GM Gabe Paul that he'd retire before he went to the minors. Hoak made the club and had a great year in 1957, batting .293, and leading the league in doubles. After the 1958 season, he was traded to Pittsburgh, where he batted .294 and .282 the next two years. In 1960, he hit 16 home runs and drove in 79 runs, while infusing the Pirates with his internal fire. "He carried us last year," one Pittsburgh player said in 1961. "He kept us alive. We couldn't have won the pennant without him."

Hoak was an interesting, complex individual. He survived a difficult childhood he refused to talk about, joined the Marines at 16 (lying about his age) and fought at Okinawa and Saipan during World War II. After the war, Hoak took up boxing, and had 39 professional fights, winning 29, losing 8, with two draws. Donn Clendenon, in his autobiography, recalled an incident when he played for Hoak in the Dominican Republic. A number of players were at a bar when the band started playing the Dominican national anthem. Hoak started snapping his fingers, which one of the Domincans perceived as a lack of respect, and the battle was joined. "Don punched the guy in the face," Clendenon wrote, "and all hell broke loose. Don had never won a fight in his life, so, consequently, the rest of the American ballplayers had a hell of a fight on their hands. The Guardia Nationale was called in to break up the fight."

Many teammates thought they were going to be Hoak's 40th opponent. "That Hoak was so mean," Pirate pitcher Al McBean said a few years later, "he used to bite me on the ear before

I went out to pitch to get me mean." Hoak rode his teammates hard, particularly anyone he thought was not producing at maximum capacity. Dick Stuart, the lackadaisical first baseman, was a particular target. "He really says some awful things to Stuart," said a Pirate player.

"[Hoak's] personality can change with the wind," wrote Walter Bingham in *Sports Illustrated*. "He can visit a children's hospital, be warm, gentle and encouraging, then go out on the sidewalk and unleash a torrent of foul talk that would drive a sailor to cover. 'The other night,' said [Pirate broadcaster Bob] Prince, 'I had to drag him away from some guy he wanted to fight. A minute later he was crying his heart out.'"

Hoak was as physically tough as anyone in the big leagues. He wanted to play every game, and often did, appearing in 155 in both 1959 and 1960. In 1959, he had a minor throat operation during the All Star break so he wouldn't miss a game. During the 1960 season, Hoak was at a pool party when he slipped off a ladder and suffered a long, ugly gash on his foot. Fortunately, there was a doctor at the party, who stitched Hoak's foot without the benefit of anesthesia. Hoak lay on the concrete, white as a sheet, smoking a cigarette, as the needle wove its way through his skin. When he finished, the doctor told Hoak he would be out of action for some time. "Go to hell," Hoak replied, "There's a doubleheader tomorrow and I play two." Hoak did play two and, with blood soaking through his sock, singled in the winning run in the 11th inning of the second game.*

Led by Hoak, the Pirates were a scrappy team that came from behind again and again in the late innings. Even in 1959, when the club had been so disappointing, the Pirates excelled in close games, winning 36 of 55 one run contests. Twenty nine times during the 1960 season the Pirates had trailed in the sixth inning or later and come back to win. They were a remarkable 19–2 in extra inning games. Thus far, in the Series, Pittsburgh had done what they'd always done, win the close ones. "We were definitely a team of destiny," said Bob Friend, "but we had a solid, veteran team. We didn't make many mistakes, and we won the big games down the stretch."

While Hoak got the Pirates fired up, the man who kept them on an even keel was their manager, Danny Murtaugh. Murtaugh, a 43-year-old tobacco chewing former infielder, took over the club from fiery Bobby Bragan in 1957. It seemed as though Murtaugh arrived by accident. In 1956, Tommy Tatum was slated to join the Pirates as a coach, but declined. Murtuagh took his place. The following year, when Bragan was dismissed as manager, the Pirates wanted Clyde Sukeforth to take over. Sukeforth wasn't interested, and the Pirates turned to Murtaugh again. In early 1958, it was anticipated that Murtaugh would finish the season and be replaced by a "name" manager in 1959. When the Pirates finished a surprising second, Murtaugh was named manager of the year, and two years later found himself a most unexpected World Series pilot.

The craggy-faced Murtaugh, son of a shipyard worker, looked much older than 43, and provided a fatherly, calming influence no matter how desperate the situation. He'd fought the Germans in World War II and entered burning buildings as a volunteer fireman. What was so critical about a baseball game? "The easy going Murtaugh," wrote Arthur Daley, "comfortable as an old shoe, gave [the Pirates] the relaxed feeling they never had under Bragan." In a tight situation, Murtaugh wouldn't panic. "Danny would just sit there on the bench," said pitcher Don Cardwell, who played for the Pirates later in the decade, "chewing his tobacco and watching everything going on. He was like Gil Hodges. He never got hostile to the umpires. He'd just kind of stroll out there and have his say. He would never get to the point where he was ranting and raving." Murtaugh wasn't controversial, and never knocked his own players or the opposition. "We respect everybody," he said before the Series. "We fear nobody."

After his retirement as an active player, Hoak became a manager in the Pittsburgh minor league system, and was every bit as intense as he had been as a player. On the day in 1969 that Hoak found out he was not going to be named manager of the Pirates, he died of a heart attack while chasing car thieves on his property.

Thus far, the series had consisted of games relatively devoid of drama, as each been decided prior to the fifth inning. The seventh game would be different. Said Kerry Keene, author of 1960: The Last Pure Season, "It's highly unlikely that there has ever been a game even as remotely important that had so many twists and turns, unusual occurrences and downright freak happenings."

The blowouts had been a blessing in deep, deep disguise for the Pirates, for it had given Murtaugh a chance to rest the key members of his thin staff. He'd used a lot of pitchers, but they weren't his best. Pittsburgh had been out of the games early, and Murtaugh had let the Yankees feast on the bottom half of his pitching staff. Labine, Tom Cheney, George Witt and Fred Green were spent, but Face, the one reliever who really mattered, was rested. Friend, who'd been knocked out early in Game Six, was ready to pitch in relief, as was Haddix. Law, the Pirate ace, was ready for his third start of the Series while Ford, the Yankee ace, had gone nine innings the day before and would not even be available to pitch in relief.

Using starters in relief was very common in the World Series. In 1958, Turley pitched a complete game shutout in Game Five, came back in relief to get the final out in Game Six, and won Game Seven with 6⅓ innings of relief. Ford, whose arm was stiff as a board after Game Six, would not emulate Turley's performance in 1960.

Who would pitch Game Seven for the Yankees? Stengel was coy. It would be either Turley, who had pitched adequately six days earlier in Game Two, or Stafford. The night before the game, Stengel told Stafford he would start. In 1956, Casey had surprised everyone by naming young Johnny Kucks to start Game Seven against the Brooklyn Dodgers. Kucks pitched a three hit shutout as the Yankees beat the Dodgers 9–0. Perhaps Stafford could do the same in 1960. There was no question as to Murtaugh's choice. The Pirate manager said he hoped to get five good innings from Law, whose ankle was still very tender, then finish up with Friend and Face.

Sometime between the evening of the 12th and the morning of the 13th, Stengel changed his mind. It was customary for the starter to find a ball in his shoe before the game, to let him know he was the chosen one. Before Game Seven, Turley had a ball in his shoe, while the only thing Stafford had in his shoes were his feet.

When the Pirates came to bat in the bottom of the first, however, both Turley and Stafford were pitching, Turley on the mound and Stafford in the bullpen. While the Yankees batted in the top of the first, before Turley had even taken the mound, Stafford and Bobby Shantz were throwing in the New York pen. Stengel evidently planned to yank Turley at the first sign of trouble, which came soon enough. Rocky Nelson's home run gave Pittsburgh a 2–0 lead in the first, and when Burgess led off the second with a sharp single, Stafford was summoned from the bullpen. The young righthander was shaky and yielded two more runs for a 4–0 Pirate lead.

In the third, Hector Lopez pinch hit for Stafford and Shantz entered the game. The little lefty had a chronically bad elbow and his ribs were heavily taped. "He really wasn't in good shape," said Terry. "He was hurting." Bad elbow, aching ribs and all, Shantz put forth a gutty performance, shutting the Pirates down while the Yankees chipped away at the lead. Skowron hit a solo homer in the fifth to make the score 4–1. Shantz blanked the Pirates in the bottom half of the inning, as Terry and Coates warmed up in the bullpen.

In the sixth, the Yankees pulled in front 5–4 on a three run homer by Berra. Law, whose ankle was worse than ever, departed, and the Yankees battered Face to take a 7–4 lead in the eighth. The situation looked bleak, for Murtaugh had seen his two best pitchers, Law and Face, hit hard. Even if the Pirate manager could find someone who could stop the Yankees, his hitters, who hadn't scored since the third inning, would have to get three runs in the last two frames. It was a desperate situation.

"I think we had them right where we wanted them," said Schofield. "It was the late innings and we were going to win. That's how we won games all year." Sports Illustrated, which had been remarkably prescient in its Series predictions, had stated, "Anyone who has followed the adventures of the Pirates knows the miracles they can brew late in the game."

Labine had joined the Pirates in August. "I got to Pittsburgh," he said, "and, my God! We would be six runs behind in the eighth inning and we'd score seven runs and win. I thought this was a club like the old Dodgers." The old Dodgers, however, had almost always come up short against the Yankees in the big game. Could the Pirates do better?

Elston Howard had his hand broken by a Friend pitch in Game Six and missed the final game. In another of his unorthodox moves, Stengel put little-used Johnny Blanchard behind the plate and stationed Berra, who caught 63 games during the regular season, in left. Cerv and Lopez, who'd played much of the season in left, stayed on the bench.

Blanchard had not worked with the Yankee pitchers very often, and Yogi was no gazelle in the outfield. He usually held onto what he reached, but he was by no means an accomplished outfielder. Stengel could always remove Berra for defensive purposes, but then he would lose his bat in the late innings. "I always wondered," said Blanchard recently, "if putting me behind the plate and Yogi in left was the best move in the world. I might have put me in left and Yogi behind the plate." Casey could have moved Berra behind the plate and removed Blanchard for defensive purposes, but that didn't seem to cross his mind.

While the Yankees batted in the eighth, Casey told utility infielder Joe DeMaestri to warm up. He would go to shortstop, the versatile Kubek would move to left field, and Berra would come out of the game. As DeMaestri started to run onto the field, however, Stengel stopped him (Hold that shield?). Berra was due to bat fifth in the ninth inning, and DeMaestri should wait. He didn't have to wait very long.

Cimoli, batting for Face, led off the bottom of the eighth with a looping hit to right, in virtually the same spot as his single that started the winning rally in Game Four. The next batter, Virdon, hit a ground ball to Kubek. It looked like a sure double play. Anywhere but Forbes Field, it probably would have been. The Pirates' stadium was the oldest in the major leagues, having opened in 1909. "It wasn't the nicest place you ever played," said Schofield, "unless you played there all the time." "The Forbes Field infield is adapted for the Pirate style of baseball," wrote pitcher Jim Brosnan in his diary of the 1959 season. "Swift runners beat out many base hits because of the abnormally high bounces that batted balls take off the hard ground." Players referred to it as 'the brickyard.' "The infield is sure hard," said Richardson after the first game. "The trouble is it is not consistently hard all over."

"In a short series," Murtaugh said prior to the first game, "there is a lot of luck involved.... We'll see who has the luck." Just as Kubek bent down to pick Virdon's grounder up, it took an erratic bounce and hit him solidly in the Adam's apple. He "flipped over like a fish out of water," according to broadcaster Jack Quinlan, and landed in a sitting position. The ball rolled free in the infield and the Pirates had runners on first and second base. Trainer Gus Mauch ran out to attend to Kubek and the entire Yankee team gathered around him. Tony was spitting up blood from his bruised larynx and couldn't speak. He indicated through gestures that he could continue playing, but Stengel summoned DeMaestri and sent Kubek off to the hospital.

Shantz had pitched five courageous innings, and was running out of gas. The little lefty hadn't pitched that long in a game all year, and had had to run the bases after singling in the seventh. When Dick Groat drove in Pittsburgh's fifth run with a hard single, Stengel went to the mound. Coates and Terry were warming up, as they had been for several innings. Ford was unavailable. Ditmar was certainly well-rested, but Stengel didn't dare bring him in. Duren, the relief ace of 1958 and '59, was a possibility. He had appeared in Games One and Five, pitching four strong innings, striking out five. Now, in the season's ultimate game, he sat on the bullpen bench fuming, as Stengel signaled for Coates.

For once in the Series, one of Stengel's maneuvers seemed to work, as Coates retired the next two batters, while the runners moved up to second and third. Arroyo joined Terry in the bullpen. Roberto Clemente hit a ground ball to Skowron, a replay of the incident which had undone Terry in Game Four. This time, Skowron fielded the ball cleanly, pulled it out of his glove and prepared to throw to Coates at first base, a play teams practice from the first day of spring training. "We knew we had that game won," said Hector Lopez, "because we were scoring runs all the time. Then there was one miscue. The pitcher didn't cover first base."

For some reason Coates had broken for the ball rather than first base. "The first reaction of a pitcher," Coates said recently, "is to go for the ball. That's what I did. That was one of my boo-boos. I made a mistake." As Clemente crossed an unguarded first base, Virdon scored and Groat moved to third. The score was now 7–6.

The next batter was Hal Smith, who had gone in to catch when Burgess was removed for a pinch runner. Smith was a former Yankee farmhand who had played five years in the American League with the Athletics and Orioles. Traded to Pittsburgh in 1960, he formed a hard-hitting platoon with Burgess. Burgess batted .294 and Smith .295, and the two receivers combined for 18 home runs and 84 runs batted in. The Yankees knew Smith better than they knew most of the Pirate batters. Some had played with or against him in the minors and nearly all of them had played against him in the American League. "Hal Smith was a high fastball hitter," said Duren, who was still smoldering in the Yankee bullpen. "You could jam Smith," said Terry, "and Coates had a real good fastball."

On the mound, Coates, though shaken by his fielding blunder, was confident he could get Smith out. "Smith could never hit me," he recalled, "not even in the minors." Coates' first pitch was a fastball across the letters for a strike. "Oh, god," thought Duren, "Don't throw him another one up there." Coates, however, kept challenging Smith, who took a fastball high, took a mighty rip at another, and barely checked his swing on the next. The fifth pitch, according to Coates, was a hanging slider, not inside where he wanted it, but right out over the plate. Smith hit a line drive to left field. "I knew he hit it awfully hard," said DeMaestri, "but I didn't think it was high enough to go out. It took off like a two iron shot and went over the fence." Coates threw his glove ten feet in the air. Smith's dramatic home run gave the Pirates a 9–7 lead, as pandemonium broke loose at Forbes Field. Broadcaster Chuck Thompson told his partner Quinlan, "We have seen and shared one of baseball's all-time great moments. This is one of the most dramatic home runs of all time."

Smith's blow finished Coates. Terry, who had been warming up since the second inning, entered the game. "I hadn't relieved in two months," Terry said, "and I'd warmed up virtually the whole game. It's the seventh game of the World Series and when they say get up and warm up, you can't pace yourself. You've got to get with it because there's no tomorrow. Usually after a guy warms up hard a couple of times, they'll sit him down and switch to somebody else. But it was a high-scoring ballgame and both clubs had run through their staffs."

"I suppose I'm second-guessing forty years later," said Blanchard, "but Ralph Terry was a starter. I'll never understand for the life of me why he brought in Ralph Terry. Duren was a reliever all year. Sometimes starters can't come in and relieve because it takes them an inning or two to get their rhythm going. Relievers can start from scratch. On the first pitch, they're ready to go." "We had all those hard throwers on the ballclub," said Lopez, "and they bring in Ralph Terry! Ralph's not a strikeout pitcher. He wasn't a relief pitcher. We had a couple of guys who threw the ball really hard."

No one threw harder than Ryne Duren. "You've got Ryne Duren available," exclaimed Eli Grba, "and you bring in Terry!" Duren's biggest problem was control, but with no one on base, that wasn't a concern. If Duren couldn't get the ball over the plate, Stengel could always take him out and bring in Terry. Casey, however, had lost confidence in Duren.

In addition to having thrown for almost the entire game, Terry faced another problem when he arrived on the scene. "I'd warmed up on this little anthill of a mound down the left field line," he said. "It was the smallest mound I'd ever warmed up on-very steep. Then I got into the game and there was a big old wide mound with very little taper to it. When I came down, my foot would hit the ground early and everything was going in high. I had a hard time adjusting to the slope of the mound."

The first batter Terry faced was Hoak. "I was practically trying to bounce the ball up there to get it down," Terry said. "Everything I threw was high. I threw Hoak a high slider that had nothing on it." Fortunately, Hoak hit an easy fly to Berra in left and the Yankees, down by two runs, went in for their final at bat of the season.

Friend came in to start the ninth inning for the Pirates. Thus far, he'd had a rough Series. In Game Two, Friend struck out six in only four innings but, trailing 2–0, was removed for a pinch hitter, after which the Pirate bullpen allowed the game to degenerate into a rout. "I threw the ball real good in my first start," Friend said. The sixth game was a different story. "I had nothing," he said. "It was one of those games where you hope they hit it at somebody."

Shutting down the Yankees in the ninth inning and closing out the Series would make up for the two losses, but Friend couldn't do it. Richardson led off with a looping single to left, his twelfth hit of the Series. "None of us got Richardson out," Friend recalled. Left handers Harvey Haddix and Vinegar Bend Mizell warmed up in the Pirate bullpen and Ford began to throw in the Yankee pen. Dale Long, a former Pirate, batted for DeMaestri and singled to right. Friend left the game without having gotten anyone out. "I thought I made two good pitches," he said.

With the left-handed Maris up, Murtaugh called in Haddix, his last reliable pitcher. Maris, who had homered off Haddix three days earlier, fouled out to Smith, and the Pirates needed just two more outs to win their first World Championship since 1925. Mantle, the next batter, lined a single to right field. Richardson crossed the plate to make the score 9–8, and Long went to third when Clemente had difficulty picking the ball up.

After the first pitch to Berra, Stengel sent Gil McDougald in to run for Long. On a 2–0 pitch, Berra hit a ground ball to Rocky Nelson at first. Nelson stepped on the bag for the second out and turned to throw to second. Mantle was just a couple of steps off first. With the force play removed, Mickey realized he could return to the base and dove in just under Nelson's attempted tag. "That was just great instincts," said Friend. "That's why he was such a great athlete." It was a brilliant play under the greatest pressure, and it saved the Yanks from defeat, as McDougald crossed the plate with the tying run. Haddix retired Skowron for the third out, and Terry trudged out to the mound for the last of the ninth.

Bill Mazeroski was the leadoff hitter for the Pirates. After his poor 1959 season, Mazeroski had taken a cut in pay. He lost weight and staged a comeback in 1960, improving his batting average and fielding as well as ever. Mazeroski had seven hits in 24 at bats in the Series and, prior to Nelson's first inning blast, had accounted for the only Pittsburgh home run. He'd hit 11 during the regular season.

Terry, still having trouble with the mound, delivered the first pitch high. "Our scouting dope on the Pirates kept repeating one thing," Ford said later. "'Remember, these guys are high ball hitters.'" High was definitely not the place to pitch Mazeroski, who had hit a homer off Coates in Game One on a fast ball across the letters. "Maz would jump up and hit a ball over his head," said teammate Joe Christopher. Blanchard called time and went out to talk to Terry. "You've got to get the ball down," he said. "This guy's a high ball hitter." "I know. I know," said Terry. "I'll get her down."

Blanchard went back behind the plate, gave the sign and prepared for the next pitch. It never reached him. "It was a hanging, Harry High School slider," he said. "I mean, it was not doing nothing. It didn't spin good. It was in a bad spot." A pitcher can often get away with an ill-placed fastball, but not a bad breaking ball. "If you make a mistake with a breaking pitch," said infielder Bobby Klaus, "it's a lot more serious than a mistake with a fastball. A fastball can overwhelm you and get by you."

A pitcher didn't usually escape the consequences of a hanging slider. "A bad slider is the easiest pitch in the world to hit," said Jack Fisher. "There's nothing like a hanging slider. Man, it's like it's out there on a pedestal just sitting still. When you let it go, your heart stops. When it's halfway there, you're thinking, please just hit it for a single."

Terry's pitch came floating in. "It was a high fastball," a breathless Mazeroski told Pirate broadcaster Bob Prince in the wild Pittsburgh dressing room. "It looked like a high slider," said Friend, who was sitting in the Pirate dugout. "It was a fastball with a little cut on it," Terry said recently. "Isn't that a slider?" Friend asked.

Whatever it was, Mazeroski hit it high toward the distant left field fence. "Sometimes it's difficult from the dugout to tell just how hard it's tagged," said Friend. "The way Berra was going back to the wall, I thought he might catch it." Berra, his back to plate, reached the wall and backed off, ready to play a carom that never came. It was the first "walk-off" home run in Series history, and only the third time a series had been decided in a team's final at bat. The Yankees, who had outscored the Pirates 55–27, had lost the game 10–9 and the Series four games to three. Mazeroski half danced, half ran around the bases as the crowd surged onto the field.

Labine had been suffering from the flu for four days, and spent much of the game in the dressing room, near the Pirate bullpen. When the Yankees rallied in the ninth, he was watching the game on television. He thought, "We're going to lose and that's all there is to it." Labine made his way out to the bullpen just as Mazeroski's shot cleared the fence. "As sick as I was," he said, "I ran out of the bullpen toward home plate to see if I could get to him. It was the greatest thing I'd ever seen in my life. I never saw people go so crazy. They didn't do anything bad, they just went crazy. I've been in a lot of clubhouses, but being in that clubhouse was the greatest thing I ever experienced."

The Yankee clubhouse, on the other hand, was like a morgue. "I can still see it now," said Eli Grba. "There was no talking when the ball went over the fence. We just grabbed our gloves. It was unreal watching him run around the bases." Duren and Ford, standing side by side in the bullpen with Grba, started walking silently toward the clubhouse. Inside, Mantle put his head in his hands and began to sob. "It was the first time I ever saw Mickey cry," said DeMaestri. "Everybody just sat there with their head hanging down, but Mickey was actually crying. That shook me up more than anything."

As soon as Mazeroski hit the ball, Stengel, who had seen thousands of home runs in his long career, knew it was gone. The Series and his Yankee career were over. Nearly every gamble he had taken turned out poorly. Casey never saw Mazeroski's hit leave the park. He turned immediately and headed for the clubhouse. One of the first people Stengel met was Terry. There had been so many key plays during the long afternoon. What if Stafford had started? What if Virdon's grounder hadn't taken a bad hop and hit Kubek in the throat? What if Coates had remembered to cover first base? By the ninth inning, however, all that had been forgotten. What everyone would remember was that Ralph Terry had given up the home run that lost the World Series.

Yet, when he encountered Stengel, Terry felt terrible, not for himself, but for the old man. Terry was 24 and would have opportunities to redeem himself. Casey was 70. "We all sort of knew it was his last year," Terry said. "He talked to us before the game started. It was kind of a farewell talk, although he didn't say he was leaving. He said, 'I want you guys to know you've had a great year and I'm really proud of you.'"

"How were you trying to pitch him?" Stengel asked Terry. "I was trying to keep the ball down and away and I got it up," Terry replied. "As long as you pitch," Stengel said, "you're not always going to get the ball where you want to. That's a physical mistake. As long as you weren't going against the scouting report, trying to throw him high fastballs. If you did that, I wouldn't sleep good tonight. Forget it, kid. Go back and have a good year next year. Give 'em hell."

Nothing could have made Terry feel good at that moment, but Stengel, who had wanted desperately to win the game, had momentarily put aside his own disappointment to console his young pitcher. Many portrayed Stengel as a crotchety old man in his final years with the Yankees, and he often was, but Ralph Terry is forever grateful for Casey's support at the lowest moment of his young life. "I loved Casey," Terry said. "He was good to me. I'd run through fire-through a brick wall-for him. That was the greatest counseling in the world." Terry, a psychology student, had always had two favorite psychologists: Adler and Jung. He now added a third — Casey Stengel.

◆ 4 ◆

The Major Takes Command
The 1961 Season
(Part I)

In 1961, for the first time since 1948, the Yankees would not be managed by Casey Stengel. For the first time since 1932, George Weiss would not be a member of the Yankee organization. Weiss and Stengel had been quite a team, one that had taken ten pennants and seven world championships in twelve years. They had personalities as opposite as two personalities could be. Weiss was dour, uncommunicative and avoided the press whenever possible. Stengel was voluble, charismatic, and courted the media with a skill equaled by few. Weiss appreciated the fact that Stengel kept the media away from him and Stengel loved not having to share the limelight. Despite their numerous triumphs, the two men each had one glaring weakness in the Fall of 1960. Stengel was 70 years of age and Weiss was 66.

For the past several years, Stengel had hinted of retirement. Before the 1955 Series, New York papers speculated that Casey might not manage in 1956. Edna, they said, wanted her husband to return to California full time. The following spring, Stengel came back, but startled reporters when he said, "I'm building ahead for two years, when I won't be here any more." He spoke of youngsters like Richardson, Kubek and Blanchard that he wanted to bring up to leave a strong club for his successor. Yet, two years came and went, and there was Stengel, still in the dugout for the 1958 season.

In 1960, the rumors were stronger than ever, with one sending him from the Yankees to manage in his birthplace, Kansas City. In the spring, Stengel intimated that if he didn't win the pennant, he would step down. Most fans and reporters assumed the decision would be Casey's, and many appealed to him to remain. "They keep trying to chase old Casey Stengel back to his bank and oil wells," wrote Jimmy Powers in June. "I don't know why there is so much unseemly shoving. When Casey leaves, it is going to be mighty dull around the New York baseball beat — what there is left of it." As the season wound down, veteran writer Dan Daniel, who generally had a direct line to the Yankee hierarchy, reported that Stengel did not want to leave but might be forced to step down because of his age.

A few days before the end of the regular season, Arthur Daley penned a column praising the Yankee manager and lamenting the possibility of his leaving. "New York would become a baseball desert with his departure," Daley wrote. "The Giants are gone and the Dodgers are gone. The only oasis left is Stengel.... It will be a sad day for the sport — and the Yankees— when Stengel has managed his last game. Hurrying that day would be a sinful waste. Don't quit, Case.

44

You come closer than anyone else to being the irreplaceable man." The New York chapter of the Baseball Writers Association drafted a petition urging Stengel to stay. As the season came to a close, everyone, including Casey, speculated about his future.

Since Weiss rarely spoke, no one knew what his plans might be. One could only surmise, and since Weiss had no life outside of baseball, it seemed relatively certain that, as long as he was in good health, Weiss would not step aside voluntarily. In late September, a rumor surfaced to the effect that Weiss would retire at the end of the season. Dan Topping called it "the damnedest story I ever read." He didn't say, however, that Weiss would return. He merely said that he and his general manager had not discussed any plans for 1961.

On October 18, just five days after the Yankees lost the seventh game of the World Series, the club held a press conference to announce that Stengel was leaving the team. Topping, puffing on a cigarette, made a brief prepared statement, giving no indication whether the departure was a retirement or whether Stengel had been dismissed against his wishes. When Casey took the microphone, he left no doubt as to what had transpired. "Mr. Topping and Mr. Webb paid me off in full," he said, "and told me my services were no longer desired because they want to put in a youth program." Topping had instituted a new policy which mandated retirement at the age of 65. "If retirement at 65 is good for the president of General Motors, U.S Steel and other vast organizations," Topping told Daniel, "it should work just as well in baseball." "Left to his own decision," Topping continued, "Stengel would force us to tear the uniform off him at 80." He said Stengel would have been fired even if the Yankees had swept the World Series. Casey was only the sixth manager fired after winning a pennant, an exclusive fraternity that would be increased to seven in just four years.

The dismissal of the most popular manager in baseball drew an immediate reaction. Bill Veeck offered him a job with the White Sox. Paul Richards said the Yankees would never find a better manager. "[Stengel] imparted warmth to a cold organization," wrote Daley, whose earlier wish had not been granted, "giving it a colorful appeal that it couldn't have bought for millions of dollars. He was priceless.... After reading [his statement], Topping faded into the background as if ashamed of himself. He should be." The opinion of New York fans and baseball lovers everywhere was uniformly in favor of the septuagenarian manager. A one hundred year old clerk from Florida fired off a one word telegram that said, "nonsense."

Two weeks after Stengel was fired, Weiss walked the plank. Always non-controversial, Weiss played along with the notion that he was stepping down of his own volition. The Yankee general manager had been the most distant of men, but at his retirement announcement, he broke down in tears. He had not been fired, he emphasized, but had accepted a five year contract as a consultant, a contract which contained a clause that he would no longer be paid if he accepted a general manager's post with another organization. Although Weiss's departure was not greeted by the outrage that marked the firing of Stengel, baseball sent the message to Topping more subtly. Shortly after leaving the Yankees, Weiss was named Major League Executive of the Year by *The Sporting News*.

In place of the antiquated Weiss and Stengel, the Yankees promoted 58-year-old Henry Royal (Roy) Hamey, Weiss's assistant, and 41-year-old Ralph Houk, the Yankee first base coach. Both were fully qualified for their new posts. Hamey had had a long career as a baseball executive. Following youthful stints as a shorthand specialist with Standard Oil and as treasurer for an assortment of theaters, Hamey became secretary of the Springfield club of the Three-I League in 1925. In 1934, he first became associated with the Yankees as business manager of their Binghamton farm club. Hamey remained with the Yankees until becoming president of the American Association in 1946. He served as general manager of the Pirates, then returned to the Yankees from 1951 through 1954 as an assistant to Weiss. Hamey then left again to be the Phillies' GM before joining the Yankees for a third tour of duty in 1959, again as Weiss's assistant. He accepted the post, a demotion from his position in Philadelphia, with the expectation that he would eventually succeed Weiss.

Houk first became a Yankee in 1947, following distinguished service in World War II. Enlisting as a private following Pearl Harbor, Houk went to Officers' Candidate School, rose to the rank of captain and earned the Silver Star, the Bronze Star, four campaign stars and a Purple Heart. He started out like many players in the service, managing an army baseball team. Then, unlike most, Houk got into the thick of the fight. He landed on Omaha Beach a few days after D-Day, and was decorated for his role as a platoon leader during the Battle of the Bulge. At the end of the war, Houk received an automatic promotion to major, which gave him his baseball nickname.

Houk was a Yankee catcher for parts of eight seasons, but appeared in only 91 games, 41 of them in his first year. In his last six years, he never appeared in more than 10 games in a season, and spent most of his time sitting in the bullpen, warming up pitchers and studying the game. Houk's status with Yankees was so tenuous that one year he shared an apartment lease with fellow catcher Gus Niarhos, figuring that one of them would be farmed out during the season, and the one that remained would assume the lease.

After serving as bullpen coach for the Yanks in 1954, which represented little change from his previous duties, Houk went to Denver to manage the American Association Bears in 1955. He spent three years in Denver, always finishing well above .500, leading the Bears to the Little World Series championship in 1957, and developing future Yankee stars Bobby Richardson, Tony Kubek, Johnny Blanchard and Ryne Duren and future Met Marv Throneberry.

The Denver players loved Houk. "He fought for his team," said Denver player Jim Pisoni. "We had a real tough kind of togetherness. If we didn't have enough beer in the clubhouse, he'd open up the gates, pick up a couple of cases and bring 'em on down. He fought for us on the field, too, getting into some fights with managers of teams that were throwing at us. Ralph was a man who didn't brag about anything. He just fought for his men and got the job done. That's what you do in the Army and that's what he did in baseball."

In 1958, the Yankees brought Houk to New York to serve as first base coach and, it soon became obvious, heir apparent to Stengel. During the first week of the 1958 season, Dan Daniel wrote an article hinting that Houk would be the next Yankee manager. When Stengel was hospitalized and missed twelve games in 1960, it was Houk who took over the team.

Other organizations were well aware of Houk's ability. The Tigers wanted him as manager, as did the Athletics. Houk turned them both down. He had been in the Yankee organization since 1939, cashed several World Series checks and wanted to manage the Yankees, not the Tigers or Athletics.* Topping also wanted Houk to manage the Yankees, but was worried that, with Stengel showing no signs of bowing out, Houk would tire of waiting and take another managing job. If Stengel decided to retire in a couple of years, Houk might not be available.

Casey's leaving had not come as a complete surprise, but the hiring of Houk to succeed him was one of the most open secrets in many a year. Nearly everyone knew that Houk was the man. Prior to the official announcement, reporters staked out his house, and his neighbors hounded him for information. On October 20th, just two days after Stengel's departure, the Yankees staged another press conference, at which Topping introduced Houk as the new manager.

Although Houk had been a Yankee coach for three years, few of the writers knew much about him. Stengel had always been the man they sought, and the coaches said little. "When I

---

*In 1968, there was a rumor that Houk would leave the Yankees to manage the Tigers. "Houk will leave the Yanks," wrote Jim Ogle, "right after the Statue of Liberty swims the Hudson River." Or until an abrasive shipbuilder from Cleveland tried to tell him how to manage.

was a Yankee coach and the writers asked me questions," Houk said, "I used to shrug and say, 'I don't know, ask Casey.'" Now Houk was the man on center stage, and he proved a master with the press, a skill he'd first exhibited at Denver. When Houk began managing, he found that one Denver writer ripped him and his players regularly. Rather than ban the reporter from the clubhouse, vilify him, or try to turn the players against him, Houk went to see him. He didn't mind if the writer criticized him, Houk said, but lay off the players. He went on at length about how good his young players were, and got the writer to like him. The negative articles stopped.

Houk had a string of humorous stories from his days in the minors, and told self-deprecating tales about his life as a third string catcher. He almost always minimized his own accomplishments. After being named manager of the year in the Puerto Rican League one winter, he explained, "It was a five club league and two of the managers were fired during the season. Another finished behind me. The fourth one hit a sportswriter. That left only me for the award."

At the press conference, many of the writers' questions were predictable. Would Houk manage like Casey? "There's only one Casey Stengel," he replied diplomatically. "I'm Ralph Houk." Houk would, in fact, do very little of what Stengel had done. Casey talked non-stop. Houk listened and conversed. Casey yearned to be the center of attention, Houk did everything in his power to shift attention to the players. Houk wasn't as entertaining as Casey, but at least he was understandable. Casey talked in circles to confuse, while Houk got right to the point. "It was strange to listen to a Yankee manager speak English," wrote Daley.

There was one other major difference between Houk and Stengel. Casey loved to maneuver, shuffling players in and out of the lineup. He was Casey the Genius, winning ballgames with his brain. Stengel was a pioneer of platooning, playing his right handed hitters against lefty pitchers and vice versa. The success of the strategy is debatable, but there was no doubt that it invariably infuriated the platooned. Each platoonee assumed that, if Stengel picked one starter, it would be him. They never considered the possibility that the alternative to being platooned might be a full time seat on the bench. "What really gets me," said former Met Frank Thomas, "is that the managers who played never liked to be platooned and then, when they become managers, they platoon the hitters. I just think it's wrong. You have some pitchers that are going to give you trouble, but the only way you're going to learn to hit those pitchers is to stay in there against them."

Stengel won pennants alternating players like Hank Bauer, Gene Woodling, Billy Johnson and Bobby Brown, and when he managed the Mets, he continued the same practice, but didn't win any pennants. "When you don't have a real strong team," said Met pitcher Craig Anderson, "platooning isn't really the way to go, because you don't have that many good players. You might as well play your best players."

Houk believed in a set lineup. His talent was not in making strategic moves, but instilling confidence in his players, putting them on the field and letting them win ballgames. Casey liked to rile a player up by getting under his skin. Houk believed in positive reinforcement. He never criticized a player in public and never made sarcastic comments about his team to the press. In the spring of '61, Houk was asked about the incident in 1960 when Stengel pulled Mantle for not hustling. He did not believe in showing a player up, Houk said. "If he had a problem with you," said pitcher Rollie Sheldon, "he never chewed you out in front of people. He'd call you into the office, close the door and you'd sit down man to man. He'd lay it on the line and tell you what he wanted you to do."

Houk was an optimist through and through. "If [Houk] found a bomb on the *Queen Elizabeth*," wrote Dave Anderson, "he'd tell the passengers how much they'll enjoy the lifeboats." While everyone else complained about the coast to coast travel that accompanied expansion, Houk raved about the restful plane flights and the ability to sleep in hotel rooms rather than railroad cars.

In the early '60s, of course, it was easy for the Yankee manager to be a positive thinker. With bashers like Mantle and Maris, a three run homer was always just around the corner. From 1965 through the end of his tenure as manager, however, Houk was still the cheery optimist even while the Yankee dynasty crumbled around him. No matter how bleak the situation, better days were ahead. Mantle was about to break out of his slump and start hitting like he did in '61. Those young pitchers were going to come through and surprise everyone. It would be a close race and anyone could catch a few breaks and take it all. If it weren't for those injuries, the Yanks would have been right in the thick of it.

When Houk took the reins, he paid homage to Stengel's skill but, even though Casey was unemployed in 1961, Houk never consulted him. It was Houk's team, for which most of the players, especially those who had played for the Major at Denver, were grateful. In his last years with the Yankees, Stengel had become increasingly crotchety, and the Yankee players were ready for someone who emphasized the positive. When Houk was a coach, he, not Stengel, was the man the players went to when they had problems.

Boyer, who had been humiliated by Stengel during the World Series, marveled at the confidence Houk showed in him. Richardson, always quiet and reserved, thought Stengel had preferred scrappy, holler-type players like Billy Martin, and he was right. Bobby had never been one of Stengel's favorites. Casey liked the rough-and-ready type, and referred to Richardson sarcastically as a "milk drinker." Kubek was equally abstemious in his habits, but Stengel liked the fact that Tony was feisty and opinionated. Richardson took whatever Stengel dished out with quiet calm. Casey liked to agitate and get under a player's skin, but he couldn't penetrate Richardson's serene epidermis.

Houk knew exactly what buttons to push. At Denver, he'd given the shy youngster the confidence he needed to get to the big leagues. Houk was as rough-and-ready as anyone, and always up for a good fight, but he and Richardson developed a deep mutual respect.

"Ralph was more of a player's manager," said Joe DeMaestri, "more of a friendly, pat-on-the-back kind of guy. I think the guys really enjoyed playing for Ralph. There was nothing wrong with Casey. That's just the way he was. He was always grumpy, but that's the way he was."

"Casey was kind of a professor of baseball," said Jim Coates. "He liked to do a lot of talking to the media. He'd go into the hotel bar where he did his drinking and talk to the sportswriters. Ralph was more of a players' manager. You could talk to him. He was a good man."

"Houk was the best I ever played for," said Bud Daley. "All managers make the same moves. But you've got 25 guys and can only play nine at a time. The guys who are playing are fine, but it's those other guys sitting on the bench that you've got to keep happy. The good managers are the ones who do that, and Houk was really good at that." Daley was traded to the Yankees in June, 1961, and proceeded to pitch very poorly. "The day after I lost my fourth game," he recalled, "I was sitting in front of my locker when Ralph came over. I said that maybe he should put me in the bullpen. 'Hell, no,' he said, 'the law of averages says you're going to win one eventually.' That took all the pressure off me."

"The first fifteen guys on a club," Stengel once said, "you don't have to bother with. They're playing and don't need the manager. The next five play once in a while, so you gotta spend some time buttering them up. The last five you gotta be with all the time, because they may be plotting a revolution against you."

"When you're managing," said longtime utility player Lou Klimchock, "you've got 25 different personalities. If you can keep the role players happy, which is the thing good managers do, you don't need clubhouse meetings." Houk, who sat on the bench his entire major league career, had not only sympathy, but empathy for the man who played occasionally and got little of the glory or wealth. "Ralph was a very straightforward guy," said Jack Reed, a substitute from 1961–63. "He told me exactly what my role was." "If you were going good and pitching every fourth day," said Sheldon, "he'd pat you on the fanny. But if you were down in the bullpen on the lowest rung of the ladder, he would still treat you like a man. The utility players knew exactly how and when they were going to be used."

"Ralph knew how to work with people," said pitcher Tex Clevenger. "He was always upbeat and always talking to you. If you did something bad, he'd tell you what you should have done, and if you did something good, he'd congratulate you." "Ralph always had some kind word to say," added Johnny Blanchard. "He'd pat you on the back and tell you to hang in there." "I trusted Houk," said Tom Metcalf, "and I've never been around anybody I respected more than him. He was always in charge. He never, ever let anyone get a leg up on him."

"Of all the managers I played for," said Andy Kosco, a Yankee in 1968, "Ralph was probably the best, from a player's standpoint. He would visit with guys at their locker, and might say, 'Even though you're playing well, I'm going to give you a day off. The rest will do you good.' He communicated with his players very well. The players respected him and played very hard for him. Ralph made you love the game a little bit more, because he looked at it from a different perspective." Did Kosco ever think Houk was merely 'blowing smoke?' "No. Never, never."

Much more than most managers of his era, Houk understood his players, and realized the importance of their mental state. "I always said that Ralph was the greatest manager I ever had the chance to play for," said Tom Tresh. "He had a very good understanding of the pressures of the everyday life of a major league player, not just baseball, but what was happening off the field. Are you married? Do you have children? Is your wife pregnant? He always made a point of knowing what was happening so he would know how to act when players were struggling — when to get on them and when to sit back. One time Ralph came up to me when Pepi was struggling a little bit. Joe was my roommate, and Ralph asked if there was anything going on with Joe.* Was he having problems at home? He would try to see if there was anything going on off the field that might be bothering someone and affecting their performance." "I remember him walking up to me a few times," said Phil Linz, "and sensing something was wrong. Even at Old Timers' Games, he'd say, 'Is everything OK with you?' It wasn't and he noticed that."

For all his sensitivity, Houk was not Mr. Rogers or Oprah Winfrey in baseball togs. His toughness was legendary. When Pedro Ramos came to the Yankees in 1964, he remarked, "He doesn't want your money. He wants your ass." Houk wasn't afraid to mix it up, which earned him respect in the physical world of baseball. "Ralph was my father figure," said Eli Grba. "I admired him more than anyone in baseball. I liked him because he was tough. I heard about what he'd done in the military. He was a nice man, and you'd never think that this was a guy who could tear your head off. But that was the kind of guy I needed."

"Ralph Houk was a toughie," said former *New York Times* reporter Gordon White. When Houk opposed Cincinnati skipper Fred Hutchinson in the 1961 Series, fellow manager Birdie Tebbetts observed, "Here are the two toughest managers, physically and spiritually, ever to appear against each other in a World Series. Each man can lick any man on his ballclub. In fact, each could knock the stuffings out of any two men at the same time."

Houk had long had a reputation as a brawler. "He doesn't fight at the drop of a hat," wrote Ben Epstein in 1947. "He'd slug you before tipping the bill." The biggest moment of Houk's playing career came during the final week of the hotly contested 1949 pennant race between the Yankees and Red Sox. Ralph, making a rare appearance on the field, took a throw at home plate as the Red Sox's Johnny Pesky slid in with the go-ahead run in the eighth inning. Although Houk thought he had the plate blocked, umpire Bill Grieve called Pesky safe, precipitating a ferocious argument. Houk went completely berserk. "Any competent dramatic critic," wrote Red Smith, "would have Houk banished for overplaying his impersonation of a homicidal maniac."

---

*There was always something going on with Joe.

On one occasion at Denver in 1957, following an exchange of beanballs, Houk got into a fistfight with St. Paul manager Max Macon, a battle that was far more realistic than most baseball fights. "At the finish," wrote Frank Haraway, "Macon and Houk were the principal combatants, with the Denver pilot apparently getting in the best licks."

If necessary, Houk also fought his own men. Don Larsen was sent to Denver with a well-deserved reputation for carousing, which had prevented him from realizing his potential in the major leagues. In New York, they had tried to keep him in his room and out of trouble, but Houk took a different approach. He told Larsen he didn't care what he did away from the park. "But if you ever come into this ballpark not ready to pitch," he said, "I'll kick the hell out of you."

"One time in Washington," former Yankee Ray Barker recalled, "I thought the plate umpire made a few bad calls during the first game of a doubleheader. Between games we went back to the clubhouse. The players and umpires went by the same runway, and then split off to different locker rooms. We were walking and the umpire was sort of mouthing off to Ralph. Ralph said, 'You SOB,' and he took off after him. I happened to be near Ralph and me and a couple of other players had to grab him to keep him away from the umpire."

There was a method to much of Houk's madness. "If we were losing," recalled Bob Friend, who played for Houk in 1966, "he'd say, 'Well, boys, we're going to have to shake it up. We're going to have to start a fight here.' He started a fight in Baltimore to kind of shake things up."

Once, during a Yankee losing streak, Houk took off from the dugout to argue a ball and strike call, even though he knew it meant an automatic ejection. "He got in that umpire's face," said Barker, "and gave him a nose-to-nose ass chewing. The umpire cleaned off home plate twice and Ralph took his spikes and covered it back up with dirt. When he finally came back to the dugout, we were all breathing lightly, because we didn't want him to jump on us. He looked at the whole row of players sitting there and said, 'How was that performance, guys?'"

Today, Houk's psychological tactics and his understanding of human nature might not seem unusual, but in 1961, they were revolutionary, compared to the methods employed by most major league managers. Even the good managers, like Walter Alston, were uncommunicative. Some, such as Hutchinson, were feared. Charley Dressen was in a class by himself. A self-proclaimed genius who couldn't put a properly-worded sentence together and boasted that he never read books, Dressen believed it was he, not the players, who won ballgames. "No matter where the Braves finish," someone once said when Dressen led Milwaukee, "Charley will finish five games ahead of them."

"I never could impress Charley Dressen," said Clem Labine. "Nobody could impress Charley Dressen." That was not exactly true, for Charlie was very impressed with himself. Arthur Daley described him as "the amazing Mr. Dressen, who knows everything about everything and is never too reluctant to admit it." "He knew all the answers," said former Brave John DeMerit. "He tried to tell Spahn how to pitch. Spahn would laugh at him."

Labine played for Dressen in the early '50s. DeMerit played for him in the late '50s. John Sullivan played for Dressen in Detroit in the mid–'60s. He hadn't changed a bit. "Charley was a little different," Sullivan said with a laugh. "He was definitely an I-I, me-me guy." Hold the other team for seven innings, Dressen was famous for saying, and he would think of something to win the game. One year, when he was a coach for the National League All Star team, Dressen was asked what signs he would use. "I'll give every man the signs he uses on his own ballclub," he replied. "I've been stealing them and I know what every team uses."

Another self-professed genius was Leo Durocher, who spawned a school of disciples that mimicked his brash, swashbuckling style without the same results. The most notorious of Durocher's pupils was Eddie Stanky, known, generally without affection, as "The Brat." Herb

Moford, who played for him in St. Louis, said, "Stanky was a ... well, he was a ... well ... he tried to be tough. He had kind of a complex against big men."

Stanky had a tumultuous tenure as manager of the Cardinals in the 1950s. The players hated his autocratic ways and frequent temper tantrums, and were in a constant state of discontent. Opposing teams hated him and played harder than ever against the Cardinals. Umpires hated him, and once forfeited a game which Stanky delayed by carrying arguments to ridiculous proportions. In 1952, Stanky engaged in a shoving match with umpire Scotty Robb, which resulted in Robb's resignation.

Stanky alienated everyone. He treated the press with disdain. He earned the enmity of his coaches. In the first inning of his first exhibition game as Cardinal manager, Stanky berated coaches Mike Ryba and Johnny Riddle in front of the entire club for blowing a sign. A third coach, Terry Moore, told Stanky he'd punch him senseless if he ever did that to him. "He's the only man I ever disliked," Moore said.

In 1955, Stanky was fired as Cardinal manager, and slipped into the background for over ten years. Like Winston Churchill emerging from his wilderness period, Stanky re-surfaced and was named manager of the White Sox for the 1966 season. When Churchill was recalled to power in 1940, with the Germans pounding on the gates, he was the right man at the right time. Stanky was the wrong man at the wrong time. He had been out of step in 1955, and his timing had not improved in the intervening years. Stanky's earlier troubles could be blamed on his relative youth; he was only 35 when he took the Cardinal reins. He was 49 when he took over the White Sox, but no wiser. Had he mellowed during his hiatus? "I don't like the word mellow," Stanky replied. "It reminds me of a piece of fruit that's gone soft." On the day he was named manager, Stanky proclaimed that Durocher, who had just become manager of the Cubs, was the greatest leader he had ever played for. "I believe talk of 'handling men,'" he said a few weeks later, "is exaggerated when managing is discussed. I believe the biggest factor is knowledge of baseball." "I try to treat my players the way I was treated," he added. Of course, Stanky was treated by the arrogant Durocher.

Stanky was an equal opportunity agitator in Chicago. As he had in St. Louis, he offended everyone. In his first year, Stanky couldn't get along with his coaches, so in the second year, he got new coaches. He infuriated the opposition and demeaned his own players, comparing managing a ball club to managing a child. He ordered batting practice after his club had played three games in 24 hours, and said, "They can either do it or get out."

Stanky also fought with reporters. After being criticized for throwing a tantrum following a loss, he said, "From now on when we lose, I'm going to offer the writers champagne, and then I'll roll on the floor and laugh and say, 'Hi, fellas, we just lost a tough one 3–2, ha, ha." The day the White Sox clinched the pennant, he declared, he would lock the clubhouse door for an hour. Not wanting to leave anyone out, Stanky took a few shots at the fans. "The fan," he said, "the butcher, the baker and the man who sells green stamps— doesn't know anything about this."

"Eddie Stanky came in," said White Sox catcher J.C. Martin, "and he was the most [here Martin, like Moford, paused for a long time trying to find the right word] ... different guy I ever played for. He was an intimidator. He tried to take people's money and intimidate them. He was not a people person. He was a high pressure person, and that didn't work on the White Sox. After the first year, the growl and bite didn't work. He knew baseball as good as anybody, but he didn't know how to get it across. He had no patience with people and just couldn't handle the players."

Stanky instituted a series of fines for failure to perform. Failure to score a runner from third with less than two out cost a player five dollars, as did an inability to sacrifice or to advance a runner from second with less than two out. He fined pitchers who refused to obey his orders to hit opposing batters. Most managers had fines for behavioral transgressions or mental errors, such as missing signs, but not many fined players for failure to execute.

One of Stanky's proteges in St. Louis was Solly Hemus. While he was manager of the Cardinals, Hemus was repeatedly ejected by National League umpires. In 1959, Hemus, then player-manager, was hit by a pitch thrown by Pittsburgh's Bennie Daniels. He called Daniels a black bastard, which precipitated a fight. Hemus said afterward that he meant no harm, and was just trying to fire up his team. Like Durocher and Stanky, Hemus made many enemies, who never forgot his blunders. He told Curt Flood in 1960 that he'd never make it as a major leaguer, a remark repeated with glee after Flood became an all star.

In July, 1961, having thoroughly worn out his welcome with the players (by his behavior) and the fans and owners (by failing to win) Hemus was replaced as Cardinal manager by Johnny Keane, and signed as a Met coach shortly thereafter.

Most managers were grizzled, tobacco chewing types who had paid their dues in the bushes and spat out clichés along with their tobacco juice. Houk followed their style only in the matter of tobacco chewing. He chewed constantly in the dugout and, when he was named general manager, had a spittoon installed in his office. "Houk is the only manager you need a couple of oars to get to see," said writer Clif Keane.

"Outside of staining the entire end of the Yankee dugout every year," said former reporter Gordon White, "Ralph was a good guy. Christ, that guy chewed the biggest wad of tobacco I ever saw and it just drained all game long. Ralph went to the left end of the dugout, put one leg up on the first step, leaned forward a little bit, and just kept spitting juice and spitting juice. There were three steps in the dugout, and by the time the season was over, there was a brown stain about three feet wide on all three steps. Yecch!" "[Houk] is known as the 'pool' chewer," wrote Jerome Holtzman. "Houk takes great delight in cloud-bursting one location, a drenching that frequently irrigates even the most drainable of dugouts."

The players loved Houk, but a successful manager cannot be buddies with his players, as Billy Martin proved a few years hence. Unlike Martin, Houk knew where to draw the line. Late in 1963, the Yankees were scheduled to play at Fenway Park. During the Yanks' visit to Boston, Mantle had given an interview to a local paper in which he praised Houk profusely. Houk was a great manager, Mantle said, and if he asked him to run through a stone wall, all they had to do is show him where the wall was. He went on at great length about how much he respected Houk, and what a fine manager he was. "He meant it," said Tom Metcalf, "and Houk had to be feeling pretty damn proud, because it was a great story."

Before the game, it began to rain. The Yankees sat in the dugout, waiting to see if they would play, and hoping they wouldn't, for the pennant race was nearly over and the field was rapidly becoming a quagmire. "It was raining cats and dogs," said Metcalf, "and we just wanted to get out of there. We're sitting in the dugout killing time, and a number of raunchy jokes were going around, with Mantle the main perpetrator. I won't get into the details, but he wanted to know if guys had done a certain thing. 'You're from a farm, Metcalf,' he said, 'did you ever do that?' Just then, Houk walked out of the tunnel and Mantle said, 'Hey, Ralph, have you ever done this? You were a kid once. Don't bullshit us.' I'll leave it to your imagination what he was asking about. We all sat there wondering whether Mickey had crossed the line. Mantle or no Mantle, that wasn't something you say to the manager. We all wanted to see how Ralph would handle it."

Houk never responded to Mantle's question. He stood on the first step of the dugout and said, "Come here, Mickey. I want to ask you something." Mantle walked over to him and Houk spoke in a very low voice. "Mickey," he said, "I want to thank you for those real nice words in the paper. They made me feel good. It would make me feel good coming from anybody, but coming from you ... I want you to know how much I appreciate those words." Mantle, unsure of where Houk was going, was getting a little nervous. "You know I meant every damn word of it, Ralph," he replied.

Houk moved in for the kill. Mantle had been injured for some time and had spent most of the past three months on the bench. The Yankees were cruising to the pennant because reserves like Lopez and Blanchard were playing in place of Maris and Mantle and knocking the cover off the ball. "Can I count on you in center field tonight?" Houk asked. Mickey looked out at the field, which was covered with a half inch of water and getting soggier by the moment. The last thing he wanted to do was test his injured knee in a swamp. "Remember what you said in the paper," Houk told him.

Mantle thought for a minute. "Hell, yeah, Ralph," he finally said. "If you want me to go out there and play, I'll play, but why?" "Well," Houk replied, "I don't want to take a chance of getting any of my regulars hurt." Houk turned and walked away, with Mantle's "You son of a bitch!" trailing after him. "We almost fell off the bench laughing," said Metcalf. "It was a defining moment between those two great men. It showed how gracefully Houk could handle the strong personalities on that team. To be able to handle a guy like Mantle and a guy as off the wall as Joe Pepitone and keep everybody on the same page and happy, you've got to be great."

One of Houk's first initiatives after taking over the Yankee club was to tell Mantle he wanted him to be the team leader. That had not been the case under Stengel, who had a father-son relationship with the Yankee superstar, scolding him when he acted up and being proud of him when he did well. Mickey was polite and guarded in his remarks after Stengel left the Yankees. "The things he said to me and about me I always figured were for my own good," he said. Under Casey, however, Mickey was clearly a youngster looking for Dad's approval. Houk told Mantle he was an adult, 29 years old, and with his ability and charisma, should be the leader of the Yankees, as Dimaggio had been. Mantle would be a much different leader than Dimaggio, whose teammates were either in awe of him or intimidated by him. Mantle had seen that side of Dimaggio and had no intention of being that kind of leader. He was one of the guys, but the one who would lead by example.

Buoyed by Houk's expressions of confidence, a new Mantle arrived in St. Petersburg in the spring of 1961. The moody, sometimes surly young man of the 1950s was replaced by a more friendly, outgoing individual whose quick wit became less caustic and more jovial. "He waved and hollered hello at me in the parking lot a little while ago," said an incredulous photographer. "What's happened to him?" "He's grown up," said Houk. "He's a man now."

Turning Mantle into a leader was the first step in Houk's plan. The second was to lighten the heavy attitude that had prevailed on the Yankee team during Stengel's final years. The new manager told Hamey he wanted the players to be happy, and urged him to be generous in salary negotiations. Generosity was a relative term in 1961, but Hamey was munificent by 1961 standards. No Yankee player took a cut in pay.

Houk also believed in a set lineup. He made Howard his every day catcher and abandoned Stengel's constant shuffling in the infield, putting Richardson at second, Kubek at short and Boyer at third. McDougald, a Yankee since 1951 who had shifted around the infield in 1960, retired. His skills were declining, he had four children at home, and he had a growing maintenance business. "I told Casey and George Weiss," McDougald said, "at the end of the 1959 season that I was retiring at the end of the 1960 season no matter what. It didn't matter if I was MVP. I said that I was through. I really didn't want to play ball anymore. I just made up my mind that I was going to play ten years and that's it. I'd started a business in 1957 and it had gotten to a point in 1960 that I could make a living for myself and my family."

Richardson, Boyer and Kubek were delighted by the turn of events. Before the 1960 season, Stengel had called Richardson the most valuable second baseman in the league, better than MVP Nelson Fox. When he got off to a slow start, however, Bobby found himself on the bench. Stengel even talked about replacing him with Hector Lopez. It seemed as though every time Richardson had been scheduled to bat in a clutch situation, Stengel pulled him for a pinch hitter. Hamey gave Bobby a raise for the 1961 season, despite a 49 point decline in his batting average, and Houk told him he would play second base every day. When Richardson got off to a slow start, Houk kept him there. Bobby was batting just over .200 in May, but he was fielding well, and Houk kept telling him he would hit.

The Yankees were glad Houk was their manager, but in spring training, they didn't show it. The club was sluggish in Florida, finishing with a 9–19 record. For championship teams, however, spring training is a time for learning, not for winning games. What Houk was finding out about his team, however, was sometimes disturbing. Maris, the 1960 American League Most Valuable Player, wasn't hitting at all and, other than Mantle, neither was anyone else.

When he started the training season, Houk believed his starting rotation was well-manned. Based upon Ford's two World Series shutouts, it appeared that Whitey's arm was sound again, and Houk could expect him to rebound from his mediocre 1960 season. Terry was young and resilient and appeared not to have been scarred by Mazeroski's home run. Stafford, who was released from the Army in mid–March, had great stuff and seemed ready to contribute. With veterans Turley and Ditmar on the scene, there was plenty of depth.

The bullpen was another matter. Shantz, Grba and Maas had been lost in the expansion draft, leaving the relief corps alarmingly weak. Luis Arroyo had been placed on the list of expansion eligibles, but with his advanced age and mediocre major league record, neither the Senators nor Angels was interested. Duren, the best reliever in the American League in 1958 and 1959, had been wild and unreliable in 1960. In the ninth inning of Game Seven, with the Series on the line, he sat idle in the bullpen. Houk talked about using Duren as a starter in '61. Other bullpen possibilities were Coates, who shuttled between starting assignments and the pen in 1960, Danny McDevitt, a sore-armed lefty purchased from the Dodgers, and Billy Short, still trying to get over his elbow trouble. "Unless that arm of mine goes haywire again," Short said in the spring, "the Major's search for another pitcher is over." Unfortunately, Short's arm went haywire again, he had arm surgery in April, and the Major's search continued.

If the Yankees were to have a strong pitching staff, Ford, its anchor, had to have a good year. Whitey had frequently suffered from a tender arm, and Stengel coddled him, giving him extra rest, saving him for the tough teams, and often skipping his turn when it came up at tough parks like Fenway. Whitey had a terrific winning percentage, but had never won 20 games in a season. In the spring of 1961, Houk approached Ford with the notion of pitching every fourth day, rather than every fifth day, which he had done most of his career, and staying in rotation no matter who the opposition and what the location. Houk suggested Whitey speak with Warren Spahn and others who started every fourth day to get their impressions.

Another person in the Yankee camp urging Ford to consider a four day schedule was pitching coach Johnny Sain, the other half of the famous "Spahn, Sain and two days of rain" rotation that won the 1948 National League pennant for the Boston Braves. In 1948, Sain pitched so frequently, often with just two days rest, that it took a severe toll on his arm, and he went from a 24–15 mark with a 2.60 ERA to 10–17 with a 4.81 ERA in 1949. Eventually, Sain's arm recovered and, after another 20 win season with the Braves, he was traded to the Yankees, where he became one of the best relief pitchers in the American League. In 1954, he led the league with 22 saves, an unimpressive total in today's game, but seven saves higher than the 1954 runner up.

While spending more than four seasons in the Yankee bullpen, Sain had the opportunity to hold frequent conversations with bullpen catcher Ralph Houk about his pitching theories. Houk was planning on managing, and made up his mind, sitting in that bullpen, that if he ever got a major league job, Johnny Sain would be his pitching coach.

Sain coached for the Kansas City Athletics in 1959, but resigned after just a year to operate his Chevrolet agency in Walnut Ridge, Arkansas. Business at the agency was good, but when Houk asked him to return to the game, he accepted without hesitation. Selling cars couldn't match the excitement of coaching major league pitchers.

Sain was one of baseball's most interesting personalities, and, by the mid–'60s, the sport's highest paid coach at $25,000 per year. He changed jobs frequently, and wherever he went, two things were sure to follow: twenty game winners and disputes with the manager. With the Yankees, Ford and Terry, neither of whom had ever won 20 games in a season, had the best years of their careers. After Sain left, neither won 20 again. For two years, Sain coached the Twins, where Mudcat Grant and Jim Kaat, two good but heretofore unspectacular pitchers, entered the 20 game circle. In Detroit, Denny McLain won 30. When Sain joined the Tigers in the Fall of 1966, manager Mayo Smith told him his first project was Joe Sparma, who'd slipped from 13–8 to 2–7. In 1967, under Sain's tutelage, Sparma was 16–9. With the White Sox in the early '70s, Wilbur Wood and Stan Bahnsen each joined the 20 win club.

Coaching was a very inexact science in the 1960s. "I think the philosophy of the Yankees in those days," said pitcher Bob Meyer, "was to go out and sign the best talent, grow them in the minors and let them learn by doing." Most coaches were pals of the manager, and their skills, other than being likeable individuals, were often difficult to discern. Houk had a simple formula for selecting coaches. They should be "Heroes who command the attention of young players and who have a solid grounding in the fundamentals of the game." Such men, however, proved hard to find.

"There was no communication between the players and the coaches," said pitcher Gary Kroll. "They were chosen on a friendship basis from the old days. Mel Harder was our pitching coach with the Mets and I don't think I ever talked to him. Wes Westrum caught Maglie and all those guys. He's a guy who could have helped the pitchers, but no one ever said, 'This is the plan,' or 'Let's work on this.'"

"I had a hitting coach in Allentown," said former Met Ted Schreiber, "and if you stood on home plate and he was the batter and he swung at you, he'd miss. That's how bad this guy was." "We weren't coached," said pitcher Dave Hillman. "Most places I went there was just a bat, a ball and a glove and you'd just go out and go to it. We didn't have a pickoff play. We didn't have nothing. That's the way it was with the Mets. We had a bunch of coaches there, but, bless their hearts, there was no coaching."

"In those days," said Eli Grba, "you were supposed to know what the hell you were doing when you got there. In 1960, Eddie Lopat was our pitching coach, but he never talked to me about changing speeds, never said, 'Hey, we've got to get you a changeup,' or 'Let's go work on your mechanics.' It was nothing like it is now." "We had so many pitching coaches," said Met pitcher Ron Locke. "One would tell you to throw a slider this way. One would tell you to throw a changeup. You're trying to work on all kinds of different things."

Many pitching coaches were advocates of what had made them successful as players, and some insisted on having every pitcher throw the same way. Met pitcher Bill Denehy believes that one of the factors which led to his arm trouble and rapid demise as a major league pitcher was Johnny Murphy changing his motion from overhand to three quarters in order to make him a better fielder.

Denehy later became a minor league pitching coach for the Red Sox, where he was able to put his theories into practice. Each pitcher, he believed, needed to be coached based upon his unique attributes. In the early '80s, Denehy coached Oil Can Boyd and Roger Clemens in the Eastern League. Boyd was a skinny, bony right hander, while Clemens was a heavily-muscled, broad-shouldered stud. "I noticed that Oil Can would get tired late in the season," said Denehy, "so I limited the number of pitches he threw between starts. When he went in the outfield to shag fly balls, I made him wear a left-handed glove. He led the league in strikeouts and innings pitched in 1982."

"Clemens was different. He was so big and strong and bulky. Between starts I'd put him on one foul line and I'd go three quarters of the way to the fence on the other foul line and have him throw like an outfielder. He'd throw the ball 300 feet to stretch out his arm. I didn't want his muscles to tighten up. I wanted to keep them as long and elastic as possible.

"I really believe that you have to look at each pitcher individually. I look at their anatomy, their makeup and their delivery. You absolutely don't make changes to someone unless they show they can't get people out. Then, if they want to make a living playing ball, they make the change."

Psychology and building self esteem were not the long suits of most coaches and executives. Catcher Norm Sherry recalled meeting Branch Rickey, Jr. during his first year of professional ball. "I had a bad uppercut swing," Sherry recalled. "Branch said, 'How many times have you swung the bat?' I said, 'I don't know.' He asked how long I'd been playing and how many times I thought I'd swung a bat. I guessed about ten or twelve thousand times. 'Well,' he said, 'That's how many times you've swung it wrong.'"

"The only way we had to gain experience was to talk to each other or to the older players," said Met Jim Hickman, "simply because we didn't have any hitting coaches. We had Rogers Hornsby for a year. Then he was gone [Hornsby passed away after the 1962 season] and we didn't have a hitting coach for a number of years." Hickman, now a minor league batting coach in the Reds organization, is not certain, however, that the lack of coaching was a hindrance. "I think maybe we see too much coaching now as opposed to what we saw years ago. I think hitting has changed in the fact that people try to clone hitters more than they did years ago. Stan Musial hit his way and Smoky Burgess hit his way. Now you see more guys trying to do the same things."

The quintessential coach of the 1960s was Frank Crosetti, who manned the third base box for the Yankees from 1947 through 1968. Prior to becoming a coach, Crosetti had played shortstop for the Yankees since 1932. Managers and players came and went, but Crosetti remained. He was never a threat to the manager, for Crosetti stated repeatedly that he had no desire to manage. He stayed contentedly in the background, rarely spoke to the press, and always played the part of the company man. Until the early '60s, he refused to appear on radio or television. The most exposure he received was when he was photographed shaking the hand of a Yankee rounding the bases after a home run.

The role of company man paid well, for Crosetti collected 21 World Series shares, totaling well over $100,000. He didn't part with much of it, for in the midst of a Yankee team known for its high lifestyle, the Cro led a frugal, abstemious existence. During the 1962 World Series, as the Yankee players waited out the rain in San Francisco, Elston Howard looked out the window of the hotel and saw an armored car pulling up. "Here comes Crosetti," he announced. Once when a sore arm prevented the Crow from throwing batting practice, Phil Rizzuto surmised that he must have tried to lift his wallet with one hand.

"Crosetti is an odd character," wrote a *Sporting News* columnist, "the oddest in the major leagues." On a typical day (there were few night games in the 1960s), he was in bed by 10 P.M. and up and about by 6 A.M., often running into players returning from a night on the town as he took his morning stroll. Crosetti almost never attended social functions and, as soon as the season was over, returned to his home in San Francisco and left the bright lights of New York behind, generally without bothering to attend the annual Yankee victory celebration.

Since a coach would be judged by the success of his pupils, the natural tendency was to work with the more talented subjects. "Most hitting instructors will take somebody who's a good hitter and maybe give him another ten points or so on his average," said Phil Linz, "like Charley Lau with George Brett. To me, a good hitting coach will take somebody like me who's hitting .230 and get them up to .260, like Ted Williams did with Ed Brinkman. Wally Moses was a nice guy, but he didn't want to deal with me. I was a slap hitter who put the ball in play. He wanted to work with a guy like Tresh, who was going to be a good hitter anyway."

"In those days," said former Met Don Bosch, "if you were hitting .167 [which Bosch often was] you were the guy who needed batting practice, but you weren't the guy who was going to get it. The Rusty Staub's who were hitting .312 got the extra batting practice and they looked at you like you were a waste of time. I remember going up to Yogi Berra and saying, 'I need some extra BP,' and he'd say, 'Well, I don't know if we can find anybody to pitch to you,' or 'the balls cost money.' There was always some excuse. I would have hit until my hands bled, but you never got the opportunity, so it was very difficult to improve your skills."

Tresh and Steve Whitaker swore by Moses, a longtime Philadelphia Athletic outfielder during his playing days. As a young prospect, Moses had been discovered by none other than Ty Cobb. "I really had a lot of confidence in Wally," said Whitaker, "whether he did anything or not. I just loved the guy. It's hard to explain. He made you feel special. He made you feel like you could do anything. In the minor leagues or the big leagues, whenever Wally Moses was around, I bet I hit .500. One time, Ralph Houk told him, 'Just stay here, don't leave.' When he was in town, he gave me that comfort." Perhaps Moses' most unique skill was that, although in his playing days he had been a singles hitter, he could adapt to the style of power hitters like Tresh and Whitaker. Most coaches, such as Harry Walker, wanted players to hit like they hit.

Former Met Don Rowe has been a major league pitching coach and has also coached football. "Here's where baseball gets screwed up and football doesn't," Rowe said. "In baseball, they fail to practice. First of all, the coaches aren't teachers. There are very few major league managers or coaches who are teachers. Let's say we're in spring training and we have all these drills and get everything worked out. Then the season starts and we don't work on those plays. So you see rundowns in the middle of the year and there's ten guys running back and forth. In spring training, they got the guy out because they practice it. It would be like a football team saying, 'We're going to run this play in August and then we'll never run it again until the Pro Bowl.' What do you think their chances are of being successful? Baseball teams get lazy because they play every day. You can work out your schedule and not work them so hard that they can't play but still review what happens."

Johnny Sain was an anomaly among major league coaches for two reasons. First, he was an excellent teacher and, second, he didn't need the job. Sain was financially independent, unlike most coaches, whose livelihood depended upon pleasing the manager and not making waves. Sain's loyalty was not to the manager but to his pitchers. "I guess I get attached to my pitchers a little too much," he once said. "I like to see all the pitchers have success, even the ones leaving us for other clubs."

Sain loved his pitchers and they in turn loved him. "He's the guy who made my career," said Rollie Sheldon. "It was brief, but it would've been a lot briefer without Johnny. He would sit on the bench and point things out to you. He would work with you in the bullpen on certain pitches. I thought he was a psychologist. He was always in our heads. I thought he was the finest pitching coach in the game at that time."

When the Twins cut Sain loose after the 1966 season, Jim Kaat, who'd won 25 games that year, blasted the Twins' management in a letter to a local newspaper. "If I were ever in a position of general manager," Kaat wrote, "I'd give Sain a name-your-own-figure contract to handle my pitchers. (And, oh, yes, I'd hire a manager that could take advantage of his talents.)" Kaat, who has become a respected authority on pitching as a coach and broadcaster, gave Sain credit for his development as a pitcher, called him the most knowledgeable baseball man he knew and equated Sain's departure with the Green Bay Packers letting Vince Lombardi, then at the height of his fame, get away. Not only were Kaat's remarks a paean to his pitching coach, they were a direct slap at Twin manager Sam Mele, and an indication of the gap Sain created between his pitchers and the manager.

Sain's talent lay in the combination of his thorough knowledge of pitching mechanics with a keen psychological insight into his charges. He'd never been an overpowering pitcher, and had to acquire knowledge and guile in order to succeed. Sain's father was a mechanic and John had always tinkered with machines to find out what made them work. He adapted his knowledge to tinkering with pitchers to find out what made them work. "Johnny helped me a lot with mechanics," said Jim Coates. "He'd really pinpoint it. He'd say, 'You're sliding too far. You've got to stay on top a little more.'"

After the 1963 season, Sain asked the Yankees for a sizable raise, which he knew wouldn't be granted. As he expected, Sain's demand resulted in his replacement as pitching coach, and he began his odyssey as a roaming professor of pitching. When the Yankee staff struggled in 1964, the pitchers signed a petition asking that Sain be re-hired. Whitey Ford, who'd replaced Sain and was serving as player-coach, was one of those who signed.

Why didn't managers like a pitching coach who could produce 20 games winners on a consistent basis? "Sometimes," said Sheldon, "I think he expressed himself in a meeting with the coaches and it might have been taken the wrong way. He did make a lot of moves." After leaving the Yankees, Sain engaged in one power struggle after another, for he wanted total control of the pitching staff. They were his pitchers, and he didn't want any manager interfering. "Sain and [Hal] Naragon [the Tiger bullpen coach] thrive in any situation by building a wall around their pitchers," wrote Detroit columnist Watson Spoelstra. "Anyone who comes busting through the gate to second-guess the pitcher encounters troubles. Sain's broken relations with Billy Martin and Sam Mele stemmed from a small incident. For Sain, you lay off his pitchers, or else.... You'll never catch Sain putting the knock on any pitcher."

The incident with Martin occurred when the fiery Twin coach was instructing base runners about breaking from third on a squeeze bunt. "It isn't that simple, Martin," Sain interjected. "It is easy," Martin replied. "And that's why we [meaning the Yankees] always won and you always lost. Any time you have something to say to me, Sain, say it in private and not in front of the players." Mele listened to the exchange and said nothing, which infuriated Sain. He moved his gear out of the coaches' locker room and into the players' section, which infuriated Mele. Earlier in the season, with the Twins headed for the American League pennant, Mele had praised Sain's work ethic and the results he was achieving with the Minnesota staff. Now Mele said either he went or Sain went. Sain went, and was immediately hired by the Tigers. "I don't care what happened with that club," said Tiger manager Mayo Smith, "Sometimes situations occur. I only know that Sain is a capable man and I'm glad he's with Detroit."

The Tigers had always been a hard-hitting team that couldn't win a pennant because their pitchers couldn't stop opposing batters. Under Sain's tutelage in 1968, Denny McLain won 31 games, the Tigers allowed the fewest runs in the league (the first time the team had ever done so), and Detroit won its first World Series since 1945. The Series was Sain's ninth, his fifth as a coach. Yet, he was soon on his way once again, leaving Detroit in the middle of the 1969 season. Sain was angry because Smith didn't consult him on pitching choices, and because of front-office interference with his work, the same trouble he'd had with the Twins.

Sain spent five years in Chicago under Chuck Tanner, and one year in Atlanta in 1977. He returned to coaching nearly a decade later for two final years with the Braves, finishing his career under Tanner in 1986. By that time he was 69 years old, and the magic apparently was gone. In his final year, the Braves finished last in the National League's Western Division and Atlanta pitchers were ninth in the 12-team league in ERA.

In 1961, however, Sain was at the top of his game, and probably the best pitching coach in baseball. He urged Ford to consider changing his routine, for Sain was a strong believer in the four man rotation, which he felt enabled a pitcher to keep his rhythm and routine. Ford agreed and set up a regular schedule. On the first day after he started, he threw easily for a few minutes to get the stiffness out of his arm. On the second day, he ran a lot and threw hard for about fifteen minutes. On the third day, he did very little, tossing the ball around a bit and shagging flies. On the fourth day, he pitched.

Routine is like a security blanket to starting pitchers. "The night after you start," said Bob Shaw, "you can stay out late. The second day, you run and watch your diet. Two nights before you're going to pitch, you go to bed early and get a good night's sleep because the night before, you're dreaming half the time about the game and who you're going to pitch against, so you don't get a real good night's sleep. You run so many laps each day. Everything's organized."

Bill Denehy was thrown off stride when the Mets went to a five man rotation. "I didn't want that extra day's rest," he said. "With a four man rotation, the day after I pitched, I'd take the day off and do a lot of heavy running. The second day I'd throw on the side. I'd take the third day off and the fourth day I'd pitch. With a five day rotation I could never figure out how to work it. Should I take two days off, throw on the side, then take a day off and pitch, or take a day, throw and then take two days off? I never found the right sequence."

As a pitcher, Sain understood the importance of maintaining a steady routine. Early in 1948, he said, he was pitching sporadically, due to off days and rainouts, and not pitching all that well, when manager Billy Southworth told him, Spahn and Vern Bickford that they were going to pitch every fourth day. The schedules of the other pitchers would be adjusted to compensate. Sain strongly believed that the same program would be of great benefit to Ford. He liked to peg his rotation around the top three pitchers and plug in two other spot starters as needed.

The four day rotation worked almost immediately for Ford. He had an outstanding spring, with no sign of the arm trouble that had been a feature of virtually every previous training camp. "Whitey's arm hasn't looked this good in the spring in I don't know how many years," Houk said. Sain also taught Ford a slightly different grip on his slider. Whitey started throwing the slider in 1960, but it hurt his arm. Sain taught him to use a longer follow-through rather than jerking the ball, and his arm no longer hurt. The slider also had a bigger and sharper break, and became his best pitch.

The new slider made Ford a much better pitcher. He'd never been overpoweringly fast, and relied on a varied assortment of pitches and pinpoint control. "It wasn't even a day's work when you caught Whitey," said Jake Gibbs. "Ford wasn't fast at all," said John Blanchard, "but he could hit the black nine out of ten times. Unbelievable what control he had. In Yankee Stadium, he would take that big right hand power hitter and put it on the outside corner and just let him hit it. It was just a big 420 foot out." "The keys to Whitey's success," said Bud Daley, "were his curve ball and his control. He had a pitch he threw to right handers that would start almost at them and come back over the inside corner. He got a lot of strikeouts that way." "He had so many pitches," said Lee Thomas. "He could cut you up and you wouldn't even know it."

Or, many thought, he could cut the ball up, or maybe load it up. "One day he was pitching," said former Indian outfielder Al Luplow, "and I hit a foul ball. I picked it up and looked at it. The ball was all cut up. I showed the umpire and he threw it to the ball boy and didn't say a word. He knew." "He always had that wet one," said Joe DeMaestri, "once in a while in the right spot."

During the first two months of the 1961 season, Ford was terrific, but the rest of Sain's pitchers were disappointing. An unusually rainy spring, which limited the Yankees to just two games in the first week of the season, made it difficult for Houk to give his pitchers much work. Ditmar and Turley followed good outings with bad ones and Terry, who was one of the spot starters worked around the top three, pitched infrequently. By the middle of May, Terry had just one win and an ERA of nearly 6.00. Stafford got a late start after being mustered out of the service in March, and developed a sore shoulder. During one fourteen game stretch, Houk didn't get a single complete game from his starters. The bullpen was mostly ineffective, with Arroyo emerging as Houk's only reliable relief man. It was clear that pitching was the Yanks' number one problem.

In early June, Houk showed he was not afraid to make bold moves. He traded McDevitt, who had been wild and ineffective, to Minnesota. He removed veterans Ditmar and Turley from the rotation and replaced them with youngsters Sheldon and Stafford. "There is no use in kidding," Houk said. "The starters are not doing the job. They have had ample opportunity and can't kick. I've been with them 100 per cent, but I cannot go any farther with them." It was a gutsy move for a rookie manager. No one could have faulted him for sticking with proven veterans like Ditmar and Turley. On the other hand, if the youngsters failed, Houk would look foolish.

Fortunately for Houk and the Yankees, Sheldon and Stafford came through, Terry started pitching better, and Ford continued to be the best pitcher in the American League. In midsummer, however, a second crisis hit the Yankee pitching staff. Stafford injured his shoulder again. Terry, in the course of pitching eleven innings against the Indians, hurt *his* shoulder, and was out of action for almost a month. Turley was given another chance, but failed. He was put on the disabled list in July and had an operation during the Fall.

When the Yankees needed help in the past, they looked to Kansas City. Dan Topping's buddy Arnold Johnson had passed away, and the new owner of the Athletics was a flamboyant insurance executive from Chicago named Charles O. Finley. Finley hired controversial Frank Lane as his general manager, a pairing that was bound to end in disaster. The new owner was a visionary with a sharp edge who knew little about baseball, while Lane fancied himself a baseball genius. He loved to trade, and wound up executing more than 500 swaps during his career. There was not enough room in one organization for two egos the size of Finley's and Lane's.

Despite his cantankerous personality, Finley was often a positive, if grudgingly accepted, force. When baseball discovered marketing in the 1960s, the leader in innovation, if not in attendance, was Finley. He was Bill Veeck, without Veeck's puckish charm. Finely was never without a new idea, and never hesitant to share it. "I think I can sell anything," he once said. His best idea, which was eventually adopted, was to start the World Series on a Saturday, and play the weekday games at night.

Finley's primary goal was to increase the abysmal attendance in Kansas City, but his secondary aim was to end Yankee dominance of the American League. He accused the Yankees of gaining an unfair advantage from the short right field porch in Yankee Stadium. The Yankees packed their club with left handed power hitters, Finley claimed, who hit easy home runs into the inviting right field stands. A major weakness in Finley's argument was the fact that the Yankees hit roughly the same number of homers on the road as they did at home. In 1961, Maris hit 31 home runs in Yankee Stadium and 30 on the road. Mantle hit 24 at home and 30 on the road. The previous year, Maris hit 26 of his 39 homers on the road. When the Yankees set a major league record with 240 circuit clouts in 1961, 128 of them came on the road.

No matter. Finley said he was going to change the dimensions of his park to conform to those of Yankee Stadium. What Finley lacked, of course, was a crew of sluggers to hit the ball over the fence. Moreover, his gambit was against the rules, for each park constructed subsequent to 1958 had to have fences at least 325 feet from home plate at the foul lines.

When Finley moved his right field fence to within 296 feet of the plate, American League President Joe Cronin told him he had to move it back. Finley had another idea. He moved the fence back, but cut it in toward the plate at such a sharp angle that there was a narrow alley going to the right field pole and a fence that was 296 feet from home plate just a few feet from the foul line. Cronin told him that had to go. Finally, Finley contented himself with drawing chalk lines on the field marking off the dimensions of Yankee Stadium. Every time a ball was caught within the field of play but beyond the chalk marks, the public address announcer informed the crowd, "That would have been a home run in Yankee Stadium."

Yankee publicity man Bob Fishel had his own idea. While Yankee Stadium's right field fence was much closer to the plate than the Kansas City fence, the Stadium's left field wall was a healthy shot away. Fishel brought a battery powered megaphone to Kansas City, and when Clete Boyer hit a home run over the 353 sign in left field, switched it on and prepared to deliver his speech: "That would have been an out in Yankee Stadium." The devil in most ideas is in the details, and when Fishel spoke, the only people who could hear him were those within 20 feet. His batteries had failed.

Finley outfitted his A's in colorful green (Kelly Green), white (Wedding Gown White) and gold (Finley Gold) uniforms and white shoes (supposedly made from albino kangaroo leather). The white shoes were perhaps the most controversial. When the Athletics first wore them in 1967, Cleveland manager Joe Adcock protested, claiming that white shoes on a pitcher were an illegal distraction to the batter. The unusual garb caused Athletic players to be subjected to no small degree of bench jockeying. "Hi, there, beautiful," came a cry from the opposing dugout. "Aw, isn't that sweet," said crew-cut former KC manager Hank Bauer, no doubt greatly relieved Finley had fired him a year earlier. "Say one word," the Athletics' Gino Cimoli said to a reporter on opening day, "and I'll deck you." "When we went to the kelly green and gold uniforms," said catcher Bill Bryan, "everybody around the league laughed at us, but Charley said that eventually all games were going to be televised in color. Gray and white don't show up in color."

When Finley and Lane took over the Athletics in 1961, one of the first acts of the new partnership was a vow that the parade of quality young players to New York would come to an end. Lane, in Cleveland at the time, had blasted the Maris trade. "The good young players we'll keep in Kansas City," he vowed, "and they will not find their way to Yankee Stadium or any other stadium if they are good." In early February, Finley staged a publicity stunt in which he set afire a bus affixed with the label "Kansas City to New York Shuttle Bus."

In April, 1961, Athletic manager Joe Gordon joked, "In view of the fact the Yankees keep yammering that they want to make a deal but insist all that's offered in return is junk, we stand ready to make this offer. We'll trade any twenty five on our roster for any twenty five on theirs." When the Yankees obtained Bob Cerv and Tex Clevenger from the Angels in May, Lane said that Los Angeles had replaced Kansas City as the Yankees new farm club.

Lane's resolve lasted until June, when he helped alleviate Houk's pitching problems by trading lefty Bud Daley, a 1960 All Star, to the Yanks for Ditmar and talented young prospect Deron Johnson. Ditmar was out of baseball less than a year later. Johnson would eventually become a star, but not with Kansas City, while Daley played a key role in two Yankee pennants. The As had been taken again.

The shuttle was running once more, and Finley and Lane soon became embroiled in the bitter dispute everyone knew was just a bruised ego away. Manager Gordon was in a difficult position. In 1959, when Lane was general manager at Cleveland, he fired Gordon at the end of the season, only to rehire him a few days later. In 1960, Lane traded Gordon, the Indian manager, for Jimmie Dykes, who had been managing the Tigers. He hadn't wanted Gordon then, didn't want him in 1961, and succeeded in convincing Finley that Gordon had to go. Finley fired Gordon, who would later re-appear in Kansas City as manager of the expansion Royals in 1969, and replaced him with Hank Bauer.

Lane didn't like Bauer's managing any more than he'd liked Gordon's, so he went to Finley and told him to fire Bauer. One night, Lane climbed aboard the team bus after a loss and blasted Bauer in front of the players. The Athletics were in tenth place, and it couldn't possibly be the fault of the genius who was in charge of providing the players. It had to be the manager's fault.

In August, Lane committed the unpardonable sin of affronting the dignity of one Charles O. Finley by making trades without Finley's permission. Finley fired Lane just two years and four months before the end of the general manager's three year contract. Lane departed in a blaze of invective. "I have my pride, even though I have been working for a crackpot," he said the next day. "All Finley needs to do to see who is responsible for this mess is to look in the mirror." Lane also said he had been a big supporter of both Gordon and Bauer.

The episode was a preview of Finley's tenure as the Athletics' owner. In less than a year, he'd had two managers and two general managers. One thing he eventually did, however, was end the shuttle from Kansas City to New York. Daley was the last major acquisition the Yankees made from Kansas City for several years.

Even after the arrival of Daley, the New York pitching situation was problematic. The Yankees became so desperate that 19-year-old left hander Al Downing was recalled from Double A Binghamton and given a start. Downing, the first African-American to pitch for the Yankees, was in his first season of professional baseball, having thrown less than 100 innings as a pro. "I had to have a pitcher," Houk explained, and it could be a raw rookie or someone who'd been in the minors for several years without being deemed good enough to come up before. Downing clearly wasn't ready for the majors, but the youngster had fantastic stuff and there was no one at Triple A Richmond who could help. Like Elston Howard, Downing was also the "right kind of Negro." He was a college student, well-read, and articulate, and had been president of his high school class for three years.

The inexperienced Downing wasn't much help, and by July, with Stafford and Terry ailing, Daley and Sheldon were the only starters other than Ford who could be relied upon to consistently put forth major league performances. Sheldon, one year removed from D ball, was the club's top right hander. Yet, the club was winning. During June and July, when the rotation was in shambles, the Yankees posted records of 22–10 and 20–9, respectively. It didn't take great pitching to win when it was backed by a few homers, and the Yankees were hitting more than a few. Maris, who had slumped so badly during the latter stages of the 1960 season, started out equally poorly in 1961, not getting his first home run until April 27. In his first 27 games, Maris batted just .215, with three homers and 15 RBI. Suddenly, his dormant bat came alive. In his next 16 games, Maris hit 12 home runs.

The other Yankees were coming alive as well. In the club's first 33 games, they hit 34 home runs, an impressive pace. In their next 17 games, they hit 32 homers, an American League record. The Yankee lineup was probably the strongest any team had fielded since the 1930s. "Richardson led off," said Bob Shaw, who pitched for the Athletics in 1961, "and he was a tough hitter. Then you had Kubek, another tough hitter, and then here they come. You had Maris, Mantle, Berra, Skowron and Howard. The out man was Boyer, and he ended up hitting almost 30 home runs for Atlanta."

Red Sox pitcher Bill Monbouquette recalled, "After we took batting practice, one of the grounds keepers would go up a ladder with a pail and collect all the balls we'd hit into the stands. Then, after the Yankees finished batting practice, he went up there with two pails."

The Yankees were not the only team hitting home runs, nor were Maris and Mantle the only individuals knocking the ball over the fence. With two additional teams and eight more games on the schedule, the American League hit 1534 home runs, shattering the league's previous high of 1091. The National League, with the same schedule as in previous years, posted the second highest total in its history. The Angels, playing in Los Angeles' cozy Wrigley Field while awaiting the opening of Chavez Ravine, hit 189 homers and the Tigers, with Rocky Colavito and Norm Cash leading the way, connected for 180. In mid–June, the Angels, an expansion team, had more home runs than the Yankees.

What was happening? Was the ball juiced up? Commissioner Frick and National League President Giles said it was not. A.G. Spalding and Company said they were manufacturing balls the same way they always had. Extensive testing proved inconclusive. Scientists gathered in Central Park to fire baseballs out of an explosive-driven ram, and said the ball was no livelier than older balls. One must remember, of course, that the older balls had been laying around for twenty or thirty years. *Sports Illustrated* commissioned the engineering firm of Joseph S. Ward and Associates, whose study showed the 1961 ball to have 10 percent greater rebound than the 1952 version.

Non-scientists had their own opinions. Baltimore pitcher Skinny Brown insisted that the seams were not as high, and the ball felt different in his hand. It was lighter and therefore would go farther. Oriole pitching coach Harry Brecheen agreed. "It's livelier, all right," said Satchel Paige, who had been handling baseballs for several decades. "You just cut it open," growled Early Wynn, "and you'll find a carburetor."

Maybe it was the bats, which were lighter, with thinner handles, and were being swung harder, even with two strikes. Ten years earlier, most bats weighed 34 or 35 ounces. In 1961, the most popular models were 31 or 32 ounces, with very thin handles. Players were also more aggressive. Forget about guarding the plate. The hitters of 1961 were swinging for the fences at all times.

Was there another reason for the home run explosion? Forget about the balls and bats, said Mantle. The players were livelier. They were more talented than ever before, he said. Golfers were hitting the ball farther, and athletes were better in every other sport. Why not baseball?

Maris and Mantle grabbed the headlines with their pursuit of Ruth's home run mark, but virtually every Yankee hitter contributed. Howard, catching regularly for the first time, was hitting at a pace that would give him a .348 average at the season's end. Kubek and Richardson were getting on base and Maris, Mantle, Skowron and Berra were driving them home. Only Boyer and Lopez weren't hitting. "I had a terrible season," said Lopez. "Everybody was hitting home runs and I only hit three." There was a logical reason, however. "I blame it on my wife," he said recently, "because I got married after the 1960 season."

The 1961 Yankees are generally rated one of the best teams of all time, along with the 1927 Yankees, the 1998 Yankees, the 1954 Indians and the 1929 Athletics. "I still say it's the best team that ever set foot on a ballfield," said Clevenger. "The comraderie was really, really strong. Whenever the games got tight, you knew that somebody was going to hit a home run, or pinch hit a home run or do something to win."

The '27 Yankees won the pennant by 19 games, and the '29 As won by 18. In 1961, however, the Yankees were locked in a tight pennant race for nearly the entire season. Cleveland and Detroit broke quickly from the gate, but the Indians soon fell off the pace. The Orioles had been the Yankees' toughest rivals in 1960, and with a youthful team, especially its terrific young pitching staff, figured to be even better in 1961. "It Can be Done in '61," was the slogan that was plastered all over Baltimore, and translated into Russian, Greek, German, Italian, Yiddish and Polish. Before the season, Paul Richards said, "All this team really needs is that one big man, a monster who can hit 40 home runs and drive in 130 runs for you." Richards found his monster in Jim Gentile, who hit 46 home runs and drove in 141, but the rest of his team fell apart. Baltimore started slowly and couldn't get it done in any language.

Bob Scheffing's Tigers, however, stalked the Yankees into September. The Tigers had finished sixth in 1960, twelve games under .500 and 26 out of first place. They were last in team batting. Detroit had employed two managers in each of the previous three years before deciding on Scheffing, a 47-year-old former National League catcher, to lead the club in 1961. Scheffing's Tigers were a powerful team, with Al Kaline and Rocky Colavito in the outfield and Norm Cash at first base. Kaline, rebounding from a terrible 1960 season, hit .324, Colavito rapped 45 homers and Cash led the league with a .361 average, while adding 41 homers and 132 RBI. In addition, two rookies, second baseman Jake Wood and third baseman Steve Boros, came up from Denver to have excellent first seasons.

The Detroit pitching staff was anchored by Jim Bunning and Frank Lary, a 31-year-old workhorse who won 23 games and continued his uncanny mastery over the Yankees. He'd beaten them seven times in 1958, and in 1961, bested them four times. After coming to the majors in 1954, Lary won 24 of his first 32 decisions against the club that was dominating the American League. Overall, he was 28–13 against the Yankees and 95–97 against the rest of the American League. How did he do it? "I guess with my bat," Lary said, laughing. Once he beat the Yankees by dropping a perfect bunt with two out. On another occasion, he hit a game-winning home run. It was his pitching, however, that generally overwhelmed the Bombers. "Playing the Yankees as many times as we did," Lary said, "I thought I knew them pretty well." The Tigers' principal weakness was a lack of depth, which would haunt them when injuries struck late in the season.

For most of the year, it was the Yankees who were chasing the Tigers. Houk and Scheffing attended a dinner in late April, after the Tigers had gotten off to a fast start. If the Tigers kept up their present pace, Houk said, they would win 141 games. If that happened, he said, the Yankees would win 142. Scheffing said he'd take his chances with 141 wins. The Tigers didn't keep up that heady pace, but they were a game ahead when they came to Yankee Stadium for a July 4 doubleheader. The largest Stadium crowd since 1947 (74,246) turned out on a gorgeous midsummer afternoon. The Yanks pulled even with the Tigers by winning the opener 6–2, behind Ford's complete game five hitter, which boosted his record to 15–2.

A victory in the second game would put the Yankees in first place. Turley, given a rare start, exited early, but solid relief pitching stopped the Tigers, leaving the score 3–3 after nine innings. Stafford was pitching for the Yankees and Lary, the Tiger starter, was still on the mound for Detroit. Lary came to bat in the tenth with runners on second and third and two out. He dropped a beautiful bunt down the third base line, beat it out and drove home the winning run. The Yankees were back in second place.

Meanwhile, Mantle and Maris were putting on a demonstration of power that hadn't been seen since the days of Ruth and Gehrig. "It got to the point," said Joe DeMaestri, "where we would stand up to watch when they came to the plate." After the doubleheader on the 4th, Maris had 31 home runs and Mantle 28. For the first time, the chance of catching Ruth became a topic of discussion. Houk was more interested in whether the Yankees would catch the Tigers.

• 5 •

The Bootstrappers—Looie, Shelley and Blanch

The 1961 Season
(Part II)

Throughout the summer of '61, the saga of Roger Maris and Mickey Mantle captivated America. Fans in every American League city turned out to see the two Yankee sluggers hit home runs. If the home team won but there were no homers, they went away disappointed. A reporter in Kansas City asked 30 fans why they had come to a Yankee-Athletic game. Three went to see every Yankee game, two were season ticket holders, four others were there for various reasons, and 21 were there to see Maris and Mantle.

Whitey Ford, without the manic level of media attention generated by Mantle and Maris, was sculpting the finest season of his career. He won eight games in June alone, and, by the end of July, had accumulated 19 victories. On the 10th of August, Whitey became a 20 game winner for the first time. By the end of the season, Ford was 25–4, set a Yankee record for left handers with 209 strikeouts, and won the Cy Young Award as baseball's best pitcher.

Outstanding seasons by two or three players, however, do not guarantee a championship. In 1958, Ernie Banks won the National League MVP award while his Cubs finished sixth. The following year, Banks repeated and so did his team, coming in sixth again. Willie Mays, Willie McCovey and Juan Marichal were phenomenal during the '60s, but the Giants captured the pennant just once, and never won a World Series.

Former Met pitcher and long time Brewer pitching coach Don Rowe coined the phrase 5-10-10, to explain the way in which a team wins a pennant. "There are 25 guys on a team," Rowe said. "There are five stars, ten average players and ten who are just hanging on by their bootstraps. You know the stars are probably going to have good years. To win the pennant some of the ten average guys have to have great years and just one of the guys hanging on has to have a great year."

In 1961, the Yankee stars, Mantle, Maris and Ford, had the best years of their illustrious careers. The second echelon, which included Howard, Terry, Kubek, Berra and Skowron, came through with strong performances. Kubek had his finest all-around season. Howard led the league in hitting at one point in July, and batted .348, by far the highest average of his career. Terry was 16–3, and Skowron hit 28 home runs, the highest total of his career. Berra, playing less frequently at 35, hit .271 with 22 homers.

What about the bootstrappers? Which one of them would come through? One of the Yankees who was hanging on by his bootstraps in the spring of '61 was Luis Arroyo, who had been purchased from Jersey City the previous July, and was back with the Yankees only because he had been ignored in the expansion draft by the Angels and Senators.

Arroyo was born in 1927, in Penuelas, Puerto Rico, and began pitching on the island in 1946. By 1948, he was in the St. Louis Cardinals organization, where he impressed with an overpowering fastball and a 21–10 record at Greensboro in 1949. Arroyo pitched summers in the United States and winters in his native Puerto Rico, playing the equivalent of one and a half seasons each year.

In 1952, Arroyo developed a sore arm and sat out most of the next two seasons. Some writers described his arm injury as imaginary. Latin players were believed to be temperamental, superstitious and odd, just the type to develop psychosomatic ailments. Arroyo, who by the time he reached the major leagues, was affable, likeable and congenial, was invariably described, as were most Latins, as hot-headed and erratic in his early years.

Finally, in the spring of 1954, Arroyo's arm came back. After he made the Cardinal team the following year, a New York reporter showed up at his hotel room, woke him up and asked how his arm had been cured. Luis didn't really know, but realized that the reporter was not going to leave without a story, and he wanted to go back to sleep. Arroyo told him a tale that fit the pre-conception of Latin players so neatly that everyone believed it had to be true.

Arroyo told the reporter he had met a mystical old medicine man in the mountains, who told him to climb a certain tree and pluck some of the leaves. The leaves should then be heated and wrapped around Arroyo's sore arm. He followed instructions, Arroyo said, and, almost immediately, he was throwing bullets in the Puerto Rican League. The story appeared in the New York papers, leading one of the St. Louis reporters to ask him about it. "Good story, eh," Arroyo told him. It sure was, the scribe agreed. "But," Arroyo added, "not true."

The little lefthander, who spoke excellent English, always had a terrific sense of humor. In 1961, on a flight from Minneapolis to New York, pitcher Tex Clevenger took out his hunting rifle to show his teammates. Needless to say, security was not as tight in 1961 as it is today, when bringing a rifle aboard a plane would be cause for concern, if not incarceration. Tensions were high in those days, however, because of the situation in Cuba, and planes had been hijacked to the island on a few occasions. "Lend me the rifle," Arroyo told Clevenger, "I want to show it to the pilot and say a few words in Spanish to him."

Even in his 20s, Luis looked old. He was only 5'8" and chubby, with hair that began graying long before he reached 30. Off the field, he often wore glasses and smoked big cigars; few who saw him in civilian clothes imagined that he was a professional athlete. "He looked like an earmuff salesman rather than a pitcher," wrote Dan Daniel. On one Yankee flight, a stewardess was busily gathering autographs from the players. Til Ferdenzi, *The Sporting News* correspondent, asked her if she had gotten them all. She had, the young lady answered, and by the way, what paper did that man sleeping over there write for? That was star reliever Luis Arroyo, Ferdenzi told her. "What a commotion he'd cause on What's My Line?" she replied.

How did Arroyo get the gray hair so early? In *The Sporting News* of June 29, 1955, he said, "It's the liners those hitters knock back at me." In the March 21, 1956 issue, he said, "It isn't old age which made me look this way, but worry over line drives hit right through the box." In the April 10, 1957 issue, from Fort Myers, Florida: "It isn't old age which makes me look this way, but worry over the line drives hit right through the box." Mercifully, April 10, 1957 was the last time any *Sporting News* correspondent asked Arroyo about his hair.

In 1954, after returning from his arm injury, Arroyo had an outstanding season in the minor leagues. After posting an 8–6 record at Columbus, he was moved up to Houston of the Texas League, where he was 8–3 and helped the Buffs into the Dixie Series. Arroyo pitched a no hitter, struck out 17 in one game, and fanned 131 in 117 innings. His arm was back. In addition to the 227 innings he pitched in Columbus and Houston, he hurled 131 in the Puerto Rican League, for a total of 358 in one calendar year.

Arroyo made the Cardinal team the following year, became a regular starter and got off to a phenomenal start. Many couldn't believe that the portly, gray-haired lefty, who had spent so long in the minor leagues, could be pitching so well. After he beat Birdie Tebbetts' Reds in April for his first major league win, Tebbetts said Arroyo wouldn't be in the National League by July. Not only was Arroyo still in the league in July, he was named to the All Star squad because of his 9–3 record.

Arroyo was the only National League player who didn't appear in his team's dramatic 6–5 twelve inning win, and his season went downhill in the second half. He finished the year with an 11–8 record and a 4.19 ERA. The following spring, Cardinal manager Fred Hutchinson sent Arroyo to the minor leagues, and then traded him to Pittsburgh. He pitched sporadically and ineffectively for the Pirates and was dispatched to Hollywood in the Pacific Coast League.

Arroyo spent 1957 with the Pirates, pitching in 57 games, mostly in relief, and posted a 3–11 record. If line drives caused him to go gray, his hair would have been snow white. They said Arroyo didn't have a major league fastball or a major league curve and, in 1958, he didn't have a major league job. Arroyo went back to the minors and learned how to pitch in relief. He still had a decent fastball, even after his arm injury, and while pitching in the minors, Luis developed a fine screwball.

In 1959, Arroyo was with the Reds for a time before Hutchinson, now managing Cincinnati, sent him to Havana. Although he didn't pitch enough innings to qualify for the title, Arroyo had the lowest ERA in the International League at 1.15, and allowed just 74 hits in 117 innings. The Sugar Kings won the International League playoffs, taking the final game 1–0 before more than 13,000 exuberant fans in Havana. "This is a happy day for Cuba," Fidel Castro, the island's number one fan, said after the final game.

During the winter, Arroyo was available to all big league teams in the draft, but despite his fabulous statistics at Havana, there were no takers. He was 32, and feared he was destined to play out his career as a wintertime hero and summertime minor leaguer. Many a fairy tale story begins with the premise that the hero is just about to throw in the towel before he is rescued from oblivion. Arroyo, however, had no thoughts of giving up, and intended to keep pitching as long as some team, somewhere, would have him. "Baseball," he said in 1960, "it is my only business." Pitching both summer and winter was an economic necessity, for Arroyo was now divorced and remarried and had four children.

Luis returned to Havana with the Sugar Kings in 1960, but before long found himself in New Jersey. Castro loved baseball, and the Sugar Kings, but he did not like the United States and the United States did not care for him. That did not bode well for the continued existence of the Sugar Kings. The future of baseball in Havana first came into question when the revolution began in 1957, before Castro assumed power. When the trouble started, Sugar King owner Bobby Maduro said he had enough financial strength to weather the storm, and the International League said Maduro could stay in the league as long as he was able.

When the Buffalo Bisons made their 1958 trip to Havana, dictator Fulgencio Batista provided overwhelming security, to demonstrate convincingly that the Americans faced no danger. In fact, the presence of armed guards on every corner made just the opposite impression. The players and reporters also noticed that the once-bustling tourist haven was now a ghost town. "You virtually name your cab fare," wrote Cy Kritzer. "Watches, jewelry, perfume and alligator bags, diamonds, etc. were being sold at one-tenth their value in this country." Maduro struggled through the 1958 season, after which the International League established an emergency plan in the event Havana was forced to drop out.

The aftermath of the Communist takeover included political unrest and economic distress, neither of which was good for baseball. Maduro started the 1959 season but said he would sell the franchise if he lost money. Castro pledged his support, and the Cuban Sugar Stabilization Institute (which apparently also believed in stabilizing Sugar Kings) donated $20,000 to the team. Maduro also received a subsidy from the Cuban Tourist Commission. Still, attendance was poor and the team suffered financially. In order to help the club's finances, fans threw foul balls back from the stands. The biggest crowd of the season (more than 26,000) appeared on June 24, when Castro pitched an inning in an exhibition game. He struck out two, getting some assistance from the plate umpire, who apparently had a very broad strike zone for dictators.

The championship season of 1959 provided a respite from the troubles of the past two years, as the crowds which attended the playoff games were the largest in Havana since 1947. Prior to the 1960 season, in order to assure Americans that Communist Cuba would be hospitable, a group of ten journalists was invited to Havana and entertained in lavish fashion. During the regular season, however, some International League players complained that they didn't like going to Havana. The trip was too long, they said. It was no longer than it had been in prior years, but at least under the Batista dictatorship the players could enjoy Havana night life, which was better than that in Buffalo, Rochester, or Columbus. Now that Castro had taken all the fun out of Havana, it was just a long plane flight to visit what was rapidly becoming an economic wasteland. Diminishing attendance, a function of the sorry economy, made it difficult for visiting clubs to recoup the extra travel expense.

Safety was an increasing concern. In May, the Richmond Virginians' plane was delayed when outfielder Bob Martyn was taken off and questioned in a case of mistaken identity. There had been no incidents, but with political tensions with the United States running high, there was always a chance of violence.

There didn't seem to be many advantages to leaving the struggling Sugar Kings in Cuba, and International League President Frank Shaughnessy decided to act before there was an incident, rather than after. In July, Shaughnessy ordered the transfer of the Havana franchise to Jersey City, New Jersey, which was happy to accept them. The city had not had a minor league franchise in ten years, their only recent brush with professional baseball coming in 1957, when the Brooklyn Dodgers played some of their home games in Roosevelt Stadium.

The new players were welcomed with a parade, and left-handed pitcher Bob Miller, soon to gain fame as an original Met, was presented with a cake to mark his 25th birthday. Nap Reyes took over as manager of the club, and was provided with a contract, a uniform, a pair of spikes and a squadron of detectives. Reyes, a Cuban, had been denounced by Castro as a "traitor and public enemy No. 1 of Cuban baseball" for taking over the team that had been stolen from his country. For their first few days in Jersey City, the detectives followed Reyes and his Reds (baseball version) everywhere they went.

On July 15, the Reds took the field with silk patches containing the script letters "Jersey City" sewed over the spot on their shirts where *Cubanos* had appeared. A crowd of over 7,000 came to Roosevelt Stadium, far greater than the crowds that had been appearing in Havana. Unfortunately, the newly-christened Reds lost to Columbus. One of the four pitchers they used that night was Luis Arroyo.

Arroyo's stay in Jersey City was brief, lasting only until the Yankees purchased his contract in late July. "Who'd have ever thought a guy like that would be laying around dead somewhere," Stengel said. "If they brought back Walter Johnson for me," he added on another occasion, "I couldn't like it more than this man with the screwball." When the regular season was over, Stengel said, "I want to give special tribute to pitchers Luis Arroyo and Billy Stafford, who came to me late in the season and did more than I expected of them. I don't think that we could have done it without them."

Despite his fine pitching in the stretch run, Luis was not a factor in the World Series, pitching just briefly in Game Five. He sat in the bullpen with Duren while Terry gave up the decisive hit to Mazeroski. Arroyo, now 34, wasn't sure what 1961 would bring. His hair was grayer than ever, and his paunch was a little bigger. Back then, 34 was rather old for a ballplayer, particularly one who had never distinguished himself in the major leagues. "Luis Arroyo was sharp in spots last year," wrote *Sports Illustrated* in its pre-season preview, "but cannot be regarded as a day-in, day-out stopper." Each year, *The Sporting News* produced a summary of the players on each team who were the best in a particular category, such as best hitter, most likely to win the home run title, fastest player, best newcomer, etc. For the Yankees, the box labeled Best Relief Pitcher said None.

In his first appearance of the '61 exhibition schedule, Arroyo entered a tie game in the bottom of the ninth, put the first three runners on base, and then gave up a grand slam game-ending home run to the Twins' Earl Battey. The next day, Arroyo was pitching batting practice when rookie catcher Jesse Gonder hit a line drive right at him. Luis threw his hands up to protect himself, and the ball fractured the ulna bone of his left arm. There was no medicine man handy to point Arroyo to a tree with magic leaves, so the arm was set and placed in a sling, shelving the lefty for the rest of the spring. He later claimed the injury was a blessing in disguise, for it gave him a chance to rest his arm, which had been pitching winter and summer for almost fifteen years.

Arroyo returned at the end of the exhibition season, and when the regular schedule began, Houk's bullpen consisted of Arroyo, Duren, Coates, McDevitt, rookie Roland Sheldon, Johnny James, back from Richmond, Ted Wieand, a 28-year-old who'd had a couple of brief trials with the Reds, and Duke Maas, who had been taken by the Angels in the expansion draft but traded back to New York just before opening day. It was not a formidable array.

Houk's plan to start Duren had been quickly abandoned, and the manager's desire to use Duren in any role diminished when the big right hander returned from a night in St. Petersburg and began banging on Houk's door at 4 A.M. It was not Duren's first transgression of the spring, but it was one that couldn't be ignored. Houk fined him $200 and, despite his bullpen troubles, began thinking of where he could send his troublesome reliever. Duren was ready to leave. "My drinking situation was advancing," he said. "I embarrassed the club. There was an incident on the plane on the way out to Los Angeles [see below]. I was ready to leave the Yankees. I liked the guys alright, but I hated the front office. I thought they were cruel, cheap and cold."

The many open dates in April, plus the inevitable rainouts, enabled Houk to mask his bullpen deficiencies by using Stafford and Terry in relief. On the 14th of April, Arroyo returned from his injury and pitched three hitless innings in an exhibition against the West Point cadets. He made his first appearance in a regular game on the 23rd, but was unimpressive. Three days later, he pitched well against the Tigers and got his first victory, as the Yankees won a wild 13–11 game. He saved a win for Terry, one for Ford, then one for Coates. By early May, Luis had established himself as the stopper in the Yankee pen.

When Pirate manager Bobby Bragan sent Arroyo to the minor leagues in 1956, he told him he needed a pitch to get right handed hitters out. Al Hollingsworth, a former big league pitcher who managed Arroyo at Hollywood, helped him learn to throw the screwball, and in Puerto Rico he got help from countryman Ruben Gomez, a veteran right hander who had once been a star with the New York Giants.

Gomez threw a wicked screwball, and many thought he was a screwball. Ruben was a certifiable eccentric, whose most famous episode occurred when big Braves first baseman Joe Adcock charged the mound after Gomez hit him with a pitch. Gomez, a spindly 175 pounder, threw the ball at Adcock and sprinted for the dugout, with Adcock in hot pursuit. On numerous occasions in the winter leagues, Gomez was accused of faking an injury or illness to avoid pitching. He said he couldn't pitch in cold weather, which created difficulty in New York in April and May. As odd as he was, however, Gomez could always pitch. With his help, Arroyo developed his screwball into one of the best in the major leagues. He threw it hard to left-handed hitters so that it broke in quickly on their hands, and slower to right handers, so that it functioned as a change of pace.

With Arroyo established as the Yankee relief ace, Duren was expendable. On a flight to the West Coast, an inebriated Duren grabbed the breast of a flight attendant. When the Yankees reached Los Angeles, Hamey traded Duren, James and rookie outfielder Lee Thomas to the Angels for former Yankee Bob Cerv and veteran reliever Truman (Tex) Clevenger.

Clevenger was a 28-year-old right hander who had been an effective reliever with the Senators for several years, leading the league in appearances in 1958. More important, he came without Duren's baggage. Clevenger, surprisingly, hailed not from Texas but from California. He got his nickname when he reported to the Red Sox in 1954 and everyone noticed a striking resemblance to former Boston pitcher Tex Hughson. Houk dearly hoped he would bear a striking resemblance to a capable relief pitcher.

James, the sensation of the Yankee camp just over a year earlier, had appeared in only one Yankee game thus far in 1961. He pitched in 36 games for the Angels, and posted a record of 0–2 with a 5.32 ERA. James' most vivid memory of the season was pitching against the Yankees at the Stadium in June. The home run derby was in full swing, and Mantle and Maris had each hit one that day, leaving them tied. James relieved in the second game and struck Mantle out. The two Yankee sluggers came up again and James walked Maris with two out. "That irked me," he said, "so when Mantle came up, I struck him out again. I'll never forget it. It was the third out and Mickey just flipped his helmet away. He made eye contact with me and said, 'If you pitched like that when you were here, you'd still be here.'"

Unfortunately, Clevenger was not the answer to the Yankees quest for a right handed stopper and, with Duren gone, there was no question as to the identity of the number one reliever. Whenever a Yankee starter faltered in the late innings, a 34-year-old, gray haired, short, portly gentleman from Puerto Rico made his characteristic hop over the bullpen fence in right field and trudged slowly to the mound.

It seemed that Arroyo was Whitey Ford's personal reliever, partly because Ford's strong hurling usually enabled him to go into the late innings with a lead and partly because Whitey was 32 years old and didn't go the distance often anymore. In 1961, Arroyo relieved Ford on 24 occasions, and saved 13 of Whitey's 25 wins. One day Ford was at a batting cage with his seven year old son, and was having difficulty operating the machine. "Too bad you can't put in another quarter and bring in Arroyo," someone shouted at him.

By the end of the 1961 season, Arroyo had pitched in 65 games, setting a league record for appearances by a left hander, posted a league-leading 29 saves, a 15–5 record and a 2.19 ERA. The bullpen question, which loomed so large for Houk when the season started, had been answered by one man.

Arroyo was not the only marginal Yankee to come through in a big way in 1961. When the season started, Johnny Blanchard was the third string catcher, behind Howard and Berra. He had been in the Yankee farm system since 1951, when he turned down a basketball scholarship from the University of Minnesota to sign for a $20,000 bonus. Blanchard had been an outfielder and third baseman, but when he went to his first spring training camp in 1952, the Yankees decided that, because he had good hands and a strong arm, he should be a catcher. "I'd never caught a pitch in high school, American Legion, or even Little League," said Blanchard, "but if [Yankee coach and Hall of Famer] Bill Dickey thought I could make it to the big leagues as a catcher, I was going to give it a try." Blanchard worked hard to learn the new position, under

A journeyman pitcher for most of his career, Luis Arroyo had the year of his life in 1961, with 15 wins, 29 saves and a 2.19 ERA. Two years later, his career was over.

the tutelage of Dickey, and later, at Denver, under another old catcher, Ralph Houk. "Ralph taught me footwork," Blanchard said, "how to make the feet work fast when the runner's going, how to stay light on my feet and take that extra step toward second base."

Blanchard fought his way through the New York farm system, establishing a reputation as a power hitter and a mediocre defensive catcher. In his first minor league season, he batted .301 and led the Western Association in home runs with 30, RBI with 112 and total bases with 257. Blanchard led the Eastern League with 34 homers in 1955, while Berra was winning the MVP award and Elston Howard joined the Yankees as Berra's heir apparent. In 1957, Blanchard batted .310 at Denver, with 18 home runs, and led the Bears to the Little World Series championship. "Looks to me," said Stengel, "that he could be the greatest major league catching prospect of 1958." Blanchard was also rated by scouts as the best catcher in the minor leagues, but the next spring, despite winning the James Dawson Award as the outstanding rookie in the Yankee camp, he was back in the minor leagues. Blanchard batted .291 at Denver, with 19 homers and 96 RBI, and came to the Yankee camp again in 1959.

Blanchard was 25 years old, with seven seasons in the minor leagues behind him. Other teams needed catchers, especially left handed hitting catchers with power, but Blanchard never wanted to play for another team. "I wanted to be a Yankee," he said. Stengel talked about playing him at first base, or maybe the outfield, but Blanchard kept ending up back in the minors.

Finally, in 1959, Stengel decided that Blanchard was ready to catch in the big leagues. Mostly, however, he sat on the Yankee bench and watched Berra and Howard catch, batting only 59 times. The next season was even more difficult. Although he was with the team from opening day, Blanchard did not make his first plate appearance until May 29. He batted only five times through the end of June and did not get his first hit until the middle of July. He developed ulcers, and had to be operated on in mid-season. In August, with Howard and Berra both injured, Blanchard finally got to play and did well. By the end of the month, in just 60 at bats, he was hitting .300. Still, Stengel wasn't impressed. "It's not that I'm dissatisfied with the way John Blanchard has been filling in," Casey said, but he wished Berra was back.

As further insurance, the Yankees signed Jim Hegan, a veteran catcher who had been released by the Cubs. Blanchard felt that Stengel didn't have confidence in him and would use Hegan until Berra and Howard recovered. After all the years he had spent in the Yankee farm system and all the tank towns he had played in, Blanchard was irate. He had finally proved he could play in the big leagues and now he was going to be pushed aside for a 40-year-old. Blanchard therefore did something Yankee reserves were not supposed to do. He spoke up. "I guess I said some things I shouldn't have," he recalled. "I'd waited all that time and they still didn't have confidence in my ability behind the plate. I said, 'I've been here long enough. I've got to get a yea or a nay and I might as well find out right now.'"

Speaking up paid off. The Yankees activated Hegan, but he never appeared in a game. Blanchard stayed in the lineup until Berra and Howard were well, and had a terrific World Series, starting the seventh game after Howard's hand was broken. Still, he had batted just 158 times in two full years in the major leagues.

During the winter, Blanchard was the subject of a number of trade rumors, the strongest indicating that he might be on his way to San Francisco. When spring training camp opened in 1961, however, he was still a Yankee, with more opportunity than ever before. Berra was spending most of his time in the outfield. Hegan retired and became the Yankee bullpen coach, leaving Blanchard as the only full time catcher behind Howard. In the early season, with numerous off-days and rainouts giving the regulars plenty of rest, Blanchard played sparingly, as he had in 1960. As summer approached, however, he began to appear more often, catching, playing the outfield, and becoming the most feared pinch hitter in the American League.

Pinch hitting has always been one of the most difficult jobs in baseball. "I don't see how anybody could enjoy it," said Lee Thomas. "When you pinch hit," said Tom Shopay, who did quite a bit of it, "it's either against somebody who's having a heck of a game or against one of the top relievers." Bob Johnson, who set an American League record with six consecutive pinch hits, was one of the few who enjoyed the role. "I loved pinch hitting," he said. "I liked it because nobody else liked it. It kept me in the big leagues a little longer."

Johnson was a rarity. Most players hated to pinch hit. Joe Hicks, former White Sox, Senator and Met outfielder, really disliked coming off the bench. "If I could play regularly," Hicks said, "I was OK, but pinch hitting is a tough job, particularly early and late in the season. At Comiskey, it got cold out there early in the season, and you're sitting on the bench freezing. In the ninth inning, you're asked to go up and hit. You have somebody out there closing the game throwing BBs, and you have trouble getting loose."

Hicks' first at bat as a Met was as a pinch hitter. "We were playing the Dodgers," he recalled, "and Koufax was pitching. Casey loved to platoon, so he had all his right hand hitters in the lineup. The pitcher was due up in the ninth, and he didn't have any right handed hitters on the bench. He went down to the end of the bench where Snider was sitting and said, 'Duke, do you want to hit?' Duke said, 'Not particularly.' So he turns around and heads my way and I know he's going to ask me, but before he does, I jumped up and said, 'Hey, skip, I'll give him a try.' From the dugout, Koufax didn't look that tough. He had an easy motion. I ran the count to three and two. He was missing with his curve. I'd seen two fastballs and I knew the fastball was coming. I was right on it, but then it had a little rise to it and I'm struck out. I walked back to the bench shaking my head."

"You go from the dugout to the field," said Al Luplow, "and all of a sudden you're in the lights, and it's not the same as when you're in the dugout. A lot of times I'd go out and warm up the pitcher between innings, so I could get to see the ball a little better."

Most players claim they needed to play steadily to hit well. Everyone who made it to the majors had been a regular in the minors, and arrived with little pinch hitting experience. Almost no one, however, is handed a starting major league job as soon as they come up. Making an impression as a part time player is the only way to earn a spot in the lineup, but very few youngsters could handle the role. "How many times do you see a good young pinch hitter?" Stengel once asked rhetorically.

There are many theories on pinch hitting, but nearly everyone agrees on one thing. With only three strikes to work with, there is no point in giving any of them away. "Hector Lopez used to say," recalled former Yankee Archie Moore, "'swing at the first fastball you see. You'd better go up there looking for a fastball.' If you're sitting there for any period of time, it's really tough to adjust to anything else." "If you're a good fastball hitter," said Chuck Hiller, "you can be a good pinch hitter."

Blanchard was a notorious first ball hitter. "Some idiot, years ago," he surmised, "must have said, 'Look at the first pitch.' What the heck are you going to look at? I don't believe in that philosophy. What if he throws it right down the middle? Sorry, pal. I'm going." It was the perfect attitude for pinch hitting. "I was always a wild swinger," said Billy Cowan, another good pinch hitter. "The first pitch I saw that I liked, I wanted it. You have to realize that you're not going to get many good pitches to hit and you've got to concentrate so you can hit the first good pitch you get." "You can't be real selective," added Hawk Taylor.

Lou Klimchock credited Alvin Dark, his manager at Cleveland, for his success. "Alvin told me how he was going to use me," Klimchock said. "If a manager said, 'Lou, this is what you're going to do. We're going to use you as a pinch hitter to get on base and then somebody else is going to pinch hit to drive you in,' I could prepare myself for seven innings. You play right alongside the manager and you could pretty much sense the flow of the game. I'd always have a bat in my hands and I'd be swinging it in the tunnel." "I worked hard to prepare myself for situations," said catcher John Stephenson. "I tried to manage along and to anticipate what was coming up — when I should be ready. I think that's one of the reasons I stayed around as long as I did."

Klimchock also believed that few players excelled solely as pinch hitters. They needed to start often enough to maintain their timing. "Blanchard caught a lot," said Klimchock, "and played a bit in the outfield. To be a good pinch hitter, you've got to play some." Blanchard got more than 200 at bats each year from 1961–63, as did Lopez, the Yankees top right-handed pinch hitter. "Ralph Houk would usually try to give me a game or two during the week," said Lopez, "to keep me sharp. He wouldn't let you just sit on the bench and then try to go up and pinch hit."

As difficult a job as it was, Blanchard was determined to become a valuable pinch hitter. Dale Long was lost in the expansion draft, and Kent Hadley was cut in spring training, leaving the number one left handed pinch hitting job open. Lopez was the right hand pinch hitter when he wasn't starting, and Blanchard wanted to fill the role from the left side.

Blanchard knew he wasn't going to beat out Howard, Berra or Maris, and if he wanted to remain a Yankee, which he desperately did, he would need to prove his worth coming off the bench. "I accepted it as a full time job," he said. "I worked at it mentally. Guys say it's the hardest job in baseball. It is. There's no doubt about it. You know you only have one shot at it. When you're starting, it's a different ballgame. You strike out or pop up the first time and you know you've got a shot at the pitcher again. But when you pinch hit, you've got to go up there ripping and really bear down, because there's no second chance. I worked hard at it and of course a few Hail Marys didn't hurt either." As the backup catcher, Blanchard spent most of the game in the bullpen, warming up the relievers. When he came in to the bench to hit, he'd ask the other players what the pitcher was throwing, what he could expect on the first pitch.

Johnson, Hiller and Klimchock were primarily singles hitters, as were most good pinch swingers. "The main thing when you're pinch hitting is to concentrate on hitting the ball through the middle," said Johnson. Blanchard, with a big power hitter's swing, couldn't do that. His timing needed to be more precise, for he didn't punch at the ball with a compact stroke. He was expected to hit it into the right field bleachers.

In 1961, Blanchard had the finest season of his career, producing time and again in the clutch. Houk gave Blanchard the praise that he had coveted but never received from Stengel. Hamey, the new general manager, made him feel wanted as Weiss had never done.

At first, 1961 did not seem as though it would be anything special. As in '60, Blanchard saw little action early in the season, not getting his first hit until May 3. After eleven unsuccessful trips to the plate as a pinch hitter, he homered on May 7, and the floodgates opened. On June 5, Blanchard connected for a three run pinch homer and on the 18th hit two home runs in a game against the Tigers. The Yankee bench, which had been so weak in 1960, suddenly became one of the strongest parts of the team. For the year, Yankee pinch hitters batted .273 with nine home runs. Blanchard hit .259 with four homers.

The highlight of Blanchard's season, and his career, came in late July. The Yankees had fallen to second place, and their pitching staff was in shambles as they went to Fenway Park for a three game series. Ford was knocked out in the first game of the series, and in the ninth, Blanchard batted for Clete Boyer with the bases loaded and the Yanks trailing 8–7. He hit reliever Mike Forneiles' first pitch for a grand slam and an 11–8 win, putting the Yankees back in first place by a half game over Detroit. The next day, Sheldon was knocked out in the 4th and the Yankees trailed 9–8 in the ninth. Blanchard led off, again batting for Boyer, and homered to tie the score. Arroyo, who had already pitched three innings, batted for himself because Houk had no fresh arm in the bullpen. He doubled off the left field wall and chugged around to score the winning run on Richardson's single.

There were no heroics on Sunday, and the Yankees lost in the ninth inning. Houk left Daley in the box on a sweltering afternoon in order to allow his bullpen to catch its collective breath, and the lefty ran out of gas. The Yanks nearly pulled the game out of the fire as, losing 4–2 in the ninth, they tied the game on a two run homer by Howard. Blanchard, who had been on deck to bat for Boyer, went back to the bench after Howard tied the game. He remained there until a Wednesday game against Chicago. "Houk got a little excited," Blanchard recalled, "and started me against the White Sox." Houk was even more excited when Blanchard homered his first two

In 1961, Johnny Blanchard hit 21 homers in just 243 at bats. He was the most dangerous pinch hitter in the American League, with four home runs. Blanchard was traded to Kansas City in 1965, and was devastated to leave the Yankees.

times up, tying the major league record of four consecutive blasts. His third time up, in the sixth inning, he narrowly missed a fifth consecutive homer, as his long fly to right was caught by Floyd Robinson against the right field fence.

One of the keys to Blanchard's success was the fact that he finally learned to relax. "I had no butterflies of any kind," said the man who had been operated on for an ulcer the previous year. "It was all due to Mickey and Roger taking all of the pressure off everybody because of the home run chase. All the media was concentrated on the M&M boys. I just got up there and swung the bat. I was relaxed the whole year."

The home runs and base hits kept on coming. Blanchard won a game with a home run on August 4, and another a month later. By the end of the season, he had batted .305 with 21 home runs in only 243 at bats and drove in 54 runs with just 74 hits. "Play him every day," said hitting coach Wally Moses, "and the chances are good that he'd hit more than 40 homers a season."

Despite his success, Blanchard never felt secure in the major leagues. "There was no such thing as a long term contract," he said. "I had to work awfully hard, and I didn't have real good ability behind the plate." No matter how much success he experienced, Blanchard always felt he was a step away from being sent back to the minor leagues. "I used to wake up every morning," he told an interviewer in 1962, "and say a prayer of thanks that I was up here." After his great '61 season, Blanchard didn't go into Houk's office and demand a starting position; he just hoped that he had gotten a reprieve and bought himself another year in the big leagues and a bit more playing time.

Roland Sheldon shaved three years off his age when he signed with the Yankees, made it to the big leagues and was a key pitcher during the 1961 season, posting a record of 11–5.

Don Rowe said that one of the bootstrappers had to come through in grand style for a team to win the pennant. With Arroyo and Blanchard, the Yankees had exceeded the quota, yet, there was one more. The third surprise of the 1961 season was not even hanging by his bootstraps when spring training began. He was a 21-year-old rookie pitcher from Class D ball. Or was he?

"It wasn't my fault," pitcher Roland Sheldon said recently when asked about the confusion concerning his age. In recent years, there have been a number of players from the Caribbean whose true ages were discovered to be slightly different than those listed by major league baseball. Decades earlier, players commonly shaved a year or two off their ages. Perhaps the most audacious fib was revealed when, in 1963, first baseman Luke Easter revealed that he was 52 years old, not 42 as he had previously claimed. Easter, however, came from the Negro Leagues, where records were as hazy as in the Caribbean. Sheldon shaved three years off his age the hard way, in the United States, where meticulous records are maintained of every birth, death, strikeout and ground rule double.

Upon his graduation from high school, Sheldon joined the Air Force, served for four years and matured from a 5'10" 135 pound boy to a 6'4"

190 pound man. After his discharge, he attended Texas A&M for one semester, then transferred to the University of Connecticut, where he joined the basketball team in the middle of the '59-'60 season. "I couldn't jump very well," Sheldon said, "But I had a pretty good shot." He averaged eleven points a game and played against NYU in the first round of the NCAA tournament. In those days, the NCAA tournament teams were an elite group. For the most part, only conference champions qualified, and there were no at-large berths.

If Sheldon had any aspirations of continuing his basketball career, they were dashed in that game, when he was guarded by future Celtic defensive star Tom (Satch) Sanders. "I had six or eight points," Sheldon recalled, "and they were all on fast breaks when he was at the other end of the court. He had me covered like a blanket."

Following UConn's loss, Sheldon began pitching for the baseball team, and showed enough to impress Yankee scout Harry Hesse. Hesse asked Sheldon to fill out a questionnaire, on which he gave his age, 23. Hesse felt that Sheldon's ability was worth a modest bonus, but didn't think his superiors in New York would want to spend much money on a player who had been out of high school for five years. Hesse knew what his superiors wanted to see in a prospect, and he intended to accommodate them, no matter what the facts might be. A few years later, he was scouting outfielder Tom Shopay, who stood only 5'9". "You're kind of small," Hesse told him. He suggested Shopay get a chin up bar, put it up in a doorway and hang from it. "Maybe you'll stretch a little bit and get taller," Hesse said.

There was no device to make a man younger, so Hesse took matters into his own hands. Although Sheldon never saw Hesse's questionnaire again, it apparently arrived in New York in slightly altered form. Negotiations began, and Hesse increased his offer from $7,000 to $14,000 and finally to $20,000.

Sheldon agreed on $20,000 — spread over four years — and was ready to sign. Hesse told him he couldn't sign, since he was underage. This was news to Sheldon, but for $20,000, he could be underage if that was what Hesse wanted. "I went to the kitchen," said Rollie, "where my mom and dad were drinking coffee and whispered to them, 'Mr. Hesse thinks I'm only 20 years old and I need to have you sign this. You know I'm 23, but would you please sign this contract?'"

Mr. and Mrs. Sheldon obliged, and Rollie left for Auburn, New York, home of the Yankees' Class D farm club, the lowest rung on an extended minor league ladder. Typically, clubs would start a college player in Double A or at least A ball, but an untested 20-year-old started at the bottom. Sheldon had a terrific season at Auburn. "I was 23 playing against kids who were 18 or 19 and just out of high school," he said. "I had a good catcher and a team that scored five or six runs every time I pitched." The result was a 15–1 record and an invitation to St. Petersburg to train with the major league club the following spring. Sheldon was not the typical wild young phenom, walking only 56 while striking out 127, displaying remarkable control for a 20-year-old. Had the Yankees known he was older and sent him to Double A with the other 23-year-olds, the results might have been different, but the 15–1 record was in the books.

During the winter, Sheldon attended a dinner in Connecticut at which new manager Ralph Houk was the featured speaker. "What about our boy Sheldon?" someone asked. "Here's a guy who was 15–1," Houk responded. "I don't care if he was 15–1 in a girl's league. I'm going to take a look at him."

Houk gave the youngster a good look in spring training. So did a reporter from the *Hartford (Ct.) Courant*, who recognized Sheldon from his basketball days. He noticed Sheldon's age in the media guide and approached Yankee PR director Bob Fishel. Shortly thereafter, Fishel cornered Sheldon in the Yankee dugout and asked if he was really 21. "It wasn't my fault," Sheldon told Fishel, and explained that he had given his true age on the questionnaire. The discrepancy discovered, Sheldon went from a 21-year-old kid in need of more seasoning to an experienced 24-year-old with a legitimate chance to make the team.

With the Yankees having lost so many pitchers in the expansion draft, there was a lot of opportunity in St. Petersburg. Sheldon had gone to spring training early and was in good shape when the regulars arrived. "I guess I didn't understand what batting practice was." he said. "You're supposed to lay the ball in there, but I threw as hard as I could. A lot of guys would just take two or three swings and walk out of the cage. I got in a couple of exhibition games and pitched pretty well. I pitched against Hank Aaron and got him to pop up to the infield. I pitched against the White Sox and struck out Roy Sievers twice on curve balls. He was supposed to be a pretty good curve ball hitter. I think that's when they felt maybe I had the maturity and stuff to go north."

Sheldon won the Dawson Award in St. Petersburg, and was still a Yankee on April 11th, when the club opened its season against Minnesota. He didn't pitch that day, and saw little action in the early weeks. The Yankees had to cut their roster to 25 a month after the season started, and Sheldon knew he had just 30 days to impress Houk enough to stick. He threw whenever he could find someone to catch him, trying to perfect his changeup, and began to learn about the hitters in the American League. With the help of Ralph Terry, Sheldon compiled a book. "We'd stand around in the outfield," he said, "and discuss the hitters we were going to face in a particular series. Ralph just took me under his wing and taught me a lot about the hitters in the league. When I got to the clubhouse, I'd run to my cubicle and write everything down in my book." For the rest of his career, Sheldon took the book on the road with him and referred to it constantly.

After a few weeks, Sheldon got a chance to apply his knowledge. When Turley came up with a sore arm, and Ditmar was ineffective, the rookie got a couple of starts and pitched well in losing causes. Houk and Sain were impressed and began to use him more often. As the season wore on, the Yankee staff wore down. When Terry and Stafford came down with sore arms, Sheldon became a bulwark of the rotation.

What was truly remarkable about the rookie pitcher was his poise. In 1960, pitching in D ball, Sheldon performed before crowds of a few hundred. Yet, before thirty or forty thousand at the Stadium, or screaming fans on the road, he never seemed to lose his cool. Sheldon ran off a series of wins, and when the season ended, had an 11–5 record. "The Yankees were generating a lot of runs that year, and if you happened to be pitching on a day they were hitting, it was pretty easy." To say that the Yankees hit well in 1961 was an understatement. "I just went to the ballpark," said Sheldon, "sat on the bench and marveled at what was going on. I couldn't believe what they were doing. It was a fabulous time."

From their three bootstrappers, the Yankees got 26 wins, 29 saves, and 21 home runs. According to Rowe's formula, they should have waltzed to the pennant. But it wasn't that easy.

• 6 •

Chasing the Babe
The 1961 Season
(Part III)

Throughout July, the Yankees and Tigers ran neck and neck, as for the most part, no more than a game separated the two teams. Although the Yankees had moved into first place in late July, Detroit stuck stubbornly to their heels, arriving in New York on September 3 for a three games series just 1½ games behind. Those three games, which drew crowds almost as large as those that had watched the two teams in July, decided the pennant. The close race, combined with the excitement generated by Mantle and Maris, had been good for attendance. The Yankees drew 1.7 million for the season, their highest total in ten years.

On Friday night, Ford started for the Yankees, but had to leave the game in the fifth inning with a hip injury. Daley and Arroyo were outstanding in relief, and the game went to the bottom of the ninth in a scoreless tie. Skowron bounced a single past third base to score Howard with the winning run and increase the New York lead to 2½ games. The next day, Maris hit two home runs, as Terry beat the Tigers 7–2 for his 12th victory.

Sunday was a crucial game. If the Yankees won, their lead would be 4½ games with less than a month to play. If the Tigers salvaged the final game, they would be just 2½ back with another series coming up in Detroit. The Yankees had been remarkably injury-free all season. Ford and Mantle, who had been among the most fragile Yankees in previous years, had been virtual iron men. Now, with the season on the line, Ford had injured his hip on Friday and, on Saturday, Mantle hurt his left arm while batting. He couldn't swing hard, he said, but insisted on staying in the game and intended to bunt every at bat if he had to. There appeared to be no way, however, that Mickey would play Sunday.

When Houk brought the lineup card to home plate, Mantle's name was in its customary fourth position. Mickey decided to use Bob Cerv's 35 ounce bat, much heavier than his usual model, just meet the ball and try for singles. After the Tigers scored a run in the first off Stafford, Mantle came to the plate with Maris on first. Against hard-throwing Detroit right hander Jim Bunning, Mickey swung Cerv's bat and pulled his 49th home run into the right field stands to give the Yanks a 2–1 lead. Berra followed with another homer.

In his next two at bats, Mantle struck out, and the Tigers slowed pecked away to pull within 4–3. It was ninety degrees and Stafford, struggling in the heat, was wearing his third uniform of the day. He was removed for a hitter in the seventh. Arroyo, who had performed so magnificently all season, entered the ninth needing just three more outs to put the Tigers in a deep hole. He couldn't get them. Rookie second baseman Jake Wood hit a bases loaded single to give the Tigers a 5–4 lead.

Mantle, leading off the ninth against 41-year-old reliever Gerry Staley, hit #50, again into the right field stands, to tie the game. Berra followed with a single and Ronnie Kline replaced Staley. Arroyo sacrificed Yogi to second. Another single would win the game. Skowron was intentionally walked and Boyer flied to right. The ninth position in the order was due up, and Howard, who batted for Stafford and stayed in the game, stepped to the plate. All he needed was a single. Howard got much more than that, a three run homer into the left field stands that ended the game and, for all intents and purposes, the Tigers' title hopes.

With the pennant race decided, all eyes turned to Maris and Mantle ... and Commissioner Ford Frick. Maris had 53 home runs and Mantle 50. Roger was eight games ahead of Ruth and Mickey three. Although the American League would play 162 games for the first time in its history, Frick had declared that any records that were to be established in 1961 would need to be done in the old standard of 154 games. The new schedule, Frick stated, would probably be temporary, with a return to a 154 game slate due to occur within five or six years.

Before the season began, Frick speculated as to the impact of the additional eight games upon the record book. "It is a question that has been bothering me for some time," he told an interviewer. "But the longer I thought about it the more convinced I became that our fears were groundless. Certain records are bound to be affected but I doubt that the great marks we treasure will even be approached, despite the extra eight games.... My opinion on that is almost a conviction. I don't think the Babe's record is vulnerable." Frick didn't explain why a commissioner, even one who had been a close friend of Babe Ruth's, should cherish existing records, nor why he should be alarmed about the possibility of their being broken.

Fred Lieb, the veteran sportswriter, who had been covering baseball since the teens, also thought that an additional eight games wouldn't put long-established records at risk. However, of all Ruth's records, Lieb opined, the one most likely to be broken was his mark for most home runs in a season. He mentioned Maris as a potential challenger, but said, "[H]is history has been one of batting sprees, followed by dismal slumps and a general falling-off in the second half of the season."

The implementation of the legendary "asterisk" has been attributed to Frick, but the commissioner himself never used the word. His statement, issued in July, referred to "some distinctive mark." Any records established in the 155th game or later, he said, would be declared standards for a 162 game season and the old records would remain those for a 154 game slate. Writer Dick Young suggested the asterisk, which he said was usually employed to denote exceptions. The statement led to some interesting suppositions. What if Maris hit number 61 in the 154th game, but Mantle had more homers after 162? Who would hold what record? What if a player was batting .400 after 154 games, but dropped to .395 by season's end. Would he still be a .400 hitter for a 154 game season? Houk said that if the Yankees were in first place after 154 games, he intended to wire Frick and tell the commissioner that as far as he was concerned, the pennant race was over.

Everyone had an opinion. American League President Joe Cronin said new records should be recognized even if they took 162 games. "A season is a season," was the cry of those who agreed with Cronin. *The Sporting News* conducted a poll of sportswriters, who supported Frick by a 2–1 margin. A majority of Japanese fans concluded in a poll that the record should count only if broken in 154 games. Cuban baseball fans agreed. Mantle said that only a 154 game record should count. Maris said he didn't care. He'd be proud of his season no matter what happened.

In addition to the longer season, a second aspect of expansion, the weakened state of major league pitching, gave Maris detractors another reason to minimize his accomplishment. After all, they said, he was batting against 20 pitchers who would have been in the minor leagues a year earlier. In the 34 years since Ruth set his record, however, the population of the United States had grown tremendously, and the best pitchers in Triple A ball in 1961 were probably superior to many of the major leaguers of 1927. Further, 1927 had been a terribly unbalanced season in the American League. The fifth place White Sox were 39½ games out of first place, and the eighth place Red Sox 59 games out. The ninth place Browns had a team ERA of 4.95. The list of pitchers off whom Ruth hit his 60 homers included many who were out of the majors shortly thereafter, and who were certainly no better than the expansion pitchers of 1961.

The entire debate would be academic if either Maris or Mantle could hit 61 home runs in 154 games. After the Tiger series, the Yanks had played 135 games and had 19 games remaining until the 154 mark. Maris needed eight home runs and Mantle eleven. "We were pulling for both of them" said Blanchard. "We weren't rooting for anybody. They were both tremendous, wonderful people. But I guess deep down we were all pulling for Mickey. That had nothing to do with Roger, who was a guy we all loved and appreciated. Mickey had been there ten years and was kind of the sentimental favorite. Rog was the new kid on the block." "Everybody was pulling for Roger," added Jim Coates, "but we wanted to see Mickey do it, because he was a true Yankee. Roger had come from Kansas City. Don't get me wrong, we were pulling for Roger too." "I think most of us probably wanted to see Mickey break it," added Bud Daley. Coach Crosetti, a Yankee loyalist, didn't care which of the sluggers broke the record as long as it was held by a Yankee.

The interest of the Yankees was nothing compared to the attention the fans and the media gave to the pursuit of Ruth. Mantle and Maris received about three thousand letters per week, not all of them favorable. Many fans, especially the older ones, didn't want Ruth's record broken by anyone. Many took exception to Maris's relatively low batting average (he finished the season at .269). They could accept the record being broken by Mantle, who was batting well over .300, but believed that a .269 hitter was not a complete ballplayer and shouldn't hold such a coveted mark.

Reporters who didn't know the third base coaching box from Carnegie Hall found their way to the Yankee locker room, and many asked inane questions. A Japanese paper presented Maris with a list of 18 questions. "Mantle will pass me," Roger replied. "That seems to answer them all."

Mantle, matured after ten years in the New York spotlight, played along with the press. He was no longer the shy country boy from Oklahoma. "In 1955," said reporter Gordon White, "interviewing Mantle was like pulling teeth. In 1965 and afterward, it was wonderful. The guy grew up." "When Roger came there," said Eli Grba, "he took a lot of the pressure off Mickey, and all of a sudden, Mickey became a better human being."

Mickey had gradually learned how to handle the New York press. In September, when he and Maris were being hounded relentlessly, he told reporters he had moved out of the apartment he shared with Maris and Bob Cerv. "I've actually just moved to Tenafly, in Jersey," he said. "I'll even give you the address." He proceeded to give the reporters Elston Howard's home address.

Mantle, despite his great accomplishments on the field, had endured a love-hate relationship with New York fans. When he failed to hit a home run every time up, or struck out in clutch situations, the fans let him have it. During Mantle's 1960 salary battle with Weiss, the general manager cited his lack of popularity with the fans as a factor in Weiss's salary offer.

Mantle's troubles began soon after he arrived in New York, when he failed a draft physical and was given a 4-F classification by the Selective Service. The Service had not been selective enough, many said. With the Korean War on, the average citizen couldn't understand how Mantle could perform superhuman feats on the diamond, but be incapable of dealing with the rigors of military life.

Mickey's personality didn't help him in his early years. He was friendly after a good day, but surly when he did poorly. "Despite all efforts to change him," Arthur Daley wrote in 1960, "Mantle remains at stated intervals a churlish, grumpy fellow, petulant and given to sulking and fits of temper when matters do not go well with him." In 1960, Mantle had been the villain and Maris, the new guy, was the fan favorite. In 1961, Mantle became everybody's favorite and Maris assumed the role of villain.

"In 1960," said Johnny James, "I saw Roger up close because I was in the bullpen and he played right field. The fans really liked him because he played the game so hard. For some reason, the fans started calling him Cha-Cha. They always seemed to be in his camp." Maris was named the Most Popular Yankee by the Catholic Youth Organization. Everyone liked him that year, including the press. A number of complimentary stories were written about Roger, many of which expressed relief that the new Yankee was not the brash "popoff" they'd expected him to be. "I didn't find him to be cantankerous at all," said Gordon White. "He got very short with people in '61 and I don't blame him. In 1960, he was nice enough to talk to after a game. He was an introvert. He was a short sentence guy. If you went to his locker and asked him what pitch he hit or something like that, he'd answer you. But then toward the end when he began to approach Babe Ruth, stuff was written, not so much in New York, with the idea was that he was going to demolish God, or Jesus Christ, or Mohammed. Ruth was the greatest baseball player ever and Maris was going to break his record. It was silly for people to write that kind of thing because every record is going to be broken."

While Mantle learned to laugh privately at some of the more foolish questions, Maris took severe public umbrage. No one suffered fools more ungladly than Roger Eugene Maris. Maris lacked Mantle's sense of humor and his intensity was often mistaken for surliness. And many times he was surly. Maris was a quiet, often moody, family man who hated the long separations from his wife and children. He never craved attention, and would have been happy to play out his career as a good, solid ballplayer in Kansas City. "If a ballplayer could ever be described as being the perfect player for the perfect team," wrote Maris biographer Maury Allen, "it was Roger Maris in KC."

"I felt sorry for Roger," said Bud Daley, "because he was a very shy person. They hounded him so bad. They asked him such stupid questions. One time I thought he was going to hit the guy and I think he probably should have. The guy said, 'Roger, when you go on the road, do you cheat on your wife?' What was he supposed to say, 'Oh, yeah, I do that all the time.' I really felt sorry for him." Some of the worst hatchet jobs were written by reporters who'd never even spoken to Maris. The out-of-towners didn't know Roger and had no reservations about ripping him in print. "They ought to have shot some of those writers for the garbage they wrote about him," said Ralph Terry. Some writers made up facts or distorted the truth, while others just spewed out their unsubstantiated opinions.

For the most part, Maris was co-operative with the press. He answered questions in a matter-of-fact fashion, without emotion or enthusiasm, but he answered them. It was part of his job, the part he liked least, but he did it. One of Maris's problems was that he wasn't all that interesting. While Mantle regaled the writers with tales of his extracurricular activities, Maris gave trite, factual answers to trite, factual questions. The private life of Roger Maris wasn't very exciting. He drank, but not to excess like Mantle, and he was a quiet family man. His greatest vices were fattening foods and beer, which caused his waistline to expand substantially when he finished playing.

Most of the New York writers, at least at first, were supportive of Maris, defending him against some of the more outrageous tales written by out-of-town reporters. "The picture of Roger Eugene Maris," wrote Yankee beat writer Dan Daniel, "is 100 per cent untrue." Eventually, however, the New York scribes turned on Maris and took the fans with them. "The fans in

New York weren't very kind to Roger," said Cardinal teammate Ed Bressoud, "because they wanted Mickey to do all the good things that Roger did. I thought Roger was a bit aloof [when he played for the Cardinals]. He had been so dismayed by what happened to him in New York that he didn't want the attention."

Al Jackson also played with Maris in St. Louis. "This guy was not a prick," said Jackson. "That's what I told him the first time I saw him. I said, 'Man, I thought you were a prick from all the stuff I read about you in New York, but you're a hell of a nice guy."

Until he came to New York, Maris was not known as a home run hitter. He was a fine all-around player, an outstanding fielder with a powerful arm, a fast, smart and fearless base runner, and a straightaway hitter. "He never pulled the ball until he got to New York," said Daley, who played with Maris in Kansas City, "and he never, ever got credit for being a good outfielder even though he was one of the best right fielders in the league. He had a very accurate arm and he was faster than he looked." "He never made a mistake on the bases," added Doc Edwards, "never threw to the wrong base, never missed a cutoff man. He was just excellent." Maris didn't steal a lot of bases, but he excelled on getting from first to third on a single.

"You put him in a track meet with any of the right fielders of his day," said Terry, "and he'd leave them in the dust. He should have waltzed into the Hall of Fame just on the strength of that record (61 home runs). He held it for 37 years. They souped up the ball, lowered the mound, shortened every fence in the big leagues except Fenway and Wrigley and still nobody beat it. He was absolutely fearless in the field. He'd dive into the concrete and iron bars out there in the bleachers. He'd dive in there and come out with the ball. He'd break up double plays. No fancy hook slides for that guy."

"I came into a game in Cleveland," recalled James, "with the bases loaded and Tito Francona up. He hit a long shot to right center field that had grand slam written all over it. I will never forget Roger Maris racing back to the fence. He jumped up, the top of the fence hit him right in the back and he caught the ball and turned it into a sacrifice fly. I remember standing on the mound thinking, 'There's a guy who's a star. He could've gotten hurt but he caught that ball for me.' I was really impressed that he would do that."

"He played the game the right way," said Bressoud. "If there was a runner on second base, Roger, instead of trying to hit the ball out of the ballpark and ending up striking out, always put the ball in play, hitting it to second base or first base." Every Yankee recalled Maris, at the height of the home run chase, dragging a bunt to bring in a crucial run, when he could have been obsessed with matching Ruth's record. "The players liked him," James said, "because he played the game hard. He really gave it all he had." In the minor leagues, Maris had been knocked cold a couple of times running into outfield fences. One time he ran though a fence.

Although he distrusted reporters, Maris was a different person with people that he knew and with whom he felt comfortable. "I've thought a lot about this," said Archie Moore, who played with Maris in 1964. "I really liked Roger. I thought he was one of the really great people on the team. He spent a lot of time with me and would always answer my questions. He was never short with me. I think that what happened with the press was that he just went to the other extreme. He just really wasn't interested in talking to anyone. The press has portrayed him as very difficult to get along with, but I think if you ask any of the players, they'll say that wasn't the case at all."

"Roger just wanted to play ball," said Phil Linz. "He liked hanging out with the guys. He was an athlete from a small town and one of the nicest guys I ever met. When I was a rookie, I'd walk into a restaurant or a bar and if Roger was there, he'd say, 'Phil, c'mon, sit over here with us.' The writers in New York were all nice guys, but if you didn't give them what they wanted, they could be tough. Mickey tried to give them something to write about the next day, but Roger didn't want any part of that. Naturally, he was demonized a bit. It was really awful.

He was a nice guy, but they didn't give him a chance to be a nice guy. They wanted what they wanted and he didn't want to give it to him and it became a problem. They wrote some pretty nasty things about him and he turned off."

Mantle, everyone's favorite in the home run race, had begun to fade and, just before the Yankees clinched the pennant, contracted a severe virus. On the 14th of September, he conceded to Maris. "I can't make it, not even in 162 games," he said. Mickey had become ill in Baltimore and couldn't shake the bug. He got a penicillin shot from Dr. Max Jacobson, who was a friend of Mel Allen's and physician to many movie stars, including Elizabeth Taylor and Eddie Fisher. Jacobson was known in Hollywood as Dr. Feelgood, for the euphoria induced by his miraculous injections, but Mantle felt anything but good. He wound up with a severe infection and an abscess on his hip. With Mantle's pursuit of Ruth over, all the attention focused on Maris.

On September 6, Roger hit #54. He hit #55 the next day and #56 two days later. Maris was seven games ahead of Ruth. Number 56 gave the two Yankee sluggers a combined total of 108, a new record, one more than Ruth and Gehrig hit in 1927. Number 57 was a long time coming for Maris. The pitchers were throwing him junk, and he was swinging at it. Sometimes when he didn't swing at bad pitches, the umpires called them strikes. After one game, Maris criticized home plate umpire Hank Soar, which the press was happy to report. Maris was now blaming the umpire because he wasn't hitting home runs.

On the 15th, after getting just a single in nine at bats during a doubleheader, Maris refused to leave the trainer's room, which was off limits to the writers. He said he wouldn't come out until the press was gone, because they were writing terrible things about him. The writers requested that Houk ask Maris to come out, and were rewarded with a string of obscenities from the Major, who also slapped a notebook out of a sportswriter's hand. When Maris finally emerged, he was sullen and sarcastic. His behavior gave the press reason to write even more bad things; now he was "sulking" in the trainer's room. They praised Mantle, who stayed in the locker room after the game and patiently answered everyone's questions.

The following night, Roger hit number 57. "Maris's Big Bat Speaks Louder Than He Does," read the headline in The New York Times. Maris was even with Ruth and had four games in which to hit four more homers. Casey the Computer indicated that the odds were 20 to 1 against him.

Maris improved his odds by hitting #58 the next day, off Terry Fox of the Tigers. On the 19th, in game 153, he managed just a walk in four at bats against Baltimore lefty Steve Barber, leaving Maris two home funs behind the Babe with one game left. Milt Pappas started against the Yankees on the 20th, with much of the country watching on television. There were just over 21,000 in the stands. Maris had not hit a home run in Baltimore, Ruth's home town, all season. Perhaps the ghost of the Babe was watching.

In Maris's first at bat, he flied to deep right field. In the third inning, he connected for #59, a long drive well beyond the right field fence. Maris would have three more at bats in which to hit a home run and tie Ruth. In the fourth, against Dick Hall, he struck out. In the seventh, he hit a long drive that cleared the fence but was foul by about ten feet. He then hit a second drive that right fielder Earl Robinson caught just in front of the right field wall. Maris's last at bat in Game #154 came against knuckleballer Hoyt Wilhelm. He checked his swing and hit a dribbler back to Wilhelm, and the chase, as far as Ford Frick was concerned, was over. Maris had failed to break Ruth's record in 154 games. And oh, by the way, the Yankees won the game to clinch the pennant, and staged what Dan Daniel referred to as the wildest Yankee celebration in 20 years.

On September 26, the Yankees faced the Orioles in New York, and Maris batted against Baltimore right hander Jack Fisher in the third inning. "Gus Triandos called for a curve ball,"

Fisher recalled, "and it was just one of those dumb things. I'm in my windup ready to throw the curve and just as I got ready to release it, I thought, 'Let me take a little bit off it.' I took a little bit off it and it just rolled right down the middle of the plate. He hit it off the facing of the second deck and it bounced back on the field." Maris was tied with the Babe.

The following day, Roger took himself out of the lineup. Maris was mentally exhausted, Houk said. He needed a break from the constant pressure, and decided that the game flame throwing lefty Barber was pitching was a good one to miss. The Yankees were off the following day, and the two consecutive days of rest should do Maris good. After all, 61 home runs were not the only thing Houk had to worry about. There was the matter of the World Series against the Cincinnati Reds.

The Yankees finished the season with three games against the Red Sox in New York. In the opener, against Boston ace Bill Monbouquette, Maris popped out, flied out, and walked twice. The fans booed after each walk. On Saturday, Roger had one hit and one walk, but no homers. That left one more day, Sunday, October 1.

The Boston starter in the season's final game was 24-year-old rookie right hander Tracy Stallard, a 6'5" country boy from Virginia. Stallard was a big man with a big head, in the literal sense. "He could never get a hat big enough for him," recalled Met teammate Bill Wakefield. "He was kind of like Puddin' Head. He wore about a size eight and it would just kind of perch up on top of his head." Stallard later played in New York and loved the limelight and the metropolitan scene. He was a handsome bachelor who dated extensively and, unlike many small town boys, took to New York with enthusiasm. "He was a classic character," said Gary Kroll, "one-of-a-kind, a free spirit. I don't think anything bothered him." Once in the minor leagues, during a rain delay, Stallard reached the conclusion that it was too wet to play. He pulled out a fishing rod and starting casting into the puddles.

As Maris approached Ruth's record, with the pennant race over, many theorized that no pitcher would want to give up the 61st home run, and that Maris would get few good pitches to hit. That was not Tracy Stallard's attitude. "Tracy was the kind of guy," said his teammate Bobby Klaus, "who'd say, 'Here's the best I've got. Let me see your best.'" Stallard was not going to walk Maris.

At Lenox Hill Hospital, Bob Cerv, recovering from knee surgery, had himself wheeled into Mantle's room so the two could watch the game together. In the first inning, Maris flied to left. He came up again in the fourth. The game was still scoreless, but no one seemed to care who won. They were there to see Roger Maris. With a 2–0 count, Stallard threw a fast ball over the plate. "I went after him just as hard as I could," Stallard said. "I threw him a fastball, which was my best pitch at the time." Maris connected and sent the ball well back into the lower right field stands. From the time the ball left the bat, there was no question that it was #61.

Maris rounded the bases and disappeared into the dugout. "He came in," said Joe DeMaestri, "and he just didn't want to go out. The people really wanted to get him out on the field. Today, that's all you see. Somebody hits a home run and they go out and take a bow. It doesn't have to be a World Series. It doesn't have to be anything. They hit a home run and they go out and take a bow. Moose, myself and a couple of other guys grabbed him and pushed him out there just to get him the hell outside, take his bow and get in. Roger didn't like that."

There were slightly more than 23,000 fans in Yankee Stadium, including Cincinnati Reds Joey Jay, Darrell Johnson and coach Jim Turner, and virtually all of them were packed into the right field seats, as they had been for three days. "You couldn't get a seat in right field," recalled DeMaestri. A Sacramento restaurant owner named Sam Gordon had offered $5,000, plus a trip to the World's Fair in Seattle, to anyone who caught the record home run ball.

John Drebinger, Gordon White's colleague on the *Times*, was covering the game from the press box, and White and two other *Times* reporters were stationed in the right field seats. "I spent Friday, Saturday and Sunday there waiting for number 61," White recalled. "My assignment, which was kind of silly, was to try to get to the guy who caught the ball right away. I was about 10–20 rows up, halfway between the bullpen and the foul line. The ball went about 20 or 30 rows behind us. The police had been told to grab the guy and bring him to the Yankee dressing room immediately and that's what they did. We might as well have sat in the press box and run down to the dressing room, because all we did was run after him. We never got to speak to him until he got to the dressing room."

"Him" was Sal Durante, a 19-year-old truck driver from Coney Island, who was attending the game with his 17-year-old fiancée, Rosemarie Calabrese. Durante had attended a game the previous week, and noticed that in batting practice, a lot of hitters deposited balls into Section 33. When he showed up on Sunday, he bought a ticket in Section 33, Box 163D. When Maris's drive headed toward him, he leaped in the air, caught it with one hand and dropped it as a scramble ensued. He emerged from a pile of fans with the ball, and was hustled off by the police to the Yankee locker room, $5,000 richer. While the Yankees batted in the fifth inning, Maris left the dugout to meet Durante, who offered him the ball for nothing. Roger declined, saying that Durante should take the money. "What do you think of that kid," he told Boston catcher Russ Nixon when he came to bat later, "It shows there are some good people left in the world after all." Durante got his money, a trip to the World's Fair and two free 1962 season tickets from owner Dan Topping.

What about Tracy Stallard? When Stallard came to bat in the fifth inning, after surrendering Maris's historic blast, Yankee fans gave him a round of applause for challenging the Yankee slugger rather than walking him. Was he forever scarred by giving up the record homer? "He loved it," said Met teammate Al Moran. "It didn't bother him a bit. It was his claim to fame. He said, 'They know my name, Tracy Stallard.'" "I know this isn't true," said Ted Schreiber, another New York teammate, "but if you told me that he threw the ball down the middle so Maris could hit his 61st homer, I'd believe it, because Tracy was like that." Stallard went on to pitch for the Mets and Cardinals through the 1966 season and in the Mexican League through the early '70s. He'd always been an excellent golfer and, after he retired from baseball, played almost daily. "I won Maris's golf tournament one year," Stallard said recently, "so I got back at him."

After the game, Maris went to Lenox Hill Hospital to visit Cerv and Mantle. His grueling chase of the Babe was over, and the Yankees prepared to take on the Cincinnati Reds in the World Series. They would do so without half of the dreaded M&M combination.

♦ 7 ♦

Finishing the Job
The 1961 World Series

Sandwiched between two thrilling seven game classics, the 1961 Series was a rather dull, one-sided affair that unfolded just about as everyone expected. The Reds were a surprising opponent for, like the Pirates the previous year, no one expected them to win the National League pennant. "[F]ourth place is about as high as they can aspire," said *The New York Times* before the season. "Only the Reds, Phillies and Cubs can be regarded as out of it," wrote John Drebinger, while picking Cincinnati for sixth place. Las Vegas set the odds at 60–1 against the Reds winning the flag.

The Reds were in last place on April 30th, but moved into first by mid–June. Still, even though Cincinnati was leading the league, no one seemed to take them seriously. "If it's a two team race," Dodger outfielder Wally Moon said in August, "I sure hope the other team is Cincinnati." It was a two team race, and the teams were the Dodgers and Reds, and the team that survived was Cincinnati, which finished four games ahead. It was the third straight season that a long shot had won the NL pennant.

The Reds played Rowe's 5–10–10 rule to the hilt, getting an MVP season from Frank Robinson, and an outstanding performance from a 25-year-old center fielder many thought would be a Hall of Famer. Vada Pinson was a left handed hitter with great speed who, in 1961, batted .343, with 208 hits, 16 home runs and 87 RBI. Pinson stole 23 bases, second in the league to Maury Wills. Defensively, he was in a class with Willie Mays and Curt Flood. With Pinson, Robinson (who stole 22 bases in 25 attempts) and infielder Elio Chacon, the Reds had three speedsters.

The Reds also had a strong corps of starting pitchers, led by 21-game winner Joey Jay, the first Cincinnati pitcher in 14 years to win 20. Jay, the first Little League graduate ever to appear in the majors, had come from nowhere. Prior to 1961, he was a disappointing bonus signee of the Braves who, in parts of seven seasons, had never won more than nine games. Jim O'Toole, who was 19–9, had never before won more than 12. The third starter was veteran knuckleballer Bob Purkey, who was 16–12. The Reds lacked a dependable fourth starter, and their bullpen was no better than adequate, but in a World Series, with days off for travel between the two cities, three good starters were enough.

First baseman Gordy Coleman and third baseman Gene Freese had the best seasons of their careers, and a few of the bootstrappers came through with flying colors. Jerry Lynch was Blanchard's counterpart, the best pinch hitter in the National League, batting .315 overall, with 13 homers. Pitcher Ken Johnson came over from Kansas City late in the season and won six of eight decisions down the stretch.

Like the 1960 Pirates, the Reds lacked Series experience. While most of the Yankees had appeared in post-season play several times, not one of the Reds had ever been in a World Series game. They were certain to feel the pressure. "We knew that Cincinnati didn't have a bad ball-club," said Joe DeMaestri. "That's for sure. They had some pretty good ballplayers. But I think our guys went out there with the idea that they weren't going to get beat, no matter who was out there. We thought we had the Pittsburgh series wrapped up, and to lose it the way we did was a pretty big shock."

In one respect, the Yankees were disappointed to face the Reds in the World Series. The players' shares came from the receipts of the first four games, and every year, American League clubs rooted for the Dodgers, who played in the nearly 100,000 seat Coliseum, to win the National League pennant. If teams like the Reds and Pirates, both of whom played in small ballparks (Crosley Field had a capacity of less than 33,000 and Forbes held less than 40,000) were the opponent, the players shares would be much lower than if two of the first four games took place in the Coliseum. In 1959, when the Dodgers played the White Sox, each winning share was $11,231.18, which stood as a record until 1963, when the Dodgers next played in the Series. In 1960 and 1961, the winning shares were just $8,417.94 and $7,389.13, respectively.

For most players, the World Series is a nerve-wracking experience. For Maris, it was the most relaxation he'd had in weeks, for the pursuit of Ruth was over at last. During batting practice, a writer asked Maris if he planned to aim for Ruth's record of three homers in a Series game. "Who's Babe Ruth?" Maris replied with a grin that hadn't been seen recently.

The other half of the M&M duo wasn't grinning. Mantle's long skein of injury began in a World Series, in 1951, when he caught his spikes in a drain and tore up his knee. During the 1955 Series, Mantle missed time with a pulled hamstring and two years later was hampered by a shoulder problem. His status for 1961 was a day-to-day proposition.

When the season ended, Dr. Gaynor had assured Houk that Mantle would be able to play in the Series. When he was released from the hospital, however, Mickey was in terrible shape. He couldn't run at all, and was very weak. His hip ached. On the day before the opener, all Mantle could do was walk around the outfield. "If I'm feeling tomorrow like I feel today," he said, "I don't see how I'll be able to play." Houk estimated he was asked 25,000 times whether Mantle would play. "My wife told me this morning," he said, "that all night she kept hearing me repeat in my sleep, 'I don't know whether Mantle will play tomorrow.'"

Mantle didn't play tomorrow. After watching him take batting practice, Houk knew there was no way Mickey was ready. He moved Maris to center and planned to platoon Lopez and Blanchard in right. With the left-handed O'Toole working the opener, Lopez started.

O'Toole pitched very well, but was beaten 2–0 by Ford, who was even better. Whitey posted his third straight Series shutout and set a record with his eighth win. He allowed the Reds just two singles and one walk, and was never in any trouble. Howard and Skowron hit solo home runs for the margin of victory and Boyer made two unbelievable fielding plays.

Jay, the Reds' 21-game winner, and Terry, seeking to avenge his 1960 debacle, were the pitchers in the second game. The score was 2–2 in the fifth, when Red second baseman Elio Chacon singled with two out. He went to third on another single by Eddie Kasko. With Pinson at the plate, one of Terry's pitches rolled a few feet away from Howard. Ellie went over, picked up the ball and cocked his arm, looking toward Kasko to see if he would try for second. Terry trotted perfunctorily toward the plate. There was no way Chacon would try to score. But Chacon was sprinting recklessly toward the plate. Out of the corner of his eye, Howard saw him, and realized that Terry wouldn't get there in time. Ellie made a mad dash and dove at Chacon, who slid in just before Howard landed on him with the ball. The Reds had a 3–2 lead.

Jay shut down the Yankee offense and the Reds routed Arroyo, who relieved Terry. Cincinnati had a 6–2 win and accomplished what every visiting series team wants to do, split the first two games in the opponents' park. Terry suffered his third straight World Series loss.

The series moved to Cincinnati for the next three games. On Friday, October 6, the Yankees worked out, amidst two noteworthy events. The first was the appearance of Mantle, who hit for the first time and pumped six of batting practice pitcher Spud Murray's pitches into the stands. Mickey said he would play on the morrow, but Houk wasn't so sure.

The second significant occurrence of the day was the appearance of a naked man who climbed atop a seventy five foot elevator shaft beyond the center field fence and threatened to jump. The visitor, identified as Joe Watson, a "hanger-on around the ballpark," was probably the first streaker at a sporting event. He stood atop the shaft for about 15 minutes, and flapped his arms, as if he was going to fly, before he was talked down from his perch and led to the nearest police station.

On Saturday, Mantle, although clearly not healthy, was in the starting lineup. "We had them right where we wanted them," said Red pitcher Ken Johnson. "We'd split in New York, and we wanted to win two out of three in Cincinnati and then win one more game in New York. We had them right where we wanted them. The turning point of the Series was when Mantle went out to play center field and limped all the way. When he went out there the whole Yankee team just lifted up."

Mantle was little more than an inspiration, and went 0–4, striking out twice. Ever time a ball was hit toward center field, Maris and Berra came charging over to cover for him. The game was a tight one, as Stafford and Purkey staged a thrilling pitching duel. The Reds took a 2–1 lead into the eighth inning. If they could hold on, the underdog Cincinnati club would have a 2–1 series lead and a chance to close out the Yankees at home. In the eighth, after Purkey retired the first two men, Blanchard was sent up to hit for reliever Bud Daley with one mission, hit the ball into the stands and tie the game. Had Mantle not played, Blanchard would have been in right field, but fate had placed him back on the bench, facing Purkey in a crucial spot. Providence had been cruel to John on many occasions, but now, on October 7, 1961, it was about to repay the debt, with a little self-help.

Crosley Field was an old ballpark, with irregular dimensions. Its most unusual feature was a hill that sloped up toward the left field fence. The right field foul pole was 366 feet away, a healthy distance, but the fence jutted out at nearly a straight line toward center, rather than receding as it did in most parks. The home run distance in right center was just 360, actually less than the distance down the line, and just 16 feet farther than the right center field wall at Yankee Stadium. Blanchard had more than enough power to reach the fence.

"Mickey was standing right by the bat rack as I was looking for my bat," Blanchard recalled. As always, Blanchard asked Mantle what Purkey was throwing. The Cincinnati hurler threw the knuckler about 25 percent of the time and otherwise used an assortment of fastballs and sliders. "Blanch," Mantle told him, "hit the first pitch. He's going to throw you a slider on the first pitch to get ahead of you, and then he's coming back with all knuckleballs. Don't take that first pitch." "When I got to the plate," Blanchard said, "my mind was 100 percent made up. I was swinging at the first pitch no matter where it was. If he had thrown it in the press box, I'd have jumped up and swung at it."

Purkey's first pitch was a slider, down and in, just as Mantle had predicted. Blanchard swung and lofted a long fly ball into the right field stands to tie the game 2–2. Arroyo, who had been sent to the minors by twice by Red manager Fred Hutchinson, shut out the Reds in the bottom of the eighth. In the top of the ninth, Maris, who hadn't had a hit in the Series, belted a home run to put the Yankees in front 3–2.

With a lead, Houk replaced Mantle with Jack Reed. Reed had spent the year shuttling between Richmond and New York and, since he was on the Richmond roster, would not have played in the Series had it not been for Bob Cerv's knee injury. When Cerv had to undergo surgery, Reed was named to the roster as his replacement, and appeared in Game One as a late inning defensive replacement. Now, with the Series on the line, the little-used Reed, with only 28 games of major league experience, was in center field.

Arroyo struck out the leadoff batter in the ninth, but with one out, pinch hitter Leo Cardenas ripped a long drive to left center field. There was a big scoreboard in left field at Crosley Field, which rose seventy feet in the air and extended well out toward center. If Cardenas' drive had gone just a few feet to the right, it would have been a game-tying home run. Instead, it hit about halfway up the scoreboard. Houk, in his book *Ball Players Are Human, Too* described the scene:

"Jack [Reed] had had a tough season. He would have drawn a blank in the Series if Mickey and Cerv had been in shape. But the wheels turned, and there he was, setting himself for the rebound of Cardenas' hit, taking it on the carom, whirling, throwing to Tony [Kubek] in the cutoff position holding Cardenas to a two-bagger. It was perfect outfielding."

"You kind of do things on instinct," Reed said. "I knew Cardenas. He played for Havana when I was at Richmond. When the ball was hit, I could tell I wasn't going to be able to catch it. It was going to be off the wall. All I did was position myself to be where the ball would come off. That's just instinct. It's not any great shakes."

Jack Reed, who had only one job to perform for the 1961 Yankees, had done it splendidly. Pinch hitter Dick Gernert hit a ground ball through the middle of the diamond, on which Kubek made a fine play. He threw Gernert out as Cardenas went to third. He remained there as Gus Bell grounded to Arroyo to end the game and give the Yankees a 2–1 lead in the Series. Had Cardenas gotten a triple and scored on Gernert's grounder, the game would have been tied. Had the Reds come back to win, it would have been their second straight victory, with Mantle injured and the next two games in Cincinnati. Jack Reed was good at doing the little things, and in this case a little thing had big implications.

Ford and Coates combined to shut out the Reds in Game Four. Whitey left after five innings with an ankle injury, but not before he had broken Babe Ruth's World Series mark by pitching 32 consecutive scoreless innings. If there was a seventh game, Ford's status was unknown, and his injury added to the mounting Yankee list. Mantle was out, and so was Berra, who had badly bruised his shoulder sliding into third base.

Jay, the winner in Game Two, started Game Five and was again opposed by Terry. Lopez played left field and Blanchard was in right, batting cleanup in Mantle's spot. Maris played center. Richardson led off the game with a single, but Jay retired the next two batters. Then the roof caved in. Blanchard started the onslaught by drilling one of Jay's sliders over the 360 foot marker in right center for his second home run of the Series. Howard hit a blast off the scoreboard in left center, and Skowron followed with another off the center field wall, giving the Yankees a 3–0 lead. Jay departed and Jim Maloney relieved. Maloney, a hard-throwing 20-year-old, threw an outside fastball. Lopez tripled. Boyer hit yet another ball off the scoreboard and the Yankees led 5–0. At the end of the inning, the Reds' publicity man announced that the pitchers in the sixth game would be Stafford and Purkey, but no one seemed very interested.

After three innings, the score was 6–3 and Terry was out of the game, replaced by Daley after surrendering a three run homer to Frank Robinson. "There was a key play that kind of hurt me," Terry recalled. "There was a ball hit off the end of the bat to left. Hector Lopez was playing left field and it dropped in front of him." Since Terry had not lasted five innings, he could not get credit for the win. For the second consecutive season, he had pitched in the deciding game of the World Series, picking up a loss and a no-decision, but no win.

In the fourth inning, the Yankees broke out with another five run rally, featuring a double by Blanchard and a three run homer by Lopez. The Reds threw nearly their whole staff against the Bombers and still couldn't stop them. "I had a perfect World Series record," said Ken Johnson, who relieved in the second. "The first batter hit a line drive to Gene Freese that he caught as it knocked him over backwards. The next batter hit a fly ball to center that Pinson caught against the fence. I was the fourth hitter the next inning and I was praying for somebody to get a hit. Somebody did get a hit and they took me out for a pinch hitter." "The Reds had Ken Johnson," wrote columnist Bob Broeg, "but they needed Walter." Hutchinson wound up using 21 of his 25 players, including eight pitchers, but to no avail. Blanchard later added another hit, and the Yankees won the game 13–5 and the Series 4–1.

Daley finished the game and got the win. "The saddest thing about that," he said recently, "is that I kind of look back now and kick my butt. I had a plane ticket home and had about 45 minutes to get from the park to the airport. As soon as the game was over, I went in and took a shower and got the hell out of there. I didn't stick around for the interviews or the celebration."

Blanchard and Lopez both stayed for the champagne. For the Series, they were 7 for 19 and drove in 10 runs. Johnny had four hits in ten times up, including two home runs and a double, a fitting climax to the greatest season of his career. "Gosh, I'm happy," was all he could say. For Lopez, who'd suffered through the worst season of his career, the Series was sweet redemption. He'd driven in seven runs in only nine at bats. After driving home only 22 runs all season, he'd knocked in five in one game. "It made me feel good that I could still play," he said recently. "I didn't do anything during the regular season."

Maris and Mantle, whose slugging had carried the team all season, were a combined 3 for 25. Richardson, who led the Yanks with nine hits, was named the Series' Most Valuable Player, as he had been a year earlier. Houk became just the third major league manager to win a World Series in his first season at the helm. He said it was the best New York team he had ever seen. There was more power throughout the lineup, he said, than in the teams of the '50s, and the infield defense was without equal. With a relatively easy Series win, one of the greatest seasons in Yankee history had reached a fitting conclusion.

There was one more piece of unfinished business. On October 29, Sal Durante and Rose Calabrese were married at St. Finbar's Roman Catholic Church in Brooklyn. The following day, they arrived in Sacramento on their honeymoon, and presented the 61st home run ball to Sam Gordon. Gordon put the ball in an armored truck, which carried it to a Sacramento bank, where it remained until Maris arrived in town on November 4. Gordon had arranged a police escort and parade from the airport, but Maris circumvented the plan by flying to San Francisco and driving to Sacramento. Gordon gave the ball to Maris, and Durante got his $5,000. "Thank you very much," was Maris's speech. His long season was over, but his ordeal was not.

◆ 8 ◆

He Was Hector's Hands
and Mickey's Legs
The 1962 Season

Could the 1962 Yankees hope to measure up to the standard established by the legendary '61 team? "I personally thought the 1962 team was better than the '61 team, because of the reserves," said Phil Linz, who was, coincidentally, a reserve on the '62 team. "Yogi became a reserve. I took Joe DeMaestri and Billy Gardner's place. Plus, the guys who came up were better."

The guys who came up were Linz, Jim Bouton, Tom Tresh, and Joe Pepitone. Linz, the 1960 Carolina League batting champ and the MVP of the Texas League in 1961, Pepitone, and Bouton made the jump from Texas League champion Amarillo. Tresh, who played a few games with the Yankees at the end of the '61 season, hit .315 and had been the International League Rookie of the Year at Triple A Richmond.

The presence of Tresh and Linz was of particular interest, since both played shortstop and Kubek, the Yankee shortstop in 1961, had been called to active duty by the Wisconsin National Guard. He reported to Fort Lewis, Washington, in November and was expected to miss the entire 1962 season. In January, President Kennedy activated two regular army divisions, creating the possibility that reserves like Kubek might be released early, but when spring training arrived, the Yankees were in Fort Lauderdale and their shortstop was still in Fort Lewis.

The Yanks' military losses could have been worse, for it was at one time feared that both Terry and Stafford might be inducted. The loss of 30 combined wins from an already thin staff would have given Yankee haters reason for hope. Both Terry and Stafford escaped the clutches of Uncle Sam, however, and were still civilians when training camp began.

Most of the attention in the 1962 camp gravitated toward the odds of Maris hitting 62 home runs and the competition between Linz and Tresh for the starting shortstop position. Whichever of the rookies didn't win the starting job would be the number one infield reserve, for Joe DeMaestri had retired to join his father's lucrative beverage distributing business. "That has been probably my only regret in baseball," said San Francisco native DeMaestri. "All I had to do was stay one more year and I'd have been home for the World Series."

With DeMaestri gone, the battle was between Tresh and Linz. "At the beginning of spring training," Linz recalled, "Houk called Tommy and myself into his office and said he would give us both a fair shot to compete for the shortstop job and would play us every other day. At the time I felt I had a chance, but in retrospect I realize it was just for publicity, because Tommy had gotten called up at the end of the '61 season and was the Rookie of the Year in the International League."

Tresh had more poise than the typical rookie. He was the son of Mike Tresh, a former catcher who spent twelve years in the major leagues, mostly with the White Sox. "I always felt that was an advantage," said Tresh, "not in the sense that he taught me how to play, but in the fact that I grew up believing that I could play in the major leagues. It was a mental thing. When I was a kid, my dad was hanging around with Luke Appling and those guys. They were my dad's friends. They were the guys who were coming over to the house all the time. Everyone I knew played baseball, and as I got a little older they'd say, 'So, are you going to play baseball like your dad?' I'd say, 'Yeah, I'm going to play.' I never thought I couldn't make it."

Linz was just the opposite. He'd never been considered a hot prospect. While Tresh had gotten a $25,000 bonus, Linz received just $4,000. He was skinny, wore glasses and didn't look like a major league ballplayer. Linz always seemed to get off to a slow start in the minors, and each year the Yankees were ready to write him off. "In Class D," said Jack White, then the Yankee director of scouting, "we tried everything to get rid of Linz."

Somehow, the gangly youngster managed to come on strong each summer and climb to the next rung on the Yankee ladder. "I grew up in Baltimore," Linz said, "which was a Triple A town then. That was almost like the majors to me. I felt that if I got to Triple A, that would be terrific. Then I started having these good years. I led the Carolina League in hitting, and then I jumped to Double A. By the time I got to the major leagues, I started thinking, 'I can play against these people. I can play here.' But I didn't expect to make the big leagues. Even in the Texas League, I didn't know I was going to be called up by the Yankees until I saw it in *The Sporting News*."

Linz and Tresh alternated at shortstop all spring. Linz batted .348 and Tresh hit .302, but Tresh won the Dawson Award as the spring's top rookie and was given the starting job. "I'm picking Tresh for the opener," said Houk, "simply because I've got to start one or the other." Linz was philosophical. "In Binghamton," he said, "and in Richmond, he won the top job over me. But my luck's improving. At least this time they let me stay around to watch him play."

Linz was good, but Tresh was much more impressive at first glance. He had more power, a stronger arm, and was a bit flashier. "Phil was the type of player who didn't overwhelm you if you went to see him play once," said teammate Archie Moore. "But if you watched him play over an extended period of time, you'd see that he made the plays. He didn't hit with power, but he put the bat on the ball. He would do the little things for you. He could run better than people thought. He could throw a little better than people thought." "I could do all the little things," Linz recalled. "I don't think I ever missed a sacrifice bunt. It kills me to this day when they can't bunt a guy from first base to second."

The other big story in the Yankee camp was Maris. Roger may have thought that the media attention would fade after the pursuit of Ruth ended, but he was mistaken. All winter, he worked the banquet circuit, which he loathed, and gained ten pounds in the process. While everyone else speculated whether Maris could hit 62 home runs in 1962, Roger predicted 30, and said he would quit baseball as soon as he was financially secure.

In late February, after prolonged haggling, Maris signed a contract for an estimated $70,000, nearly double the $37,500 he had earned the previous year. In Fort Lauderdale, he and Mantle co-starred in a corny movie called Safe at Home, which also featured William Frawley. As soon as Maris finished acting and started working out, the questions began again. "If I had had any sense," he said, "I would have made a master recording before I left home. It would serve for all interviewers."

Maris was booed during exhibition games, and soon found himself entangled in a feud with Met coach Rogers Hornsby, one of the greatest hitters of all time. In 1961, Hornsby, a bitter, cantankerous man his entire life, made disparaging comments about Maris's ability, particularly his relatively low batting average. The next spring, when asked to pose with Hornsby for a publicity photo, Maris declined. "That bush leaguer," Hornsby said. "I've posed for pictures with some major league hitters, not bush leaguers like he is." When asked a few days later, for the millionth time, whether he thought he could hit 62 home runs in '62, Maris replied, "My goal this year is to finish with a batting average of .425. [Hornsby had once hit .424.] Then I know I'll be able to shut up Mr. Rogers Hornsby."

Throughout Maris's tribulations, Houk defended him, relating many instances in which Maris was unfairly made a villain. As for Hornsby, Houk said, "I think Hornsby would do well to take care of his own [Met] players and leave mine alone." Houk also dismissed claims that Maris was causing dissension on the Yankees, stating that the players were all behind him.

After being hounded all spring, Maris announced that he would not grant any further interviews. Oscar Fraley (who later gained fame as a scriptwriter for The Untouchables) wrote an article critical of Roger's pronouncement and was verbally assaulted by the outfielder in a violent confrontation in the Yankee clubhouse on March 18. Maris then decided to give interviews but answer all questions with the phrase "I don't know." Jimmy Cannon, the venerable columnist who had been friendly to Maris, also turned on him. When Maris failed to show up for a scheduled interview, Cannon blasted him in his column. The more Maris fought the press, the more they vilified him, and he had no way to fight back.

In Maris's first exhibition game, he had a single in three at bats and made an error. "It was embarrassing," declared The Sporting News. "He disappointed a capacity crowd of 7,584 by failing to hit a home run." Unless he hit a home run every time up, Maris discovered, he would be a disappointment. On March 25, after he hit his second home run of the spring, reporters noted that Maris was well ahead of last year's pace, when he hit just one home run in Florida.

Things were no better when the regular season started. Someone threw a bottle at Maris in Detroit. The next day, someone heaved an empty beer can. Cleveland fans threw garbage at him. Roger was greeted by boos each time he came to the plate. He hit a home run on Opening Day, putting him well ahead of his 1961 pace, but soon fell into a dreadful slump. On April 23, Maris was batting .132, with only one home run. He had started slowly the previous year, but now the entire world was watching — and it wanted him to fail.

Like Maris, Whitey Ford had the greatest year of his career in 1961, but no one expected him to win 30 games in 1962. When he had some arm trouble and got off to a slow start, the reaction was concern, not disgust or outrage.

The Yankees weren't great in the first two months of 1962, but, fortunately for them, neither was anyone else. The Tigers, their closest pursuers in 1961, were below .500, and lost their best pitcher, Lary, and their best all-around player, Kaline, to injury. Lary wound up on the disabled list with a sore shoulder and Kaline broke his collarbone making a diving, game-ending catch at Yankee Stadium in late May. The Orioles, the Yankees' toughest rival in 1960, lost pitcher Steve Barber and shortstop Ron Hansen to the Army. The Indians were playing well and so, surprisingly, were the Angels and Twins.

The Yankees, for the most part, were not playing well. The three bootstrappers who had helped them to the pennant in 1961 were not producing. Blanchard, playing more than he ever had in the early season, started well but quickly fell off. Sheldon was hit hard, sent to the bullpen and never got untracked.

The biggest disappointment of all was Arroyo. After his surprising 1961 season, Luis was given a $5,000 bonus, a new contract with a $10,000 raise and a hero's welcome when he returned to Puerto Rico after the World Series. For the first time in many years, Arroyo played very little during the winter, pitching in only a few games at the end of the season.

Arroyo had a good spring, but when the season started he encountered problems almost immediately. On April 23, he was bombed for six runs in three innings by the Indians. The next morning, he couldn't bend his arm. For several years, Luis had been carrying calcium chips in his elbow, which had slipped into the wrong place and caused the joint to become inflamed. After nearly a month of rest resulted in no improvement, Arroyo was placed on the disabled list May 21.

Three days before Arroyo went on the disabled list, the Yankees suffered a more serious blow. They were losing to the Twins 4–3 with two outs in the ninth and Mantle at bat. Mickey hit a ground ball deep in the shortstop hole. Zoilo Versalles had difficulty handling the ball and Mantle thought he had a chance to leg out a hit. Versalles uncorked a strong throw to first, however, and nipped Mantle to end the game. Following his final lunge toward first base, Mickey crumpled to the ground with a torn muscle in his right thigh. He had to be helped from the field and taken to the hospital. Mantle would miss more than a month.

At the time of Mantle's injury, Maris was also sidelined, and when he returned, he no longer had the protection of Mantle's bat behind him. Maris saw fewer and fewer good pitches, and in one game, drew four intentional walks and one unintentional pass. He batted under .200 during Mantle's absence and, by July, his average was just .239.

Mantle was injured, Maris wasn't hitting, and neither were Howard, Skowron and Berra. Fortunately, others had taken up the slack. Tresh proved an adequate replacement for Kubek, and was hitting close to .300 and driving in runs. Boyer, who batted only .228 in 1961, was tearing the cover off the ball. He claimed to have found the secret to hitting, which was to stop lunging at the ball. At the end of April, he led the Yanks in runs, hits, total bases, home runs, runs batted in and batting average. Richardson was also hitting well and was on the way to his finest year.

As in 1961, the Yankees had pitching problems. Ford struggled with a sore shoulder all season. He developed blisters. He suffered from stiffness in his side. Sheldon was ineffective and Arroyo injured. Turley was unable to come back from his off-season arm surgery and was never a factor. Reliever Hal Reniff, who had pitched well as a rookie in 1961, was discharged from the Army in early June, hurt his arm shortly after reporting, and was useless. Terry was a workhorse, but after a 16–3 mark in '61, his '62 record hovered around the .500 mark during the first half of the season. Stafford, although hampered by some arm trouble, was pitching well. Coates and Daley were steady but unspectacular in the bullpen. Rookie Bouton, both starting and relieving, showed promise. What the Yankees really needed, however, was someone to replace the injured Arroyo.

Houk found that person in Marshall Bridges, a 31-year-old left hander obtained from the Reds during the winter. Known as "The Sheriff" for obvious reasons, Bridges had an interesting career, which began when he quit school at the age of 11 to become a groundskeeper's assistant in Jackson, Mississippi. Bridges began his playing career as a first baseman in the Negro Leagues, with the Memphis Red Sox, and had bounced around professional ball for many years. Like Arroyo two years earlier, he was a journeyman lefty who couldn't seem to establish himself in the major leagues.

Bridges had escaped from the Negro leagues in 1953. During the 1950s, major league players frequently undertook barnstorming tours after the season ended. A group of players would gather together as a team, play in towns that never saw major league players, and split the gate receipts. Although baseball was broadcast on television, many Americans didn't have televisions and for those who did, the schedule of games was limited. Barnstorming tours were their only chance to see major league players.

Even stars took advantage of the opportunity to earn extra money. In 1958, Mantle led a team of American League stars which opposed a National League team headed by Mays, in a game at Yankee Stadium. Mays took a team to Mexico and Latin America. Most barnstorming teams consisted of a core of major leaguers who drew the crowds and collected the majority of the money, supplemented by minor leaguers.

In the fall of 1952, a number of black major leaguers, including Roy Campanella, Monte Irvin, Joe Black and Harry Simpson, formed a barnstorming troupe to tour the hinterlands. Bridges, still with the Memphis Red Sox, joined them as a pitcher and first baseman. He pitched and hit with enough skill to cause a number of the major leaguers to recommend that their clubs sign him. The New York Giants listened to Irvin, and dispatched scout Alex Pompez, who signed many major league stars, to check Bridges out. When Pompez concurred with Irvin's opinion, the Giants purchased the contract of the 22-year-old Bridges from Memphis for $10,000.

In 1953, Bridges pitched and played first base. He hit well, but what really impressed the scouts was his live fastball. By 1955, Bridges was strictly a pitcher, and was 14–1, with 172 strikeouts in 135 innings, at Amarillo. He was 18–11 at Topeka the following year, and led the Western League with 213 whiffs. That earned him a promotion to the Pacific Coast League, just one rung below the majors.

In 1958, Bridges had a terrific season at Sacramento. He tied for the Pacific Coast League lead with 16 wins, and led the league with 205 strikeouts. The following year, after a good start in Triple A ball, Bridges was called up by the Cardinals. He was the long man in the bullpen, compiling a record of 6–3. In 1960, after a poor start, Bridges was traded to Cincinnati, where he pitched well at the end of the year, compiling a 1.08 ERA in 14 games.

In 1961, the year the Reds won the National League pennant, Bridges began the season in Cincinnati, but was long gone by World Series time. He injured his arm bowling during the off season, and was sent to Jersey City in July. By winter, Bridges was available. He had been erratic during his brief time in the majors, but he was a left hander with a live fastball and had led two minor leagues in strikeouts. The Yankees, who needed a strong-armed pitcher, had a surplus of catchers, with Howard, Blanchard and Berra. They also had a 25-year-old slugging receiver at Richmond named Jesse Gonder. Gonder had led the International League in hitting in 1960, but slumped badly in 1961. He wasn't much of a defensive catcher, and even if Berra was nearing the end of the line, there was no way Gonder was going to move ahead of Howard and Blanchard. He was available, and the Reds needed a catcher. They'd won the pennant in 1961 without having a regular at the position. Rookies

Like Luis Arroyo, Marshall Bridges was a well-traveled left hander who became the Yankee bullpen ace in 1962. An outrageous character, he took a bullet in the calf in a barroom incident in 1963.

Johnny Edwards and Jerry Zimmerman, who shared the job, batted just .186 and .206, respectively. Cincinnati needed a catcher who could hit, so Hamey traded Gonder to Cincinnati for Bridges. It was a good trade, picking up a much-needed pitcher for a player who wasn't going to make the Yankee team.

While Bridges may have been a borderline major league pitcher, he was a bona fide major league character. He could talk. Lord, could he talk. Bridges talked on planes. He talked on buses. He talked wherever he could find an audience. Bridges told tall tales about blue snakes, improbable adventures and, one might guess given his later escapades, of exploits unfit for young ears. Bridges liked to tell hunting stories which, as Til Ferdenzi wrote, "featured Bridges in the role of hero, a sort of Paul Bunyan, Daniel Boone and Kit Carson all rolled up into one." Bridges also fancied himself a singer, and was christened "The Velvet Smog" by his teammates—as opposed to Mel Torme, the Velvet Fog.

Houk wanted Bridges for his pitching, not his singing or story-telling, and in 1962, The Sheriff showed the manager he could pitch. With Arroyo on the shelf, Bridges became the stopper in the Yankee bullpen. He didn't allow a run until late May, and won his first six decisions. He was one of the leading contenders for *The Sporting News* Fireman of the Year award before fading late in the season.

On June 16, the Yankees were in a virtual tie for first place with the Indians and Twins, as only three percentage points separated the three teams. The Angels, less than a year and a half old, were just 2½ games behind. The Twins and Angels were the two surprise teams of the American League. Minnesota had a strong offensive club, led by sluggers Harmon Killebrew and Bob Allison. Rookie third baseman Rich Rollins led the league in hitting for a stretch, and fellow rookie Bernie Allen had taken Billy Martin's job at second base. Versalles, who would be the American League MVP in 1965, was a flashy and talented, if erratic shortstop, and Earl Battey was a sound veteran catcher. All eight of the Twins regulars hit at least ten home runs. Add two strong starters like Camilo Pascual and Jim Kaat, and the Twins had a team that could give the Yankees trouble.

The Angels seemed to be contending with mirrors. "Los Angeles has got more than the maximum," wrote *Sports Illustrated*, "out of what on paper appears to be a team made up of dead sparrows and pieces of string." The Angels' starting rotation was weak, and there were holes throughout the lineup. The Angels' top RBI man from 1961, former Yankee Ken Hunt, missed virtually the entire season with a separated shoulder. In July, Ken McBride, the Angels' best pitcher, got hurt.

Bill Rigney, the Los Angeles skipper, was a wiry, nervous, ex-infielder and former Giant manager. Rigney was 44 in 1962, but, like Danny Murtaugh, looked much older. He had thinning gray hair and an ulcer that sometimes sent him to the hospital for a few days at a time. In August, after a weekend in dry dock, he said cheerily, "No ulcer yet. Just a little gastritis. Nothing that two out of three or a sweep against the Yankees won't cure." The Angles lost two of three, and two of the games went to extra innings, none of which did Rigney's sensitive stomach any good. His crew, scratching and scrambling, however, stuck to the Yankees nearly until the end. "The Angels hung out together," said pitcher Eli Grba. "We were a bunch of rag-tags. One time they asked Rigney, of all of his teams, which one was his favorite. He said the '62 Angels."

Los Angeles' top players were Leon Wagner, one of the top sluggers in the league (37 homers) and former Yankee Lee Thomas. Thomas, like Wagner an American League All Star, batted .290 with 26 homers and 104 RBI. Second baseman Billy Moran came from nowhere to make the All Star team. A first year catcher named Bob Rodgers won the regular job and was one of the top rookies in the American League. The Angels' strength, however, was their relief pitching. Rigney had a strong bullpen at a time when most managers didn't think the bullpen was all that important. Ex-Yankees Ryne Duren and Tom Morgan, plus two other veterans, Art Fowler and Jack Spring, supported a starting staff that completed only eight of its first 57 games. Somehow, the Angels found themselves in first place on July 4.

The Yankees were just one half game behind. Mantle had returned to active duty with a dramatic pinch hit home run on June 17, and rejoined the Yankee lineup late in·the month, with the club in fourth place, four games behind the Indians. No one could replace Mickey, but Blanchard hit well in his absence, and had 10 home runs, second only to Maris's 12. For more than a month after Mantle returned, he had trouble with his leg, but, bad leg and all, he was hitting like the old Mantle. In early July, over a two game stretch, he hit home runs in four consecutive at bats.

With Blanchard, Berra and Lopez cavorting in the outer pasture, and Mantle at half speed, the Yankees were weak defensively. In the late innings, Houk usually replaced one of the outfielders with Jack Reed, who played a unique role on the Yankee team, and was soon to have a very special moment.

One Sunday in 1959, the New York football Giants dropped a couple of punts. "Who taught those guys how to field punts?" asked a press box pundit, "Hector Lopez?" Everybody laughed, for in less than a season with the Yankees, Lopez had acquired quite a reputation for adventurous fielding.

When he arrived in New York in 1959, Lopez was an infielder. After a few mishaps, including an errant throw that resulted in Moose Skowron's broken wrist, Stengel, in the spring of 1960, decided to play Hector exclusively in the outfield. "[H]e let too many grounders jump up and hit him in the chest," said Stengel, "and sometimes he did a Pepper Martin and threw the batter out, and sometimes the other way around." Even if Lopez was not much better in the outfield, at least he would be farther from the action. Since he led the Yanks in RBI in 1959, surpassing Mantle, Berra and the rest of the Yankee All-Stars, Stengel had to find someplace to play "a man which batted in ninety three runs for me and if I bench him I bench ninety three runs but I would like better fieldin' outta ninety-three runs."

Stengel, hesitant to put Lopez in Yankee Stadium's spacious left field, decided that the newly-acquired Maris would move to left and Lopez would patrol the more cozy confines of right field. "Stengel still shudders," wrote John Drebinger, "every time he contemplates seeing the well-meaning but inept Hector cutting up more capers in the Yankee Stadium left field." Maris, a right fielder his entire career, whose rifle arm was perfectly suited for the position, reluctantly agreed to try left. He played it adequately during spring training, but left field at Miller Huggins Field in St. Petersburg was not left field in Yankee Stadium. The final exhibition games were played against the Red Sox in New York. In one of the games, Maris lost a fly ball in the left field haze. Immediately afterward, Stengel, with little explanation, gave up on his experiment and returned Maris to right, where he wanted to play, and put Lopez in left. "Maris is my right fielder," he said, "and he's going to keep on playing there. Sun or no sun, Lopez will start in left; and if he can't make it, we'll have to try somebody else." Better to gamble at one position than mess up two.

In fairness to Lopez, one must remember that he had been primarily an infielder his entire career. "I'd never played the outfield before," he said recently. "I just had one spring training and they put me out there. I tried to do the best I could." Left field in the old Yankee Stadium was one of the most difficult positions in the major leagues. There was a vast expanse of ground to cover, for the fence in left center field was 402 feet from home plate. The ball came at the left fielder out of the tall grandstand behind home plate, often in a background of sun or smoky haze. At World Series time, when dusk came earlier in the day, left field at Yankee Stadium could be a nightmare. It nearly ruined Norm Siebern in 1958. "It was brutal," said Yankee outfielder Jim Pisoni. "When a line drive went out there, you'd better know where it was when it left the bat, and then try to pick it out of the stands and the sun. If it was a high fly ball, it wasn't bad, but the line drives killed you."

Even fly balls could lead to trouble. During the first week of the 1960 season, in a game against the Red Sox, Lopez went into the left field corner and dropped a fly ball for a three base error that led to a five run inning. Later in the game, he tried for a shoestring catch and let the ball get by him for a triple. As the season went on, the pattern continued. Lopez delivered key hit after key hit, and turned every fly ball and line drive to left field into a hair-raising adventure. Early in the season, Stengel replaced him with rookie Ken Hunt in the late innings, but often Hunt proved little better than Hector in the field. When Hunt was sent to Richmond, Stengel stuck with Lopez and held his breath. For a while he didn't play Lopez in the outfield at home. In September, when the roster limit expanded to 40, the Yankees recalled Pisoni from Richmond and used him to play left field late in the game.

Pisoni was a 31-year-old minor league veteran who first came up to the major leagues with the St. Louis Browns in 1953. He also played briefly with Milwaukee and Kansas City and spent a few weeks with the Yankees in 1959. Pisoni had a strong arm, good speed and a reliable glove, and in September, 1960, he appeared in left field nearly every day as a replacement for Lopez. He was in 20 games and, after his long minor league apprenticeship, got to experience a major league pennant clincher for the first time.

Since he had been recalled after September 1 and was ineligible for the Series, Pisoni watched the Yankees and Pirates on television. For his efforts during the stretch run, he received a $500 share of the Series money and a ticket back to Richmond the following spring. He never appeared in a major league game again.

Pisoni was no longer needed, for in the spring of 1961, another talented defensive outfielder appeared in the Yankee camp. Jack Reed was a southern boy who had played football and baseball at The University of Mississippi. Jimmy Patton, the future New York Giant All-Pro, played one defensive halfback position and Reed played the other. As an outfielder, Reed led the Southeastern Conference in batting one year. He was injured and missed his senior season on the gridiron, but showed enough skill on the baseball diamond to be signed by the Yankees in 1953. "You know how it is when you sign a contract," Reed said. "You say, Mickey Mantle, move over, here comes Jack Reed." That didn't happen. Mantle didn't move over, nor did Hank Bauer, nor Norm Siebern. The 1950s were a difficult time to break into the Yankee outfield and, despite a number of solid seasons in the minors, Jack kept going back to the bushes year after year.

Reed's progress was slowed when he was inducted into the service for two years. After he was mustered out, he went to spring training with the Yankees in 1959 and 1960, but didn't come close to making the team. "Back then," he said, "unless somebody retired, or you were a pitcher, you really didn't have a chance to make the Yankees." Sometimes, Reed thought it might be nice to get traded to the Senators or Athletics, but in the era of the reserve clause, there was nothing he could do about it.

In addition to facing a stacked Yankee roster, Reed was plagued by a series of misfortunes. In the winter of 1959, he contracted hepatitis, which affected his stamina. In 1960, got off to a good start in Richmond, but hurt his arm. He kept playing, but his productivity dropped off markedly and he had a poor season. His arm kept getting worse, and by the end of the year, he couldn't throw the ball more than a few feet. "I came home and thought my career was over," he said. The Yankees removed him from the major league 40 man roster, and even if his arm regained its strength, there seemed to be little hope of making the team. The Yankees had added Roger Maris to go along with Mantle, and Maris wasn't about to move over for Reed any more than Mantle was. Lopez was still there, and Yogi Berra and John Blanchard were being switched to outfield duty. "I think I was mature enough to realize that I wasn't going to take Mantle's place," Reed said, "and I wasn't going to take Maris's place and I wasn't going to take Yogi's place."

With Lopez, Blanchard and Yogi in the mix, the Yankees might need a good defensive outfielder, but Reed couldn't throw a ball across the room. He thought it might be time to take his Bachelor's Degree in Business Administration and go to work.

During the winter, Reed received a call from Jack White, the Richmond general manager. Ralph Houk wanted Reed to go to spring training with the Yankees as a non-roster player. "I asked why," Reed recalled, "because I wasn't going anywhere. I told Jack I didn't even know if I could throw." Houk still wanted him in spring training, White said. "Will you do it for me?" he asked. Reed said he would. He went to the trainer at Ole Miss and received treatment for his arm three or four times a week, but when he left for St. Petersburg, there had been little improvement.

When Reed arrived in camp, Houk surprised him by telling him that if his arm came back, he would have a job as Mantle's replacement in the late innings. Mickey was not yet 30, but the accumulation of leg injuries had already taken its toll. Reed, who ran the 100 and 220 yard dashes in college and won the Mississippi high school state championship in the quarter mile, had great speed and was a skilled outfielder, strong in the fundamentals that were taught throughout the Yankee chain. "Jack wasn't much of a hitter," said Eli Grba, "but he was a great competitor and he could run and he could go get 'em in the outfield." Reed would be the perfect defensive replacement for Mantle. Houk didn't want to put a promising young player like Joe Pepitone in that role, for he wanted Pepitone to get his at bats in the minor leagues and learn to hit. Reed, on the other hand, was 28, and not a hot young prospect. He would be happy just to make the team.

Nineteen sixty-one was the first year that Joe Dimaggio rejoined the Yankees as a spring training instructor. His role was largely ceremonial, but he appeared on the field daily and occasionally worked with the outfielders. "We'd be out there taking fly balls," recalled Roger Repoz, "and he'd walk out there and say, 'Good morning, everybody, how're you doing.' Then he'd go in, get a massage, play a round of golf and maybe sign some autographs." The younger Yankees were in awe of Dimaggio. "Just his presence impressed you and put you on guard," said Lee Thomas. "You just didn't go up and start talking to him," said Reed. "I was afraid to."

Dimaggio surprised many of the young players, who had heard of his legendary aloofness, with his friendliness. "He and I got along pretty good," said Pisoni, "I guess because we were both Italians. When we went on bus trips in spring training, Joe would always sit right behind the driver. Nobody would sit next to him. You didn't sit where he sits." Not even old teammates like Berra and Ford sat next to Dimaggio. "About our second trip," Pisoni said, "I was walking by him and he grabbed me by the arm. He said, 'Hey, Dago' and told me to sit next to him."

Richard Ben Cramer, who wrote a scathing biography of Dimaggio, recounted numerous episodes of Joe's frugality and portrayed him as a nearly obsessive miser. According to Cramer's account, Dimaggio was an overbearing freeloader who felt that, as a legend, he should pay for nothing and extend no courtesy for free. The young Yankee players, however, remembered Dimaggio much differently. It was exciting to have him in camp, Pisoni recalled, but the real highlight was the presence of Marilyn Monroe.

Divorced since 1955, Dimaggio and Monroe had begun dating again after the actress's divorce from Arthur Miller. Monroe spent some time in St. Petersburg that spring, much to the delight of the Yankee players. They saw her sitting behind home plate, took note of her outfits, and sought a pretense to meet her. Dimaggio was a very possessive man, and one didn't simply walk up to his girlfriend and start a conversation. Berra, Skowron and a few other veterans therefore plotted as to how they could arrange to meet the beautiful actress. Finally, they nominated Skowron to approach Dimaggio and tell him they wanted to take him to dinner. And, if he would like to bring a guest, which they knew he would, that guest, who they knew would be Marilyn Monroe, would be more than welcome to join them. Skowron walked over and talked to Dimaggio for a few minutes and came back bubbling with enthusiasm. Not only did Dimaggio accept, Skowron reported, he insisted on paying. For Berra, a notorious tightwad, this was a dream come true. Dinner with Marilyn Monroe, and it was free.

Archie Moore spent the 1964 season with the Yankees, and remembered walking into the coffee shop in the Yankee Clipper Hotel to get a dish of ice cream late one night. Moore found only one person there — Joe Dimaggio. He hesitated, unsure whether he should go in, but Dimaggio motioned him over to his table and talked to the 22-year-old rookie for quite a while. It was an experience Moore would never forget — just Archie Moore and Joe Dimaggio, talking like old friends. He cannot understand the portrayal of Dimaggio as unfriendly and hostile and attributed it to Joe's suspicion of the media. "He was a very kind, personable man," Moore said.

Steve Whitaker had similar memories of the Yankee legend. "I'd walk into a restaurant in Fort Lauderdale after I stopped playing," he said, "and Joe would be sitting at a table in the corner with some of his goombahs. I'd hear somebody say, 'Hey, Whit.' He'd always wave me over and include me. I'd go to a place and even if I was with other people, he'd come over, sit down at our table, be very cordial and sign autographs."

Dimaggio also helped Moore and Whitaker with their outfield play, as he did with Jack Reed in 1961. He told reporters that Reed was a fine outfielder with a natural knack for getting a jump on a fly ball. One day, Reed made two shoestring catches in an exhibition game against the Cardinals. "The next day," he recalled, "I was standing out in center field and Joe walked up to me and said, 'How did you learn to do that? I never could do that.' I thought, 'Man, are you kidding me? You're the best center fielder that ever played the game and you're telling me you couldn't do that?'" Dimaggio told Reed that he had always been weak at coming in on line drives. The ice broken, Reed started asking questions about outfield play and Dimaggio opened up. He spent the next hour and a half talking to Reed about playing center field. "He told me," said Reed, "that when you play against the same people year after year, you know their tendencies, and you know the pitch that's coming because the shortstop signals it to you. If the batter is a pull hitter and the pitch is a changeup, you know he's going to pull it, so he would take off before the pitch ever got to the plate. Every now and then you'll get burned, he told me, but 99 times out of 100 you won't get hurt and you'll probably make a catch you wouldn't have made otherwise."

In the early spring of '61, Reed played a few games, replacing Mantle in the late innings, but didn't have to cut loose with any throws. Finally, in a game against the Cardinals, Alex Grammas got a base hit to right center. Reed went over, cut it off, and knew he would have to make his first hard throw of the spring. "When I let it go," he recalled, "I thought my arm came off. It hurt that bad. I thought, 'That's it. I'm not going to be able to do it.'" About a week later, however, Reed woke up one morning and his arm felt fine. Trainer Joe Soares told him he had probably torn adhesions loose with his throw and that the arm had healed. From that day on, he had no further trouble, and made the opening day roster. For Reed, however, the 1961 season was a series of trips between Richmond and New York. He appeared in his first major league game in late April, but was injured and, when Bob Cerv was acquired from the Angels, was sent back to Richmond. After the two for one trade for Bud Daley, he was recalled, but with Mantle enjoying a rare stretch of good health, spent nearly all of his time on the bench. By mid–July, he had only two at bats, and was again returned to Richmond.

In early September, with the roster limits expanded, Reed was recalled once more. By the time the season ended, in his three stretches in New York, he had played in a total of 28 games, nearly all as a defensive replacement, and managed two hits in 13 at bats.

Reed got into three World Series games as a defensive replacement, and was on the field for the last out of the finale. It had been quite a year for a man who, during the winter, was expecting to quit baseball, couldn't throw a ball across the room, and had been dropped from the Yankee roster. In November, he received a check for $7,389.13, his share of the World Series money.

Reed spent the entire 1962 and 1963 seasons caddying for Mantle, Blanchard, Lopez and Berra. On a Sunday evening in Detroit in 1962, he had the biggest night of his career. On that evening, Reed made headlines, not with his glove or his legs, but with his bat. He started the afternoon as he began most Yankee games, on the bench, as the Yankees faced Tiger righthander Frank Lary, the "Yankee Killer." When Lary pitched against New York, the Yankees were usually in for a long day.

June 24, 1962 was indeed a long day for the Yankees, but it was a very short one for Frank Lary. On April 13, Lary had picked up where he left off the previous year, beating the Yankees again, in a game played in Detroit amidst swirling snow, drizzling rain, and temperatures that dropped as low as 36 degrees. In the seventh inning, with the Tigers trailing 3–2, Lary tripled in the tying run. While traversing the slick basepaths, he pulled a thigh muscle and had to be replaced by a pinch runner. The muscle would heal, but Lary's shoulder, damaged by pitching in the miserable conditions, would not. "I can't tell you exactly how I hurt my arm," Lary said recently. "Actually, it didn't hurt. I just lost my fastball. I didn't have the zip."

On June 24, Lary was hammered for six runs in the first inning and another in the second before leaving for a pinch hitter. Yet, his good fortune against the Yankees continued, for his Tiger teammates hit another sore-armed former star, Bob Turley, with equal effect. Turley walked the first two batters to face him, gave up a three run homer to Purnal Goldy, walked another, and made an abrupt exit.

The Tigers tied the score 7–7 in the sixth inning against Stafford. Then the Yankee and Tiger hitters went into a deep slumber. Fourteen runs had been scored in six innings, but no one crossed the plate for the next fifteen innings. Stafford, Bridges, Clevenger, Daley and Bouton stymied the Tigers, while Jerry Casale, Ron Nischwitz, Ronnie Kline, Hank Aguirre and Terry Fox throttled the Yankees. Fox, a curve-balling short inning specialist, hurled eight innings, the 14th through the 21st, without facing a serious threat.

The Tigers threatened in the eleventh when they loaded the bases against Clevenger with no outs. Rocky Colavito opened with a triple, and Houk ordered two intentional walks to fill the bases and create a force play. Chico Fernandez hit a line drive to short left, not deep enough for Colavito to score. The Tigers then attempted a squeeze play, as Colavito raced for the plate with the pitch. If Dick Brown could get the ball on the ground, the game would be over. Brown, however, popped the bunt into the air. Catcher Berra caught it and easily doubled Colavito off third.

Mantle had played both games of a doubleheader the previous day, and retired after the seventh inning in favor of Pepitone. With left hander Hank Aguirre on the mound in the 13th, Houk sent up the right-handed Linz to bat for Pepitone. In the bottom of the 13th, Reed went to right field. He had batted only nine times thus far in 1962 and had gotten his first hit of the season just a week earlier.

Three innings after Reed's appearance in right field, Bouton took the mound for New York. In the spring, the rookie right hander made the Yankee roster somewhat unexpectedly. Bouton had not been a sought-after bonus player, and was not even a very good high school pitcher. Since then, however, he had matured physically and acquired a major league fastball, discarding the assortment of junk he had thrown as a skinny teenager. In the minors, Bouton ate constantly, which was the way ballplayers added bulk in the pre-steroid era of the 1950s and '60s. The best way to get bigger (and presumably stronger) was to eat things that were especially fattening, such as milk shakes, pizza, and gravy. Bouton grew from 150 to 180 pounds and, fortunately, didn't destroy his digestive tract in the process.

After leading the Carolina League in ERA in 1960, and having a good season at Amarillo in 1961, Bouton came to the Yankee camp in 1962, but was a long shot to make the team. In dispatches from Fort Lauderdale, he was twice mid-identified as Frank Bouton.

Bouton's big chance came in an exhibition game against the Cardinals. He was not scheduled to pitch that day, but when the game went into extra innings, Houk inserted the youngster in the tenth. Bouton pitched four hitless innings, then lost the game in the 14th on an error. Houk took notice and used Bouton more and more. When the club went north, the right hander was still on the roster.

Bouton was used sparingly in the early season. He pitched a shutout against Washington in his first start, was unscored upon in his first fifteen innings, then had some rough outings. By June 24, the shutout represented his only big league win. Yet, Bouton had become a valuable man on a weak staff. He pitched whenever called upon, in any role. Many pitchers who had been much more successful than Bouton in the minor leagues didn't last in the majors because they only prospered when starting every four days. Bouton was adaptable. He could start irregularly, pitch long relief, or throw short relief.

As in spring training, extra innings proved Bouton's salvation. After entering the contest in the 16th, he shut the Tigers down, matching Fox frame for frame. Meanwhile, the game had surpassed the American League endurance record of four hours and fifty eight minutes, set by Baltimore and Boston in 1954. The major league record of five hours and nineteen minutes, established by Brooklyn and Boston in 1940, fell shortly thereafter.

"I pitched in that game," said Jim Coates. "Hell, all of us pitched. It was just a long, long, long ballgame." "There were far more players in the clubhouse than there were in the dugout," said Rollie Sheldon. "We'd consumed all the beer and they had to send out for more." Lopez pinch hit in the seventh, took a shower and snuck back to the hotel, figuring everyone would be joining him soon. He sat alone in his room watching the rest of the game on television. In the 20th inning, sportswriter Matt Dennis of the Windsor (Ont.) Star got up to leave. "My visa just expired," he explained.

In the top of the 22nd, with the crowd dwindling and the Tiger Stadium concession stands closed due to Michigan labor laws, Reed stepped to the plate with one out and Maris at first. He drove a Phil Regan pitch deep to left field. "I really thought it would be a double," Reed said. "I didn't look up, but I knew I hit it good. I didn't have the kind of power where I could stand there and watch it. I was one of those guys who had 'warning track power.' By the time I got to second base, the umpire was telling me it was a home run." Reed's drive landed in the lower left field stands and the Yankees had a 9–7 lead. "I think Jack was the only guy still strong enough to knock one out after all that time," said Sheldon.

Bouton retired the Tigers in the bottom of the 22nd. Blanchard caught Norm Cash's fly ball for the final out just as the game clock hit six hours and fifty nine minutes. Joe Falls of *The Detroit Free Press* was the official scorer. "[M]y clever little mind was still working," Falls wrote a few years later. "I figured, who will ever remember 6:59 as the longest game in baseball history. So I shouted out the time, 'Seven hours.'" It had been the longest game in major league history by nearly two hours, and broke the Yankee mark for most innings, eclipsing the 19 innings they played against the Indians in 1918.

The Hall of Fame asked for two pictures, one of Reed rounding second and another of Maris greeting him at the plate. "I got more mail than Mantle for a couple of days," Reed said. He also got 25 telegrams, including one from Yankee owner Dan Topping.

In addition to the heroics of Bouton and Reed, there were several noteworthy performances. Bobby Richardson had a record-equaling eleven official at bats. Rocky Colavito had seven hits, raising his average from .268 to .285. The seven Yankee hurlers threw a total of 316 pitches, all of them caught by 37-year-old Yogi Berra. Tiger Stadium concessionaires sold more than

32,000 hot dogs, 34,000 sodas and 41,000 bottles of beer, before the stands had to close at 8:15. Seventy six baseballs took part in the action, leaving plate umpire Bill McKinley with just 20 left by the end of the game.

The home run in Detroit was the high point of Reed's career. He hit .302 in 43 at bats in 1962 and, in 1963, with Mantle injured for much of the year, Maris out for long stretches and Blanchard and Lopez again starting frequently, Reed got in 106 games. He got off to a strong start at the plate, but faded to bat only .205 in 73 at bats. On a Yankee club that rarely stole bases, however, he pilfered five in six attempts.

Reed did not appear in either the 1962 or 1963 Series, although he collected a full share from each. In the spring of 1964, he became a player-coach at Richmond. Knowing that his playing career was likely to be of limited duration, Reed had set his sights on managing. He had plenty of time to observe from the bench and managed along with Houk, often asking the manager why he had made a certain move. "He took it the right way," Reed said. "He knew I wasn't second-guessing him. He would always tell me why he did something." Houk did the same thing for Dick Howser, who finished his career in New York. Howser sat beside Houk on the bench, and soaked up the lessons that made him a fine manager in New York and a World Series winner in Kansas City.

Richmond manager Preston Gomez let Reed manage the club for several games at the end of the 1964 season. He began his full-time managing career in 1965 at Fort Lauderdale, in the Class A Florida State League. "I had a lot of young kids," he said, "four college boys and the rest right out of high school. It was kind of like being a father to them." Reed put his acquired knowledge to good use in his first job, winning the Florida State League championship. He was moved up to Columbus of the Southern League in 1966, and managed Binghamton in 1968, before leaving baseball to join his family's soybean business. "I didn't have a real interesting career," Reed said, "but I enjoyed every minute of it. I enjoyed the whole experience. I accomplished something in my life that I'd dreamed of. It might not have been exactly what I wanted, but to play on a world championship team two years in a row — I don't know how you can beat that."

With Mantle back on a full time basis, the Yankees played well in July. By the end of the month, they held a 5 game lead over Los Angeles and 5½ over the Twins. Two days later, the club received some unanticipated good news. Kubek, who had expected to spend the entire season in the Army, was going to be discharged early. This presented Houk with a pleasant problem, for he now had two all star shortstops. Tresh had proven to be much more than a stopgap replacement. His fielding, which had been a little shaky in spring training, had improved immensely, and he had shown more power than anyone expected. Tresh drove in more runs than Houk had a right to hope for, sharing the team lead with Maris at the end of June.

With the lead and the addition of Kubek, giving them a stronger lineup than they'd had all season, the Yankees seemed poised to wrap up the pennant. Kubek had not played much in the Army, but after working out for only a few days, he started in left field. In his first game, Kubek hit a three run homer as the Yanks routed Minnesota 14–1. Tresh served notice that he was not going to be easily displaced, however, by hitting two home runs, giving him a total of 12 for the year. He hit three more home runs in rapid succession, tying the team record for shortstops held by coach Frank Crosetti.

The Yankees had not had a regular left fielder all season. Lopez, Berra and Blanchard shared time, but none of the three was having a great season. If Houk had to create an opening for either Tresh or Kubek, left field was the place. Tresh had not played the outfield since high school. Kubek played 135 games in the outfield in four years under Stengel. The logical move would seem to have been to leave Tresh at short and move Kubek to left. Houk, however, liked to demonstrate his loyalty to veterans. Kubek wasn't about to lose his starting job because he'd been drafted. Besides, Kubek made the double play better than Tresh and had more range. Therefore, Houk moved Tresh to left field and returned Kubek to short. The players kiddingly accused Crosetti of masterminding the move to preserve his share of the home run record.

Tresh adapted quickly to the outfield, and won a Gold Glove in 1965. Even at shortstop, anyone could see he had a knack for getting a jump on a fly ball or popup. "Having been a short-stop all my life," he said, "I think I developed a lot of the tools that are necessary to be a good outfielder. A shortstop has to be able to go back on a ball real well, and has to have a pretty strong arm. You've also got to be able to run. I think I had the tools to do it"

Despite the return of Kubek, the Yanks couldn't shake the Angels and Twins. On August 24, leading the Angels by 5 and the Twins by 6, the Yanks began a five game series in Baltimore, which was out of the race. "If we can get back to Yankee Stadium from Baltimore," Houk said, "with as big a lead as we have now, I'll feel we're pretty well set for the rest of the season." The series was the final leg of a 17 game road trip to four cities. It would be a grueling weekend, beginning with a six o'clock arrival from Los Angeles Friday morning. There would be a twi-night doubleheader Friday evening, a day-night twin bill on Saturday, and a single game on Sunday.

Doubleheaders were hell on the Yanks, with their lack of pitching depth. Bouton was routed in the first game of Friday's doubleheader, and lost 6–2 to Chuck Estrada. The second game was even worse. Turley gave up nine runs and Sheldon surrendered five more in a 14–2 loss.

On Saturday, the Yanks were forced to employ two more second line starters, Coates and Daley, and the result was two more losses. Daley pitched well, but in both games, the bullpen was shelled. Bridges was hammered in the first game, and Arroyo, back from the disabled list, gave up the winning run in the second. Finally, on Sunday, in the final game of the series, the Yankees were able to use a top starter, Ford, who was opposed by Robin Roberts of the Orioles.

If the Ford-Roberts match up had taken place a few years earlier, it would have featured two of baseball's top pitchers. Roberts, a graduate of Michigan State, joined the Phillies in 1948, and for six straight years, 1950 through 1955, won at least 20 games. From 1952 through 1955, he led the league in victories each season. Roberts was a power pitcher, and as he lost speed on his fastball, his performance declined markedly. From 1956 through 1960, he was 73–87, losing 22 games in 1956 and posting high earned run averages nearly every year. Even in his good seasons, Roberts had given up a lot of home runs, but for three years in a row in the late '50s, he gave up more than 40.

In 1961, Roberts hit bottom. Bothered by a shoulder injury, he was 1–10, with an ERA of 5.85. At the age of 35, the Phillies believed he was finished, and sold him to the Yankees. Philadelphia had the worst team in baseball in 1961, and was not about to rebuild with 35-year-old pitchers who had won just one game. The Yankees, who needed pitchers, believed that Roberts could be useful as a spot starter. With Terry and Stafford vulnerable to military callup, they were willing to pay Roberts' $30,000 salary for insurance. Robin was determined to prove that he was not finished, and declared that his arm was fine, but he was having difficulty adjusting from being a power pitcher to one with finesse. The Yankees had a history of rejuvenating older pitchers, and perhaps the magic of Johnny Sain could make the old veteran a useful pitcher again.

Roberts was adequate, but no more, in exhibition games, pitching just nine innings. Between off days and rainy weather, he wasn't able to get into a regular season game. On April 25, without having pitched a single inning, Roberts was released. Neither Terry nor Stafford had been drafted, and his young pitchers, Houk said, had developed more quickly than he expected. The Major didn't think Roberts could pitch in relief, and didn't believe he was better than Ford, Terry, Stafford, Sheldon or Bouton.

Roberts' prospects weren't encouraging. "Once he lost the hop on his fastball," wrote Arthur Daley, "he lost everything." "Robbie can't even throw his fastball past your Aunt Matilda," said

Phillie manager Gene Mauch. The Mets and Colts, who desperately needed pitching, had both passed him up in the expansion draft. The Mets' pitching had proven even worse than anticipated but, when Roberts was cut loose by the Yankees, they declined to sign him. "If he couldn't help the Yankees," said a Met spokesman, "how could he help us?"

Roberts contacted a number of teams asking for a tryout. He also began to work on a changeup. After almost a month of waiting, Roberts was signed by the Orioles and made his first appearance on May 21, pitching two innings of perfect relief. Soon, he was given a start and pitched well enough to join the regular rotation. By the time he faced the Yankees on August 26, he had an 8–6 record and the second best earned run average in the American League. He'd come up with a good changeup curve and had become a control pitcher who hit spots.

Roberts believed that his success with the Orioles proved that the Yankees had not given him a fair shot and wanted to show them face-to-face. He did just that, pitching a five hitter, beating Ford 2–1 and giving the Orioles a sweep of the five game series. After the final out, Roberts leaped into the air and did a complete pirouette, as if he had won the final game of the World Series. "He ran into the clubhouse," recalled Jack Fisher, "and was jumping up and down, hollering and hooting. I never saw a guy celebrate a win more than he did. To beat the Yankees and Whitey Ford, that was just great to see." It was not so great for Houk, who saw the New York lead dwindle to three games over Minnesota and Los Angeles, who were tied for second.

On August 30th, the Yanks lost another doubleheader, this time to Cleveland, again with two second line pitchers, Coates and Bouton. The seemingly inevitable pennant clinching was becoming evitable. New York had lost 13 of 21 and the Twins were just two games behind. The surge of doubleheaders, lengthy travel itineraries and virtually no off days had put a tremendous strain on a thin pitching staff. At one point, the club played 17 games in 14 days. Houk, as always, was optimistic. "We're putting a lot of pressure on those other clubs now," he said. "The closer they get to us, the tougher it gets on them." Yankee fans hoped Houk's crew wouldn't put too much more pressure on the Angels and Twins.

With six open dates in September, the pitching staff had time to rest and regroup. Nothing could rejuvenate a team like a visit from the Kansas City Athletics, who were swept by the Yankees during the first weekend in September. The Angels followed the Athletics and split four games, both of Los Angeles' wins coming, as had so many Angel wins, on dramatic ninth inning rallies. On the 9th, the Yanks lost twice to the Red Sox, their fourth doubleheader loss in three weeks. The Twins were just 2½ behind. The next day, Mantle hit the 400th home run of his great career, and the Yankees won, behind Terry's 21st victory.

On the 18th, the lead was only three games, as the Yanks just couldn't shake the stubborn Twins. There was no powerful pennant surge, as there had been in 1960 and 1961. The 1962 Yanks trudged to the flag, winning the pennant in workmanlike fashion, with 12 fewer wins than in 1961. Had the Tigers played as well as they had the previous year, they might have won. During the final month the Yankees were 17–9, while the Twins were 15–11 and the Angels 11–16. Finally, on September 25, the Yankees clinched their 27th pennant, as Ford gained his 17th win by beating the Senators.

It had been an unusual season, much different from 1961. Mantle and Maris, who combined for 115 homers in '61, hit 63 in '62. Mantle, although missing five weeks with his thigh injury, hit .321 with 30 homers and 89 RBI, good enough to win the MVP award for the third and final time. Maris hit 33 home runs, the third highest total of his career, but was a major disappointment to everyone, including himself. "I'm just counting the days until the season's over," he said in September. "I'm ready to write the whole thing off." Never again, however, would Maris have a season as good as his frustrating 1962 campaign.

Ford and Arroyo, who had 40 wins and 29 saves in '61, had 18 wins and 7 saves a year later. Ford, troubled by a sore arm, dropped from 25 wins to 17. Arroyo went from 15 wins to 1, 29 saves to 7 and his ERA ballooned from 2.19 to 4.76. Howard dropped from a .348 average to .279. Berra had the worst season of his career, batting just .228. The slack was taken up by Tresh, the Rookie of the Year, who batted .286 with 20 home runs and 93 RBI, Terry, who was 23–12, Bridges, 8–4 with 18 saves, Richardson, who hit .302 and Boyer, who improved his average from .224 to .272 and his home run production from 8 to 18.

Richardson became the first Yankee to get 200 hits since Phil Rizzuto, established a career high with eight home runs and finished second in the MVP voting. "Bobby should have been the MVP that year," said Terry. "Mantle said that himself. He had a hell of a year. The last day of the season, Mickey hit his 30th homer. That's what got him the MVP. It would have been hard to give it to a guy who hit 29 homers." Mantle agreed. That Christmas, he sent the Richardsons a card addressed to the Most Valuable Player.

The pennant-clinching celebration was subdued, with the exception of the rookies, who had never won before. "It's something we expected all along," said Maris. Most of the players seemed more interested in watching the Floyd Patterson-Sonny Liston championship fight on television than talking to Mel Allen for the cameras in the clubhouse. During the last week of the season, Houk rested his regulars, arranged his pitching rotation, and waited to see his World Series opponent emerge from the wild National League pennant scramble.

◆ 9 ◆

Ralph's Redemption
The 1962 World Series

The career of many a promising pitcher has been ended by a dramatic home run. Ralph Branca, who had been a 20-game winner at the age of 21, was never the same after giving up Bobby Thomson's historic blast. Branca was just 25 when he surrendered the home run to Thomson, but was out of baseball five years later, after winning only 12 more games. Mitch Williams totally lost his control after giving up Joe Carter's Series-winning home run in 1993. Donnie Moore lost his life, committing suicide less than three years after his dramatic failure in 1986.

Ralph Terry was 24 years old in 1960, a year younger than Branca had been in 1951. He'd signed with the Yankees in 1954, upon his graduation from high school. Bidding was heavy, and Terry actually signed a written contract with the Cardinals before he inked the Yankee pact. Commissioner Frick, however, ruled that Terry's telephone agreement and confirming telegram to the Yankees preceded the Cardinal contract, and awarded him to New York. In July, 1956, after just two years in the minor leagues, Terry made his big league debut, beating the second place Red Sox before a big crowd at Fenway Park. "That was the first game I pitched," Terry recalled, "and I said, 'Boy, this is really easy." It was not that easy. Shortly thereafter, Terry lost to the last place Orioles, and a month later he was back in Denver.

Terry pitched for the Yankees during the first part of the 1957 season, that is, he pitched a lot of batting practice, appearing in only seven games. On June 15, the trading deadline, he was called into Stengel's office and told that he was being traded to Kansas City. Terry was not the primary player in the transaction, for the big story was the departure from New York of Billy Martin, fresh off the infamous Copacabana incident. "I told Casey," Terry recalled, "'It seems like you're giving up a hell of a lot for what you got.' Casey hadn't even looked up. He was in tears. He said, 'Yeah, I didn't make the trade. George Weiss made the trade. That Martin, he's one hell of a player.' Oh, he loved Billy. He said, 'Look, kid, you go to Kansas City and you'll pitch regular there and you'll learn how to pitch.'" Terry concluded the conversation by telling Stengel he was going to be out to beat him every time he took the mound against the Yankees.

With the second division Athletics, Terry was 4–11 for the remainder of the 1957 season, and 11–13 as a regular starter the following year. As Stengel had predicted, the youngster was getting plenty of work, hurling 217 innings in 1958. In 1959, Terry got off to a poor start. "It was a rainy Friday night," he recalled, "and I was standing in short right field with Hector Lopez. There had been rumors of a trade, but we thought it might be Cleveland or Boston. There was never anything said about New York." Manager Harry Craft approached the two men and said, "We've made a little trade." "Where are we going," Terry and Lopez asked. "You're going to New York," Craft replied. Terry and Lopez had been traded to the Yankees for pitchers Tom Sturdivant and Johnny Kucks and infielder Jerry Lumpe. "Well, alright!" Terry thought. He was going where he'd wanted to be in the first place.

Terry was an intellectual, inquisitive sort, who had studied psychology at Northeastern Oklahoma, Southwest Missouri and the University of Kansas. He was calm almost to the point of eccentricity. "Ralph used to be on the mound," Eli Grba said, "and if a plane would go over, he would step off and look at the plane. Stengel used to say, 'Look at that SOB. He's crazy.'"

Many thought Terry was too smart, too calm and too nice for his own good. They said he lacked a "killer instinct" and was too hesitant to challenge hitters. In his early years, Terry carried on a passionate love affair with a tantalizing slow curve. "Ralph had great stuff," said Bud Daley, "but he was what we called a 'Ben Franklin.' He was always experimenting. He had a good fastball, a good slider, and a good curve, but he would always screw around and try to come up with something different."

"He had a great arm," said Joe Demaestri, "but Ralph would fool around with this curve ball he had. It used to drive me crazy. He could blow the ball by these guys, but he would start fooling around with that little curve ball and it would get him into trouble. Rocky Colavito used to love to see him throw it. He'd hit it so far it would take a twenty dollar cab ride to find it. I told him, 'Ralph, forget that curve ball. Just throw it by them.'"

"Bud and Joe are one hundred percent right," agreed John Blanchard. "Ralph was always thinking out there. He should have just thrown the ball instead of trying to get cute and hit the corners."

Terry had a habit of always carrying a ball with him, rotating it, fondling it and talking to it. "We used to watch Ralph," said Demaestri. "He'd take the ball, look at it, turn it, talk to it, turn it some more, talk to it." "Whenever he was on an airplane or a bus," said Blanchard, "he'd have a baseball in his hands. He was always feeling it." "The ball was a symbol for my concentration," said psychology student Terry.

Sensitivity can be dangerous when one is carrying weighty burdens, such as losing a World Series. Terry got married shortly after the end of the 1960 season and, wanting to get away from the memories of Mazeroski, honeymooned in Mexico. One morning, when room service delivered his breakfast, they also brought a Spanish newspaper. Terry,

Ralph Terry gave up Bill Mazeroski's game winning home run in the 1960 Series, then came back to win the deciding game against the Giants two years later. He won 56 games from 1961 through 1963.

who couldn't read Spanish, recognized only two words: Mazeroski and Terry. He asked his wife if she knew of any good hotels in Tibet.

Terry, however, appeared in St. Petersburg in the spring of '61 without a trace of psychological scarring. "Ralph didn't let those things bother him," said Grba. Terry had the support of optimistic new manager Houk and, more important, found that Yankee fans did not blame him for what had happened. "The Yankee fans, by god, were just great," Terry said. "They're the greatest. They never came down on me for losing that game, never held it against me. A lot of fans will just run you out of town, but, by god, they were just great." Terry would not go the way of Branca, Williams and Moore. "Hell, they loved Mitch Williams when he struck out the last guy in Atlanta to get them to the World Series," Terry said. "They thought he was wonderful." After Carter's home run, Williams discovered that things had changed. "If I was him," said Terry, "I'd go back to my ranch in Texas and see how high a stack of $3.5 million a year adds up to."

Terry had arm trouble in mid–1961, and missed several starts. He finished strong, pitching two straight shutouts in August and accumulating a 25 inning scoreless string. For the season, Terry was 16–3, and pitched the pennant clinching game in Baltimore, the second straight year he had won the clincher.

The 1962 season was easily Terry's finest in the major leagues. He won 23 games, led American League pitchers in wins, innings pitched, and home runs allowed, and set personal highs in nearly every category. During the second half of the year, Terry was 16–5, and his 23 wins were the most for a Yankee righthander since 1928. Terry had learned to challenge hitters, which resulted in 40 home runs given up, still a Yankee record, but walked just 57 men in 299 innings. With Ford bothered by arm trouble from time to time, and the Yankee bullpen a near disaster after Arroyo's arm injury, Terry was a savior. Had each league had its own Cy Young Award in 1962, Terry might well have been the American League recipient. The final test, however, would come in the World Series against the San Francisco Giants where, after two years of frustration, Terry longed for an opportunity to vindicate himself.

The Giants were an exhausted team when the Series began. With seven days to go in the season, they had trailed the Dodgers by four games. All the Dodgers needed were a couple of wins to lock up the pennant. They couldn't get them. "Oh, that was a tough week," said Dodger catcher Norm Sherry. "The Giants played a lot of their games in the afternoon and we played all of ours at night. We'd all be listening to the ballgames on the radio and we'd say, 'The Giants got beat. All we have to do is win tonight.'" So we'd tear the door off trying to get out there. But we couldn't do it. That was frustrating. All we had to do was win one ballgame. It was the worst disappointment I had in baseball." "It seemed as though everybody was in a little slump," said Dodger second baseman Larry Burright. "Sure you think about it. Maybe just thinking about trying to get that run across, you try a little too hard. Guys say there's no pressure, but you've got to think about it."

When the final weekend began, the Dodgers had a two game margin. Both teams were at home, with the Giants hosting the Colts and the Dodgers playing the Cardinals. On Friday night, the Cardinals beat the Dodgers in extra innings and the Giants were rained out. The Cardinals shut out the Dodgers on Saturday, while the Giants split a doubleheader with the Colts, making the margin a single game entering the final day. A Dodger win or a Giant loss would put the Dodgers in the Series.

Los Angeles not only couldn't win, they couldn't score a run. For the second day in a row, they were shut out, losing 1–0 on a home run by the Cardinals' Gene Oliver. A homer by Mays gave the Giants a 2–1 victory over the Colts and set up a best-of-three playoff for the National League pennant.

The Giants entered the playoffs hot, while the Dodgers were ice cold. Los Angeles had just seven hits and no runs in their last two games and hadn't scored a run in 21 innings. The trend continued in the first game of the playoff, as Billy Pierce shut out the Dodgers again, 8–0. Sandy Koufax, the Dodger ace who had been sidelined since July with a circulatory ailment in the index finger of his left hand, tried to pitch but was knocked out after one inning.

At the end of the first playoff game, the Dodgers had been shut out for 30 innings, and it looked as though their season was about to end. Leo Durocher, a Dodger coach, pulled out a lucky t-shirt, undershorts, and socks from the Giant pennant miracle of 1951, and put them on for the second game. Someone asked Dark, the Giant shortstop in '51, if he had retained any mementoes of that race. "Only Willie Mays," he replied.

Somehow, Durocher's vintage undershirt overcame Mays, and the Dodgers pulled themselves up from the mat to tie the Series with a dramatic 8–7 win that consumed four hours and eighteen minutes. The Dodgers scored the winning run in the ninth without the benefit of a hit. Don Drysdale, making his fourth start in nine days, was the first of a parade of LA pitchers. The Dodgers used nineteen players and the Giants twenty three. A total of thirteen pitchers took the mound.

The two teams were not only tied after 164 games, they had split the 20 games they had played against each other. The Giants and Dodgers were also at the point of exhaustion as they prepared for the third game. When the Dodgers went to the ninth inning with a 4–2 lead, it looked as though the Yankees, who had flown to San Francisco, might have to jet south.

Dodger shortstop Maury Wills was running the Giants ragged. The Giants did everything but erect a barbed wire fence on the basepaths to attempt to slow Wills and the other Dodger swifties, but it wasn't working. In August, they flooded the path between first and second to turn it to mud. Before one game, Duke Snider laid down and pretended to do a crawl stroke. When the Giants went to Los Angeles, they found a pink watering can next to their dugout, labeled Ed Bailey's Chavez Ravine 1st Base Watering Can. Before the playoff game in San Francisco, manager Dark had the crew put enough sand on the basepath to turn it into a beach. "Why don't you play it like men," umpire Jocko Conlan said angrily to Dark, before ordering a remake of the infield.

In the third playoff game, Wills stole three bases, including two in the seventh inning, when he scored the Dodgers' fourth run. Wills' final steal was his 104th of the season, breaking the record of 96 set by Ty Cobb in 1915. Cobb's steals, of course, took place in the course of a 154 game season. After 154 games, Wills had 95 stolen bases. Frick said he would need to conform to the 154 game standard in order to set an untarnished record, but no one seemed to notice, and Wills' record was duly placed in the books. Apparently, asterisks were only for Roger Maris who, with the setting of another record, was dragged through the muck again. *The Sporting News* pointed out Wills' co-operative nature and compared it to the attitude of Maris the previous year, failing to mention that Wills' pursuit of Cobb had none of the media hysteria associated with Maris's ordeal.

Wills' season ended two innings later. While hitting only two balls out of the infield, the Giants scored four runs and, finally, clinched the National League pennant. For the Dodgers, it was one of the most frustrating episodes of a very frustrating existence. Singer Andy Williams, a devoted Los Angeles fan, was so upset he kicked in the side of his new sports car. Former Dodger Gil Hodges, watching the games on television, wept.

In the opening game of the Series, the Giants played like a team that had just been through a grueling pennant race. Their pitching staff was in shambles, and although they were the home team, the Giants arrived in San Francisco later than their opponents. Their pitcher, Billy O'Dell, had started four days earlier and pitched in relief two days after that. The Yankees, fresh and rested, won easily 6–2, as Boyer's home run snapped a 2–2 tie. Ford's scoreless inning streak was broken at 33⅔ innings, but he got credit for the win, the last Series victory he would ever get. The Giant fans booed Maris every time he batted. After the pressures of 1961, Maris told reporters after the game, 1962 had been a comparative cakewalk. He responded to the booing with a two run double which iced the victory.

The next day, Terry pitched a nearly flawless game, but was bested by Giant ace Jack Sanford, who pitched an even better one. Terry's luck wasn't any better than it had been in past post-season contests. The Giants got a scratch run in the first inning, when Chuck Hiller, leading off, hit a pop fly into short right field. Maris came charging in, lunged, caught the ball, then dropped it as his glove banged against his knee. Hiller reached second and scored on a sacrifice bunt and an infield grounder. In the seventh, Willie McCovey hit a mammoth home run into the right field seats. Sanford, making his third start in seven days, was pitching with a bad head cold. He'd lost five pounds, and was wearing pants two sizes smaller than normal. Sanford weakened in the late innings, but every ball the Yankees hit hard was right at a Giant fielder. Sanford called it the best game he'd ever pitched. What had he done for his cold during the game, he was asked. "I blew my nose," he replied.

Following the 2–0 loss, the Yankees and Giants were even at a game apiece and Terry was 0–4 in World Series play. The next day, Tanya Terry, back in Larned, Oklahoma, gave birth to a son, Frank Gabe, to be known as Gabe. Perhaps the new baby would bring better luck.

Bill Stafford beat Billy Pierce 3–2 in Game Three, despite taking a nasty welt on his left shin from a shot off the bat of Felipe Alou in the eighth inning. Stafford picked himself up and finished the game, but his future availability was in doubt. The contest was decided on some sloppy outfielding by the Giants and aggressive baserunning by Maris, who tagged up and went to third on a fly ball to Mays. On the next play, he scored the winning run on an infield out. With the Giants trailing 3–0 in the ninth, Ed Bailey hit a two run homer that just cleared the right field wall. "If I dove for it," Maris said after the game, "I probably would have caught it. But what's the sense in diving at it? I'm not going to hit a brick wall for anyone." That was a far cry from the Maris of a few years earlier, who hit walls with abandon.

After six innings of the fourth game, the score was tied 2–2. Ford had not been sharp and left the game for a pinch hitter in the sixth. Coates took the mound to begin the seventh, but departed quickly with one out and runners at second and third. When Dark sent the powerful left handed hitting Bailey up to bat for Giant reliever Don Larsen, Houk countered by bringing Bridges in from the bullpen. It was a smart move. Dark either had to have Bailey hit against a left hander, or lose one of the biggest power threats on his bench. He elected to do the latter, sending right handed Bob Nieman up to hit for Bailey. Houk countered by walking Nieman intentionally. The Yankee manager had caused Dark to use two pinch hitters without either one of them getting to lift the bat from their shoulders.

When Harvey Kuenn popped to Boyer for the second out, bringing up second baseman Chuck Hiller, a left handed hitter, it appeared as though Bridges might escape unscathed. Dark still had McCovey in the wings, but if McCovey hit for Hiller, the bench would be barren for the last three innings. It was terrific managing. Houk had everyone exactly where he wanted them. All Bridges had to do was get Hiller out, and the inning would be over.

Hiller was in his first year as the Giants' regular second baseman, a position very few people other than Hiller ever expected him to be in. "I had a lot of people tell me I'd never play in the big leagues," he said. "From the first day I signed, it was always an uphill battle. I just said, what the hell, I'm going to keep playing and see what happens. I'm going to show you." No one was interested in Hiller when he graduated from high school, so he went to St. Thomas College in St. Paul, Minnesota. No one was interested when he graduated from college in 1956. Finally, Cleveland signed Hiller in the spring of 1957 for a $1500 bonus. After two years in the Indians' farm system, Cleveland left him unprotected in the minor league draft of 1958. The Giants selected Hiller, and sent him to Eugene, where he hit .341. The next year, 1960, he led the Texas League with a .334 mark and was named MVP.

Midway through the 1961 season, Hiller was called up to the big leagues. "It was kind of fun reminding a couple of people of what they'd said," Hiller related. "Hoot Evers was the Cleveland farm director, and he said, 'You son of a bitch, you're the only guy who ever fooled me. I didn't think you were going to play in the big leagues. You fooled me, man.'" What was the break that got Hiller to the major leagues? "If you look at my record in the minors," he said emphatically, "that's what got me to the big leagues. I was a pretty damn good player."

In the spring of 1962, Hiller, by default, became the Giant second baseman. He could hit, but his defense wasn't all that strong. His teammates nicknamed him Dr. No, after the James Bond character who had no hands. The Giants spent most of the spring talking about finding someone to replace him. They tried to obtain Joe Amalfitano, who the Colts had acquired from San Francisco in the expansion draft, but the Colts wanted too much.

Hiller played poorly in exhibition games, but with the Giants unable to acquire another infielder, he opened the season at second. Dark came to Hiller the day before the season opener and told him he was his second baseman. It wasn't a ringing endorsement, for everyone who could read a newspaper knew the Giants had been looking for a replacement. Dark said they might continue to look for one, but that Hiller was going to play until he proved he couldn't do the job. As he had done his entire career, Hiller surprised everybody but himself. He had a solid year, playing 161 games and batting .276. True to his nickname, he led the league's second basemen in errors, and hit just three home runs.

On his back, Hiller carried number 26, the number worn by Dusty Rhodes when he was the hero of the 1954 Series. Thus far in the 1962 Series, however, Hiller had not been a hero. He'd managed only two hits in thirteen at bats, and in the third game, his failure to turn a double play had allowed the Yankees to score the winning run. In his previous at bat against Ford in the fourth game, Hiller had fanned with the bases loaded.

On Bridges' third pitch, Hiller got his third hit of the Series and his fourth homer of the season, the first grand slam ever hit by a National Leaguer in World Series play. The crowd erupted as if the game were being played at Candlestick Park. The Giants were just five years removed from New York, and it seemed as though there were as many San Francisco fans as Yankee fans in the stands. Hiller's hit was the deciding blow, as the Giants won 7–3. Larsen, six years to the day from his perfect game, pitched another perfect game. He retired the only batter he faced and was the winning pitcher.

The Series was even, with Terry scheduled to oppose Sanford for a second time in Game Five at Yankee Stadium on October 9. It rained on the 9th, however, and after waiting more than an hour, Commissioner Frick postponed the game until the following day, giving Terry and Sanford four days rest. Sanford, whose Giants had been involved in a frantic pennant race, had started three times in seven days. Terry, whose Yankees had clinched the pennant on September 26, had been well-rested for Game Two. The extra day of rest figured to help Sanford more than Terry, and once again the Yankee right hander appeared to be the recipient of a bad break.

In the early innings, Terry was victimized not by the Giant sluggers Mays, McCovey and Cepeda, but by the pesky San Francisco infielders. In the third inning, shortstop Jose Pagan singled and was doubled home by Hiller. After the Yankees tied the game in the fourth on a Sanford wild pitch, Pagan hit a home run to put the Giants ahead 2–1. In the sixth, New York tied the game again on a passed ball, and Terry, despite yielding two singles in the seventh, held the Giants scoreless. Sanford was pitching a terrific game once again. In seven innings, he had yielded just three hits and struck out ten.

In the eighth inning, Tom Tresh stepped to the plate with two teammates on base and his father, ex-major league catcher Mike, watching from the stands. Tresh was a rookie, but after going through a 162 game season, making the All Star team, and playing four games in the

Series, he didn't feel like a rookie. "I felt that I belonged on that ballclub," he said. "I had produced and I felt confident I would be competitive in the Series."

Tresh was just trying to get a base hit to drive in the lead run. He did even better, connecting solidly with a Sanford fastball that was right over the middle of the plate and hitting it into the right field stands for a three run homer, a few rows above the glove of the lunging Matty Alou. "It was my biggest thrill in baseball," he said recently. "My dad played in the major leagues for twelve years and never even got into a World Series.

Anxious moments remained. In the ninth inning, with the Yankees holding a 5–2 lead, McCovey led off with a single. With one out, Tom Haller doubled McCovey home, and the tying run came to the plate. Terry had given up 40 home runs during the regular season, and four in his World Series appearances. Another would tie the game and send Terry to the showers, winless once more. Pagan, who had homered in the fifth, was at the plate. Terry retired him on a ground ball to Kubek at short. With two out, Bailey, a catcher who had hit 17 home runs in part time duty, pinch hit for Giant reliever Stu Miller. Bailey was a big left handed hitter who could reach the nearby right field seats in the Stadium. He had hit a two run homer off Stafford in Game Three. Houk considered removing Terry, but his top reliever was Bridges, who had been none too reliable late in the season and had surrendered Hiller's grand slam two days earlier. Behind Bridges was another left hander, Bud Daley. If he brought in a lefty, Houk reasoned, Alvin Dark would probably counter with Cepeda, who was on the Giant bench.

Terry remained on the mound to test his fate. He delivered and Bailey swung, lifting a high fly to deep right field. "I hit the ball good enough to go out," Bailey said after the game, "but it sank instead of taking off." Maris retreated and caught the ball a few feet in front of the right field stands. Terry finally had his first World Series win, and the Yankees had a 3–2 lead as the Series returned to San Francisco. In the Yankee locker room, Terry was congratulated by Casey Stengel, while Tresh got a bearhug from his father.

Early in the Series, columnist Arthur Daley commented on the cold that was characteristic of Candlestick Park, but added that at least it never rained. Since moving to San Francisco, Daley pointed out, the Giants had averaged just one rainout per year. But on October 12, Typhoon Freida swept down from Oregon, and it began to rain in San Francisco. Once the rain started, it wouldn't stop. The first storm passed and a second followed on its heels. The game scheduled for the 12th was postponed. It rained on the 13th and the 14th, and there was no baseball. The Yankees and Giants suffered through the longest delay in World Series competition since the Giants and Athletics were idle for six days in 1911. By the time they got around to awarding the car to the Most Valuable Player, Ford quipped, it would be last year's model. The Giants were home with their families, and had some semblance of a normal life. The Yankees sat in their hotel rooms, watched television, hung around the lobby, and tried to calm their nerves.

Every day of rain made the Candlestick turf more soggy, and sometimes it seemed as though the Series would never be completed. When Commissioner Frick went on the field to check its condition, they had to put boards down to keep him from sinking. In a rare moment of humor, Frick noted that he might have to put an asterisk on the Series. On the 15th, both teams bused down to Modesto, 75 miles south of San Francisco, and worked out on a field used by the Class C California League club and named after Yankee co-owner Del Webb. Meanwhile, helicopters hovered over Candlestick, trying to dry the soaked surface sufficiently to make it playable. The many days of rain resulted in a field badly in need of mowing, but most of the field was too wet to bear the weight of the mowers.

Finally, on the 16th, with the outfield grass soaking wet, the two clubs took the field to play Game Six. Among its myriad of problems, Candlestick suffered from poor drainage, caused by the adobe clay subsurface. Tongue in cheek, Giant groundskeeper Matty Schwab said it was the wettest the field had been since the Dodgers were in town.

Ford, who had won Game One and not been involved in the decision in Game Four, didn't have it in Game Six. He was hammered in the fourth and fifth innings, and the Yankees were soundly beaten 5–2. Pierce, who was undefeated in Candlestick all season, won there for the 13th time. The Series was tied and would be decided in a single game which, counting exhibitions, was the 200th game the Yankees would play in 1962. The pitchers, for the third time, would be Ralph Terry and Jack Sanford. Sanford and Terry had already faced off in two tense duels, and the third would turn out to be the tightest of all. "It was the toughest [game] I have ever managed," Houk said.

Facing Sanford, a 24-game winner, was no picnic. It was even tougher when your two top sluggers weren't hitting. Maris was batting .211 with one home run. The Giants were using an exaggerated shift against him, with the shortstop playing on the right side of second base, and it was bothering Roger. On one occasion, he tried to beat the alignment, and hit a hard line drive to left. It went directly at the only man on the left side of the infield, third baseman Jim Davenport.

Mantle had just two hits in 22 at bats. He had not driven in a single run, and was not happy about it. "Mantle was dreadful in the Series," wrote Arthur Daley. "It turned him into a grumpy, uncivil, unmannerly boor."

Sanford was a 33-year-old veteran who had been 28, with nine minor league seasons and two years in the Army behind him, when he reached the big leagues with the Phillies in 1957. He was the National League rookie of the year, posting a 19–8 record. Sanford was traded to the Giants after the 1958 season, and won 15, 12 and 13 games the next three years. "The worst trade I ever made," said Phillie president Bob Carpenter just before the Series. In his first three seasons with San Francisco, Sanford had been a good, steady pitcher, but not a star. That changed in 1962, when he learned to control a volatile temper, acquired pitching savvy and stopped simply raring back and firing his fastball.

Like Terry, Sanford had the finest season of his career in 1962. He won 24 games, including 16 in a row down the stretch, and was the best pitcher on a club that included Hall of Famers Juan Marichal and Gaylord Perry, plus Pierce. He won 14 of 15 decisions at Candlestick, plus his victory in Game Two. With the Series on the line, each team had its best pitcher rested and ready.

"The night before the game," said Terry, "we had a little poker game, seven card stud. Yogi was in the game, and Elston and Hector. Yogi had a pretty good hand and was trying to bluff everybody out. I stayed in until the last card. Yogi had a king-high flush, but I drew the ace of clubs and beat his king-high flush with an ace-high flush. I think the pot had $340 in it. I scooped it all up and said, 'That's it boys, I'm going to bed.' Of course they didn't want me to leave, because I had a lot of their money. They never like you to walk out a winner. I said, 'That's an omen, beating Yogi at poker.' I slept like a baby."

The next day, riding to Candlestick on the bus, the Yankees listened to a pregame radio show, which featured Joe Garagiola. Garagiola, an old National Leaguer, was asked to predict a winner. "He picked the Giants to win," recalled Terry, "because he said Terry will choke." When the players got to the park, Terry saw Garagiola near the batting cage and asked him about what he had said. "I said, 'Joe, I see you picked me to choke today.' He denied it. I said, 'Hell, you said it. We all heard it on the radio.' He said, 'You've got to say something.' I said, 'Well, you didn't have to say that!'"

For their first two seasons in San Francisco, the Giants played in Seals Stadium, while a new park was constructed at Candlestick Point. "The site is beautiful and ideal," said NL President Warren Giles after a 1958 visit. Of course, Giles didn't try to catch any pop flies. Originally scheduled to open in 1959, a series of delays pushed the date back a year. Finally, in April, 1960, Candlestick Park, constructed at a cost of $15 million, was ready. Criticism arose almost immediately. "There is no joy," wrote Robert Lipsyte, "in Candlestick Park.... It is a masculine stadium of strong bleak lines, a fortress on a hill silhouetted against a sky that can suddenly turn as dark as turtle soup. The wind whips in from everywhere carrying portents of tragedy: It is here that Oedipus could tear out his eyes; here that a little fearful governess could knock on a door thrown open by a mad and violent Rochester."

Lipsyte was a bit dramatic, but Candlestick was truly a difficult place to play baseball. It was a difficult place to hit. It was a difficult place to pitch. It was an uncomfortable place to watch a game. When the park was under construction, Giant VP Chub Feeney visited the site. Why were the workers dressed for arctic conditions, he wondered, when downtown was fairly temperate? When he got out of his car, Feeney learned the answer. Did the wind always blow this hard?, he asked a worker. No, the man replied, only between the hours of one and five. Unfortunately, that happened to be the time when World Series games are played.

The problems began the first time the Giants played at Candlestick in 1960. There was a massive traffic jam, the radiant heating didn't work, and some of the lights malfunctioned. Then, of course, there was the weather. When Candlestick wasn't oppressively cold, it was unbearably hot. At the 1961 All Star Game, there were 95 cases of heat prostration, nearly equaling the Candlestick record set two days earlier. The All Star contest brought the conditions at Candlestick under national scrutiny for the first time. Those who had never played there were astonished. After leaving the American League clubhouse after the game, one man said, "I never was in a clubhouse like this. No one talked about the ball game. Everyone talked about that damn wind." Stan Musial explained to Berra that in the National League it wasn't necessary for left fielders to make the West Coast trip. "They don't have to catch the ball in San Francisco," Musial said "because the wind blows it back to the shortstop. And in Los Angeles [where the left field fence was just 250 feet from home plate], the shortstop takes everything that doesn't hit against or over the screen."

While Candlestick's afternoons were hot and windy, the temperature dropped severely when the wind stopped blowing and the sun went down. Feeney had his choice of scheduling day games, when pop flies danced like out of control kites, or night games, when Giant fans appeared in overcoats, hats, and gloves and huddled against the wind and cold. Employees wore parkas and pitchers sitting in the bullpen wrapped themselves in blankets.

It seemed as though everything about the park was problematic. The wind caused dust to blow around and get in the players' eyes, so a compound called Turface was spread over the infield to bond with the dirt and keep it anchored. In 1962, female fans complained that splinters in the seats were putting runs in their stockings. A brigade of twelve teenagers with sandpaper was dispatched to remedy the situation.

The fans didn't always endure the elements stoically. In January, 1962, prominent San Francisco attorney Melvin Belli sued the Giants, claiming breach of warranty and fraudulent representations. Belli had purchased six box seats in the belief that they had radiant heating, which they did not.* Others suffered more serious consequences than numbed fingers and toes. On September 2, 1962, 56-year-old Joseph Costa collapsed and died of a heart attack while ascending the slope to Candlestick known as "Cardiac Hill." The Associated Press reported that Costa was the eighth fatality Cardiac Hill had claimed that season.

Death and Melvin Belli haunted the facility, but the main problem with Candlestick was the cold, created principally by a stiff breeze which blew in from San Francisco Bay. Original plans called for a roof extending over both decks, but in order to reduce costs, the roof was replaced with a wind baffle. When further cuts were required, the size of the baffle was reduced. The wind came in behind third base, was forced left by the baffle, and broke out in left field,

---

*Belli won his case and was awarded $1,597.

where there was no protective baffle and no stands. Upon entering the stadium, the breeze blew fiercely from left field to right, knocking down drives to left, aiding any ball hit to right center, but pushing those hit to straightaway right foul.

In 1960, during the first game played in the new park, the wind gusted up to 25 mph. U.S. Weather Service statisticians predicted that the wind would get worse as the season wore on, peaking in July and slacking off in August and September. Local officials claimed the conditions on opening day were an aberration. They estimated that the average wind velocity during the season would be 12 mph.

The city officials were wrong, as the Candlestick winds affected ballgames from April through October. The most famous blast was the gust that blew little Stu Miller off the mound in the 1961 All-Star game, causing a balk. Six years later, an even stronger blast knocked 218 pound Don Drysdale off the hill. When the Giants ordered a flag to commemorate their National League pennant, they chose a special re-inforced version so it would not be ripped to shreds by the wind.

"It was awful," said Chuck Hiller, who played five seasons in Candlestick. "It was a dreadful place to play. It wasn't only windy, it was cold. The night games were absolutely terrible. The wind was so strong that a ball could be foul down the third base line and wind up at second base." "It was just a cold, cold experience," said former Giant Steve Whitaker, "even in July." When Japanese pitcher Masanori Murakami joined the Giants in 1964, someone asked him how he liked San Francisco. Through an interpreter, Murakami said, "Inside, fine. Outside, too cold."

"You can't stand still while fielding a ball in this wind," said Willie Mays. "You got to keep circling around because the wind might catch the ball and change its direction." "Pop flies were ridiculous," said former Giant Ed Bressoud. "It's the most unique ballpark I ever saw with regard to fly balls and the effect the wind had on them. Clubs would come in and take pop fly practice, which I had never seen before." In an attempt to avoid the strongest winds, the Giants began all World Series games at noon. The winds peaked in the late afternoon, and the Giants hoped to finish the games before anyone was blown off the mound or into the stands.

Sanford began his third duel with Terry by retiring the Yankees in the top of the first inning with just a harmless walk to Richardson. When Terry took the mound in the bottom of the first, he had to deal not only with the Giants, but also with the wind, which was blowing a 35 mph gale in the wake of the storm. The breeze was so strong that it not only affected batted balls, it altered pitched balls as well. "You'd throw one curve ball," said Terry, "and it might break six inches. Another might break two feet." In two games in San Francisco, Ford had experienced severe difficulty trying to throw his left-handed breaking pitches into the wind. Finally, he gave up and stuck to his fastball. Terry would at least have the wind behind his breaking stuff. "After an inning or so," he said, "you make adjustments. You put an experienced pitcher anywhere and they can adjust." Sanford was also having trouble with the wind. His fastball had a natural tail to it, and the wind was increasing the tail to the point where he had problems controlling it.

There was no adjustment period for Terry, who set down the first seventeen Giants to come to the plate. Unfortunately for the Yankee defense, Terry was a fly ball pitcher. Of those seventeen outs, only three were ground balls. There was one strikeout and 13 balls hit up into the treacherous wind.

The Giants lofted several balls into the gale blowing in from left. Tresh tied a World Series record for left fielders with six putouts. "One of them was just an average fly ball to left," Tresh recalled. "I called for the ball early, not having factored in the wind. I started running in and pretty soon I'm running harder and harder and harder. Once you call for the ball, it's all yours and the shortstop is going to get out of your way. I ended up catching the ball with one foot on the infield dirt." "It was a circus," said Terry, "with guys circling around catching those balls. They did a great job. We really had a wonderful defensive ball club."

Sanford matched Terry inning for inning until the fifth. Skowron led off with a single to left, and went to third on a single by Boyer when the ball died in the wet center field grass. Terry drew a walk to load the bases. "I had a walk and a single in that game," he recalled. "I was a force." With the bases loaded and no one out, the Giants elected to play the infield back and try for a double play. It was only the fifth inning. Surely the heavy-hitting Giants would score one run in their next five at bats. Kubek slapped a hard grounder to Jose Pagan at short. Pagan threw to second to Hiller, who relayed to first for the double play as Skowron scored the first run of the game.

With two out in the bottom of the sixth, Terry jammed Sanford with a fastball, which he hit off his fists and blooped into center field for the Giants' first hit. Felipe Alou was retired on an infield grounder and the game continued to the seventh. Boyer and Terry hit singles but were left on. Chuck Hiller led off the Giant seventh by attempting to bunt, and popped up to Terry.

Then came one of the key plays of the Series. Mays hooked one of Terry's pitches and pulled a long drive into the left field corner, into the teeth of the gusting wind. In hot pursuit went Tresh, who had only been playing the outfield since August. "I got a real good jump on the ball," Tresh said. After the game, Mays complained that Tresh was playing him out of position. Since Terry was pitching him outside, Mays said, Tresh should never have been so close to the foul line.

The Yankee left fielder, playing a new position in one of the most difficult parks in the major leagues, raced after Mays's drive. The ball had been hit so hard that it was cutting through the wind, hooking toward the line. On the mound, Terry watched anxiously. "I knew he was going to have a shot at it," he recalled. "I was surprised it curved away from him as much as it did." The ball kept hooking and Tresh kept running. At the last second, he lunged, stretched as far as he could and caught the ball backhanded in the webbing of his glove. Then came the difficult part of the play, for the wire mesh fence was only a few feet beyond the foul line. "You're going to hit the fence," Tresh said, "if you catch a ball near the line running hard. It's pretty hard to stop." As soon as the ball hit his glove, Tresh got his right hand on it to keep it from popping out, then hit the fence. The ball was still in his glove. It was a remarkable play.

McCovey, the next batter, ripped a triple to center field. Had Tresh not made his fabulous catch, the score would have been tied. With McCovey on third and two out, Terry struck out Cepeda to end the threat.

The Yankees loaded the bases in the eighth with no one out. Maris hit into a force play at the plate. By now, the Giants were playing the infield in and were not going to concede any more runs. With one out, Howard hit a bullet toward third base. "I guarantee," said Terry, "if the ground is dry, that ball is in the corner and cleans the bases." Instead, the ball hit the mud in front of third base and popped up into the air, where third baseman Jim Davenport grabbed it and threw to the plate. Howard, a slow man running on a muddy track, was doubled up at first to end the inning. "The score in that game," said Terry, "probably should have been about 5–2, with all the hard hit balls."

Instead, it remained 1–0 as the Giants batted in the bottom of the ninth. Matty Alou, batting for Sanford, led off. "I was hoping to get Matty Alou," said Terry, "and then Felipe Alou and Hiller and not have to face Mays, McCovey and Cepeda." He didn't get Matty Alou. Alou hit a high pop foul toward the first base stands. Howard drifted over toward the Giant dugout, which was at field level, with no steps. "Ellie was camped under it," Terry recalled. "He's got one foot in the dugout and one out. Two guys went over and hit him with a shoulder block and he dropped the ball. He came out to the mound and said, 'I'm not sure who it was. Either Bob Nieman or Alvin [Dark] hit me.' When you go into the dugout I guess you're fair game. Dark's a throwback to the old Dodger-Giant days. He's a dear friend and a great guy, but that was their idea of playing ball, I guess."

On the next pitch, Alou dropped a beautiful drag bunt to Terry's left and beat it out. Hiller, trying to sacrifice, bunted foul twice. "They were perfect bunts," said Hiller, "but they just rolled foul. I believe I would have beaten them out." Then Terry threw a curve in the dirt which Howard blocked to hold Alou at first. With two strikes, Hiller swung and missed a slider in the dirt for the first out. Felipe Alou tried to bunt his brother to second, couldn't, and struck out on a low curve. Mays came to the plate, the only man standing between Terry and redemption for 1960. Was the Mazeroski home run on Terry's mind? "No, I never had any thoughts like that," he said recently. "Not during the game. But it was definitely the most tension I ever went through."

Mays had hit 49 home runs during the regular season, including 28 at Candlestick. It had been a grueling year for the veteran, now 31 years old. In mid–September, he had collapsed from exhaustion on the bench, remained unconscious for twenty minutes and had to be hospitalized. Still, worn down or not, there was no one more dangerous in the clutch than Willie Mays.

At the 1961 All Star Game, Ford asked Giant pitcher Billy Loes how to pitch to Mays at Candlestick. "You just wait until the wind blows," said Loes, "and pitch him low and inside." "I didn't want to give him anything out over the plate," Terry said, "because he had that right field shot down pat. He'd just hit it up in the air and, whoosh, it was gone. I tried to crowd him. If he was going to hit one off me, I was going to make him hit it through the wind to left field."

Terry's first two pitches were inside, and Mays let them go by, putting the Yankee pitcher in a hole. "'He knew what I was trying to do,' Terry said. "So I thought I'd better switch and go outside. I threw a pitch low and away, a gorgeous pitch, knee high and right on the black, with a little tail on it." Mays indeed had the right field shot down pat. He reached out and hit a rocket down the line. Maris took off after the ball as it skidded across the wet grass. Alou streaked around the bases with the tying run as Mays headed for second. Maris made a fine play to cut the ball off before it reached the corner. "Cutting the ball off wasn't the problem," said Terry. "It was basically a long single. But when he got to the ball, the hard part was that he had to stop on the wet grass without falling on his ass."

Meanwhile, Bobby Richardson was racing frantically toward Maris. He had to get as far into right field as he possibly could because Maris couldn't throw. "Nobody knew it," said Jim Coates, "but Maris had a real bad arm and he could hardly throw at all." "He didn't throw in practice a lot," said Terry. "He was good for about two good throws a game."

Whitey Lockman, coaching at third for the Giants, didn't know about Maris's bad arm. He held Alou at third. It was the right decision, for Richardson's throw to the plate probably would have cut Alou down and ended the Series. There was no point in taking desperate chances, for McCovey and Cepeda were up next. McCovey had hit a monstrous home run off Terry in Game Two and Cepeda had broken out of his long slump with three hits in the sixth game.

Houk went to the mound to talk to Terry. Right hander Stafford and left hander Daley warmed up in the Yankee bullpen. Jack Reed watched anxiously from the Yankee bench. "I don't believe I'd have pitched to McCovey," he said. "I would have brought in a left hander to pitch to him or walked him and pitched to Cepeda." Daley stood in the bullpen and observed the mound conference nervously. "I thought, 'Oh, man, he's going to bring me in to pitch to McCovey.'" Then Daley had a whimsical thought. "I'll just walk him and let Stafford deal with Cepeda."

Daley didn't have to deal with McCovey and Stafford didn't have to pitch to Cepeda. "I think it's tough bringing in a relief pitcher in that situation," said Terry. "I don't think we had anybody who really wanted to come into that game." A reliever wouldn't have time to adjust to the Candlestick wind, and with all the rain and inactivity, the Yankee bullpen was rusty. Daley hadn't pitched in eleven days and Stafford hadn't appeared since his start in Game Three.

Houk had no thought of removing Terry, and asked him if he wanted to pitch to McCovey or walk him and pitch to Cepeda. Terry remembered the National League playoff between the Dodgers and Giants two weeks earlier. The Dodgers had loaded the bases with an intentional walk in the deciding game, only to have Stan Williams walk in the winning run. Terry had not walked a single man that day. In fact, he hadn't walked anyone since passing Hiller leading off Game Five, but he didn't want to take any chances. "You're playing in a National League ball-park and you've got a National League umpire behind the plate, so the strike zone gets a little smaller," he said. Terry told Houk he wanted to pitch to McCovey. "I'll still never understand why they did that," said Hiller. "They lucked out."

McCovey became the most dangerous hitter in baseball in the late 1960s, and was elected to the Hall of Fame in 1986, but in 1962 he was a part time player, platooning with Harvey Kuenn in left field. He was known in San Francisco as "the wrong Willie." "If McCovey frightens pitchers whenever he picks up a bat," wrote Arthur Daley, "he frightens his manager and all Giant partisans even more when he picks up a glove." McCovey wouldn't have to catch a ball in this situation, however, just hit one. Terry's first delivery was an off-speed pitch, and the big left hander pulled it to right field. Maris drifted over and appeared to have a chance to catch it, but the wind kept pulling the ball, and pulling it, until it fell foul in the stands. "People dramatize it," said Terry, "and say that it was a long drive. Hell, it just barely got beyond the bullpen area. It was 40 feet short of the fence." Terry took a deep breath and wound up to throw his 102nd pitch of the game, as Alou and Mays led off their bases. From the dugout, Houk was trying to get Richardson to move closer to first base. Richardson didn't see him.

For the second time in three seasons, Terry delivered the final pitch in the seventh game of a World Series. "Where I really wanted to get McCovey out was up and in, from the belt up," Terry said. He threw a fast ball and McCovey hit a wicked line drive. "I thought I had a hit," McCovey said after the game. "I knew I hit it good." "I never could figure out how he got on the ball so well," said Terry, "until I saw a film clip taken from behind the plate. He leaned back to hit it, and had to use his hands. He couldn't get his arms extended. When he used his hands, he put a little topspin on the ball, and that's why Bobby was able to catch it shoulder-high." "There's a photo out there somewhere," said Phil Linz. "We were all pretty tense. When McCovey hit that ball, every single player on the bench went up. When Bobby leaped, we all leaped. Everyone's feet were off the ground." "Ralph Houk was always kidding at banquets," said Rollie Sheldon, "about how he'd tried to get Richardson to move over a little bit. He'd say, 'I'm so damned glad he didn't see me.'"

Terry took off his glove and threw it high into the air. The entire Yankee team surged toward the mound and carried him to the dugout on their shoulders. From a goat in 1960 to the hero two years later was a tale too improbable for fiction, yet it had happened to Ralph Terry. "I am a very lucky fellow and I certainly thank God for a second opportunity," he said after the game. "You don't often get another chance to prove yourself, in baseball or in life." "After it was over and even before the game," Terry said recently, "I said, 'Win or lose, I'm thankful for the opportunity.' I was thankful for a second chance. You couldn't ask for any more than that."

Back in Larned, Kansas, Tanya Terry sat clutching 10 day old Gabe, as Richardson clutched McCovey's line drive. "Gabe was real good today," she said, "until the Giants came up in that ninth. And then he started fussing for his bottle." Even a 10 day old could feel the pressure. "I don't know anything about the game," said Rose Terry, Ralph's grandmother, "but it seemed like it was awful close." Indeed it was-the first seventh game decided by a 1–0 score.

The 1962 Series was the apogee of Terry's baseball career. He was named the Most Valuable Player of the fall classic and given a new Corvette by Sport Magazine. In 1963, Ralph was again a stalwart of the Yankee staff, posting a 17–15 record and leading the American League with 18 complete games. With more offensive support, his record could have been much better. During the World Series, Terry was relegated to the bullpen, pushed out of the rotation by youngsters Al Downing and Jim Bouton. There would be no repeat of his '62 heroics.

The following spring, Terry experienced back trouble, tried to return too quickly and was hampered by injuries most of the season. Always plagued by the gopher ball, he had grave difficulty in 1964, surrendering 11 homers in his first 46 innings. Moreover, his excellent control deserted him. In July, Terry's ERA was over 7.00 and he was being booed by Yankee fans.

Late in the year, the Yankees acquired Pedro Ramos from the Indians for a player to be named later, in a deal that was instrumental in the New York pennant drive. Before the season was over, Terry heard rumors that the Indians had been given a choice of players and that he was one of those on the list. By this time, Mel Stottlemyre had joined Ford, Bouton and Downing in the starting rotation, and Terry, approaching his 29th birthday, was expendable.

Just before the acquisition of Ramos, Terry had emerged from the shadows of a difficult summer to have an excellent road trip. He began doing what people had always told him he should do—throw his fast ball more often. "I won three games and had two saves," he said, "and I felt really good about being able to move back into the rotation, but they just sat my ass down. I didn't pitch at all. They tried to get me to say I had a sore arm." Terry did pitch two scoreless innings in Game Four of the Series, but his last post-season appearance had none of the drama of his early World Series games. He was merely mopping up a lost cause.

Terry was indeed sent to Cleveland as payment for Ramos, and pitched very well for the Indians in 1965, posting an 11–5 record. He pitched a four hitter on opening day, but the highlight of his season was a three hit shutout over the Yankees in May. The game was a Terry classic. He didn't walk anyone, threw only 70 pitches, and completed the game in one hour and forty minutes. After a great start, Terry was used infrequently late in the season. The Indians had fallen out of contention and said they were going with younger players. Terry claimed his inactivity was due to the fact that he had been offered illegal incentives by Cleveland, which had agreed to pay him $1500 for each win above ten. After he won his eleventh, he didn't pitch. Terry said he wanted to be traded and the Indians accommodated him. At the end of the season, he was traded back to, of all places, Kansas City, where he had learned his trade as a young pitcher.

In Kansas City, Terry had another salary dispute, this one with Charley Finley, and after a lengthy battle (he staged the longest holdout of any major leaguer in 1966), Terry wound up back in New York, with the Mets. He finished the '66 season with the Mets, and performed a feat he wished he had been able to accomplish a few years earlier. In mid–September, the Mets were in Los Angeles, following a series against the Pirates in Forbes Field, when they were visited by a California banker named Charles Dillon Stengel. "Hey, Case," Terry said, "Guess what? I finally got Mazeroski out ... six years too late."

Terry was waived by the Mets during the winter, but invited to spring training as a non-roster player. The previous season, while pitching for the Athletics, he had begun working on yet another pitch, a knuckleball. When he went to the Mets, he worked on his knuckler in the bullpen, and believed he was getting the hang of it. He threw it in the Florida Instructional League, and mixed it with his other pitches during the exhibition season. Terry had a great spring, and made the team, despite some reservations on the part of manager Wes Westrum. "He's throwing too much slow stuff," Westrum said in late March. "I want to see his fastball more."

In two regular season games with the Mets, Terry pitched three innings, allowed only one hit, and struck out five. It didn't matter. The Mets had decided that, if they were going to finish last, they might as well do it with youth. It was time for veterans like Terry, Jack Lamabe, Bob

Shaw and Jack Hamilton to step aside. "A few of us would sit around in the bullpen," recalled Lamabe, "and say, 'How can they pitch those two guys and not us?' You know who those two guys were — Seaver and Koosman."

Terry was released and, as he said recently, "One door closed and another one opened." In November, 1957, Terry had been involved in a serious automobile accident, during which his car overturned several times. He suffered a broken hip, and a badly bruised back and knee. Terry spent the entire winter in traction and, when he went to spring training, his activity was severely limited. For exercise, he began walking around with some of the coaches when they played golf after practice. They suggested that he might as well rent a set of clubs and learn to play, rather than just walk with them. At first, Terry hit a lot of grounders, but he quickly picked up the game and became one of the best golfers among major league players. In 1961, he finished fourth in the national baseball players' golf championship. Terry also grew to love the game, and the people around it, befriending professionals such as Art Wall and Julius Boros.

When Terry was released by the Mets, he was named club pro at Roxiticus Golf Club, a new course in Mendham, New Jersey. He had been offered the opportunity to pitch in the minor leagues by the Cubs and Reds, but it was time to move on to a second career.

Terry saw many parallels between pitching and golfing. "Pitching was my natural, god-given talent," he said. "Golf is more of an acquired art, but the thought process is very similar. It's all about decision-making. When you're pitching, you look at the opposing lineup, and there are certain players you can challenge, while others you've got to pitch to more carefully. It's the same in golf. On every course, there are three or four holes that are really tough, and a few you can attack. Others you play more cautiously — left jab, left jab, then you throw the right.

"Pitchers have a lot of arm speed, and that translates into long drives. They can also vary their arm speed so they can hit more finesse shots. They probably have a lot more touch. When you're pitching, you've got to be committed to what you're about to do. When you start to throw a pitch, there can't be any uncertainty in your mind. In golf, uncertainty has probably ruined more shots than anything. During the middle of your swing, you think, 'Do I have enough club? Do I have the right club? Am I aiming too far to the right?' and you don't get a good, positive swing. I think that's the reason a lot of pitchers make good golfers. They're decisive. They commit to the shot and they live with it. They don't let it gnaw at them."

There is no better synopsis of the Yankee career of Ralph Terry than the preceding statement. He began the '60s by absorbing a crushing blow, one that might have ruined a lesser man, but when he had a chance at redemption two years later, he attacked it without hesitation, with total confidence in his ability. One man, Willie McCovey, stood between Terry and success. Terry challenged him and won. Ralph had his redemption.

· 10 ·

The Pride of the Yankees

In 1965, shortly before they were traded for each other, catchers Johnny Blanchard and Doc Edwards happened to meet at a delicatessen in Kansas City, where both were having a post-game sandwich. "I wonder if people know how good the Yankees really are?" Blanchard asked. "I think we do, John," Edwards replied. "You beat the hell out of us all the time." That wasn't what he meant, Blanchard said. "Every time we walk into a town, the other team is going to play the best baseball they possibly can. They're up for it and ready to play. It's not like any other team coming to town. Everybody's playing as hard as they can, doing everything they can to beat the Yankees. And yet we win the pennant every year."

Edwards, who had been in the major leagues for four years, thought about what Blanchard had said. It was true. Every time he played against the Yankees, he put forth just a little extra effort. His teams always saved their best pitchers for the Yankees. "Yet," Edwards said, "they still beat our brains out. That's a tribute to how great they were. They never felt they were out of a game. They would do whatever it took to win. I saw Mickey Mantle drag bunt with a man on third and two outs to win a ballgame."

Tom Metcalf recalled a key series with the White Sox shortly after he was called up to the Yankees in 1963. The first game was a tight one in the late innings. "I think somebody for the White Sox booted a ball at shortstop," Metcalf said. "I saw Steve Hamilton and Bill Kunkel throwing the balls in the bag, starting to put stuff away. "I said, 'What the hell are you guys doing?' They said, 'The game's over. We've got them. They're beaten. Watch them self-destruct.' Sure enough, Hector Lopez comes up, Juan Pizarro hangs a curve ball and Hector hits a towering home run to left field. The gates opened and we won all three games. Those players in the bullpen knew we had the edge mentally. I didn't believe it when I first saw it, but there was an aura about that team. Even if the game was close, we knew we were going to win and the other team knew it, too. It's like a golfer who has a two stroke lead, but knows that Tiger Woods is two holes back and he's going to do something. The Yankee mystique was there. It was a tenth man. Everybody on that team will tell you that." "We just knew we were going to win," said Joe DeMaestri, "even when we got behind." "It didn't make any difference," said Jack Reed, "if we were five runs behind."

The Yankee mystique had a long history. Pitcher Waite Hoyt, after he was traded to the National League in the 1930s, was enduring a number of barbs from the cocky Chicago Cubs. "If you guys don't shut up," he retorted, "I'll put on my old Yankee uniform and scare you to death."

Before joining the Yankees in 1961, Tex Clevenger pitched against them for many years, always on second division clubs. "You could be ahead of them by a run or two in the ninth inning," he said, "and something would happen. A ball would take a bad hop. Somebody would get on base, and you'd say, 'Oh, hell, here it goes again.'" Ed Bressoud, who played for the Red Sox from 1962 through 1965, said "You'd get ahead and you knew darn well something was going to happen in the seventh, eighth or ninth inning. They were just a great ballclub."

The Yankees were different than the other clubs. "The Yankees were winners," said Steve Whitaker. "They knew how to play the game and you had to learn to play the game before you got to come to New York. You had to play defense. You had to know how to run the bases. You had to play the Yankee way and the Yankee way was fundamentals."

"They had a pretty good system," said former Yankee farmhand Rod Kanehl. "Everybody trained the same way, whether it was D ball or the major leagues. You learned how to take the cutoff, where to go for the cutoff, and how to take the signs, so that when you advanced from one level to the next, you were right in the system. It was called the Yankee system and Stengel started it."

When a new player joined the Yankees, he was told in no uncertain terms what was expected of him. DeMaestri was traded to New York following the 1959 season, after nine years as a regular shortstop for second division clubs. "It was such a different experience," he said. "You could just feel it when you walked in the clubhouse. I'll never forget the first day of spring training in St. Petersburg. The first thing they did was— McDougald, Berra and Skowron sat me down before we even went out to practice the first day. They said, 'Remember one thing. You're playing with our money.' I'll never forget that as long as I live."

"Moose used to say, 'Don't mess with my World Series money,'" recalled Hector Lopez. "'You've got to go out there and play hard all the time. You're a Yankee now.' He always reminded the younger guys of that." When Stan Williams joined the club in 1963, he asked traveling secretary Bruce Henry, "When I want to borrow some money, do I get it from you?" "Stanley," Henry replied, "the Yankees don't borrow money."

"There was an *esprit de corps* that wasn't there on other clubs," said Ryne Duren. "The veterans kind of carried the torch for it. We played as a team. It was special to be a Yankee. There's no doubt in my mind about that."

Joining the Yankees from a second division club required an adjustment. "The Yankees' daily workouts and everything else were completely different than everyone else's," said Clevenger recently. "When I went to spring training in 1962, I could really see a difference. From the first day of spring training, all that was on their mind was to win the pennant and get to the World Series. It was talked about in the clubhouse all the time." "There's a sort of ease and relaxation," Clevenger said in 1962, "when you're with a second division club that gets in your blood.... Sure we all try to win. But if we lose, well, shucks, you're with a club that isn't expected to win too often and you shrug it off." The Yankees didn't shrug off losing until about 1967.

Newcomers were given the rules of the fraternity, but they were also welcomed. A Yankee was a Yankee, no matter what their role on the team. When Doc Edwards arrived in New York from Kansas City in 1965, he was nervous. Two popular Yankees, Johnny Blanchard and Rollie Sheldon, had been sent to the Athletics in the trade, and Edwards knew he was not of the caliber of Elston Howard, the man he was supposed to replace. The Yankees made him feel at home as soon as he arrived. "Mickey and Whitey and all of the guys would always do something to make you feel comfortable," Edwards remembered. "Whitey, with all his class and Mickey, much more so than people gave him credit for, always went out of their way to make that marginal player or rookie feel comfortable." If Mantle or Ford saw Edwards walk into a restaurant, they would invariably invite him to their table and usually insisted on paying. "When you sit at my table," Mantle once told Edwards, "I pay. Somewhere along the line, if you're making good money and some rookie sits at your table, remember it."

"Mantle always treated me great," said Fred Kipp, who spent only the first month of the

1960 season with New York. "He went out of his way to treat guys like me — I was just a humpty on that team — he went out of his way to be friendly to me. If I was shagging balls in the outfield, he'd come over and talk to me."

"Mantle came down to my locker one day," recalled Metcalf, "and asked me what size shoe I wore." Shoes were a valuable commodity in those days, for players had to pay for their own footwear unless they had an endorsement contract with a manufacturer. If they had a contract they could get all the equipment they wanted for free. Endorsement contracts generally went to established players, like Mantle, and for someone like Metcalf, making the minimum salary of $7,000, the cost of his shoes was a meaningful number.

Metcalf told Mantle he wore 11D. Mantle called his rep at the sporting goods company and told him he needed a pair of size 11D shoes with a pitching plate on the right foot. The shoes they were sending him, he said, were cramping his feet and he needed a bigger size. What about the pitching plate? Was Mickey contemplating a switch to the mound? Well, said Mantle, that was what he needed. Shortly thereafter, Metcalf found a pair of 11D baseball spikes in his locker, with a pitcher's plate on the right shoe, compliments of Mickey Mantle, who never said a word about it.

In 1987, the San Francisco Giants celebrated the 25th anniversary of the 1962 World Series, and invited the participants to an Old Timers Game. Jack Reed was getting off the bus at Candlestick Park with Dale Long, his teammate on the '62 Yanks. "You know," Long said to Reed, "those guys [the Yankees] were great players, but the best thing about them is that they liked each other. I played with the Pirates and there were guys I didn't even speak to, and ones who didn't speak to me." "I thought that was a pretty good summation of what the Yankees were like," Reed said.

Other great organizations created a similar atmosphere. Nate Oliver, who played on the championship Dodger teams of the '60s, said, "Everyone on that club was a major league player and they were treated as such," he said. "That was from Koufax on down." Oliver had a locker next to the great lefty. "I'd heard that other stars, when they had a utility player or a rookie next to them, asked to have them moved" he said, "but not Sandy."

"When I joined the Dodgers in 1962," said Larry Burright, "they treated me like I'd been there two or three years. That really made an impression on me. We were like one big family in the Dodger organization. You'd see guys going out to eat together. There were never any problems."

What created the harmony in the Yankee and Dodger clubhouses? Did great camaraderie lead to winning or did winning lead to great camaraderie? "If you win," said Dick Schofield, "a lot of things are overlooked. You put up with things that, if you were losing, would get magnified and blown out of proportion."

Bud Daley was an All-Star pitcher in Kansas City and a spot starter in New York. "At Kansas City," he said, "you thought about yourself. You'd say, 'Gee, if I don't win I'm not going to get a raise next year.' In New York, if you lost, you thought, 'Gee, I really let the guys down' and if you won, you thought, 'Oh boy, I really helped the club.'"

Former Met pitcher Larry Miller is now a management consultant, and often talks about teamwork in business situations. He believes that winning is the catalyst. "It's hard to build chemistry on a losing team," he said, "because everybody on the team knows that every time they go out, their individual performance is going to determine whether they stay or go. It's pretty hard to be thinking about the team, because baseball's an individual sport. When you get promoted to the major leagues, you don't get promoted based upon the record of your minor league team, you get promoted based upon your individual statistics. You get a raise based upon your individual statistics. You had a lot of anxiety on a club like the Mets. There's not a lot of camaraderie as much as everybody is looking out for themselves. You show me nine guys who are having a good year and I'll show you a team that's easily manageable."

John Sullivan played with the last place 1967 Mets and coached for the world champion Blue Jays in the early '90s. "Playing on a losing team is a tough situation," he said, "because you're fighting for your well-being and your family's well-being. It's kind of tough at times to keep a team-oriented atmosphere. There are people trying to hang on. There are young people trying to make a name for themselves. I believe you look to protect yourself more."

One of the few losing teams to avoid dissension was the 1962 Mets. "When you play on teams that are losing," said Felix Mantilla, the Met third baseman, "it seems like everybody starts pointing fingers. But with the Mets that year, it seemed like everybody was very cool. There were no fights. I enjoyed playing with that bunch of guys. I didn't enjoy losing 120 games, but they were great guys."

"None of the Mets seemed to be depressed by their constant losing," said reporter Gordon White. "It was a hallmark of that team. If today's Yankee team were to have a 22 game losing streak, I'll bet that by the twentieth game, the dressing room would be like a morgue. They would be totally depressed. They wouldn't know what the hell was wrong with them. I don't remember what the Mets' longest losing streak was, but they never seemed to think that way. I think they all understood where they were and what they were and why they were."

Winning fostered more winning, and for decades before the free agent draft, the Yankees were the first choice of many top prospects. Almost every talented youngster wanted to play in New York. "Everybody who's ever been in baseball," said former pitcher Danny McDevitt, "no matter what they say, wanted to be a Yankee. I can say all my life that I played in Yankee Stadium. I was a Yankee. They were the team." "I was full of that Yankee mystique," said pitcher Johnny James. "I was a real Yankee fan when I was a kid. I listened to the World Series on the radio, read the books. I was really into it."

Even when the Yankees were not offering the biggest bonuses (and they seemingly never did) the lure of World Series shares and chance to be a Yankee meant more than a large bonus to play in Philadelphia or Kansas City. "When I was a boy in the little town of Grenada, Mississippi," said Jake Gibbs, a baseball star and All-American football player at Ole Miss, "I used to lay on the bed and listen to the Game of the Day on the radio. It seemed like it was always either the Yankees or Detroit. I dreamed about playing professional baseball. I never dreamed about playing college football or professional football. I dreamed about playing professional baseball. In 1950 and 1951, I was actually a Detroit Tiger fan. I could name the whole lineup today. But they were always playing the Yankees and the Yankees were always winning pennants and always winning the World Series. Then I went to Ole Miss and in my three years of football we won 29 and lost 3. We were used to winning. So when it got down to my senior year and I could choose who to go with — the Yankees or the Cubs or the Dodgers or the Giants— I said, hell, I'm going with the Yankees. These guys know how to win. I'm coming from a winner and if I'm good enough, maybe I can make the Yankees. I could've gotten the same bonus from the Giants or the Braves, but I said, I'm going with the Yankees because I know what they are. I know their tradition. They win. That's why I chose the Yankees."

Bill Stafford turned down $20,000 bonus offers to sign with the Yankees for $4,000, thinking that if he could pitch for New York, and collect a few World Series shares, he would make more money in the long run. Getting to the Yankees was the culmination of a lifelong dream in a way that reaching the Chicago White Sox or Washington Senators was not. In 1961, young Yankee outfield prospect Lee Thomas made the opening day roster, but spent the first month of the season riding the bench, pinch-hitting only two times. In mid–May, on a flight to Los Angeles, Maris told him, "We'll take care of you." The next day, in the clubhouse before batting practice, he said to Thomas, "It doesn't look like you're going to get a chance to play here and we think you can play. Four of us are going to let you take our minutes in batting practice. So just smoke the ball." With Angel manager Bill Rigney watching, Thomas followed instructions.

"I must have hit 15 out of there," he said. "I just rattled the ball all over. For three days, I did it."

Sure enough, before the Yankees even left town, Rigney had traded for Thomas, who went from benchwarmer to All-Star outfielder. Despite the opportunity to be a regular, he hated to leave his spot on the Yankee bench. "I wanted to be a Yankee," he said. "In '61 I knew they were going to win before it even started and it would have been great to stay with them all year. As much as I wanted to play every day, I would have loved to have stayed with them." Phil Linz coined the expression, "Play me or keep me." "I chose the Yankees," he said recently. "I would rather have done that than played for Kansas City. I wanted to play for the best. I wanted to be with the best."

"When we were winning," Linz said, "every time I got into a game it was an important circumstance. When you sacrificed somebody over, it meant something. When you got a base hit and drove somebody in, it meant something. When you're on teams that don't win, nothing you do means anything except your own personal statistics."

Everyone, it seemed, wanted to be a Yankee, but while many were called, few were called up. With talent at the major league level, and more stacked up behind it in Triple A, the progress of many prospects was stalled. Deron Johnson, who became a feared National League slugger in the mid–'60s, never got more than a brief trial with the Yanks. "I thought Deron Johnson was going to be a superstar," said Lee Thomas. "I played with him at Binghamton and it was like a man playing among boys. He was 18 years old and this guy was a stud. I thought he would hit 40 home runs a year." In Johnson's first season, at Kearny in 1956, he hit 24 home runs and drove in 78 in just 63 games. In 1957, Stengel compared the 20-year-old Johnson to Mantle at a similar age. Yet, year after year, Johnson kept going back to the minors and hitting more home runs. Bob Martyn, a left handed hitting outfielder, hit 128 home runs and drove in 415 runs during five years in the Yankee system. All it got him was a trade to Kansas City.

Don Lock and Ken Hunt, right handed power hitting outfielders with great minor league home run records, couldn't dislodge Mantle and Maris and wound up as regulars for other teams. Lock set an Eastern League home run record in 1960 and wasn't even in the running for a roster spot the next spring. In 1960, Thomas hit .326 with 26 homers and 107 RBI in the minors and was lucky enough to get traded to the Angels. Marv Throneberry was the American Association MVP but couldn't unseat Moose Skowron from first base. It took Elston Howard, the Most Valuable Player in the American League in 1963, six years to supplant Berra as the regular catcher.

In 1956, seven of the American Association All Stars were Yankee farmhands. Throneberry at first, Bobby Richardson at second, Tony Kubek at short and Woodie Held at third comprised an all–Denver infield. Martyn was one of the outfielders and Ralph Terry and Jim DePalo were the pitchers. Kubek, Richardson and Terry were the only ones who made it to New York to stay.

The Yankee camaraderie was not the raucous "We Are Family" spirit of the '79 Pirates, or of St. Louis's Gashouse Gang of the 1930s. "It was quieter," said pitcher Eli Grba, "more of a Waldorf-Astoria type of camaraderie — a Joe Dimaggio type of camaraderie. When you went on the field, it was for four hours and it was all business. From the time you got to the clubhouse at 2 o'clock, you behaved like a Yankee."

The Yankee image and dignity were important parts of the mystique. Yankees dressed like the businessmen they were on the field. "One of the great things for me," Grba continued, "was the discipline as far as dress was concerned. We wore a shirt and tie and you looked nice all the time." The Yankees were fairly unique in this regard, which their players immediately noticed if they were traded to another team. When Jim Coates went to Washington, he was appalled by the way the players dressed. Needless to say, he does not appreciate the wardrobe of modern players. "If you're going to a circus," Coates said, "you dress for the circus. If you're going to play ball, you dress as a ballplayer." Coates's idea of dressing as a ballplayer was shirt and tie. "I think the greatest thing that happened to the Yankees was George Steinbrenner," he said recently. "George put that ballclub where it was supposed to be."

Steinbrenner, of course, is hell on beards, long hair, earrings and anything else modern. Coates played before the Joe Pepitone hair dryer era, when mustaches and beards were found only on poets and folk singers. As for earrings—Could Coates imagine Moose Skowron wearing an earring? "I would love to see that," he laughed. "Pepitone yes, but not Moose."

The dress, the dignity and the consistent winning all contributed to the special feeling associated with being a Yankee. "The four years with the Yankees were like being in heaven for me," said Linz. "I hardly ever look back on the Mets or the Phillies. I look back on being with the Yankees—hanging out with Mantle and Pepitone and Maris and Tresh. We had so much fun together. We were winning. We were in New York. I was single. I was happy. The whole experience in New York was wonderful for me." Marv Throneberry, the darling of Met fans during their first season, always considered himself a Yankee. "I am a Yankee," says Tom Tresh proudly. "I not only was a Yankee; I am a Yankee today."

Roger Repoz played about a year and a half with the Yankees and several years with other major league teams. "I follow the Yankees," he said recently. "They're still my first love. I have the Yankee emblem tattooed on my left arm. It was such an honor to play for them." Repoz noted with pride that he was a member of the Yankee alumni association and was pleased that George Steinbrenner was so anxious to keep the Yankee aura intact. "I wish more clubs would do that," he said. "Oakland hasn't. Kansas City hasn't and the Angels never have. I get a Christmas card and a birthday card every year from the Yankees. This year, out of nowhere, I got a package. There was a gold tie tack with the NY logo and a letter from George Steinbrenner. It said, George would like you to wear this in respect for the greatest professional franchise in America, or something like that. He's the type of owner who's made the tradition last."

Part of the Yankee mystique was the magnificent stadium in which the team played, a setting rich with the history of so many championships and Hall of Fame players. Rich Beck remembered seeing the Stadium for the first time when he was called up in 1965. "The team was on the road," he said, "and was coming back the next day, so I went to the Stadium to stow my gear. I walked out of the locker room into the Yankee dugout, which was on the first base side. I walked up to the steps and put one foot on the top step and looked straight out to left field. I was like a camera slowly panning the diamond, from left, to left center, to center, to right center and to right. I said, 'My god, I'm in the House that Ruth Built.' I'm actually here. This is unbelievable. I thought about Babe Ruth playing there. I thought about Lou Gehrig playing there—Bill Dickey, and, oh my gosh, Mickey Mantle and Roger Maris are here now. I can't believe it! I'm on their team!"

When Rob Gardner was first called up by the Yankees in 1970, he was overwhelmed by his first visit to the Stadium. "I got there early my first day," he recalled, "and did the monument walk and all that. There was absolutely some mystique to that stadium. There's no question about it. I could feel it. Maybe I'm just making it up for myself, but I could feel it. There was just something different about playing in that ballpark." "That first trip into Yankee Stadium," said Cleveland outfielder Al Luplow, "was the most exciting thing that ever happened to me in baseball."

"It's a breath taker," said Jim Coates. "You go into that dugout, walk up the steps and look across the field and it just takes your breath away. Yankee Stadium does something to you. Everything changes. That's the field that Ruth and all those guys played on and you just thank the Lord you're there."

When asked his best memory of playing for the Yankees, Pete Mikkelsen didn't mention being the winning pitcher in the pennant-clincher in '64, or pitching in the World Series. He said, "The best thing is to walk into Yankee Stadium and walk on the field. That's the biggest thrill for a young fellow and I think even for some of the older guys who get traded there. I hear about the Yankees moving to New Jersey and I can't believe it."

Mikkelsen was correct about the older guys. Bob Friend spent fifteen years with the Pirates before coming to the Yankees in 1966. "I remember walking out through the runway," he said. "Whitey looked at me and said, 'What do you think?' I said, 'Whitey, this is awesome. This is really something.' PNC Park here is fabulous, but Yankee Stadium is really something, just a sight to see."

No one was more in awe of the Yankee mystique, nor did anyone do more to promote it, than Mel Allen. Allen, whose real name was Melvin Israel, grew up in Alabama, the son of a dry goods merchant. Julius Israel's business collapsed during the Depression, helped along by a boycott organized by the Ku Klux Klan, which didn't like the idea of a Jewish merchant prospering while Christians did without. At the age of 11, Mel became associated with baseball for the first time, as a batboy for the Greensboro Patriots. A precocious student, he matriculated to the University of Alabama at age 15, and harbored dreams of playing baseball. Allen was quickly cut from the team, however, and began writing sports for the college paper.

By his senior year, Allen had a full plate, serving as editor of the paper, free lancing for other publications, and serving as student manager for the Alabama baseball team and as P.A. announcer for football games. In 1935, he obtained his first broadcasting job, earning five dollars a game describing Alabama and Auburn football contests. Three years later, after obtaining a law degree, Allen was in the CBS radio booth announcing the 1938 World Series.

Allen joined the Yankees in 1939, and soon became identified as the Voice of the Yankees. The team did little wrong in the years that Allen described their play, and Mel generally chose to ignore even the minor blemish, unabashedly cheering "his" team's exploits and making only the most perfunctory effort at objectivity. The Yankees' success was certainly not due to Mel Allen, but Allen's success was without question attributable to the fame of the New York Yankees. Listening to taped broadcasts today, one is hard-pressed to see what made Allen a premier announcer. He had a mellifluous voice, but it was marked by a noticeable Southern accent. He was not witty, nor did he turn a phrase in the manner of Red Barber or Vin Scully. Allen's description of a baseball game was straightforward, in the "ball one, strike one," fashion of early broadcasters, with long pauses between pitches, interspersed with undisguised delight at a Yankee home run or double play.

In 1954, Allen was joined in the Yankee booth by Red Barber, and in 1957, former shortstop Phil Rizzuto made the broadcast team a trio. Barber brought greater insight to the game than Allen, filling in dead spots in the action with informative tidbits, and not even Allen could approach Rizzuto in his enthusiasm and rooting for the Yankees. Unlike Allen, Rizzuto also added corny humor and warmth to the broadcast. As his Yankee career approached its end, Allen was no longer the star of the team. The only thing he had remaining was his recognizable name, which still landed him on national broadcasts.

In 1963, while working the final game of the World Series, Allen lost his voice in the ninth inning, and Vin Scully had to take over the mike. It was reported that the Yankophile had been so distressed at the thought of the Bombers losing in four straight games, he had suffered a psychosomatic illness that robbed him of his voice.

The following year, Allen's style was as desultory as ever, and noticeably out of step with the more dynamic announcers, such as Joe Garagiola, who were livening up baseball broadcasts. During his final Yankee appearance, on the last day of the 1964 season, Allen rambled endlessly about mundane topics. He reminisced about his childhood and his college days. When Cleveland catcher Duke Sims waited for someone to bring him his mitt, Allen said, "A tisket, a tasket, he's lost his catching basket." Catcher Jake Gibbs was batting second for the Yanks, which reminded Allen of other catchers who'd batted second. He proceeded to name them. Then he named catchers who'd batted third, fourth and fifth, and so on. Finally, before leaving after three innings, Allen launched into a lecture on different languages, and the incorrect pronunciation of names of players with foreign origins.

To his great dismay, Allen was left off the World Series broadcast team in favor of Rizzuto, who both he and Barber considered no better than a likable amateur. Shortly afterward, Allen was fired. A lifelong bachelor who had few interests other than the Yankees and sports, he was devastated.

Allen was replaced in the Yankee booth by Garagiola, already nationally renowned for his work with the Cardinals. Two years after Allen's departure, Barber, another link to Yankee greatness, was dismissed. No one ever accused Barber of being partial, and with the Yankees bottoming out in the American League cellar, they needed a cheerleader, not an objective reporter. When Barber ordered the WPIX cameras to pan a stadium that held 413 people, he sealed his doom. The director refused to honor Barbers's request, and the Redhead asked a second time. He was turned down again, and at the end of the season he was fired. In his autobiography, which appeared shortly after his dismissal, Barber ripped Garagiola, who he said talked too much, and Rizzuto, who he said was lazy and unprepared. After Barber's departure, seldom was a discouraging word heard on Yankee broadcasts. Ralph Houk might have written the script. For the announcers, like Houk, a return to glory was always just around the corner.

The Yankee image was very important to those who played during the championship years. The most grievous sin anyone could commit was to tarnish that image. When Jim Bouton released *Ball Four* in 1970, he broke the bond that linked the Yankees to their proud tradition.

Bouton's co-author, writer Leonard Schecter, had never been a favorite of Yankee players. "A lot of the credit, or discredit, for that book," said Johnny James, "should really go to Leonard Schecter. He was a writer who wasn't really welcome in the locker room. Whenever he'd come in, Mantle and a couple of other guys would say, in very loud voices, 'Hush up, here comes Schecter,' or something to that effect."

"There was a little distrust with Leonard," said Linz. "We wouldn't say things around him." "Leonard was always a grouchy sort of guy," recalled fellow reporter Gordon White. "He was famous for the fact that he grew a mustache at one time and the Yankees jumped him in the dressing room, took him into the trainers' room and held him down while they shaved his mustache. Leonard was just so negative. He knocked Maris all the time. He said to me once, 'If you can't knock it, it ain't worth writing about.'"

In 1969, after the Mets won the World Series, Schechter authored a book on the team. Apparently, he couldn't bring himself to write of the joy of winning, and chose as his subject matter the two losing seasons the Mets spent in the Polo Grounds. The book drips with typical Schechter sarcasm. Norm Sherry was a great catcher, he said, his only problem being that his brother Larry, a pitcher, would out hit him. Larry Bearnarth was the handsomest Met. "Now if he could only pitch," Schechter added.

Schecter was famous for printing stories that the other beat writers, respectful of the players' and team's reputation, kept out of the papers. "The writers wouldn't write about stuff they knew about," said Linz. "They were terrific. We'd go out and get smashed together and say things about the other players. We never thought about any of them printing that stuff." "You'd do an interview with a writer," said former Met Bill Denehy, "and an hour later you'd be having dinner with him and an hour and a half after that you'd be in a bar with him, and the only thing that was in the paper the next day was about your performance on the field."

Schecter didn't honor the code. After Stengel was fired by the Yankees, Johnny Blanchard, who had seen precious little playing time under Casey, was asked by Schecter for his reaction. Schecter and Blanchard were having a drink, and Blanchard asked the reporter if they were off the record. Schecter assured him they were. "Well," said Blanchard, "I'm glad the old son of a bitch is gone. Maybe some of the young guys will get to play now." The next morning, Blanchard picked up *The New York Post* to see his comments in print. He nearly throttled Schecter the next time he saw him. "Well," Schecter replied, "you said it, didn't you?"

In 1958, when Ryne Duren and Ralph Houk brawled following the pennant clinching, the writers traveling with the club supposedly agreed not to print the story. To their shock and anger, a complete account appeared the next day in *The Post*, over Schecter's byline. The other writers had to explain to their editors how they had been scooped, and why they hadn't reported the story, and they were furious.

The animosity between Schecter and the Yankees lingered, and erupted the following summer. One evening, while Stengel was entertaining the writers in the locker room, Schecter asked Stengel about an incident where Stengel and Whitey Ford supposedly "brushed off" a photographer. Stengel turned on writer Joe King, who he thought was responsible for the story, and things started to heat up. Schecter then asked what Stengel had said to his team during a closed door meeting. "You been running this club for three years," Stengel shouted at him. "You want to know what I said ... you want to join the club? I'll give you a uniform." Stan Isaacs of *Newsday* pointed out that the Yankees didn't have a uniform big enough for the portly Schecter, which led to general laughter and defused a potentially volatile situation, but Stengel was still angry.

Schecter was a writer, and one the Yankees hadn't particularly liked. But Bouton was a ballplayer, one of them, a Yankee. Most players, forty years after the fact, are careful not to speak ill of their former teammates. Several made an exception for Bouton. "Any man who would knock a man like Mickey Mantle," said Coates, who named his son Mickey Charles, "I can't say much for him. You just don't knock a guy like that. I don't care what you might think. You don't say it." Bouton also made a number of uncomplimentary references to Coates in his book. "He said a lot of nasty things about me," Coates admitted. "He dogged me pretty good because I was pegged as a headhunter. He said I hated the coloreds, which I didn't, but he just blew it all up."

The subject of Mantle was a particularly touchy one. One former Yankee pitcher was soft-spoken, humorous and gracious until Bouton's name came up. "I'm not too happy to speak about Jim Bouton," he said sharply. "He should have kept his mouth shut. The things he said about Mickey he had no business saying. I lost all respect for him and I don't even like to talk about him." "I shouldn't curse while we talk," said Blanchard, while declining to discuss the subject of Bouton. Joe Pepitone was angry that Bouton exposed everyone else's carousing and philandering, but made no mention of his own. He said that Bouton and Coates were the only two teammates he ever disliked.

Another Yankee said, "I thought that was terrible — telling personal things about people. Who knows what harm that might have done to their families. I always thought he should have gotten knocked on his ass and I would've like to have been the guy to do it." "It's a wonder he's still alive," said ex–Met Larry Miller. "There's a certain sanctity about the clubhouse. There's an unwritten code and he violated it." When Bouton became a sportscaster in 1970, the Yankee players refused to talk to him.

"I was his roommate," said Linz. "He was writing stuff on napkins. I didn't know what he was writing about and I didn't care. He'd say, 'Oh, I'm just putting some notes down.' All I can say is that he's still my friend, but if somebody had asked me I wouldn't have written the book. I never would have written a book like that. We always felt that whatever we did together, no matter what we did and what was said, it just stayed among us. That was an unwritten law in those days. I think Jim suffered a bit for writing the book. A lot of guys still don't talk to him, but he made his peace with Mantle before he died. Mickey had lost one of his sons, and Jim called him. I don't know what happened, but they made up."

Tom Metcalf, who also considered Bouton a friend, speculated, "I think he had a little bit of contempt for the game. It always bothered him that people thought the game was so smart when he thought it was kind of a dumb game — a dumb game run by dumb people — the owners and some of the coaches. It doesn't take a genius to figure out that some of the coaches are just stooges. They're good baseball men. They follow the rules. They know when to hold a guy up at third base and when to let him go. They know how to relay signs. But I don't know why he did it. He's a good guy and not as wacky as he might have appeared."

Jack DiLauro played with Bouton on the Astros in 1970, after the publication of the book. "I liked the guy," DiLauro said. "I really did. He was so honest, so straightforward. I asked him why the hell he wrote the book. He said he just had to do it because of all the different experiences he saw with the Yankees. There were so many personalities." "Christ," DiLauro continued, "everybody knew this shit was going on. We did it in the minor leagues. We were kids. In the minds of the fans, you're not that young. They think you're 30 or 40, that you're a mature individual playing a professional game. But the mentality off the field was often that of kids. Maybe it was the pressure. I don't know. But Jim was a very interesting man. He was very outgoing, very upbeat."

Why did he do it? What kind of man is Jim Bouton? For one thing, he was different than most ballplayers. While most players' hobbies tended to be hunting, fishing and golf, Bouton's were painting in water colors, jewelry-making and ceramics. He'd initially wanted to become a commercial artist, and exhibited a number of his paintings during his Yankee career. He also took creative writing courses, and published an article in *Sport* magazine about his experiences in the minor leagues in 1967. Bouton was involved in several liberal political causes, and was strongly against the war in Vietnam.

Bouton was very witty, and loved comedy. He performed two impersonations that would not survive political correctness. Bouton did a very accurate imitation of Frank Fontaine's portrayal of the drunken Crazy Guggenheim, and an impression of Robert Kennedy, which became much less funny after June, 1968.

As a player, Bouton was intense and driven. In the spring of '61, when he came to his first Yankee training camp, one of his roommates was another rookie pitcher, Bob Meyer. Early one morning Meyer was awakened by a jarring sound in the room. It was Bouton, doing jumping jacks to warm up for pitching batting practice at 11. Bouton had a unique and, to the hitters, irritating, attitude toward batting practice. He threw as if he were pitching in a World Series game. "Bouton had a yellow legal pad," said Meyer, "and he would write the names of all 20 or so pitchers we had in camp, listed in order from best to worst based upon his opinion of how they had done that day. Our third roommate was Gerry Heintz, an 18-year-old bonus kid. Heintz and I would always sneak a look at his list. Bouton always had his own name at the top of the list and Heintz's at the bottom. That was the kind of competitor he was. I have a lot of respect for Bouton. I think he's a very smart guy and certainly was a great competitor."

Bouton was clearly a very smart guy. He was not, however, the first intelligent, opinionated Yankee. Tony Kubek, although he never attended college, was one of the most erudite, well-read players in baseball. "Tony was always smarter than anyone else," said Johnny James. "He would do the *New York Times* crossword puzzle every day." A voracious appetite for reading had given Kubek an impressive vocabulary, and he was not hesitant to venture his opinion. He refused to endorse products out of principle, and decried the commercialism that he saw becoming more prevalent in baseball. Kubek saw through much of the silliness in the game, and held forth on the future of baseball, its salary structure, and numerous other topics. He never, however, talked about his teammates.

Bouton's intelligence and intellectual curiosity were the equal of Kubek's, but he didn't have Kubek's tact. "Bouton was the type of person," said Meyer, "who would really think about something, and you don't find a whole lot of that in 23 or 24 year old kids. You could ask him any esoteric question, and he would ponder it and come up with something that would make sense. If you asked most guys a question like that, they'd say, 'Ah, shut the fuck up,' or 'Why are you thinking about that for, man?' but Bouton was cut from a different cloth. A very interesting guy." Many of his teammates, and especially the baseball establishment, would have substituted "big troublemaker" for "very interesting guy."

"He was a troublemaker," Meyer said, "because he had the audacity to think for himself and state it publicly." He laughed. "You're not supposed to do that." Meyer understood the animosity many old Yankees felt after the publication of *Ball Four*. "I never held it against him," he said, "but maybe they felt that Bouton was out for Bouton. I think that he was, but so what? So was everybody else. To get to that level, you've got to be out for yourself."

Perhaps the most notable altercation Bouton had during his Yankee career was with Frank Crosetti, guardian of stray baseballs and the Yankee tradition. One day Bouton started the first game of a Sunday doubleheader and was knocked out early. The Yankees had an off day on Monday, and Bouton had scheduled a fishing trip. After he was taken out of the game, he went into the clubhouse and changed into his street clothes, intending to make an early getaway. Crosetti came into the locker room and asked Bouton what he thought he was doing, then went back to the dugout to report to Houk. Crosetti returned with orders that Bouton was to put his uniform back on, because he might be needed in relief in the second game. Bouton was furious, but he got dressed.

Between games of the doubleheader, Bouton started yelling at Crosetti, telling him to mind his own business. Elston Howard came over and told Bouton to shut up, which calmed things down for a while. Then Bouton started again on Crosetti. "Unbeknownst to anybody," said one of the Yankees, "Houk was listening to all this shit. He came out of his office and went strolling down to Bouton's locker. Bouton turned around and was nose to nose with Houk." "You were told to shut the fuck up," Houk shouted, "and you had better shut the fuck up right now." "Everybody knew," the player continued, "that Houk would hit you in a minute if you gave him any shit. Bouton didn't breathe for about five minutes. You could hear a pin drop in the clubhouse." The incident was over but not forgotten.

"Houk would call Bouton into his office about once a month," said Steve Whitaker, "and want to kick his ass because Bouton was spouting off in the paper." Whitaker was playing with the Seattle Pilots when Bouton was taking notes for his book. "I personally thought it was a cheap shot," Whitaker said, "because anybody can write a book like that. But it was a Bouton thing. He's a talented guy. I remember Gene Brabender, our pitcher, who was almost 6'6" and weighed about 250 or so, got a big blow dart gun. It was like something right out of Africa, for chrissakes. Bouton was being very secretive, and people knew his reputation so they didn't want to talk too much around him, but he was always taking notes. Finally, Brabender said, 'Bullshit, man, you're writing down everything we say.' He came in one day and Bouton was sitting there playing chess with Mike Marshall on these old goddamn wooden stools or benches we had in front of our lockers. Brabender came in with his dart gun that must have been ten feet long and started shooting nails into these rickety old lockers we had at Sick's Stadium. He started at the top and was working his way down toward their heads, and he wasn't stopping. They kept saying, 'C'mon, what are you, a moron?' Finally, we had to take that gun away from him because he was gonna kill them."

By the end of the 1960s, when Bouton wrote his book, the Yankees were no longer winning pennants. Their opponents no longer feared them. But the aura was still there. "They weren't the Yankee teams of the '50s or early '60s," said Bill Monbouquette, who became a Yankee in 1967, "but the mystique was still there. To walk into the clubhouse and think of the great players who had played there. When you walked into the stadium, you were in awe."

"You had to be aware," said Lindy McDaniel, who arrived a year after Monbouquette, "that when you join the Yankees it's kind of an international name and a Yankee is a Yankee, regardless of what era they come from. You're aware of their great history and the accomplishments of the Yankee organization. I became very aware of that. I became a Yankee."

In the early 1960s, the Yankee mystique was more than just a memory. In inspired those who wore the pinstripes and cast doubt in the hearts and minds of their opponents. The ghosts of Ruth, Gehrig and Dimaggio weren't coming to the plate, or patrolling center field, but many of the Yankees felt their spirit, and it gave them strength. If that didn't work, they always had Moose Skowron telling them not to mess with his World Series money. They knew that being a Yankee was special, that they were expected to win, and their opponents knew they were expected to lose. Most often in the first half of the decade, that is exactly what happened.

• 11 •

I Shot the Sheriff
The 1963 Season

The Yankees' 1963 training camp began with a bang. Fort Lauderdale was still a segregated city in the early '60s, and had a number of establishments known as "Negro clubs" that provided entertainment for African Americans. One such club was The Fort Lauderdale Elks Lodge. On the evening of February 13, Yankee pitcher Marshall Bridges was at the Elks Lodge, making a concerted effort to attract the attention of a 21-year-old woman named Carrie Lee Raysor. Bridges, married and the father of three children, kept asking Ms. Raysor if she would go home with him. She said she wouldn't. When Bridges persisted, she pulled out a small revolver and put a .25 caliber bullet into Bridges' left leg, just below the knee.

The damage to Bridges' leg was minor, with the bullet merely chipping a small bone and injuring the fleshy part of his calf. Doctors told him that if they operated to remove the slug, he would be sidelined for the entire year. Otherwise, he would be up and walking within a week. Bridges elected to keep the bullet as a souvenir of the occasion, and, after a few days in the hospital, went home to Jackson, Mississippi to recuperate and explain the episode to his wife. Although police arrested Raysor and charged her with aggravated assault, Bridges declined to press charges, for obvious reasons. He didn't relish the prospect of recounting the evening's events on the witness stand, under oath.

In late March, having explained the situation as well as he could to Mrs. Bridges, the Sheriff returned to Fort Lauderdale. While Bridges was in the hospital, Houk had visited and, in those politically incorrect days, brushed the incident off with a joke. "I'm going to have to get you a holster," he said. "You're too slow on the draw." Houk told Bridges that the boys would be expecting some good stories when he returned.

In the good old days of the early '60s, alcoholism, philandering and gunplay were funny. Columnist Melvin Durslag wrote that Ms. Raysor appeared to have eyesight and aim like Ryne Duren. When Bridges returned to the Yankee clubhouse, he found that someone had posted a cartoon on his locker, showing a pitcher pulling out a gun and shooting a runner leading off first base. The caption read, "He has the best pickoff motion in the league." At first, Bridges' teammates were silent, virtually ignoring him as he sat on his stool. Suddenly, Mantle burst out of a side room with a toy pistol, shouting, "Bang, bang, bang." Things were back to normal.

The Yankees had won in 1962 despite a thin pitching staff. Turley, Arroyo, Clevenger and Sheldon had contributed little all season. Houk used only six pitchers in the World Series, with Terry and Ford throwing 45 of the 61 innings. While the bullpen could use some help, the club's most pressing need was for a solid fourth starter to join Ford, Terry and Stafford in the rotation. In 1962, Sheldon, Coates, Turley, and Daley had been tried in the fourth slot and all had been found wanting.

Houk and Hamey believed they had filled the hole in the rotation with the acquisition of strong, hard-throwing right-hander Stan Williams, who came to the Yankees from the Dodgers for Moose Skowron. The trade had the look of a winner. Skowron was still a valuable player, but was 32 and had a history of injury. The Yankees had Joe Pepitone, ten years younger, in the wings.

Only 26 years old, Williams was a five year veteran who had been a consistent winner with the light-hitting Dodgers. He was a big, tough, burly man with a good, hard fastball, reminiscent of Vic Raschi. Williams had garnered 43 victories in the past three years and, in 1961, struck out 205 National League batters, second in the league behind teammate Sandy Koufax. The big righthander, hampered by arm trouble, struggled in 1962, despite winning 14 games. His ERA was 4.45, and he ended the season by walking in the winning run in the Dodgers' final playoff game. Williams' arm now seemed fine, and he had a good spring. Supported by the New York sluggers rather than the popgun Dodger attack, Houk expected Big Stan to win 20.

With Ford, the 1961 Cy Young winner, Terry, coming off the best season of his career, Stafford, who'd won 14 games each of the last two seasons, and Williams, Houk believed he had a solid starting rotation for the first time in his three years at the helm. The bullpen was not as promising. Bridges, the best reliever in 1962, was in drydock for nearly all of spring training. His condition wouldn't be critical, however, if Arroyo, who had been virtually useless in 1962, could return to anything resembling his 1961 form. Luis avoided winter ball completely for the first time in many years, and when he reported to Fort Lauderdale, said his arm felt as good as it did in 1961. In thirteen exhibition innings, he allowed just one run and struck out 17, looking like the Arroyo of '61.

The starting lineup, with the exception of Skowron, returned intact. Since Kubek would be with the club from the start, the Yankees had an even stronger starting eight than that which had opened a year earlier. For the first time since 1958, the team had a regular left fielder. Tresh, who looked so good at the end of the 1962 season, would have an entire spring to work on his outfielding. One of the keys to the Williams trade, of course, was whether Pepitone could adequately replace Skowron. "We have just about the same team as last year," Mantle told an interviewer, "except for first base. So if we lose, you can blame it on Joe Pepitone."

Pepitone started off slowly in the spring, but Houk, with his usual confidence, said he wouldn't be surprised if Pepitone drove in 90 runs. He said Pepitone was better than Tresh, the 1962 Rookie of the Year, had been a year ago. Just to make sure the rookie wasn't too relaxed, however, Houk had Lopez work out at first base, and hinted that if Pepitone didn't make it, he'd go with Hector.

Pepitone, as cocky as ever, was certain he would succeed, and said he was much more mature than he had been the previous year. "His self-confidence sticks out all over him like a badge," wrote Newsday, "almost to a fault." In late March, Pepitone's hitting caught up with his confidence, and he wound up with nine spring home runs. When he hit two round trippers in the opening game of the regular season, it seemed as though the Moose wouldn't be missed. In August, Leonard Koppett described Pepitone as, "the loose-limbed first baseman who has turned Bill Skowron into a dim memory."

Bridges was the only gunshot victim of 1963, but his injury was the first of many that were to plague the Yankees throughout the year. During training camp, Kubek experienced a mysterious swelling in his right armpit, which was eventually diagnosed as a pulled muscle. Ford's arm bothered him all spring. The wave of injuries was not limited to players. In February, at his home in Hillside, New Jersey, broadcaster Phil Rizzuto caught his fingers in a snowblower and required a three hour operation to save the mangled digits.

In the second game of the season, on a cold day in Kansas City, the injury bug hit the pitching staff. Stafford was breezing along in the seventh inning, shutting out the Athletics, when he felt a sharp pain in his elbow, and had to leave the game. The injury didn't appear serious, and Dr. Gaynor, the Yankees' team physician, said Stafford might not even miss a turn. Stafford did miss a turn, and when he pitched again, he wasn't the same. In fact, Stafford was never again the pitcher he'd been in '61 and '62. Later in the season, he suffered a groin pull sliding into a base, developed a terrible rash all over his body, and gained weight. He went two months without a win, and finished the season 4–8 with a horrible ERA of 6.00.

When Stafford had to leave the game in Kansas City, Bud Daley came on to preserve his win. That night, Daley was awakened by a shooting pain in his arm, and the next day his elbow swelled up like a balloon. A floating bone chip had lodged in a joint. "About two years earlier," Daley recalled, "I felt a little pop and I think that's probably when I broke off the bone chip. It probably didn't go down into the joint until that day in Kansas City." When the swelling and pain persisted, Daley was forced to undergo an operation that finished his 1963 season, and effectively ended his career. "My arm just kind of got worse and worse," he said. Daley attempted a comeback in 1964, and stayed with the Yankees almost the entire season, although he rarely pitched. "My arm was really killing me," he said. "The last time my wife saw me pitch in New York, she said, 'I'm not going to see you pitch again. Every time you throw, I can hear you say, 'Ow, ow.'"

The season was only two games old, and Houk had already lost two pitchers. It wasn't long before he lost another. Arroyo, who'd looked so good in the spring, pitched well and picked up a win in his first appearance of the regular season. That was his last good game as a Yankee. On May 28, Arroyo was hammered for five hits and four runs in just two thirds of an inning. On June 6, having appeared in just six games, he was sent to Richmond. His major league career was over. With Arroyo and Daley gone, and Bridges carrying a bullet in his leg, the Yankees were without a reliable left hander in the bullpen. To remedy the problem, Hamey traded Jim Coates to Washington for 6'7" lefty Steve Hamilton. "Well," Houk said when he saw the gawky, prematurely gray Hamilton, "we've gained two inches in height but nothing in looks. The reason we traded for you was you were the only guy who could fit Coates' uniform."

Coates, who'd been a valuable contributor to three Yankee pennant winners, had been in the Yankee organization for more than ten years. He pitched poorly and sparingly for the Senators, was sent to the Reds, and then to the minor leagues. Knocking hitters down as frequently as he had in his younger days, Coates fought his way back to the majors and pitched for the Angels in parts of the 1965, 1966 and 1967 seasons. "I will never give this game up," he said in 1966. In 1968, Coates returned to the Pacific Coast League and was 17–10 for Seattle. He hoped that his record would get the attention of one of the expansion clubs, but when he was ignored, Coates signed with the independent Hawaii Islanders, and began his 17th season in professional baseball at the age of 36.

In June, Coates was leading the Islanders with seven victories when, just a few hours after pitching nine innings, he was stricken with a severe ruptured stomach ulcer which required emergency surgery. He nearly died during the operation. Coates missed the rest of the year, but vowed, with his characteristic stubbornness, to return in 1970. He did, pitching a complete game victory as Hawaii's opening night hurler. Later in the season, Coates moved to the bullpen and set a team record for saves. That was his last season in pro ball.

Hamilton, possessor of a sweeping sidearm slider that was devastating against left hand hitters, was a graduate of Morehead State College who played professional basketball with the Minneapolis Lakers for two seasons in the late '50s. Although just 27, he had begun to turn gray at 15, and by 1963 there was little dark hair to be found.

The big lefty was thrown into action shortly after he arrived in New York. On May 11th,

Hamilton was called on to relieve Williams in the first inning of a game against the Orioles. He pitched eight and a third innings, allowed only three hits, no walks and no runs, and even hit a two run triple, as the Yankees won 13–1.

Hamilton's performance was very encouraging, but the fact that he was called on to relieve Williams in the first inning was not. Stan had a great spring, the best of any Yankee starter, and pitched a five hit complete game victory in his American League debut. Then he had a few good games mixed with some very bad ones. In three consecutive starts, he lasted one inning, two thirds of an inning, and three and a third innings, looking more like the Williams of 1962 than that of 1960 or 1961. "Just what has suddenly come over the big righthander," wrote John Drebinger, "is puzzling everyone." Stan was wild, walking more than he was striking out. In the game in which Hamilton relieved him in the first inning, he walked three and threw a wild pitch.

In the spring, anticipating his starting rotation to be strong and his bullpen in need of help, Houk had put young Jim Bouton in the relief corps. Not only did Bouton have a crackling fastball and sharp curve, plus a slider he'd picked up from Johnny Sain, he had the mental toughness a reliever needed.

For the first month of the season, Bouton was outstanding. He ran off fourteen scoreless innings in a row, picking up a couple of wins in the process. In the 1960s, good relief pitching was often rewarded with a "promotion" to the starting rotation, which is what happened to Bouton, who made his first start on May 12. He retired the first 19 batters and finished with a two hit, 2–0 win. Bouton walked just a single batter, a pleasant contrast to Williams' wildness the day before. Bouton became a fixture in the rotation, and was selected to the American League All Star team.

Ford and Terry were pitching well, although their won lost records didn't reflect it. With the addition of Bouton and the subtraction of Williams and Stafford, there remained one opening in the rotation. When the Yankees sent Arroyo to Richmond, they recalled a 22-year old lefthander from Trenton, New Jersey, Al Downing, who'd spent part of the '61 season in New York.

Downing had signed with the Yankees in 1961, just after Weiss retired. Knowing the former Yankee executive's reluctance to engage black athletes, Downing said later he would not have signed if Weiss had remained. When he was called up in '61, Downing, then only 20, showed terrific speed and great potential, but was clearly not ready to pitch in the big leagues. Downing pitched at Richmond in 1962, where he threw a no hitter, but overall had a mediocre year, finishing 9–13 with a 4.10 ERA. Still, he struck out 180 in 169 innings, and anyone who saw his live fastball knew he had a chance to pitch in the major leagues. Downing had 64 strikeouts in 57 innings when he was recalled in 1963. He was also more confident than when the Yankees had last seen him, and was no longer the nervous youngster he'd been in 1961.

The day after he joined the Yankees, Downing mopped up a lost cause with a hitless inning. On June 10th, he made his first start and delivered more than even the optimistic Houk could have hoped for. In the first game of a doubleheader, Downing shut out the Senators on two hits. Best of all, the youngster, who had always had trouble with his control, walked only three. In the nightcap, Bouton pitched another excellent game, but lost, 1–0, only his second defeat against seven victories. When Downing won his next start, another complete game, it appeared as though Houk had found the other half of his rotation.

Ford, after starting slowly, nearly equaled his 1961 record. He was 24–7, and his 2.74 ERA was much better than his 1961 earned run average of 3.21. Bouton, despite starting the season in the bullpen, was 21–7, winning 18 games between May 1 and August 31. Downing, who began the year at Richmond, was 13–5, with 171 strikeouts in 176 innings, including 14 in one game, just one short of the Yankee record. He had a one hitter, two two hitters, two three hitters and a four hitter. Any club whose top three starters are 58–15 has an excellent chance of winning the pennant.

With the exception of his won and lost record, Terry's performance was nearly identical to that of the previous two years. He posted ERAs of 3.16 in 1961, 3.19 in 1962 and 3.22 in 1963. Each year, he was stingy with walks (1.3 per nine innings in '63), generous with home runs (an AL high 40 in '62) and a workhorse (a league leading 18 complete games in '63). Yet, his won and lost record went from 16–3 in '61 to 23–12 in '62 and 17–15 the following year.

With the addition of Hamilton, and the development of Hal Reniff, who'd lost the entire 1962 season to military service and a sore arm, the bullpen, although not great, was adequate. Reniff was a portly, outspoken righthander who hadn't shown much in his first few seasons in the minors. He kept asking for his release, thinking he could do better with another organization, but the Yankees wouldn't give it to him. Suddenly, at Modesto in 1959, Reniff found himself, winning 21 games. He was called up to the Yankees in '61 and pitched well, then suffered through his lost 1962 season. After a great spring in '63, he made the team and led the club with 18 saves.

Yankee starters led the league with 59 complete games, so the relievers weren't needed that much. During a 13 game stretch between August 20th and 30th, the starters completed 11 games. In the other two games, the relievers appeared only in the ninth inning. By that time, not only were Houk's top four starters humming, Williams seemed to have found himself. He discovered a sinker, finished in spectacular fashion, and wound up 9–8, with an ERA of 3.21.

While pitching had been a problem the previous two years, hitting had not, and with the same cast returning in '63, there was no reason to believe that the club would have trouble scoring runs. Yet they did. The Yankees, who led the league with 817 runs in 1962, scored only 714 in '63, due in part to the overall decline in scoring which followed a broadening of the strike zone. Not a single Yankee drove in as many as 90 runs. Moreover, the men who produced the runs in 1963 were very different from those who drove them home the previous two years.

When asked about the Yankees' pennant chances before the start of the season, Washington GM George Selkirk said that if Mantle were injured, the Yanks would not win. For the first few weeks of the season, Mickey, who had signed his first $100,000 contract in the spring, stayed in one piece for the most part, something few of his teammates were able to do. In May, he hit a home run off Kansas City's Bill Fischer that struck the right field facade and narrowly missed going completely out of Yankee Stadium.

During the first week of June, the Yankees took a road trip to Cleveland, Baltimore, Detroit and Washington. By the time the club returned to New York, five Yankees had gone down with assorted injuries. Bouton was hit in the face by a line drive in Baltimore. Maris bruised his big toe during batting practice in Detroit. Linz, filling in for Kubek, who was out with a sore hamstring, twisted his right knee in Detroit. Boyer had a sore shoulder.

On the evening of June 5, in Baltimore, the Yankees lost the man they could least afford be without. They were leading the Orioles 3–2 in the sixth inning when Brooks Robinson hit a fly ball to deep center field. Mantle sprinted back and leaped up against the unpadded chain link fence. The ball went over the fence and Mantle crashed against it, catching his left foot in the intertwined metal. When he fell to the ground, Mantle's foot was twisted at a grotesque angle, and he knew immediately that something was seriously wrong. Mickey had broken the third metatarsal bone. He was carried from the field on a stretcher, and taken immediately to the hospital. "It looks as if we're going to go to our bench more," said Houk.

Mantle estimated he would be back in the lineup within three to four weeks. "If we can stay at .500 until Mickey returns," Hamey said, "we can still make it." The Yankees hesitated before placing Mantle on the disabled list, hoping he might be back sooner than 30 days. Dr. Gaynor was not as optimistic, and estimated that Mantle would not be back until just after the All Star break, at the earliest.

Hamey finally decided to put Mantle on the disabled list. About three weeks after the injury, Mickey, who had been recuperating at his home in Dallas, flew to New York to have the cast removed. Although still on crutches, Mantle said he thought he would be able to play in about three weeks. On July 11th, about five weeks after the injury, he joined the Yankees and worked out for the first time. "It wouldn't surprise me if we had him back in the lineup in ten days," said Houk, "maybe sooner." No one who watched Mantle work out, however, could believe he would be back in action that soon. All Mickey had done was limp around the outfield a bit, and take a few swings right handed. He couldn't push off his left foot well enough to hit left handed. The next day, Mantle was taken off the disabled list and restored to the active roster, even though he clearly wasn't ready to play.

On July 16, Houk said he expected Mantle back within a week. Mickey wasn't so sure, for a complication had arisen. When he hit the fence in Baltimore, Mantle had also damaged cartilage in his knee, an injury that had gone undiscovered due to focus on the broken bone. "He may be able to play in a week," Houk said on July 25, about seven weeks after the injury, "or he may be unable to play for the rest of the season." An operation could correct the knee problem, but surgery would put Mantle out of action for the year. He and the Yankees decided to see if he could play through the pain, as he had so many times before.

Finally, on August 4, Houk decided Mantle was ready. In the second game of a doubleheader, with the Yankees losing 10–9 in the seventh inning, Houk sent him up as a pinch hitter. When the familiar Number 7 emerged from the first base dugout for the first time in 61 games, the fans erupted. Lefty George Brunet was on the mound for Baltimore, which meant that Mantle could bat right handed, the only way he was capable of hitting. Mickey took a strike, then drove Brunet's second pitch deep into the lower left field stand. The crack of the bat precipitated a second roar that dwarfed the first. The game was tied and Mickey had returned in dramatic fashion.

Mantle was not ready to return to the lineup on a full time basis. He pinch hit a few more times, getting four walks in his next five appearances, and added a second homer, again off a Baltimore left hander, Mike McCormick, on September 1. The following day, he started a game for the first time in nearly three months. Although he wasn't running well, Mantle put a scare into Houk by trying to steal a base (he was thrown out) and sliding hard into second to try to break up a double play. Mickey played sporadically during the month of September, and finished the season with just 65 games played, by far the fewest of his career. Thirteen of those were as a pinch hitter. Still, he batted .314 with 15 homers in just 172 at bats.

By the final week of the season, the second member of the M&M brigade was also ailing. While the Yankees made their final road trip of the year, Maris was in New York receiving treatment for his back. Roger's season had been little better than Mantle's. He missed the opener due to a pulled hamstring. As soon as he returned to the lineup, Maris aggravated the injury and was out for several more games.

The series of injuries didn't improve Maris's disposition. In May, during a game in Minneapolis, Maris hit a ground ball to second base and jogged to first base. When Twin second baseman Bernie Allen bobbled the ball, Maris made a belated effort to get to first, but was thrown out. As he returned to the dugout, the fans let him have it. Maris, in return, made an obscene gesture toward the stands. Unfortunately, WPIX cameras picked up the gesture and beamed it back to New York. Roger was under orders, said Houk, not to run hard because of his bad leg, but Houk did not indicate that Maris was under orders to flip off the fans. Maris was wrong, Houk admitted, but he said he couldn't believe what the fans were saying to his right fielder.

Despite his leg problems, persistent trouble with his back, the absence of Mantle behind him in the lineup, and an overactive middle finger, Roger had an excellent first half. On July

12, Maris was batting .294, with 19 home runs and 42 RBI. He led the club in average and home runs. Then his back began acting up again. Shortly thereafter, he had minor surgery to correct a rectal fissure. Then he sprained his wrist, and a few days later sprained his hand. Maris finished with a .269 average, 23 homers and 53 RBI, having batted .212 with just four home runs during the second half of the year.

Selkirk had said that the Yankees wouldn't win if Mantle got hurt. No one asked him what would happen if both Mantle and Maris were hurt and two of the four starters, Stafford and Williams, were ineffective. He probably would have said that the Yankees would be hard-pressed to finish in the first division. Yet, when Mantle returned to the starting lineup on September 2, the Yankees held a 12 game lead over the second place White Sox. After taking first place in early June, the club had gradually pulled away from the field.

How did it happen? There were several reasons. First, the teams expected to give the Yankees the most difficulty floundered. The Tigers got off to such a terrible start that manager Bob Scheffing was fired. The Twins and Angels, the Yankees' closest pursuers in 1962, also struggled. The Twins, in last place in mid–May, righted themselves and won 91 games, but the Angels never recovered, and ended up ninth, 34 games behind. The projected contenders had gotten off poorly, but since all ten teams played each other, everyone couldn't be losing. The teams that surged toward the top in the early going, however, were Boston and Kansas City, who everyone knew were eventually destined for the second division. They didn't disappoint, finishing seventh and eighth, respectively. By the time teams like the Twins and Tigers finally got going, it was too late.

A second reason the Yankees outpaced the pack, of course, was the sterling performance of Bouton and Downing, who won 34 games between them. A third reason for the Yankee success was the play of Pepitone, Tresh and Howard. Pepitone had a fine first year, hitting 27 home runs and driving home 89, just missing Houk's prediction of 90. Tresh, although bothered by a series of nagging injuries, most notably a sore right hand, hit 25 home runs.

Before the season started, Howard said his goals were a .300 average, 25 home runs, and 85 to 90 RBI. He was almost right on the nose. With Mantle and Maris injured, Howard emerged from their shadow to become the first African-American to win the American League Most Valuable Player Award, hitting .287 with 28 home runs, while driving in 85. The MVP balloting wasn't even close. Howard received 248 votes, with Detroit's Al Kaline a distant second with 148.

Howard's first experience with professional baseball was a Cardinal tryout camp in 1947. After four days of workouts, during which the Cards sent a number of players home, Howard was still there. He expected an offer, but none was forthcoming. Jackie Robinson may have been playing for Brooklyn, but the color line was not about to be broken in St. Louis. Howard played with the Negro semi-pro St. Louis Braves, then the Kansas City Monarchs in the Negro leagues, and was signed by the Yankees in 1950. His rise to the big leagues was delayed by two years of military duty, and when he reported back from the service in 1953, Stengel decided to convert Howard (who was identified in *The Sporting News* as "Liston Howard, Negro outfielder") from an outfielder to a catcher. Many thought the switch was simply a ploy to prevent another black player from reaching the majors. Berra was on the verge of two MVP seasons, and with a number of other young prospects in the wings, the Yankees didn't seem to need a catcher.

The lack of alacrity with which the Yankees integrated was unimpressive both from social and competitive aspects. George Weiss was a leader of the old guard, and had no desire to change the status quo. He thought that hiring black players might hurt him at the gate. By 1954, 14 of the 18 major league teams had employed black players. The only holdouts were the Phillies, Tigers, Red Sox and Yankees. Whether Weiss liked it or not, change was coming, but if he was forced to have an African-American player, he wanted to be certain that the first black Yankee was his type of player.

Prior to Howard's emergence, it had been presumed that farmhand Vic Power would be the first to break the Yankee color barrier. Power was one of the best fielding first basemen in baseball, and a good hitter, but he was not George Weiss's type of player. He was flamboyant on the field and off, and was reputed to have a fondness for white women. Once, when he was arrested for jaywalking, Power said, "I saw the white people crossing with the green light, so I crossed with the red one." The Yankees didn't find such remarks funny. In 1953, despite having led the American Association in batting with a .349 average, Power was traded to Kansas City before he ever played a game with the Yankees.*

If Yankee scouts were trying to find the "right kind of Negro," they weren't doing a very good job. In addition to Power, one of their other prime prospects in the minor leagues was eccentric pitcher Ruben Gomez. They stood silently aside while solid citizens were signed by other organizations. Yankee traveling secretary Bill McCorry scouted an 18-year-old outfielder with the Birmingham Barons, but reported that Willie Mays could not hit a curve ball and was not a prospect.

In 1954, Howard became the first black ever invited to a Yankee training camp. He was sent to Toronto, learned to catch, and had a phenomenal season. Howard hit .330, with 22 home runs and 109 RBI and was named the International League's Most Valuable Player. He made the major league club the following spring and, for the next six years, played about a hundred games a season, spelling Berra behind the plate, pinch hitting and playing left field. He was named the MVP of the 1958 World Series. More important, Ellie demonstrated that he was the type of man the Yankees had wanted to be the first black Yankee. He was articulate, polite, and above all, willing to look the other way when racial trouble appeared. There wouldn't be any embarrassing situations involving Elston Howard.

Howard was a nice man and well-liked by his teammates. In his first year in the minor leagues, when an opposing pitcher threw at him and called him names, the other players came to his defense. When he reached the major leagues, Phil Rizzuto befriended him. "After that," Howard said later, "no racial trouble, all the way." Of course, Howard's definition of trouble was limited. As late as 1961, he had to endure racial prejudice. When the Yankees visited Orlando, the black players stayed behind, for no restaurant would serve them. Howard remained in St. Petersburg and said nothing. He ignored and endured. "This situation is solving itself," he said.

By 1961, at the age of 32, Howard finally became a regular and, in 1963, he had the best season of his career. Howard was not only a good hitter, he had become an excellent defensive catcher. "He was real agile," said Bud Daley. "He moved from side to side real well and he would think with the pitcher. He'd get in a groove with you and he'd know what you wanted to throw. I just really enjoyed pitching to him." "He really wanted to work hard with you," said Rollie Sheldon. "I just loved to throw to him. He knew me and I knew him. I never shook him off. That first year I never shook off Elston Howard."

The fourth, and perhaps most important, reason the Yankees ran away with the pennant was the performance of the bench. From June 1 through September 25, Houk was not able to post a lineup that included his eight best players. Yet, it seemed as though whatever eight Houk put on the field played as well as his starters. Lopez played 130 games and hit 14 home runs and drove in 52. He'd worked hard at his defense, and his fielding had improved immensely from the adventurous days of 1960. He was even used occasionally as a defensive replacement, and writer Til Ferdenzi called Lopez one of the best left fielders in the league. "I know you guys used to get a good laugh out of me playing the outfield," Lopez told reporters. "But no more."

Linz filled in around the infield, as he had in 1962, and played in the outfield as well. Berra,

---

*Weiss was right concerning Power's penchant for trouble. He courted controversy throughout his career and, in 1965, was jailed briefly for failure to pay alimony.

now a player-coach, batted .293 in 64 games as Howard's backup. In July, with Maris injured, Blanchard came off the bench to play right field.

For the first three months of the season, Blanchard had been a forgotten man. With Berra no longer playing the outfield, it was 1959 and 1960 all over again. On the few occasions that Howard didn't catch, Berra did, and Blanchard sat. By mid–June, he had batted just twelve times with but one hit. He didn't get his first home run of the year until June 22. It was just his second hit. When Maris was injured, Houk first indicated he might move Kubek to the outfield and Linz to short, rather than play Blanchard. Rather than disrupt two positions, however, Houk decided to give Blanchard a chance, and Big John made the most of it. On July 7, he was batting .135, but once he began to play regularly, his potent bat came alive. After Blanchard hit two home runs to beat the Angels, one of the Los Angeles fans said, "Gosh, I hope Mantle and Maris get back soon." They didn't return soon enough, as Blanchard hit a three run homer the next day to beat the Angels again. Two more home runs against the White Sox followed on August 3. After that game, his record showed 21 for 67 (.313) since he began playing regularly, with eight home runs and 21 RBI.

Blanchard was hitting like it was 1961. On the 15th of August, he hit two home runs against the Red Sox, including a grand slam. A week later, he hit another grand slam. Two days after that, Blanchard hit his tenth home run in little more than a month. By the end of the season, he had 16 home runs, all but one of them coming after July 7. Blanchard and Maris, who logged most of the time in right field, combined for 530 at bats, in which they hit 39 home runs, a pretty good season for a full-time outfielder.*

The final member of the sterling Yankee bench was utility man Harry Bright, a right handed batter with some power, who was purchased from Cincinnati on the same day Hamilton was acquired from the Senators. Bright was originally signed by the Yankees and began his professional career at Fond du Lac in 1946. The Yankees released him, but Bright found a job with another organization and began a lengthy pilgrimage through the minor leagues. He took a brief hiatus after a .202 season in the Evangaline League. "When you can't hit better than .202 in the Evangaline League," Bright said later, "well, I decided I had had it." He took a job in a furniture factory, but when he was laid off, decided to give baseball another whirl. He asked his new wife what she thought. She was surprised, since she had met Bright after he'd stopped playing and didn't realize he had been a ballplayer.

With Mrs. Bright's blessing, Harry returned to seek his fortune on the diamond. It was a long time coming, despite some very good years in the minor leagues, including one season during which he batted .413 for Clovis in the West Texas League. Finally, in 1958, 12 years after he began his journey, Bright surfaced in the National League with the Pirates. He was 28 years old.

In parts of three seasons in Pittsburgh, Bright batted just 76 times, and found himself back in Salt Lake City in 1960. He had a terrific year in Salt Lake, hitting .314 with 27 homers and 119 RBI. It was a fortuitous time to have a good season, for the major leagues were expanding and there would be 50 new jobs available. The Senators, one of the new American League expansion teams, drafted Bobby Shantz from the Yankees, then traded him to the Pirates for promising pitcher Bennie Daniels, infielder R.C. Stevens and Harry Bright.

With the Senators, Bright finally got a chance to play. He was in 72 games in 1961 and had his best year in the big leagues the following season, batting .273 with 17 homers and 67 RBI in 113 games. Washington finished last in 1962, however, and wasn't about to rebuild with a 33-year-old utility man. They traded Bright to the Reds for a younger first baseman, 24-year-old Rogelio Alvarez. The Senators would have been better off with Bright, for Alvarez got stuck in

---

With most of the bench players employed as starters, the Yankees had the lowest pinch hitting average (.187) in the American League. Blanchard, the most dangerous pinch hitter in the league in 1961, was just one for fourteen.

Cuba and never played for Washington. Bright didn't play much for Cincinnati, either, getting into just one game before he got a call from the Reds' front office on April 20th. Bright thought he was going back to the minors. "When they told me I had been traded to the Yankees," he said later, "I fainted dead away."

Why did the World Champion Yankees want a journeyman minor leaguer who would turn 34 in September? The last place Senators had traded him and the Reds had no place for him. At last, however, Bright was in the right place at the right time. The Yankees weren't looking for a star. They were seeking a spare part and few could fill the role of spare part better than Harry Bright. He had played all nine positions in the minor leagues, and had been in the minors so long he wasn't about to complain about a lack of playing time. Like Jack Reed, he was perfect for his role. Many have used the expression, "I'm just happy to be here," but Bright truly meant it. He could play first base when Houk wanted to give Pepitone a rest against tough left handed pitchers. He could play third and the outfield, and could catch in an emergency.

Bright started hitting as soon as he joined the Yankees. For a while he was over .500, and by mid–July, was still batting close to .290. He platooned with Pepitone for a while, then played third when Boyer went into a slump. Bright hit with some pop, and fielded better than many thought he would. He became a favorite of the fans and press for his enthusiasm and graciousness. By the end of the season, Bright was down to .236, but he'd hit seven home runs, had a number of clutch hits and played a key role in many Yankee wins. In one late season game, with so many regulars injured, Houk started Lopez, Reed and Bright in the outfield. Bright homered and the Yankees won 2–1.

Nineteen sixty three was nothing like 1961 or 1962. Nineteen sixty three was the year Bouton and Downing established themselves in the starting rotation and a collection of substitutes named Lopez, Blanchard, Berra, Linz and Bright banged out one key hit after another. The Yankees also had a terrific defense, particularly in the infield. With Pepitone replacing Skowron, the Yankee inner defense was undoubtedly the finest in the league, if not in baseball. Not only did Pepitone have a better glove than the Moose, he had terrific range, which enabled Richardson to play closer to second, cut off more balls that had gone through the middle, and turn the double play more easily.

On the 13th of September, behind Bouton's twentieth win and Blanchard's 16th home run, the Yankees clinched their 28th American League pennant. "In one respect," wrote Arthur Daley, "this was the most remarkable pennant. They did it with surprisingly little help from the M-boys, Mickey Mantle and Roger Maris." Mantle and Maris combined for 115 homers in 1961, 63 in 1962 and just 38 in 1963. In contrast to the businesslike ceremony which marked the '62 clinching, the '63 celebration was loud, boisterous and filled with youthful enthusiasm. Potato salad and tomatoes were heaved across the locker room in a manner that, according to *Sports Illustrated*, was "very un–Yankee-like." The Yankees had expected to win in '62. In '63, with all the injuries, the runaway championship was a matter for enthusiastic celebration.

Houk said that the '63 club was the best he had had in his three years at the helm, even better than the '61 club. That was discouraging to the rest of the American League. If they couldn't beat the Yankee second stringers, what did that say about the competitiveness of the league. "Under Casey Stengel," wrote John Drebinger, "the Yanks at least gave the other fellows a nibble." "This has to be a reflection of a weak, miserably balanced league," Arthur Daley opined in September. "If there ever was a time when Ralph Houk's heroes were sitting ducks and ready to be knocked off, this was it. But no other club had enough class to take advantage of an opportunity such as none of them may ever get again."

• 12 •

Too Much Pitching
The 1963 World Series

Late in the 1963 season, *Sports Illustrated* ran a story titled "A Success Is Killing the American League." New York's domination was so complete and so accepted by fans, *SI* stated, that the Yankees were the only team that could draw a crowd. In August, with the race all but over, the Yankees, at home and on the road, had accounted for 40 percent of the league's attendance. Eight of the top ten crowds had appeared at games where the Yankees were one of the participants. "I used to think that the league couldn't get along without the Yankees," said Jack Dunn, administrative assistant for the Orioles, "but now I'm starting to think we'd be better off without them." "The greed of the Yankees," said Bill Veeck, "has brought baseball to a dangerous position.... The American League is made up of four divisions. The Yankees by themselves are the first division. Chicago, Minnesota and Baltimore are the second division. Cleveland, Boston, Kansas City and Detroit are the third division. Los Angeles and Washington have the fourth division to themselves." Veeck did not point out that the Angels had challenged for the pennant the previous year, nor did he explain why the Yankees' continual success was an indication of greed. Were they supposed to lose on purpose once in a while to be good sports?

William Leggett, author of the article, made some suggestions as to how to level the playing field. First, broadcast revenue should be equally divided in order to negate the economic advantage of the Yankees' presence in the New York market and their repeated appearance on the national game of the week. Second, there should be a free agent draft similar to that conducted by professional football and basketball leagues. Finally, the American League should "beg" the National League to consent to interleague play. It was generally acknowledged that the senior circuit had superior talent, and its appearance in American League parks would boost attendance. The month of October provided another possible solution to the problem of Yankee dominance. Maybe they should be forced to play all their games against the Los Angeles Dodgers.

The Dodgers had rebounded from their disastrous collapse of 1962 to win the 1963 pennant, principally due to the phenomenal pitching of Sandy Koufax, Don Drysdale and Ron Perranoski. Koufax had been 14–4 in 1962 when he had to leave a game because of numbness in his finger. No one realized the severity of the injury, but by late August, the finger was raw and it didn't appear that the ace lefty would pitch again that season, or maybe ever. With the Dodgers stumbling, Koufax tried to come back a few times, but didn't win another game. After the season, doctors said he had been suffering from Reynaud's Phenomenon, caused by a blot clot in his palm, and that there had been thought of amputating the digit if the situation had worsened.

Koufax recovered from the career-threatening circulatory problem to win the 1963 Cy Young Award with a 25–5 record, 1.88 ERA and 306 strikeouts, all league leading figures. Drysdale, the 1962 Young Award winner, was just 19–17, but his mediocre record was a result not of diminishing performance, but of the Dodgers' feeble offense. Drysdale posted a 2.63 ERA and his 251 strikeouts were third in the league. He and Koufax pitched a combined 626 innings, the most of any duo in the major leagues, and had 37 complete games between them. When a Dodger starter didn't finish, manager Walter Alston waved to the bullpen for Perranoski, who appeared 69 times, posted a 16–3 record, 21 saves (second to Lindy McDaniel's 22) and a 1.67 ERA. The three pitchers combined for 60 of Los Angeles' 99 wins, and the Dodgers' team ERA of 2.85 easily led the league.

The Dodger hitters were not nearly as impressive as their pitchers. Tommy Davis won his second straight batting title, but five NL teams scored more runs than Los Angeles, and their 110 home runs placed them seventh. The last time a team had scored as infrequently as the Dodgers and won a pennant was 1945. Skowron, expected to add power, batted just .203 with only four home runs. He no longer had to contend with Yankee Stadium's Death Valley in left center field, but, coping with a new set of pitchers and Dodger Stadium, which was big all over, he slumped terribly. The Moose had learned to reach the right field seats at Yankee Stadium, but the right field fence at Dodger Stadium was as distant as the one in left. By the end of the season, Dodger fans were booing him during his infrequent appearances.

The Dodgers weren't very good fielders, either. Skowron was no gazelle at first, and the rest of the team was equally unsteady. They made 159 errors compared to 110 by the Yankees. Most disconcerting to Alston was the fact that some of his best hitters were his worst fielders. Slugger Frank Howard couldn't play the outfield very well. Tommy Davis couldn't play third base, where Alston put him to try to cope with his overabundance of outfielders. Alston's solution was to start a good offensive lineup and make a host of defensive changes late in the game if the Dodgers had the lead.

The Dodgers lived and died on pitching and speed. "Just because it was a pitchers' season," wrote Red Foley, "doesn't mean it will be their World Series, too. Or does it?" It did, said *Sports Illustrated*. "The Series will be decided by pitching," *SI* reported. "The Dodgers should win," they said.

The Yankee invalids claimed to be healthy for the Series. Mantle said his knee bothered him a little when he turned the bases, but other than that he felt fine. Maris discarded the bulky apparatus he had been wearing for his sore back. Healthy or not, the two Yankee sluggers hadn't hit well in Dodger Stadium, which the Dodgers shared with the Angels. In 91 combined at bats, Maris and Mantle had just one home run. Against the sterling Dodger staff, they didn't figure to do much better.

In the opening game, for one of the few times all year, Houk was able to send his eight starters out on the field. Since each team had won the pennant rather handily, the pitching rotations were arranged so that each team was able to start its ace, Koufax and Ford.

Ford, winner of 24 games, didn't look like an ace. With a lefty pitching for New York, Alston selected Skowron, despite his woeful average, to start at first base rather than Ron Fairly. "Moose is the kind of man who can get hot and have a big Series," Alston said. "He has played here and knows their team." In the second inning, Skowron came to the plate after Frank Howard had blasted a 460 foot double off the distant center field fence. Skowron touched his old buddy Ford for a single through the middle to give the Dodgers a 1–0 lead. Two batters later, John Roseboro snuck a three run homer around the right field foul pole and the score was 4–0.

Four runs looked as though they would be plenty for Koufax, who appeared untouchable while striking out the first five Yankees. After Howard managed a foul pop to Roseboro to end the second, Koufax struck out Pepitone to begin the third. He fanned the side in the fourth, giving him nine strikeouts in the first four innings. Richardson, who struck out just 22 times during the season, went down three times during the game. The Yankees got their first hit and loaded the bases in the fifth, and Koufax experienced a streak of wildness in the sixth, but emerged unscathed both times. Tresh hit a two run homer in the eighth, leaving the Dodger lefthander with a 5–2 lead and 14 strikeouts, tying the Series record, entering the ninth. Carl Erskine, the Brooklyn righthander who was the co-holder of the record, sat in the stands and rooted for Koufax to break it.

With two outs, Harry Bright came to the plate as a pinch hitter, and a very strange phenomenon occurred. Despite the fact that the game was being played at Yankee Stadium, virtually every one of the fans was rooting for Koufax to strike Bright out and set a new record. "Everyone was pulling for Koufax to break Erskine's record," Bright said after the game, "and I guess I'm the only guy in baseball to have 69,000 people cheering for me to strike out." Bright didn't disappoint them. With two strikes on him, he hit a slow roller toward third. The fans cheered when it kicked foul. Koufax then threw a fastball past Bright for his fifteenth strikeout, a new record and a 5–2 Dodger win. "I don't see how he lost five games during the season," Berra said.

Johnny Podres was not nearly as overpowering as Koufax, but he was good enough to win the second game. The vaunted Dodger speed stung the Yankees in the very first inning. Wills led off with a single. Downing, with a quick move, caught Wills well off first. Marv Breeding, the former Oriole infielder who had been traded to Los Angeles late in the season, told the Dodgers that Downing's move to first base was usually a soft toss. With that knowledge, Wills made up his mind to run on the first pitch, figuring that even if Downing threw to first, he could beat a throw to second. That was exactly what happened, as Pepitone's throw was wide and Maury slid in safely. Willie Davis hit a drive to deep right field. Maris misjudged the ball, fell down, got up and fell down again. Davis's double drove in Wills and Gilliam, who had singled, and the Dodgers held a 2–0 lead. The Yankees were behind again, and would become the first team never to hold a lead at any time during a World Series.

Skowron, who had hit just four homers all season, connected off Downing in the fourth. The key to his resurgence, the Moose said after the game, was Breeding. Marv remembered Skowron from the American League and, when he came to the Dodgers, asked him why he wasn't holding the bat up as high as he used to. "By golly, that was it," Skowron said. "I never realized I was letting the bat droop. Since I got back holding the bat high, I've been doing much better."

Tommy Davis tied a Series record by hitting two triples. On the first, Maris injured his arm running into the fence, and had to leave the game. The wound didn't appear serious, but when his arm swelled afterwards, Maris's availability for the remainder of the Series was in jeopardy. Podres nursed a 4–0 lead into the ninth inning, when he tired. Perranoski closed out a 4–1 win that sent the two teams to Los Angeles with the Dodgers holding a commanding 2–0 lead. It was Podres' first win at Yankee Stadium since he clinched the Dodgers' first world championship in 1955.

"We're not throwing in the towel," Houk said. "We just aren't hitting. But we'll do some hitting before this thing is over. We're overdue." His club was even more overdue after the third game, as they got only three hits off Drysdale. Bouton, who, like Downing, was making his first Series start, also pitched an excellent game, but it was not good enough. "The night before the game," said Tom Metcalf, "Bouton and I went out to dinner. After dinner, we went into a store on Hollywood Boulevard and Bouton bought a gorilla mask that was unbelievably realistic. It scared me even though I knew it was him wearing it. He walked up and down Hollywood Boulevard, scaring people. I was leading him around by the hand, like he was some kind of nut, and he was just cracking up. We went into a little newspaper print shop and had about a dozen copies of a newspaper headline made up. It said 'Bouton beats Drysdale 1–0 in Game Three.' We went back to the hotel and he left a bunch of copies on the floor of the elevator. Then we went up to the room and went to bed."

The next day it was Drysdale who scared the Yankees. If they seemed impotent against Koufax and Podres, they were totally powerless against the big Dodger righthander. Mantle beat out a bunt single in the second, his first hit of the Series, and Kubek had singles in the seventh and ninth. The only time the Yankees got more than one runner on base was the second, when they loaded the bases. Bouton ended the threat by striking out.

Bouton had trouble with his control, walking five, but was tough in the clutch. The only Los Angeles run scored in the first, in typical Dodger fashion. Gilliam walked with one out and went to second on a wild pitch. With two out, Tommy Davis hit a hard ground ball which kicked off the pitching rubber toward second base. The infield at Dodger Stadium was kept hard to help the Dodger speed burners, and the ball jumped off the turf. Richardson moved to his right, but was shielded by Bouton, who had lunged for the ball. The ball hit Richardson square in the shin and bounded into short right field. Gilliam, running hard with two out, scored easily, giving Drysdale the only run he needed. The best Yankee threat came with two out in the ninth, when Pepitone hit a long fly ball toward the right field bullpen. Ron Fairly backed up and caught the ball about five feet in front of the fence.

"They still got 27 more men to get out," Houk said after the game. "It isn't the end. That last victory can be the toughest one of all." If the Series held to form, it would take only about 32 batters to get those 27 outs, for the Yankees had just 16 hits in the first three games. It might take less than 32 batters, for in the fourth game, New York would be facing Koufax for the second time.[*]

Although he didn't strike out 15, Koufax pitched even better in the fourth game than he had in the first. He had a better fastball, he said, which was bad news for the Yankee hitters. Koufax retired the first 13 batters, and only gave up a hit when center fielder Willie Davis lost Richardson's popup in the sun. Through six innings, only two Yankees had reached base. The Dodgers took a 1–0 lead in the fifth inning on a mammoth home run by Howard, which traveled about 450 feet into the second tier in left field, but Ford was pitching as brilliantly as Koufax, yielding just two hits in six innings. In the top of the seventh, Mantle, who had just a bunt single in three games, hit his 15th World Series homer to tie the score.

The game didn't remain tied for long. Gilliam led off the Dodger seventh with a grounder that bounced high off the hard Dodger Stadium turf. Boyer leaped, grabbed it, and uncorked a perfect, belt high throw to first. Pepitone saw only a white blur coming toward him from a mass of white shirts behind third base. He completely lost sight of Boyer's throw, which struck him on the right wrist and skittered down the right field line. "When Boyer comes down," said Metcalf, "he's throwing. And Pepitone is watching. When he saw Boyer catch the ball he said, 'Oh, my god, I've got to get over to the bag.' He ran over, looked down to get his foot on the base, and when he looked up the ball was right in front of him." Gilliam raced to third, and scored the lead run on Willie Davis's fly ball to deep center.

Koufax, pitching with Novacaine numbing an infected toe, was as strong in the ninth as he was in the first. Yet, the Yankees put up a battle. Richardson led off with a single, but remained on first as Tresh and Mantle struck out. Howard hit a ground ball to shortstop Wills, whose throw to second baseman Dick Tracewski beat Richardson to the bag. Koufax saw second base umpire Tom Gorman give the out sign and leaped off the mound. Tracewski dropped the ball, however, and Richardson was safe at second. Koufax's celebration was merely one batter

---

[*]*"People always ask me what it was like pitching against Koufax," said Met pitcher Galen Cisco. "I tell them I never minded at all, because he wasn't that good a hitter."*

premature, as he got Lopez to ground out, completing an unbelievable sweep of a team that on paper was the best in baseball. Fittingly, Skowron, who played every inning of the series, made the final putout.

The Yankees, so accustomed to setting Series records, established a number of marks they would rather not have held. Their .171 team average was the worst for a four game series, and the second lowest ever, and their 37 strikeouts dwarfed the former high of 29. They had scored a total of just four runs in four games, the worst ever in a four game series, and just two runs in the last three. Their 22 hits tied another record for futility. Other than his fourth game home run, Mantle had his third consecutive subpar Series. In '61, '62 and '63 he was just 6 for 46, with just the single home run. "I never saw pitching like that," he said.

In the Yankee dressing room, Pepitone patiently explained how he managed to miss a perfect throw. "When Clete made the throw," he said, "I could see the ball halfway across the diamond. Then it disappeared in the white shirts. All I could do was stick out my glove and hope I guessed right. I guessed wrong." "That's the kid I feel sorry for," said Howard. "He's young, he's new, and he'll be thinking about it all winter."

When Pepitone returned from Los Angeles, he spent the night at his grandfather's house in Brooklyn. During the night, a group of fans hoisted an effigy of Pepitone to a lamp post across the street. Pepitone and his 81-year-old grandfather went running out into the street, Pepitone swinging his fists and grandpa flailing away with a baseball bat, until the police arrived and broke up the fracas.

The Dodger locker room was jubilant. Alston, who had been on the verge of losing his job after the Dodgers folded in 1962, suddenly attained genius status. "It's amazing to discover how many people have discovered Walt Alston in the last several days," wrote Dick Young. "You never saw anybody get so smart so fast." There were many happy Dodgers, but perhaps the happiest of all was Skowron, who had redeemed himself in the course of four games. He was the Dodger batting star while Pepitone, his replacement, was the goat.

In New Jersey, a jury considering an abortion conspiracy charge against Dr. Thomas D. Russo had listened to the first game of the Series while reaching a guilty verdict. When the judge heard that the jury had been listening to the game, he set the verdict aside and ordered a new trial. Houk wished he could do the same, but there would be no new trial for the Yankees. They had been dethroned as champions in a most humiliating manner.

· 13 ·

The Cowboy, the Kid and Mary's Little Lamb

The 1964 Season

The 1964 Yankee pitchers were reminiscent of the 1960 staff. There were some solid veterans but, by mid-season, it was obvious that there were also some gaping holes. In 1960, the Yanks had solved their problems by bringing up Bill Stafford from Richmond and acquiring Luis Arroyo from Jersey City to bolster the bullpen. By the spring of 1964, Arroyo had retired and Stafford was a sore-armed reliever. If the Yankees were looking for a savior, it wouldn't be either of them.

The 1964 club was very different from the teams that started the past few Yankee seasons. There were changes in the starting rotation, the bullpen and, perhaps most important, the dugout, where Yogi Berra was beginning his first season at the helm.

The Yankees not only lost the World Series in 1963, they were in the process of losing a financial battle to the Mets. The upstart team, in their first two National League seasons, proved horribly inept on the field, but remarkably successful at the box office. In 1958, the Giants and Dodgers had moved to the West Coast, leaving the Yankees alone in New York. Despite winning the World Series, the Yankees saw their attendance actually decline by about 70,000, for National League fans were not coming to Yankee Stadium. When the Mets opened shop in 1962, people who had been staying at home came out to the Polo Grounds. Finishing last in 1963, and playing in a dilapidated facility, the Mets drew 1,080,104. The Yankees, while winning the American League pennant, played before 1,308,920, their lowest home attendance since the war year of 1945 and well below the 1.7 million of 1961, the last year they played without National League competition.

The Yankees, with their staid corporate image, were losing the younger fans to the Mets, who encouraged banners, which were forbidden in Yankee Stadium, and rabid enthusiasm. In 1964, the National Leaguers were scheduled to move to sparkling new Shea Stadium, constructed in the shadow of the World's Fair. Both Shea and the Fair were scheduled to open in April. If the Mets could draw in the Polo Grounds, what would they do in a brand new park, with the world's premier tourist attraction just outside the gate?

The Yankees had always been compared to U.S. Steel in terms of lovability and imagination. After the firing of Johnny Keane in 1966, Los Angeles columnist Jim Murray wrote, "The Yankees hold the same warm spot in the affections of American people as the Krupp Iron Works.

I mean these guys would drown kittens. They shouldn't play in pinstripes, they should play in spiked helmets."

Prior to the 1964 season, the Yankees made a concerted effort to change their image. Suddenly, they began to think like Bill Veeck. For the first time, the Yankees hired a sales promotion manager, Eugene Lynn. They hired 24 hostesses to assist fans. "It is to be doubted," wrote Til Ferdenzi, "if there has been a similar renovation job on the trademark of a big league team in the history of the game." The Yankees scheduled six Suburban Night games, which started at six P.M., in order to give those who lived outside New York the opportunity to visit the Stadium and still return home at a decent hour. The agenda for Suburban Night featured box suppers and a pre-game cocktail hour at the Stadium Club. There were 34 night games on the schedule, the most in Yankee history, and eight more than in 1963. The club also severed its 41-year relationship with its concessionaires, the Harry M. Stevens Company, the only provider Yankee Stadium had ever known, and engaged Automatic Canteen Company of America in their place. Automatic Canteen promised cuisine well beyond peanuts, beer and hot dogs, including pizza, shrimp rolls, hot ham and roast beef sandwiches, and nine different kinds of beverages, including milk shakes. In addition to its novel fare, the new concessionaire boasted another characteristic in its favor. New York co-owners Del Webb and Dan Topping, Sr. both served on Automatic Canteen's board of directors.

A further attempt to woo new fans to the Stadium was the giveaway of 20,000 tickets to New York City cabdrivers. Cabbies were renowned as promoters of sports events and bringing them to the Stadium gratis was a good way to urge them to pitch the Yankees to their fares. The promotional gimmick was creative, but not original, for two years earlier, the Mets had distributed 3,400 free tickets to the drivers, and two years before that the AFL's ill-fated Titans had done the same. A fifty percent success rate was enough to convince the Yankees to follow suit.

The Mets had done something which contributed to their popularity far more than giving away a few tickets. The hiring of Charles Dillon Stengel as manager was a public relations stroke of genius. When the Mets visited other National League cities, the loudest ovation of the day often went to Stengel when he brought out the lineup card or made a pitching change. If the Mets did not have quality baseball to sell, they would sell Casey Stengel. As Arthur Daley wrote, "There has never been anything like the job this wily old codger performed. He stole newspaper space from the Yankees. He attracted more attention and interest with his losers than the Bombers could do with their winners. He created the strange and wonderful collection of wild-eyed fans known as the New Breed. His television commercials were so wackily delightful that viewers suffered through Met games just to catch Ol' Case on the commercials." The sponsors of Met broadcasts were Kool cigarettes and Rheingold, the dry beer. Only Casey could explain how something on fire could be cool and how a liquid could be dry.

Ralph Houk had done as much as a manager could in his first three seasons at the helm, with three pennants and two world championships. But Houk was not Casey Stengel. No one went to Yankee Stadium to watch Ralph Houk manage. To combat Casey in Flushing, the Yankees needed a personality in the Bronx, and had one, or so they thought, on their own coaching staff.

Yogi Berra had been a Yankee since 1946, and became a folk legend shortly thereafter. In 1962, Berra, then 37, had an off season, batting only .224 with 10 homers, the worst performance of his career. During the winter, there were rumors that he would manage the Boston Red Sox. Yogi had said he wanted to manage, and there were many who spoke favorably of his chances, but too many of the endorsements consisted of phrases like that spoken by Hank Greenberg in 1962. "He is far more intelligent than anyone realizes," Greenberg said. "Anybody who thinks Yogi is dumb," added Dodger executive Red Patterson, "just isn't a smart man."

Yogi elected to remain with the Yankees in 1963 as a player-coach. During rookie camp during the spring, Houk took him aside and asked if he would be interested in managing the Yankees in '64. "Where the hell are you going?" Berra asked Houk, who explained that he would assume the general manager's post. Roy Hamey, who'd had a gall bladder operation the previous year, and walked with a permanent limp as a result of a serious auto accident, wanted to retire. Houk wasn't thrilled about leaving the field, but he'd been a loyal Yankee employee since 1939, and if that was what Webb and Topping wanted, he would do it. The deal was sealed that day on Topping's yacht, but was to remain a secret until after the season.

On October 24, two weeks after the Yankees had been swept by the Dodgers in the World Series, they announced the change. Once the shock had worn off, people began wondering first, if Houk would continue calling the shots from the front office, and second, whether the easygoing Yogi would be able to effectively discipline long-time teammates like Mantle and Ford. Berra solved the latter problem by naming Ford pitching coach. "Now that the merry southpaw is part of the top brass," observed Daley, "he'll have to act in a more dignified manner and withhold his fire." While the move may have prevented a potential disciplinary problem, the loss of Johnny Sain, one of the most successful pitching instructors of all time, would have a measurable impact on the Yankee staff.

The Yankees had always outperformed the Mets on the field and now, with Yogi and Whitey, two of the most popular Yanks of all time, elevated to management, perhaps they could compete in the newspapers and at the box office as well. New York subways featured ads that showed Berra, in a business suit, and the caption, "Mr. Lawrence Peter Berra cordially invites you to purchase your Yankee tickets this season...." The new Yankee era of friendliness had begun.

The rookie skipper was faced with the pressure of managing the best team in baseball, one that had captured pennants in eight of the last nine seasons and was expected to do the same in '64. "It's a nice job," Berra said in the spring. "All you have to do is win." Winning might not be good enough, however. If Berra won, people would say that anyone could have brought the Yankees home first. If he didn't win, those who said he wasn't ready to manage would declare their opinion vindicated. "The Yankees seem as sure as death and taxes to win the pennant again," said the New York Times. "We got the best club and should win," said Berra, "if everything goes to Hoyle."

Yogi's managerial career started slowly, plagued by rain and a lack of offense. By the end of April, 16 days into his tenure, Berra was .500. His club had played eight games and had eight off days, including six rainouts. When the Yankees did play, the results were discouraging. Berra's club lost their first three games, and got off to the club's worst start since 1930. Spotty pitching was a problem, as was a lack of power. Yankee home run production was in the midst of a steady decline, from a record 240 in 1961, to 199 in '62, 188 in '63 and 162 in '64. The vaunted New York bats did not produce their first home run until Clete Boyer connected in the team's seventh game. By the first of May, the team batting average was .221, with but two round-trippers. Neither Mantle nor Maris had a single home run.

Part of the decreased production was due to injuries, as the Yankees were unable to place all eight starters on the field at the same time until May 10th. The re-united lineup lasted only three innings, after which Kubek was forced to leave with a muscle pull. With Kubek, Mantle, Maris and Tresh all injured at various times, there were precious few occasions during the summer when Yogi was able to write the names of his best eight players on the lineup card. On May 3, all three starting outfielders were suffering from hamstring injuries, and the New York outfield consisted of Lopez in left, Linz in center and Blanchard in right. It was 1963 all over again.

Buoyed by the numerous off days, the starting pitching held up well in the early going. After losing an 11 inning complete game in the opener, Ford won his next ten decisions (including six shutouts) and had an ERA of less than 2.00. On April 21, he beat the White Sox to post the 200th win of his Yankee career, second only to Red Ruffing on the all time list. Despite back and shoulder miseries, Bouton pitched well and often, but his luck was frequently bad and his record hovered around .500 for most of the season. Downing was hampered by a bad back, as was Terry. Berra hoped that Stan Williams would bounce back in '64, but, bothered by arm trouble, Williams had some horrible outings during the exhibition season. On April 2, in order to give the big right-hander some work, Yogi sent him to the minor league camp to pitch in an exhibition game for Richmond. Williams surrendered seven runs to the Denver Bears in seven innings, including five home runs.

With all the rain, neither Williams, Terry nor Stafford made a single appearance during the month of April. When Williams finally pitched, he developed a sore shoulder. Through May 22, Ford and Bouton had pitched a combined total of 120 innings, while no other Yankee hurler had logged more than 23. That was fine as long as the rain continued, but unpropitious for a 162 game season. As the season wore on, Terry found himself and had a brief stretch of strong performances. Williams never did find himself. Bouton, Downing and Ford, when he was healthy, were the only starters who could be counted upon for consistently solid outings. By early August, Houk and Berra were badly in need of another starting pitcher. When they looked to their Triple-A affiliate in Richmond, they saw one pitcher towering above all the others. His name was Melvin Stottlemyre.

Stottlemyre was the 22-year-old son of a construction worker who was born in Hazelton, Missouri and grew up in the small Washington town of Mabton (pop. 1500). At Mabton High, Mel played baseball, football and basketball and was the student body president. In three seasons as a pitcher, he lost only one game.

After graduating from high school, Stottlemyre attended Yakima Valley Junior College, where coach Chuck (Bobo) Brayton taught him to throw a sinker. "He was just a tall, skinny, bashful kid," Brayton recalled. "He was probably one of my top two pitchers his sophomore year, but I think I had better college pitchers than he was." Yankee scout Eddie Taylor watched Stottlemyre pitch and reported, "He has a good sinker and the courage and control to use it right. I would recommend signing him for a small bonus."

Taylor was a dogged, short, bespectacled man who hated to part with the Yankees' money. He kept following Stottlemyre, and managed to sign him for no bonus at all in June, 1961. Other scouts were interested in boys who threw harder, but Taylor was impressed by Stottlemyre's sinker and the fact that, although he was not overpowering, he always seemed to

Mel Stottlemyre arrived in August, 1964, posted a 9–3 record, and pitched three strong games in the World Series. In ten subsequent years with the Yankees, he was their best pitcher, but never again appeared in a post-season game.

win. One night, Taylor knocked on Coach Brayton's door and asked if he could borrow his car to drive over and sign Stottlemyre.

After a decent 1961 season in the low minors, Stottlemyre blossomed the following season at Greensboro. He changed the grip on his sinker and posted a record of 17–9, which earned him an invitation to the Yankee camp the following spring. Johnny Sain was so impressed that he recommended a jump all the way to the major leagues. Houk didn't agree and Stottlemyre was sent to the Triple-A Richmond Virginians, where he struggled against International League hitters. He split time between starting and relieving, was inconsistent with his control and finished 7–7 in 39 games. When Stottlemyre had control of his curve, he was impressive. When he didn't, he wasn't.

In the spring of 1964, Mel was not invited to spring training with the major league club, passed over in favor of $100,000 bonus baby Howard Kitt and other long-forgotten names such as Jim Marrujo, Gil Downs, George Shoemaker and Rich Marcy. Even in the Richmond camp, Stottlemyre was not a big name. Berra, who liked relievers who could induce infield grounders, wanted him converted to relief work, but Houk disagreed, insisting he remain a starter.

Stottlemyre was a starter, but was well down in the Virginians' rotation. Kitt was virtually guaranteed a Triple A starting spot to justify the Yanks' sizable investment. Rollie Sheldon, a Yankee in '61 and '62, would also be a starter, as would Jack Cullen, who had pitched briefly for New York in '62.

Even the bullpen was crowded, with veteran player-coach Billy Muffett, Tom Metcalf and Leonardo Ferguson, the Vees' top reliever in '63. Stottlemyre would be a spot starter and reliever. "Mel was a real good pitcher," said Bob Meyer, "but he wasn't blowing guys away, and he didn't get a lot of money to sign. He was a guy who really had to earn his way up."

Stottlemyre had an inconsistent spring, looking steady at times and very hittable at others. On April 12, he pitched four shutout, hitless innings against the parent club in an exhibition game and was the winning pitcher. Stottlemyre displayed an almost unhittable sinker, but his control was shaky, as he walked four and was consistently behind the hitters. Mel started the second game of the regular season and was hit hard, giving up five hits and four runs in only 3⅔ innings. His ineffective performance, plus the unusually rainy spring, kept Stottlemyre in the bullpen for more than a month.

Stottlemyre's relief pitching was spotty, and he had particular difficulty getting his curve over, but his time in the pen turned out to be very beneficial. One day he had a long conversation with pitching coach Muffett. They talked about Mel's control problems and Muffett suggested that Stottlemyre open up more and take a longer stride in order to achieve better balance.

At this point, the rain which had cost Stottlemyre his place in the starting rotation finally worked to his advantage, for doubleheaders had begun to accumulate. On Memorial Day, Mel got to start the second game of a doubleheader against the Columbus Jets. To that point, he had appeared in 14 games, pitched 23 innings and had a 1–2 record with a 3.91 ERA.

Against the Jets, employing Muffett's advice, Mel pitched a four hit shutout and, more importantly, did not walk a single man. The fine performance earned him another start, which resulted in another four hit shutout, this time against Jacksonville. Stottlemyre walked only one, and was now permanently in the rotation.

With the Yankee staff struggling, Houk recalled Sheldon on June 12. If the parent club's pitching woes continued, more pitchers would be summoned to New York. Cullen, who was under consideration for recall, allowed only one earned run in his first 37 innings. On June 3, however, with Yankee scouts Mayo Smith and Johnny Nuen watching from the stands, Cullen was knocked out in the third inning by Jacksonville. That was the start of a long downhill slide, which included seven straight losses, and by mid–August, Cullen was 3–10. He had as much chance of getting to Yankee Stadium as he had of reaching Mars. Kitt, the highly touted bonus boy, was 0–7, and experiencing monumental control problems when Richmond manager Preston Gomez finally convinced the Yankees to allow him to send Kitt to Double-A.

Meanwhile, the stock of the unheralded Stottlemyre continued to climb. A loss to Rochester on June 8 evened his record at 3–3, but that would be the last defeat Mel would suffer in the International League. On June 12, the day of Sheldon's recall, he shut out Syracuse. Four days later, he beat Toronto 2–1. "Right now, he's one of the best pitchers in the league," said 30-year-old George (Sparky) Anderson, the manager of the Maple Leafs. "The big difference in Stottlemyre this year," said veteran Richmond catcher Bob Schmidt, "is that he's getting his curve ball over."

"His sinker ball was so good," said Jake Gibbs, the Virginians' other receiver. "One day, Mel was pitching in Toronto and Ozzie Virgil came up to hit. The first time up, he took his normal stance and Mel threw the sinker ball in on his hands and broke his bat. The second time he came up, I noticed he'd moved a couple of inches back from the plate. Mel broke his bat again with a sinker ball in on his hands. The third time, he backed up a little more and said, 'I ain't gonna get jammed this time. Nobody's gonna break my bat this time.' Well, Mel broke his goddamn bat again. The fourth time he came up, Ozzie was almost out of the batters' box. That's how much Mel's ball was running in '64."

Stottlemyre's success was a mixed blessing for manager Gomez. The manager liked having a pitching ace, but if Mel were too good, he wouldn't be in Richmond much longer. After the win over Toronto, which boosted Stottlemyre's record to 5–3, Gomez said, "There's the next man to go up, if the Yankees need another pitcher." Gomez managed to hang onto his ace for a brilliant stretch of eleven more starts. After a no decision on June 20th, Mel logged eight consecutive victories, including three shutouts and four games in which he allowed only a single run.

The phenomenal streak gave Stottlemyre a 13–3 record and fueled constant speculation as to when he would be called to New York. Berra wanted him badly, but Houk felt that Stottlemyre should spend the entire season in Triple A. In mid–July, scouts Johnny Nuen and Steve Souchock arrived in Richmond. "I think he's ready," Souchock wrote. Shortly afterward, Houk came to town and, according to Gomez, said that, absent a dire emergency, he would leave Stottlemyre in Richmond.

Houk visited Richmond again in early August to watch Stottlemyre pitch against Toronto. Mel didn't win, but if Houk was thinking of calling him up, the youngster did nothing to discourage him. Stottlemyre pitched ten scoreless innings of five hit ball and departed with the score 0–0. "He's got to go up," said Gomez. "I wouldn't hesitate if I was them."

Houk had said that he would not summon Stottlemyre to the Yankees unless there was a dire emergency. In early August, the emergency arrived. Ford had been bothered by a sore hip all season, and, as the summer wore on, the hip got worse. Strangely, it bothered him when he threw his breaking pitches, but not when he threw fastballs.

On July 5, in the last game before the All-Star break, the Twins snapped Whitey's ten game winning streak and knocked him out of the box after only four innings. Ford bounced back with two wins, the second a three hit shutout, to run his record to 12–2. Then, on July 19, he lost to the Indians and, in his next start, left after two innings when his hip became so painful he could not push off the mound. Ford stayed out for ten days, then pitched seven strong innings against Kansas City. After that game, however, he said he was in pain from the fourth inning on and would probably miss his next start. "I'm discouraged," Whitey admitted. "I think I will go to the bullpen and maybe be of some use there." Ford tried to start on August 8 against the Orioles, but had to leave after two innings. Dr. Gaynor diagnosed the problem as a ligament strain of the right hip joint, which had become chronically inflamed. He prescribed radiation treatments.

Houk didn't know much about radiation therapy, but he knew he had a kid at Richmond with a good hard sinker who could take Ford's place in the rotation. After his last Richmond start, Stottlemyre had a 13–3 record, and his 1.42 ERA was the best in the International League. He had tied Billy Short's Richmond club record with ten straight wins, and thrown six shutouts. Since entering the rotation on Memorial Day, Mel had made sixteen starts, completing ten. In 127 innings, he had given up only 88 hits, 18 walks (1.1 per nine innings) and fashioned a 13–1 record and a 0.99 ERA. After the season, he would be named *The Sporting News* Minor League Player of the Year.

On August 11th, a day on which New York lost a doubleheader to Chicago to fall to third place, the Yankees purchased Stottlemyre's contract from Richmond and dispatched Bud Daley to the Virginians. Mel was scheduled to start against the White Sox the following day.

It was a spectacular debut. Berra, filling out the lineup card in his office before the game, struggled with the spelling of his new pitcher's name. He appealed for help to the writers, none of whom were able to provide assistance. Once the game started, however, the name "Stottle-myre" was trouble only for the White Sox. With the Yankees trailing 2–1 in the bottom of the fourth, Mantle came to the plate to face Chicago pitcher Ray Herbert. J.C Martin was the White Sox catcher. "I said, 'Boy, this is a good time to throw him a sinker low and away," Martin recalled, "and let him hit it to center field. Herbert threw him a sinker low and away and Man-tle hit the ball and sort of turned and threw the bat down in disgust because the ball just went straight up into the air. I said, 'We got you, Mickey.' He was just trotting down to first base. But that ball never came down."

The "fly ball" was the 443rd home run of Mantle's career. Of his previous 442, only one, hit in 1955, had been deposited into the Stadium's center field bleachers. The fourth inning blast was the second, a 500 foot shot that cleared the black tarpaulin which rose 22 feet above the 461 foot marker.

Two innings later, Maris broke the tie with a two run homer, and Mantle added another circuit blast in the eighth. Even Stottlemyre contributed to the offense, stroking a single on the first major league pitch he saw. It was his pitching, however, that caused the most excitement. Mel threw 116 pitches in the complete game 7–3 win, inducing 21 infield grounders with his sinker. Stottlemyre also demonstrated marvelous poise for a 22-year-old. "He might have had butterflies," said Blanchard, "and I'm sure he did, but you'd never know it. He was just as cool and calm as could be."

It looked as though Berra would have to struggle with the youngster's odd name for a while longer, a battle Yogi was happy to wage if it meant more complete game victories. "He looks like a pitcher to me," Berra said. "Anybody who keeps the ball low and doesn't walk men can pitch." "He sure knows how to serve up those grounders," said catcher Blanchard. Jim Hegan compared his sinker to Bob Lemon's.

"Mel was a natural sinking fastball pitcher," said Blanchard. "If you asked Mel how he made the ball sink, he couldn't tell you. The ball would be about eight feet in front of the plate and guys would start their swing. The ball would just drop and they'd hit on top of it all the time." "He had a sinker that was like catching a brick," said Doc Edwards. "One time I caught him in Chicago and he threw 86 pitches in nine innings. I think 80 of them were sinkers. That's how good his sinker was."

Stottlemyre was a perfectionist who worked tirelessly at his trade. He could pitch, hit, field and run the bases. "After ballgames," said Lindy McDaniel, "they'd have a spread of sandwiches, and I'd watch Mel put his sandwich together. It had to be absolutely perfect. That's the way he pitched. He perfected every little thing."

"Mel was a great pitcher," said catcher Johnny Ellis. "Statistically, he may not have been as great as Fergie Jenkins or Gaylord Perry or others I caught, but he had the same demeanor.

He was comfortable in difficult situations; in fact, he almost looked like he enjoyed them. Mel had a nasty sinker and could throw a double play ball to get out of a jam when he needed to. He'd pitch a ten hit shutout. I was always amazed by that. Mel wasn't a hard thrower, but he had a great sinker, a great slider, a great curve and a great changeup. They were as good as anybody's I caught."

Just after Stottlemyre arrived in New York, the Yankees made an announcement that shook the baseball world. The most significant economic development in New York baseball in the 1960s, and one of the most important in all of professional sports, was the purchase of a majority interest in the Yankees by the Columbia Broadcast System in August, 1964. Topping, suffering from emphysema and a heart condition, wanted out, and Webb didn't want to run the club alone. In 1962, the two owners had reached agreement to sell the club to Lehman Brothers, but the deal fell through just a month before the sale to CBS was announced. The network acquired 80 percent of the club, with the understanding that it would purchase the remaining stock at some point in the future.

Commissioner Frick said he knew nothing about the transaction. It was league business. The American League had approved the acquisition by an 8–2 vote, with Arthur Allyn of the White Sox and Charley Finley of the Athletics opposed. Everything had been done with lightning speed, which was one reason for Allyn's negative vote. He had been contacted at 11:45 A.M., he said, asked to approve the transaction in three hours, and told that his vote didn't matter anyway, since a majority was already in favor of the proposal. Why, he and Finley asked, if there was nothing wrong with the purchase, couldn't it be subject to discussion and deliberation? And why wasn't it brought up at the league meetings, which had just ended two days earlier? Finley, who had a running one-way feud with the Yankees, accused the club of conspiring with the American League to gain an unfair advantage over the other clubs.

The purchase had significant ramifications. It was the first time such a large corporation had acquired a majority interest in a major league club. Just a month earlier, The *New York Times* had written, "Baseball was once a game involving sportsmen who gloried in their profitable years and suffered through their bad ones.... The Great American Game has become as commercial as General Motors." Or CBS. CBS was not just any corporation, of course. It was a major player in the television industry, which was so intimately connected to baseball. As owner of the Yankees, CBS would have a vote in all television negotiations. Wasn't that a conflict of interest? Would the corporation's nearly limitless resources spell the end of whatever competition was left in the American League? Would there be so much televised baseball that crowds would dwindle and the remaining teams would go broke? What would the Justice Department think of the anti-trust implications? Would Phil Linz get a recording contract for his harmonica skills? (See below.)

Was the CBS purchase the tip of the iceberg? Houston owner Roy Hofheinz stated that the Mets and the AFL's Jets would probably be sold to corporations soon. Even the Soviet newspaper *Izvestia* weighed in with its opinion. "In the best tradition of trade in human bodies," it reported, "the New York Yankees were not even told about the deal."

On September 9, the American League, which had been accused of acting in haste, met for a second vote. The result was the same, eight owners in favor and Allyn and Finley opposed. Finley threatened to sell the Athletics in protest and Allyn talked about bringing the matter to the federal courts.

Meanwhile, the season continued on. Stottlemyre's second start came on August 16 against the Orioles. Mel was brilliant, allowing only five hits and one run in 8⅔ innings. His third start, pushed back when an infected tooth caused his jaw to swell to twice its normal size, was six days later. Stottlemyre threw his first major league shutout, against the Red Sox in Fenway Park. Maris and Mantle again homered, and the victory broke a six game losing streak.

Still, the Yanks were 5½ games behind the Orioles, and many had given up on them. On August 21, Joe Trimble wrote, "[T]he Yankees today made it quite certain there would be no pennant when they were blanked 5–0 by the White Sox." "Frankly, I thought we were out of it," said Mantle after the pennant clincher. "When we lost those four in Chicago and everything was going bad, I gave up on it." New York was fighting against history, for of their 28 pennants, none had come in a year ending with a '4.' Further, a quirk in the schedule rendered a September stretch run improbable, for after August 20th, the Yanks would not play either of their two top rivals, Baltimore and Chicago.

As September and the stretch run dawned, both the Orioles and White Sox continued to win. Baltimore was a well-balanced team with a decent offense led by Brooks Robinson, Boog Powell, who slugged 39 home runs in his first big season, and rookie Sam Bowens, who hit .263 with 22 homers. The infield defense was outstanding, with Robinson, shortstop Luis Aparicio and second baseman Jerry Adair. The Oriole pitching was strong, despite the fact that the ace of the 1963 staff, 20 game winner Steve Barber, struggled in '64, as did promising young lefty Dave McNally. Robin Roberts was steady and consistent, while Milt Pappas came on strong at the end, throwing three consecutive shutouts in late August and early September. Stu Miller, Harvey Haddix and Dick Hall were spectacular in relief.

The ace of the Baltimore staff, however, was a 19-year-old who was on the roster only because he was a second year player who, under the rules, had to spend the entire season in the major leagues or risk being lost in the major league draft. The Oriole rookie was Wally Bunker, a brash youngster whose professional experience consisted of only 14 games in Class A ball and one with Baltimore in 1963. He'd gotten a $70,000 bonus, and, since the Orioles were not going to let another club draft him, the only thing they could do was put him on the major league roster. Most players in Bunker's position sat on the bench gathering rust all year. Bunker appeared destined for the same fate, as Manager Hank Bauer kept him out of sight for the first fifteen games. Then, when the veterans struggled, Bauer gave him a start. At least, Bauer, reasoned, the rookie was well-rested. All Bunker did was throw a one-hitter at the Washington Senators. The first victory was no fluke, and the youngster went on to finish 19–5, including a second one-hitter.

Bunker was an unusual rookie. Stottlemyre was poised but quiet. Bunker was confident and cocky, and reminded many of a more talented Bo Belinsky, the Angels' flashy young lefty. After his one hitter against Washington, reporters commented that it was too bad that the Senators' Chuck Hinton had ruined the no hitter. Who was Hinton?, Bunker asked. Moose Skowron was the only Washington player he knew.

While Baltimore was a balanced club, Chicago relied primarily upon its pitching. The White Sox finished sixth in team batting with a .247 mark and hit only 106 home runs, ninth in the league. Their pitching, however, was magnificent. Left-handers Gary Peters and Juan Pizarro were 20–8 and 19–9, respectively, and right-hander Joe Horlen was 13–9 with a 1.88 ERA. Ageless knuckleballer Hoyt Wilhelm, 41, led the bullpen with a 12–9 record, 27 saves and a 1.99 ERA.

As August ended, the Yankees were 3 games behind Baltimore and 2½ in arrears of Chicago. Since joining the Yankees, Stottlemyre had won four games, his only loss a 2–0 decision to Leslie (Buster) Narum of the Senators. "Who would have guessed," wrote Dick Young, "that one of the critical games of the pennant drive would pit Buster Narum against Mel Stottlemyre."

Who also, Young might have added, would have thought that Narum would shut the Yankees out. Now that their pitching had recovered, the hitting went sour. Mantle suffered a knee injury, which he thought at first might end his season. After a few games, however, and a cortisone shot, he was back, limping around left or right field, depending on the ballpark. Kubek and Maris continued to be plagued by minor injuries. The batting slump culminated in a 25 inning scoreless string which included back to back shutouts at the hands of Chicago's John Buzhardt and Boston's Bob Heffner, neither of whom was a Cy Young candidate.

The club reached its nadir in Chicago. The Yanks arrived three games out of first place, but four consecutive defeats dropped them 4½ games off the pace. Ford was shelled in the final game, and Berra was in a foul mood as the team bus pulled away from Comiskey Park. To make things worse, the air conditioning system wasn't working. As Yogi smoldered in the first row, he heard the discordant strains of a novice harmonica player emanating from the rear of the bus. The performer was Phil Linz.

After losing the shortstop battle to Tresh in 1962, Linz had become the Yankees' top utility infielder. Unlike most youngsters, Linz was happy to be a substitute, and, although many teams, particularly the Senators, wanted him, Linz wasn't clamoring for a trade and a regular job. He became a good pinch hitter and filled his role well. "Phil loved the organization," said Tom Metcalf. "He was a great Yankee. He'd play when they wanted him to play and if he had to sit, he'd sit and be a cheerleader on the bench." "My locker was next to Mantle's," Linz recalled, "and the first day I walked into the clubhouse I thought I was walking on air because I looked up and saw my name on the locker, and the name on the next locker was Mantle. I was just happy to be there. I wanted to be as nice as I could to everybody."

Linz joined the Yankees the same year as Tresh, Bouton and Pepitone. Tresh, although only 23 years old, was conservative beyond his years. He spent the off-season attending college and playing guitar. After he came up to the Yankees late in the 1961 season, the club offered to let him travel to Cincinnati with them for the World Series, even though he wasn't eligible. Tresh declined, for he had to get back to school to begin classes. "I think I was more of an old-timer," he said, "because of my dad and the things he believed you were supposed to do—keep your mouth shut, play when you're injured and do whatever the manager says. I think the other guys were a little more free-spirited."

That was an understatement, for Pepitone, Bouton and Linz were not Yankees from the traditional mold. "I guess you could call us '60s kids," Linz said. "We were pretty open-minded." Pepitone's extracurricular activities were legendary. Bouton was a free-thinking iconoclast who eventually became the Judas Iscariot of the Yankees, selling out Mickey Mantle for thirty pieces of silver. Linz was irreverent, but not self-destructive like Pepitone and without Bouton's sharp edge. He was just fun to be around. "Nobody has more fun

Phil Linz was a fun-loving, happy-go-lucky utility infielder who caused a nationwide furor by playing a harmonica on the bus during a Yankee losing streak. Following his impromptu performance, the Yankees went on a streak that gave them the 1964 pennant.

than Phil Linz," Steve Jacobson wrote in the spring of 1963. "There are Yankees who earn more, and Yankees who play more, but none of them enjoy it any more."

A bachelor, Linz liked the aura of being a single Yankee in New York. "As soon as [women] find out I'm in the big leagues," he said, "you can see the difference in their attitude. You can see the dollar signs light up in their eyes just like a cash register." Imagine what an impact Linz would have made if he were making more than $7,000 a year. Phil refused to pose with his glasses on during his rookie year, thinking he looked much more handsome without them. During the winter, he got contact lenses, but had trouble hitting with them, and found they didn't help him off the field either. "I must be just ugly," he surmised. "I used to be able to blame the glasses. Now I'm getting a complex."

Many of the older players viewed the writers as a necessary evil, and some, like Maris, thought they were totally unnecessary, but Bouton, Pepitone and Linz reveled in the attention. "We actually liked the writers," Linz said, "and we liked the attention. We were thrilled with the fact that somebody would come up and talk to us. A lot of the writers were about the same age as we were. We were just kids who were so thrilled to be in the big leagues. Most of the players were very reticent about speaking to the writers, but we didn't know that and we didn't care. We thought it was great to pick up the paper the next day and see our names in it. We were thrilled when they came over to talk to us. Since a lot of the guys wouldn't talk to the writers, they naturally gravitated to those of us who would try to give them something to write about. I always felt they had a job to, so why not talk to them? They were nice guys. They were writers, but to me they were celebrities. I loved reading Dick Young's column."

One of Linz's activities in spring training was to organize auto races from the Yankee Clipper Hotel to the ballpark. The commute was normally about 15 minutes, but Linz's objective was to make it to the park as quickly as possible. "He would have a road race with two or three other guys," recalled Roger Repoz. "They'd get in their cars and race to the stadium. Phil usually won because he was a little crazier than the other guys." "Yeah," Linz said, "There was a Dodge dealership down there that gave each player a car to use for spring training. We used to race every day. We had all kinds of shortcuts. It's a wonder we didn't get a ticket every day. I would go down a lane the wrong way and things like that. In those days, you could get away with a lot of stuff. We'd be in jail today.

"When I was in the California League," Linz continued, "they gave us station wagons. They gave us four wagons and we'd put six players in each one. If we were on a trip from Modesto to Reno, we'd race, and the first one to Reno would get a case of beer. What happened — I shouldn't even tell you this — is that we'd buy the beer before we started. By the time we got to Reno, we'd be pretty well smashed. Our manager would pull off to the side of the road to watch us. We'd be playing king of the hill on top of the roofs of the cars. We'd only had two or three beers apiece, but that was enough for eighteen or nineteen year olds."

Linz experimented with hypnotism to help his play. "When I first came up," said Metcalf, "I stayed with him in a hotel. He had a session with a hypnotist. When he came back, he had this little-bitty light that he kept on at night. We're both lying in bed, and he's staring at that light, and there's a record playing. It would put him into a deep sleep, and when you get to a certain point, you're supposed to start telling yourself what to do, stating it positively. 'I will hit the ball to centerfield.' The next few days he gets into the lineup and gets some hits. He was smoking the ball right up the middle. The reporters came around his locker and he's telling them it wouldn't be possible without hypnosis. Now they've really got a story and Phil was loving it. He didn't get a lot of ink, as a utility guy, and this is his day in the sun. He got teased about it quite a bit, but I believe that what he did worked."

In 1964, with Kubek injured much of the season and Boyer slumping, Linz played far more than he had in his first two years with the Yankees. "Yogi was my favorite manager," Linz said recently. "He believed in me. Houk was my first manager in the big leagues and he gave me a lot of confidence because he made me feel valuable, but he had locked me into being a utility guy and I was never going to get out of that."

Linz played a lot in 1964, but he didn't play in either game of the doubleheader against the White Sox. "I thought, how could they bench me against two lefthanders?" he said. "I hit the White Sox well. They were always emphasizing the plays I didn't make at third—the plays I didn't make at short. Hey, I'm in and out and I'm playing three different positions—plus the outfield! I couldn't believe I didn't play those two games."

Linz, who had recently purchased his harmonica at Marshall Fields for $2.25, had a tenuous connection with show business. He and Met pitcher Tracy Stallard sub-leased a Manhattan apartment from actress Julie Newmar, best known for her portrayal of Catwoman on the Batman television series. "She came to the apartment once," Linz recalled. "She came up and said hello and that she just wanted to see the apartment. She noticed we were playing stickball with a wadded up piece of paper. She had these really nice decorated canes, which we were using for bats. One day I swung and missed and broke this gold-plated mirror she had. I told her not to worry. We'd replace it. We never did replace it."

On August 22, Linz decided to venture into show business himself. He pulled out his harmonica and begin playing Mary had a Little Lamb, the only song he knew. "I had really forgotten about the games," Linz recalled. "We'd been sitting on the bus for at least an hour waiting for the traffic to clear so we could get to the airport. They give you a sheet of music when you buy a harmonica and they would have numbers and the arrow down would mean draw out and an arrow up would mean blow in. Mary had a Little Lamb was the first song on the list."

Berra had also been sitting on the bus for an hour, and he had not forgotten about the games. When he heard the inexpert squealing of Linz's harmonica, Yogi spun around in his seat. "Put that thing in your pocket," he was reported to have growled, although those on the bus remembered Berra telling Linz to put the harmonica someplace else. Mantle was sitting across the aisle. "We were all kidding around in the back of the bus," Linz recalled. "We were having a pretty good time back there. The same people always sat in the back—Mantle, Maris, me, Pepitone and Bouton, and we were always kidding around. I wasn't sure if it was Yogi who had told me to put that thing you-know-where. So I asked Mickey what he said" "He said to play it louder," Mantle replied. "I just went ahead and did it and thought it was fun," said Linz. "I didn't realize he was so upset."

Berra leapt from his seat and stormed to the back of the bus. "He came running back at me and I thought, 'Oh, shit,'" said Linz. "He was coming fast. I'd never seen him mad before." Linz flipped the harmonica toward Berra. "'Here,' I said. 'Take it. Take the harmonica.'" Berra caught the harmonica and threw it back at Linz. "He didn't throw it softly," said Linz. "He threw it hard. He was pissed off." The instrument bounced away, hitting Pepitone on the knee. Pepitone threw himself to the floor, screaming as if in great agony. "Corpsman, corpsman!," he shouted. "I'm wounded!"

Berra stood in front of Linz. "He stood over me and raised his arm," said Linz. "I turned my head and thought, 'Oh, shit, he's going to hit me.' It was like he was my father and I was the son. He said 'ooohhhh,' turned away and walked back to the front of the bus. I stood up on the seat and said 'What are you getting on me for. I give one hundred percent.' Some of the other guys were kind of dogging it."

"Yogi's not going to challenge Pepitone," said Metcalf, "and of course he's not going to challenge Mickey or Whitey if they laughed after a loss. But Linz he could challenge." "Shut up and sit down," Berra told Linz. "I sat down," Linz said, "and the guys in the back of the bus were kidding me. Mickey said, 'You can be the third base coach. When you do one toot, I'll bunt. Two toots and I'll swing away.'"

Frank Crosetti, a Yankee since 1932, didn't think it was funny as Mantle did. "I had a little thing against Crosetti," Linz said. "He was kind of an old timer and a little cranky." "Shut up," Crosetti shrieked in his high pitched voice. "You're acting like a kid." The Crow later said that was the worst thing he had ever witnessed in his 33 years with the club.

The incident created front page news all over the country. "In those days," said Linz, "UPI traveled with a team that was in the pennant race, and they must have all gotten off the bus in Boston and called their papers, because it became national headlines all over the country."

The writers had a ball with the story. Would Linz get a performing contract with CBS, the Yankees' new owner? In fact, Linz did endorse Hohner harmonicas for a reported $5,000, far more than the amount of his fine. A radio station mailed harmonicas to each Yankee player, and Hohner reported a sharp spike in sales. "You should have carried a piano on the bus," ventured Pepitone. "You would have made more money." "At least," said Bouton, "it takes everybody's mind off Vietnam." Some players on the Richmond club sent Linz a telegram saying they had reserved a room for him at the Holiday Inn. Even the Mets got into the act. Rod Kanehl admitted he also played the harmonica. "But I play it real good," he said. "I wouldn't make anybody mad." When the Yankees played the Mets a few days later in the Mayor's Trophy Game, some Met players threw harmonicas on the field. The prime suspect was Linz's roommate, Tracy Stallard.

Linz received ten harmonicas in the mail, plus $65 in checks to cover part of his fine. "You know what I'm thinking of doing?" Linz said the following spring. "I know this little fellow — he's a midget really — who plays with a harmonica group. I thought I'd get a great big raccoon coat and keep him under it, and have him play some really complicated pieces ... or maybe I could get one of those papoose things, like the Indian mothers wear on their backs, and keep him in that."

The old Yankees would have been mortified by the publicity, but these Yankees had changed their tune. They were the new, kinder, gentler Yankees, competing with Casey Stengel for headlines. Houk commented on reports that Boston radio stations were urging fans to bring harmonicas and kazoos to Fenway. "That would be funny, wouldn't it?" he said. Houk did add that he didn't think it was a good idea to play a harmonica after four straight losses. Berra said, "But it's exciting, isn't it? That picture of me in one of the papers isn't bad. We're getting the publicity, aren't we?"

All winter long, as Linz pitched Yankee tickets, he played the harmonica, was asked about the harmonica and listened to harmonicas. At a dinner in Baltimore, the audience serenaded him on 100 harmonicas. In 1965, Hohner paid the Yankees $2,300 to place an ad on the back cover of the Yankee yearbook. Linz had done more for harmonica sales than anyone of his generation.

The more serious implication of the harmonica incident was the question of Berra's ability to handle the men he had so recently played with. Houk "would have slapped Linz's ears off," said one Yankee veteran. Had Berra lost control of the team? Many thought he had.

The players loved Yogi, but they didn't respect him the way they did Houk. "I don't think we were ready to get rid of Ralph in our minds," said Tresh, "and I don't think we gave Yogi as good a chance as we should have. It was hard on Yogi because he was a teammate of ours. To be a teammate, then a coach for a year, then a manager, that's a tough role to play. It was tough for us and it was tough for Yogi. If you've been going out with the guys and hanging out with them, and then you've got to separate yourself from all that, it's tough."

"Yogi was fine," said Johnny Blanchard, "and by George he won the pennant, but you could tell he had never managed. There was a big difference in decision-making. I think he needed more experience." Berra had been thrown into the fray long before he was ready. Stengel had a lifetime of experience when he took over the Yanks in '49. Houk managed at Denver for three years and coached in New York for three more before taking the helm in 1961. Yogi had just a single season as a player-coach, with his coaching role mostly limited to slapping players on the fanny after they reached first base and hitting fungoes before the games. "I think Yogi was best suited to being a coach," said Rollie Sheldon. "He was a good guy, and fun to be around, but as far as pulling the strings and making all the moves, I just don't think he had it."

Jim Gosger, who played for Berra on the '73 Mets, concurred. "As far as looking ahead a couple of innings," Gosger said, "he didn't have a clue. "One night he had one guy pinch hit, another pinch run, and a third go in to play the outfield. He used three guys for one job." "He was a nice man," said Met Jim McAndrew, "but as a manager he was a day late and a dollar short. He wasn't in the same league as a Hodges or Houk as far as his acumen, his discipline between the lines and his knowledge of the game."

"Yogi's a wonderful person," said Gordon White, "and Yogi was a great baseball player. The one thing he wasn't was a great manager. I think he was a good manager, but he wasn't in the class with Stengel, Hodges, Torre or Alston. The thing he did was that he didn't screw it up. That's an awfully big part of managing and coaching at the major league level. These guys know what they're doing most of the time and sometimes a manager can screw it up. Yogi didn't screw it up."

One of Yogi's biggest defenders, surprisingly, was Linz. "To this day," he said, "I don't think they gave Yogi enough credit for managing. He was a damned good manager. I really loved the guy. He was as nice as you could possibly be to me. I felt bad when he got fired. I felt I was partially responsible."*

Metcalf, shocked over being cut in the spring of '64, is not one of Yogi's defenders. He recalled a Campbell's Soup commercial he and a few other players made with Berra in 1963. "We were getting three or four hundred dollars for doing it," Metcalf recalled, "and in those days we'd do anything for money. Yogi was the catcher. I was the umpire. Linz was the batter and Marshall Bridges was the pitcher." The basic premise was that Bridges was to throw a pitch, Metcalf was to call it a ball and Berra was to say, "C'mon. Bob. Throw strikes so we can go in and have some good hot Campbell's Soup." "I can remember that verbatim," Metcalf said, "because it was written in big black letters on a piece of cardboard about three feet wide and six feet high, and because of how many times we had to do it. I'll bet we did fifty takes. On the first one he said, 'C'mon, Bob throw strikes so we can go in and eat that soup.' Cut. C'mon, Yogi, what kind of soup? 'Oh, yeah,' he'd say. Then he'd do it again. Linz and I said we wished we'd never done it. We were out there til damn near batting practice for him to get that one line done."

As soon as the Yankees arrived in Boston, Linz went to Berra's office and apologized. "We hugged and shook hands," Linz recalled, "and he said, 'Forget about it, but I've got to fine you, because of the writers. How much do you want me to fine you?'" "You're the manager," Linz replied. Berra decided on a two hundred dollar fine and, as far as Linz was concerned, the matter was closed.

The harmonica incident was a fleeting amusement. The Yankees bullpen problems were neither fleeting nor amusing. In 1964, the Oriole relievers jokingly introduced a new statistic — the scare. A scare occurred when the mere sight of a pitcher warming up resulted in the end of an opposition rally. The only person the Yankee relievers were scaring was Berra.

When Yogi called on one of his relievers, he was rolling the dice. Stafford was perhaps the best right-hander, finishing 5–0 with a 2.66 ERA, but he was plagued by tendinitis in his shoulder and made only 31 appearances. Reniff, who had led the Yankees in saves in 1963, also had a sore arm. Steve Hamilton was 7–2, but erratic, and, like Stafford, hampered by tendinitis that

*Linz later named his dog Yogi.

sidelined him for nearly a month. In early August, Hamilton was quoted in *The Sporting News*, saying, "I've never had a sore arm." About a week later, he had his first sore arm. Hamilton was in only 30 games, and often when he did pitch, was unable to throw the wide-sweeping breaking ball that was so devastating to left-handed hitters. Both Hamilton and Stafford, despite their gaudy won-lost records, often failed in clutch situations.

The rest of the relievers were equally questionable. Big, twenty-four-year-old, bespectacled rookie Pete Mikkelsen was a surprising addition to the roster in spring training. Mikkelsen had been a power pitcher until he'd gotten hurt in the minor leagues. He couldn't lift his arm above his shoulder, and was doing nothing but pitching batting practice. Mikkelsen, who had always thrown overhand, noticed that when he threw sidearm, which was all he could do, the ball sank and no one could hit it. He also developed a deceptive and very effective palm ball. Switched to relief work in 1962, Mikkelsen was 11–6 with a 1.47 ERA at Augusta in 1963. Yogi, with his penchant for relievers who could throw double play grounders, took an immediate liking to the big righthander. Rube Walker, who had managed Mikkelsen in the minor leagues, was close to Berra and urged Yogi to take a long look. "Rube was probably the reason I made it to the big leagues," Mikkelsen said. "He and Yogi were friends, and I guess that helped." All spring, Yogi praised the work of Mikkelsen, who won the James P. Dawson Award as the outstanding rookie in camp and beat out Metcalf for the final bullpen spot. "Somehow," Mikkelsen said, "I think it was kind of a pre-done deal."

Metcalf felt the same. He'd been the front-runner in the battle for the final bullpen spot, for he had pitched well in late '63 and had an excellent spring. He had the best ERA on the staff, having yielded just one run in 13 innings. Yet in Berra's view, it was Metcalf, not Mikkelsen, who had to win the job. Mikkelsen went to New York and Metcalf, devastated, was sent to Richmond. "When Yogi called me in and told me about it, I almost fainted, I was in such shock," Metcalf said. "I said, 'I don't believe you. You're lying. You're putting me on. You can't do that.' He said, 'No, I'm serious. I've got to keep Mikkelsen.' I got pissed and turned around and walked out of the office. Houk came by. He was probably bullshitting me, but he said he knew I was upset and that it wasn't his decision. It was Yogi's decision. It was his team and he had to make those decisions." "I wouldn't have done it that way," Houk told Metcalf. "I would have kept you and let Mikkelsen prove himself in Triple A ball. But Yogi doesn't want to do that."

Nearly forty years later, Metcalf couldn't get that spring out of his mind and hasn't forgiven Berra for sending him down. "I actually ended up having a slight case of ulcers because of it," he said. "Pete did a good job, but we were going head to head and the results were in black and white. It really soured me. I wish I'd handled it better."

Metcalf was determined to show Berra he'd made a mistake. If Berra wanted him to learn a sinker, he would develop the best sinker ever seen in Richmond. "I said, 'If it's sinker balls you want, it's sinker balls you get,'" he said recently. Metcalf relieved Stottlemyre in the exhibition game against the Yankees, and took the instructions to keep his pitches low very seriously. He bounced several balls in the dirt and was lucky to get the save. What Metcalf didn't realize was that the sinker was not a natural pitch for him and put incredible strain on his arm. One night, he threw a sinker to strike out a hitter for the final out of the inning, and felt a slight tug in his elbow.

The next inning, when Metcalf delivered his first warmup pitch, it landed about halfway between the mound and home plate. Catcher Jake Gibbs came running out to the mound and asked what was wrong. Metcalf didn't know. "Let me throw one more," he said. The second pitch landed in about the same place as the first. "I didn't have any pain," Metcalf said, "but I lost all the feeling in my forearm, my thumb and my index finger." After the second bounced warmup toss, manager Preston Gomez went to the mound and took Metcalf out of the game. He was flown to New York for tests, which revealed that he had pinched a nerve in his elbow.

Metcalf tried to come back, but without the feeling in his fingertips, he was unable to get any snap on his curve ball. His fastball was gone, and so was his hope of a big league career. "I wish I'd had more confidence in myself," he said recently, "and said, 'I'm just going to keep doing what I'm doing and prove that they're wrong.'"

The other bullpen operatives were Williams, Bud Daley, the soft-throwing veteran left hander coming off arm surgery, and Bob Meyer, a hard-throwing left-handed rookie who was out of options. Meyer and Daley presented an interesting contrast. Meyer threw hard. Daley threw junk, including a knuckleball and a big curve. Meyer had a young, live arm. Daley had to soak his arm alternately in ice and hot water after a game to reduce the swelling. Meyer has an extremely long 37 inch arm sleeve, which gave him terrific leverage, while Daley has a withered right arm that was crooked and shortened by a childhood disease.

Since he was a young boy, Meyer had wanted to be a major league ballplayer, but for most of his youth, it seemed a ridiculously impossible dream. He was a short, scrawny boy, whose athletic career began as a freshman football player in high school. He was a fourth string guard who never appeared in a game the entire season. At halftime of the year's final game, with his club losing, the coach launched into an inspirational talk. "He looked at me," Meyer recalled, "pointed to me and said, 'I want you guys to go out in the second half and start trying like this little Meyer kid, who's always hustling, but he doesn't have any ability.' That's what the SOB said. I never forgot it."

In his sophomore year, Meyer switched to basketball and made the squad as the 15th man. "I hustled my ass off to make the team," he said, "but then some tall kid who'd been too lazy to come out for pre-season practice decided to play, so I got cut." That left only baseball, and Meyer, who had grown to 5'9", decided to go out for the team in his junior year. He made the squad, but never pitched in a game.

That same year, Meyer had the football coach, the one who'd said he had no athletic ability, as a teacher. "We had to get up in class," Meyer recalled, "and give a five minute talk on what we were going to do when we were an adult. The title of my talk was, 'I'm Going to be a Big League Baseball Pitcher.' He never said a word, but I could tell by the look on his face that he doubted what I was saying — and probably my sanity."

Finally, in his senior year, Meyer's physical maturity caught up with his ambition and he became a star pitcher, good enough to get an invitation to play for the University of Toledo. During his sophomore year at Toledo, Meyer set a school record with 18 strikeouts in a game. In his last four games, he struck out 15, 16, 17 and 18. "I could throw the ball very, very hard," he said, "and I had a good curve ball, but I didn't have good control."

Meyer signed with the Yankees in 1960 and pitched in their minor league system for the next four years. "Within a short period of time," he said, "you get branded. They say 'This guy's got a great arm' 'This one's got a ten cent head,' or 'He can run like a deer' or 'He can't run.' You can never change that image." Meyer was branded as a guy who could throw hard but not straight. In 144 innings at Modesto in 1960, he walked 129 and struck out 156. The following year, in 132 innings, he walked 128 and fanned 147.

In 1963, after pitching well in Amarillo, Meyer was recalled to Triple A Richmond. "The first game I started after I got called up was in Toronto," he recalled, "and I lost 1–0 in the ninth inning when Sparky Anderson hit a home run off me." He laughed. "Of all guys! Sparky Anderson! They had a short left field fence and the ball just made it over."

By the spring of 1964, Meyer was out of options and the Yankees needed to find out whether he could harness his great speed. He pitched frequently in the spring, but when the club prepared to go north, Meyer had not learned of his fate. "Yogi is not the most communicative guy," he said, "and nobody really told me I was going north except the equipment manager. The last day, when things were being packed up, I went to him and he said, 'Yeah, you're going with the club.' Nobody ever said, 'Bob, you made the team' or 'Congratulations,'"

On April 20th, Meyer made his first major league appearance, starting against the Red Sox at Fenway Park. "Ed 'Red Ass' Hurley was the umpire," Meyer recalled. "Elston Howard came up to me before the game and said, 'This guy doesn't like rookies, so don't show any emotion or anything if something happens.' The first pitch of the game was right down the middle. 'Ball one.' I walked the first two guys and somebody got a hit and they got two runs in the first inning."* Meyer pitched decently for the rest of the game, but lost. With the numerous rain-outs and off-days, he pitched in only six more games through mid–June, losing his only three decisions.

With the Yankees struggling, and the pitching staff in disarray, competition was brutal. Meyer discovered that one of the veteran pitchers had gone to Berra and told him Meyer was out carousing at night. "I didn't go to movies," Meyer said. "I didn't run around. I didn't drink much. I'd go to the library and read business publications for two or three hours a day. I couldn't understand why he would do that, but in retrospect I see that he was just trying to keep his job and get his years in."

In June, when the Yankees returned from a West Coast trip, Meyer was sound asleep when his phone rang. "Yogi called me about four in the morning," he recalled, "and said, 'Hey, Bob, we've sold you to the Los Angeles Angels.'" That was the end of his Meyer's Yankee career.

Meyer wasn't overly concerned when the Yankees sold him to the Angels. "I was pretty confident," he said. "I knew there were very few guys in the American League who could throw as hard as I could. If you're a left hander and you can throw hard, somebody will take you." Meyer stayed with the Angels less than two months, and was sold to the Athletics in late July. He pitched a one hitter against the Orioles, and finished with a combined 2–8 record for the three teams.

Daley, the veteran lefthander, remained with the club until mid–August, but rarely left the pen, making only 13 appearances. Williams was inconsistent as both a starter and reliever. He had a handful of good outings, including a stretch in which he did not allow an earned run in 20 innings. More often, Williams pitched poorly, and wound up with a 1–5 record in just 84 innings.

"It was kind of a funny team," said Mikkelsen. "The pitching staff was more helter-skel-ter. I don't think anybody knew their job." Mikkelsen, the only truly healthy reliever, pitched well in the early going, but became increasingly unreliable as the season wore on. He had a rough May, and in late June, after the Yankees had finally reached first place, blew a 7–2 late inning lead to drop them to second. When Stottlemyre was about to be recalled, it was speculated that Mikkelsen would be the one sent to Richmond.

In the Yankees first 46 losses, they blew a lead in the sixth inning or later 15 times. This caused Berra to leave his starters in the game longer and longer. Downing was often wild, accu-mulating a great number of strikeouts and walks, and tended to throw a lot of pitches. On July 14, in a key game against the league-leading Orioles, Berra let Downing throw 149 pitches in a 4–3 win, not daring to turn the game over to his shaky relievers. In subsequent starts, Down-ing was not so lucky. On July 31, he gave up a two-run, game-winning homer to Harmon Kille-brew of the Twins in the ninth inning. On August 18, he gave up a three run, ninth inning, game-tying home run to Chicago's Floyd Robinson and lost in the tenth. "On two occasions," wrote Leonard Koppett after the White Sox game, "Downing might have been lifted if Man-ager Yogi Berra could have counted on first rate relief. He can't, so he had to sink or swim with Downing. He sank." In his next start, Downing squandered a 3–2 lead in the eighth when Boston's Lee Thomas hit a two-run homer. The Sox did it again five days later, this time on

---

*Hurley had been the home plate umpire when midget Eddie Gaedel batted for the St. Louis Browns, and perhaps Gaedel's strike zone was the one he used for rookies.

Felix Mantilla's three run homer in the seventh. In none of these games did Berra go to his bullpen until after the damage had been done.

In desperation, Yogi began using his starters in relief. They threw between starts anyway, Berra reasoned, so why not let them pitch against live hitters? On August 16, he brought in Downing with two out in the ninth to strike out Baltimore's Earl Robinson and preserve Stottlemyre's 3–1 win. Bouton and Downing again hurled in relief in late August. While each struck out the side in their only inning, using starters was not a long term solution to the Yankee bullpen troubles.

With the trading deadline long past, the only way for a team to acquire a veteran reliever was through the waiver route. When a club placed a player on waivers, all the other teams had the opportunity to put in a claim for his services. The claim process began with the league team with the worst record, and progressed in ascending order until moving to the teams in the other league. If a claim was made, the player could be withdrawn from the waiver list, sold to the claiming team for the waiver price of $20,000, or a deal could be negotiated between the two clubs. If a player was not claimed, the club was free to sell or trade him, even if the trade deadline had passed.

With ten teams in each league rather than eight, it was becoming increasingly difficult to consummate the type of September acquisition that had brought past Yankee teams veteran hurlers such as Sal Maglie, Jim Konstanty and Johnny Sain. "It's very difficult for the Yankees to get a player on waivers," Houk said in late August. Virtually every serviceable veteran, he stated, was being claimed by the teams below the Yanks in the standings.

On September 5, however, a veteran pitcher managed to slip through the waiver net, and the Yankees acquired 29-year-old righthander Pedro Ramos from the Cleveland Indians for $30,000 and two players to be named later. Ramos, a handsome, cigar smoking, tobacco-chewing Cuban, was a ten year veteran, having arrived in the major leagues with the Washington Senators at the age of 19. "Pete was happy-go-lucky and liked to have fun," said Doc Edwards. "He was a very handsome Latin guy who knew he was good looking." Early in his career Ramos told Joe Cambria, the scout who signed him, that he was quitting baseball. "No time for girls," he told Cambria. "Baseball takes up too much time." He was kidding, Ramos said after Cambria nearly went into a faint.

Ramos was a talented all-around athlete who was frequently used as a pinch hitter and runner. He was a free swinger who hit 15 career home runs, twice hitting two in a game, but struck out 316 times in 703 career at bats. "He loved to hit," said Johnny Blanchard. "Oh, gosh, he loved to swing." "He always thought he could hit," said Al Luplow, who played with Ramos at Cleveland. "A lot of pitchers think they can hit," he added.

Ramos and Mantle had a long history. In May, 1956, Ramos surrendered a mammoth home run to Mantle that would have been the first fair ball hit out of Yankee Stadium had it not struck the right field facade eighteen inches from the top. Pete was disappointed the ball had not left the stadium and earned him an historical footnote. What was the difference between giving up a home run off the facade and one that left the park completely? Each counted for but one run. In 1960, Ramos got into a beanball war and was fined $50 for hitting Mantle with a pitch.

Ramos loved taunting Mantle. "Pete would say," Doc Edwards recalled, "'Hey, Meecky, remember the time I strike you out with a speeter?' Mickey would just grin. 'Hey, Meecky,' he'd say, 'remember the time I got you with a speeter?' Then Mickey said, 'Pete, if they put the home runs I hit off you back-to-back, they'd reach around the world.' Pete turned around and said with a straight face, 'He's got a point.'"

Ramos, one of the fastest men in the major leagues, was always looking to challenge someone to a race. He beat Richie Ashburn in a sprint. He agreed to face Luis Aparicio, but backed out when Aparicio wanted to race around the bases rather than in a straight line. Ramos constantly boasted that he could beat Mantle, generally considered the fastest man in the majors. Finally, Mantle challenged him to a race for a purse of $1,000 (according to some versions, it was Ramos who challenged Mantle). Ramos declined, saying he didn't have that much money. He approached Indian GM Gabe Paul, who said the club would put up the money, and why not double it. At that point, Mantle's swift feet turned cold, as he realized he might 1) lose $2,000; 2) mar his reputation or; 3) injure himself. After Ramos joined the Yanks, he still wanted to race Mantle. "Houk got hold of it," said Blanchard, "and said he'd have none of it. Oh, my god, if Mick had pulled a muscle, they'd have sent Pedro so far into Cuba...."

Ramos also had a couple of encounters with another American League superstar, Ted Williams. Once, after striking out Williams, Ramos went up to him after the game and asked him to sign the ball. Williams signed. Shortly thereafter, he tagged Ramos for a long home run. As he was rounding the bases, Williams shouted toward the mound, "If you find that ball, sign it yourself."

Ramos played with bad teams most of his career, and had compiled a record of 104–142, leading the American League in losses four consecutive years. He had only two winning seasons, and lost 18 or more games in every season between 1958 and 1961, including an 11–20 record in the latter year. Ramos was a workhorse, always among the leaders in innings pitched. In 1960, he tied for the American League lead with 274 innings, then pitched 217 more in Cuba during the winter, for the astounding total of 491 innings in a season. From 1955 through 1959, Ramos pitched more innings and won more games than any other Senator pitcher. He was prone to the gopher ball, yielding an average of 33 homers per year from 1957–63, with a high of 43 in '57.

Despite his lack of statistical success, Pete had good stuff, a crackling fastball, a fine curve and good control. He was also alleged to throw a wicked spitball, which he referred to as his Cuban palm ball. "He had the Beech-Nut working," said Blanchard. "He'd put it on his fingers, nobody would see it and she would dip. Boy, she'd really explode!" Luplow recalled one incident when Ramos was playing for Cleveland, and Baltimore manager Billy Hitchcock complained that Ramos was throwing a spitter. After finding Vaseline on his uniform, the umpires took Ramos into the locker room and made him change his clothes. The game was delayed for 15–20 minutes. "Finally," said Luplow, "they came back out. The first pitch he threw was wetter than hell. The home plate umpire turned to the Baltimore bench, looked at Hitchcock and shrugged his shoulders, as if to say 'What do you want me to do?'"

Ramos' failure to win consistently was always a puzzle to his managers. "The man who can do as many things with a baseball as Ramos has no business losing anything like 19 games," Senator pitching coach Bob Swift once said. "He should be ashamed of himself.... Unless he is facing one of the good hitters, he doesn't bear down."

Finally, in 1964, Cleveland decided that Ramos, 29, was never going to realize his potential. Indian manager Birdie Tebbetts said Ramos had a great arm and wanted to use him in relief, but Pete wanted no part of it. Ramos began the 1964 season in the Indians' starting rotation. He was erratic, with more bad performances than good. In early July, he was dispatched to the bullpen with a 4–6 record.

A few days later, Cleveland called up rookie Luis Tiant, who had a sparkling 15–1 mark with Portland of the Pacific Coast League. During the winter, the Indians had left Tiant unprotected, and any club, including the Yankees, could have claimed him for $8,000. No one did, and in his first major league appearance, Tiant beat Whitey Ford, hurling a four hit shutout. He won four of his first five decisions, burying Ramos deep in the bullpen.

With the emergence of Tiant, and the development of another youngster, fireballing Sam McDowell, Ramos became expendable. He had aggravated Tebbetts in early August by conversing with fellow Cuban and former teammate Camilo Pascual of the Twins in the outfield prior to a game. This violated the club rule on fraternizing with the opposition, a transgression for which Ramos was fined $50. "I don't care if I get fined for that," he replied defiantly. "I was talking with my best friend. It was worth the fine to talk to Pascual."

Ramos' eccentricity also irritated Tebbetts. When he joined the Senators, Ramos understood virtually no English. In order to learn the language, he watched a number of western movies, and acquired a love of western clothing. He loved to dress in ten gallon hats (of which he owned ten), studded belts and six-shooters, and dubbed himself "The Cuban Cowboy." "He and Sam McDowell would go through stages," said Edwards. "One of them was when they started wearing western garb and acting like they were cowboys. Of course, Sam was a cowboy and Pete was a ranchero."

Tebbetts had missed the first half of the season, after suffering a heart attack in spring training, and the presence of The Cuban Cowboy was not contributing to his recovery. Believing the Cleveland manager had reneged on a promise to keep him in the starting rotation, Ramos asked to be traded. Tebbetts told him no one wanted him. In September, when the Yankees expressed an interest, Ramos was gone.

A Yankee fan since childhood, Ramos was delighted to leave Cleveland for New York. When he pitched for the Senators, he kept asking Stengel to trade for him. Ramos and Pascual, the two best Washington pitchers, were the subject of constant trade rumors, often involving the Yankees. In 1960, a McDougald for Ramos trade was discussed but never consummated. After the 1961 season, they talked about a trade for Blanchard.

While Ramos may have been excess baggage to the Indians, to the Yankees, any pitcher with a live arm was worth a gamble. If he was inconsistent, Ramos was no less reliable than the group that had paraded from the Yankee bullpen all season. Like Stottlemyre, Ramos was rushed into combat immediately upon joining the club, despite having pitched the previous day. He came in to face the Athletics in the ninth inning to protect a 3–0 lead for Rollie Sheldon. Sheldon departed apprehensively. All three of his victories had been complete games, and on three other occasions he had left the game with a lead, only to watch the bullpen squander it. Ramos did little to bolster Sheldon's confidence, yielding singles to Rocky Colavito and Jim Gentile, making the score 3–1, with runners on first and third and no one out. That was it for the Athletics, however, as a double play grounder and a popup let in a meaningless run but ended the game.

Ramos went back to the mound the following day, pitching effective middle relief against Minnesota. The Yanks pulled within a game and a half of Baltimore by winning 5–4, as Ford came out of the bullpen to get the final out.

From September 13 through the end of the season, the Yankees' new reliever was sensational. He appeared nine more times and posted one win and six saves. In 15⅓ innings, Ramos allowed just six runners to reach base, none on walks. On the 13th, he replaced an injured Ford and worked five innings of two-hit ball for the win. Pete saved both ends of a doubleheader on September 23 and again on September 30. With quality relief pitching for the first time all season, the Yankees went 21–7 after The Cuban Cowboy rode into town.

While Ramos was finishing, Stottlemyre was starting and finishing, with five complete games in 12 attempts. The Cowboy and the Kid were combining to win the pennant for the Yankees, but rarely did they appear in the same game. With Stottlemyre pitching so many complete games, Ramos was called upon to relieve him just twice.

Several other players contributed to the stretch run. Mantle and Maris, slowed by injuries all season, came alive in the final month. Mickey, dragging himself around on two bad legs, finished with a .303 average and 35 home runs. It was his last big season. For most of the year, Mickey tore the cover off the ball hitting right handed, but his bad knee gave him trouble from the left side. He had a difficult time maintaining his balance and getting out of the way of close pitches. Maris, taking Mantle's place in center, hit 26 homers and delivered one clutch hit after another in September. Along with Al Kaline, Maris had been among the best defensive right fielders in the league. Now he was one of the best in center.

Pepitone hit 11 homers in a month and wound up with 28. Downing led the league in strikeouts, and Bouton won 18 games. Terry, plagued by back trouble, had been 2–8 with a 7.11 ERA at the All-Star break. In the second half, he was 5–3 and lowered his overall ERA to 4.54.

On September 8, Stottlemyre pulled the Yanks to within a game of first place with a complete game 2–1 victory over the Twins, New York's fifth straight win. In the eighth inning, with the Yanks ahead by a run, Minnesota put runners at second and third with two out. Berra declined to bring in Ramos and left the rookie in to face dangerous slugger Bob Allison. Stottlemyre needed only one pitch to induce a grounder to Clete Boyer for the third out.

Over the next few days, despite another complete game victory by Stottlemyre, New York was able to gain little ground. Finally, on September 17, the Yankees moved into first place, as Mel notched his seventh win by defeating the Angels 6–2, with relief help from Sheldon. Mantle capped the scoring with his 31st home run. The race could not have been tighter:

	W	L	Pct.	GB
New York	86	59	.593	—
Baltimore	88	61	.591	—
Chicago	88	61	.591	—

Since August 22, the Yanks had been 17–7, Baltimore 12–14 and Chicago 13–12. Over the weekend of September 18–20, New York swept a three game series from the A's to open a one game lead over Baltimore and two over the White Sox. On the 23rd, the Yanks extended their winning streak to nine with a doubleheader sweep of the Indians. The stretch drive was becoming reminiscent of 1960, a long winning streak powered by a rookie starter and a journeyman Latin relief ace. Ramos saved both games on the 23rd, striking out four in 1⅔ innings in the nightcap. The starting pitcher for Cleveland in the first game was Sam McDowell, one of the youngsters who had supplanted Ramos in the rotation. The other, Tiant, was the loser in relief. The Yankees now held a four game lead over the Orioles and White Sox, with ten to play. The magic number was six.

On September 26, Stottlemyre shut out the Senators 7–0, New York's fourteenth straight win. After the game, no one wanted to talk to Mel about his fine pitching, which was now almost taken for granted. The big story was his five hits in five times at bat. Mel hit a double, beat out a bunt, had three other singles and drove in two runs off four Washington hurlers. The magic number was four.

It was still four prior to a doubleheader against the Tigers on September 30th. As he had a week earlier against the Indians, Ramos saved both games as the Yanks reduced the coveted magic number to two. The Tigers reversed the result in yet another twinbill the following day, as two youngsters, Dennis McLain and Mickey Lolich, beat Stottlemyre and Sheldon. Mel's record dropped to 9–3.

Entering the final three games of the season, versus the Indians at the Stadium, the Yankees needed one win to clinch a tie and two to wrap up the pennant, regardless of what the Orioles and White Sox did. Ford, recovered from his hip injury, won his 17th game on Friday night to assure at least a tie. On Saturday, Downing started on just two days rest. By the eighth inning, the score was 3–3 and Mikkelsen had replaced Downing. "The thing I remember most about that game," said Mikkelsen, "is that there was nobody there." For the clincher, the Yankees had drawn less than 15,000.

In the bottom half of the eighth, Mikkelsen departed for a pinch hitter and the Yanks got runners on second and third with one out. Richardson hit a line drive over the head of Cleveland shortstop Dick Howser. Howser leaped, got the ball in his glove, but couldn't hold it. Clete Boyer scored and New York led 4–3. Before the inning ended, four more runs came across. Ramos worked a 1-2-3 ninth and the Yankees, after a long, hard struggle, claimed their 29th pennant, their fifth in a row. The victory was their 23rd in 29 games. As Ramos walked off the mound, he made an obscene gesture at Birdie Tebbetts.

"They should consider 1964 a classic year for us," said Linz, "because we were behind by 6½ games at the end of August and went ahead and won the thing. You had strong competition. A lot of clubs were starting to get really good. Besides, we had a lot of injuries. Mickey was out for a long time. Whitey had a bad arm. Kubek was hurt a lot. That should be considered a classic season for us."

It had been a monumental struggle, but the Yankees were going to the World Series for the fifth consecutive year. "Seldom have pennant winners been less convincingly superior to their rivals than the Cardinals and Yankees," wrote Leonard Koppett. In a short series between two evenly-matched teams, anything could happen. Berra hoped that his famous luck held out for another week.

◆ 14 ◆

Yogi's Last Hurrah
The 1964 World Series

Not since 1949 had the pennant race in both leagues gone down to the wire. The Yankees won with a day to spare, while the Cardinals, with a magnificent closing burst that overtook the fading Philadelphia Phillies, took the race down to the final out of the final inning. Perhaps the biggest question was whether the Cardinals would be able to regroup after the draining pennant race. Previous National League teams in similar situations had not fared very well. The 1949 Dodgers, 1950 Phillies and 1951 Giants, all last day pennant winners, were beaten soundly by the Yankees in the Series. Bob Gibson, the Cardinal ace, had pitched a complete game on Friday night and won in relief on Sunday. He was in no condition to pitch the first Series game on Wednesday, so Keane selected southpaw Ray Sadecki as his opening game starter. Based upon won-lost records, there would not appear to be much difference between the two pitchers. Gibson was 19–12, while Sadecki had an even better record (20–11). Gibson, however, was beginning a period of dominance that would land him in the Hall of Fame, while 1964 was the only time in an 18-year major league career that Sadecki won more than 14 games.

The Cardinals, although they barely eked out the pennant with a desperate stretch run, had a very good team. They had three Hall of Famers, Gibson, Lou Brock and backup catcher Bob Uecker, who was elected to the Hall as an announcer in 2003. Brock had a good series, Gibson an outstanding one, and Uecker provided an entertaining pregame exhibition before Game Two, borrowing a tuba from the band in left field and demonstrating as much musical ability as Linz had shown on the harmonica a few weeks earlier. Roger Craig played straight man by hitting fungos into the tuba as Uecker played.

The Cardinal infield, with Bill White at first, MVP Ken Boyer at third and former MVP Dick Groat at short, was the equal of any in baseball. Groat, who was acquired in a trade before the 1963 season, filled a hole at shortstop that had existed since Marty Marion left in 1950. He helped turn the Cardinals from a sixth place club in 1962 to one that challenged for the pennant in 1963. Curt Flood ranked with Willie Mays as a defensive center fielder, and batted .311, leading the National League with 211 hits. Tim McCarver, in just his second year, emerged as a standout catcher, and the Cardinals had three solid starting pitchers, plus veteran knuckleballer Barney Schultz in the bullpen. Schultz, like Ramos, had been rescued from the scrap heap, and proved a savior down the stretch.

The final piece of the championship puzzle arrived on June 15, the trading deadline. Lou Brock came out of Southern University in 1961 with rave recommendations and a $30,000 bonus from the Chicago Cubs. He was fast as lightning, had excellent power, and in his first year of professional baseball, led the Northern League in batting with a .361 average. In fact, Brock led the Northern League in just about everything, including games, runs, hits, doubles and putouts by an outfielder.

The following year, 1962, with just one year of professional experience, Brock found himself in the Cubs' starting lineup. During the next two years, he was no better than adequate. There were flashes of brilliance, such as a mammoth home run off the Mets' Al Jackson which landed in the center field bleachers in the Polo Grounds, just the second time the feat had been accomplished. But Brock's batting averages were just .263 and .258, and there were too many strikeouts, 96 in 1962 and 122 the following year. Further, he was not a polished fielder and, although he had great speed, not an accomplished base stealer. Brock stole 24 bases in 1963, but was caught 12 times.

In mid–June of 1964, Brock, a few days shy of his 25th birthday, was batting about .250, with two home runs. The Cubs were playing .500 ball, and were just 5½ games out of first place, led by power hitters Ernie Banks, Ron Santo and Billy Williams. If they could get some pitching, they might have a chance for the pennant that had eluded them since 1945.

Ernie Broglio won 21 games for the Cardinals in 1960, and was 18–8 in 1963. He was only 28 years old and, although he'd had a little arm trouble, was a solid starting pitcher, just what the Cubs were looking for. The Cardinals traded Broglio to the Cubs along with veteran reliever Bobby Shantz and outfielder Doug Clemens for Brock and two second line pitchers. The trade was not considered a blockbuster. Dick Young wrote, "The Cardinal-Cub trade wasn't especially exciting, but I'll say this for the two clubs: It's better to move a few players around than to fire the manager."

The trade soon became very exciting, at least for the Cardinals. Broglio suffered from arm trouble and won only seven games during the next three years, his last three seasons in the majors. Shantz was traded to Philadelphia and retired at the end of the season. Clemens played one season as a regular and batted .221.

Brock was an instant success in St. Louis, hitting .348 and stealing 33 bases in 103 Cardinal games. He also hit 12 home runs for St. Louis, more than he had hit in any full season in Chicago. During the World Series, someone asked Stan Musial, who had retired after the 1963 season, if he wished he'd stayed one more year so that he could have played in the Series. If he had been in left field rather than Brock, Musial said, the Cardinals wouldn't be in the Series.

The Yankees and Cardinals were each missing a starting player. St. Louis second baseman Julian Javier had strained his hip in the last series of the year, and was replaced by utility man Dal Maxvill. The Yanks were without Tony Kubek, whose season had consisted of a frustrating series of injuries. Kubek missed the opening of the season with a mysterious injury, which, after a painful week, was diagnosed as myositis, an inflammation of the muscles of the upper back. It was May before he was finally able to appear in a game. Late in May, he was sidelined by a pulled muscle in his rib cage. In August, he had to leave a game after jamming his hip sliding into second base. In and out of the lineup, and often below par when he played, Kubek had a poor season, batting just .229 in 106 games. Finally, in the last week of the season, Kubek's frustration got the better of him, and he punched a door in anger. The door survived, but Kubek's right wrist did not. He was out for the Series.

Linz, who because of all the Yankee injuries, played in 112 games, would start. He was capable of playing a steady shortstop, but no one could turn the double play like Kubek and Richardson, who had been doing it gracefully and efficiently since their days at Denver. At a number of crucial moments, the Yankees inability to convert double play opportunities would cost them dearly.

Kubek's place on the roster was taken by 22-year-old Mike Hegan, son of the Yankee bullpen coach, a left-hand hitting first baseman who spent the season with Columbus of the Southern

League and had been called up in September. He'd batted just five times in the major leagues. The Yankee bench, once the team's strength, was woefully weak for the Series. Two of the left-handed hitters were the green Hegan and Archie Moore, carried all year as a first year player, who batted just 23 times. Since Linz would start at shortstop, Berra was without another valuable substitute.

With Linz at shortstop and Hegan sitting on the Yankee bench, the first game took place in St. Louis on Wednesday, October 7. Sadecki was paired against Ford, who held virtually every World Series pitching record, but had lost his last three Series decisions, one against the Giants in '62, and two to Koufax in '63. Sadecki was no Koufax, and the Yanks entered the bottom of the sixth with a 4–2 lead. With one out and Ken Boyer at first, right fielder Mike Shannon came to the plate.

Shannon was a swarthy-looking 25-year-old who had been with the Cardinals for parts of three seasons. When Musial retired after the '63 season, Charley James, a former University of Missouri football player and a Cardinal reserve for four years, was slated to replace him. Carl Warwick, who'd started for the Colts, was slated for right field. James, however, didn't hit. Warwick wasn't impressive either, and both wound up on the bench. Rookie Johnny Lewis was overwhelmed by big league pitching and was sent back to the minor leagues. Brock was acquired to play left and Shannon, who hadn't even been considered for a starting job in the spring, and had been sent to the minor leagues in May, was called up from Jacksonville in mid-season. He wound up starting almost every game in right field during the Cards' frantic run to the pennant.

Shannon ripped Ford's pitch deep to left center field. On a calm day it would have been well beyond the left field fence. On this day, however, a stiff breeze was blowing to left and Shannon's blast caught the jet stream. The ball was finally stopped by a sign on top of the scoreboard, roughly 450–475 feet away. The score was tied and, when McCarver followed with a double, Ford was gone.

Since Ramos joined the Yankees after September 1, he was ineligible to pitch in the Series, leaving Berra with the erratic crew that had given him fits throughout the summer. With two off days built into the series schedule for travel, Yogi decided to go with Ford, Stottlemyre and Bouton as his starters and use Downing, who had led the American League with 217 strikeouts, in the bullpen. Would he have liked to call on Ramos to relieve Ford, Berra was asked after the game? "But we don't have him," Yogi replied, neatly ducking the obvious answer. The two batters following McCarver were right handed, but with a tie score in the sixth inning, Yogi went with the best pitcher he had, who was Downing. After getting the second out, Downing faced pinch hitter Carl Warwick, making his first appearance since having his cheekbone fractured ten days earlier. Warwick singled in McCarver with the go-ahead run.

Curt Flood, the next batter, lifted a high fly to left field. Left field in Yankee Stadium was renowned as the most difficult field in all of baseball, especially in October. As Tom Tresh was soon to discover, Busch Stadium's left field was no piece of cake. The sun shone directly into the fielder's eyes, and a stiff wind, about 16 mph, was blowing from right. Further, the playing surface was atrocious. "They were circulating a scouting report on Lou Brock," recalled Archie Moore. "They said that he wasn't particularly good at fielding ground balls, and we should look to take the extra base. We went to St. Louis and found out why he couldn't field ground balls. The outfield was terrible. It wasn't even equivalent to a good high school field."

Flood's drive went up into the sun, and Tresh lost sight of it. When he picked it up again, the wind blew it toward the wall. The ball hit off the base of the wall, and Flood steamed into third with a triple which gave the Cards a 6–4 lead.

The Yanks were never able to make up the deficit, and suffered their fifth consecutive World Series loss. Ford was the losing pitcher, his fourth straight Series defeat. Mikkelsen and Sheldon succeeded Downing and gave up three runs in the eighth. The Yankee loss was bad enough, but even worse, two weaknesses had emerged, shortcomings that were to plague the team throughout the series. First, the bullpen had failed, giving up four runs in 2⅔ innings. The defense, always a key to Yankee champions of the past, also broke down. In addition to Tresh's misplay, Boyer made a key error and Mantle, in right field, made a wild throw to the plate.

One game down, the Yankees were reduced to starting Stottlemyre, with less than two months of major league experience, against Gibson, the Cardinals' ace. "He's a rookie," Berra said, "but he beat Chicago and Baltimore the first two times he pitched, so why can't he pitch in the World Series?" Who was available in the bullpen if Mel should falter? Berra said Downing would be his number one choice, if his arm could bounce back. The young lefthander had relieved only twice during the regular season, and had never pitched two days in a row.

Fortunately, Stottlemyre didn't need any help. He had not been rattled by the pressure of a pennant race, and was not bothered by the hoopla of the World Series, or by the loud St. Louis fans. Stottlemyre blew through the top of the Cardinal order in the first, striking out two. After yielding a run in the third, Mel shut the Cardinals down. Unfortunately for the Yankees, however, Gibson was terrific. He had the best stuff, he said, that he had in any game during the Series. Gibson retired the first nine Yankees, striking out six of them. Not one of the first fifteen batters managed to get the ball out of the infield. "I was amazed by how hard Gibson threw," said Moore. "Everything he threw had great velocity, and he had no problem moving people off the plate."

The Yankees tied the game in the fourth, and got their big break two innings later. With one out and Mantle on first, Pepitone checked his swing and pulled away from a low inside pitch. He stood at the plate, and seemed surprised when umpire Bill McKinley waved him to first base, indicating that the ball had hit him on the right thigh.* Catcher McCarver jumped up in disbelief. "The ball hit the bat first," he said after the game. "When the ball hits a leg, it doesn't sound like wood, unless it's a wooden leg." "When a guy gets hit by a ball," said Dick Groat, "he doesn't just stand there like Pepitone did and wait for the umpire to tell him to go to first. He drops his bat and takes off." Wasn't it strange that he just stood there? "Not if you know Pepitone," said umpire Hank Soar. After the game, Pepitone insisted he had been hit, and pointed to his left thigh, which had a distinct red mark on it. Wrong leg, he was told, and Joe quickly corrected himself.

That was the break the Yankees needed. Tresh singled in Mantle, driving home his fourth run in two games. New York scored two more runs in the seventh and, after the Cardinals had scored once off Stottlemyre in the eighth to close the gap to 4–2, broke the game open in the ninth. Linz, who had two singles earlier in the game, hit a home run off Barney Schultz to lead off the inning. One out later, a single kayoed the Cardinals' ace reliever. With Mantle up, Keane brought in rookie left hander Gordon Richardson. It was a curious choice, for Mantle's troublesome right leg made it difficult to bat left handed. During the past two seasons, he batted just .244 from the left side but an incredible .422 right handed. In mid–July, 1964, he was hitting an even more amazing .515 right handed.

*This was not the first time McKinley had become embroiled in controversy. In 1960, he and fellow umpire Ed Runge were photographed in a series of compromising situations at a hotel with a pair of exotic dancers. While the per diem rate for umpires was notoriously low, apparently it was enough to afford cocktails and some extracurricular activity at the Gaiety Supper Club, followed by a nightcap at the hotel. Male acquaintances of the women soon came forward, asking for $5,000 in cash to keep the pictures from becoming public. The two umpires spent an agonizing night, then decided to go to the police. Both men were married, and the photographs would help neither their marriages nor their careers. The police commenced monitoring the umpires' activities, and told them to continue communicating with the extortion artists. When the umpires said they couldn't come up with $5,000, the blackmailers suggested $3,000, plus throwing a game. With evidence in hand, the police moved in, the extorters were arrested, and the umpires requested and received a leave of absence for the remaining month of the season. Both returned the following April.

Richardson surmised that Keane wanted to turn Mantle around so he couldn't shoot for the short porch in right field. "I knew he was about a .400 hitter against left handed pitching, and it was my first World Series experience," Richardson said. The young pitcher had little experience of any kind, having worked only 47 big league innings since being called up in late August. "I'll never forget what Johnny Keane said," Richardson recalled. "He said, 'Don't give this guy nothin' good to hit, but don't walk him.' That kind of left me in a hot spot. They told me to give him nothing but off-speed curve balls."

Mantle doubled down the left field line, and Richardson gave up two more runs before departing. His replacement was Roger Craig, the first former Met to appear in a World Series game. Craig struck out Stottlemyre to end the inning with the Yankees ahead 8–2. Stottlemyre gave up another run in the ninth, but finished with a complete game 8–3 victory. He got 19 outs on ground balls, and four on strikeouts. The first five batters in the St. Louis order managed to hit only three balls beyond the infield, and got just one hit.

The Cardinals, who had never seen the Yankee rookie before, were impressed. Cardinal manager Johnny Keane knew Stottlemyre had a good sinker, but was surprised at the velocity of his fastball. "Stottlemyre is a real good young pitcher," said Ken Boyer, who had gone hitless in four at bats. "He's going to be around for a long while." "For three innings," said Dick Groat, "we tried to think of somebody in the National League who pitched like this kid. There isn't anybody in our league who's like him. We were all impressed and that's an understatement." A fan from Mabton, Washington chimed in. "I thought Mel did a real good job," said Mrs. Vernon Stottlemyre, who had watched the game on television with her husband, who also thought their son had pitched well.

The Yankees had split the first two games on the road, which is the goal of most Series teams, and after an off day, returned to New York for Game Three. There was no game Friday, and both teams worked out at the Stadium. Pepitone emerged from the Yankee dugout and limped noticeably to third base. When the Cardinals began hooting at him, he made his limp even more pronounced. He had just taken whirlpool treatments, Pepitone said with a straight face, and the doctors were considering putting a splint on his leg. When he walked back to the dugout, someone asked what had happened to the limp. "Oh, that's right," Joe said, and commenced limping once again. Wrong leg, he was reminded, and with a graceful skip, Pepitone began limping on the proper leg.

The third game took place on a chilly Saturday afternoon in New York, fifty one degrees with a brisk wind, as Bouton hooked up with veteran left hander Curt Simmons. For eight tense innings, the two pitchers were locked in a tight duel, the hard-throwing youngster against the soft-tossing 35-year-old, who was appearing in his first Series game. In 1950, Simmons, along with Robin Roberts, led the Phillie Whiz Kids to the National League pennant, but before the Series started, he was drafted into military service and missed the four game Yankee sweep.

In 1960, at the age of 31, Simmons was released by the Phillies and it appeared his career was over. He'd had an accident with a lawn mower, in which he lost part of a big toe, had an elbow operation, and pitched only seven games in 1959. Cardinal manager Solly Hemus called Simmons after his release, and Simmons assured him that he was fine, physically. Like his old teammate Roberts, Simmons made a stirring comeback, winning seven games in 1960, nine the next year, and 10, 15 and 18 the next three seasons. Simmons threw his fastball, which wasn't too fast any more, sparingly, but changed speeds expertly. He'd transformed himself into that time-honored baseball cliché, a crafty lefthander.

Bouton, Simmons' mound opponent, not only had a crackling fastball and a sharp curve, he had mental toughness. Bouton bore down even harder with runners on base, and Game Three was a classic example of his combination of skill and grittiness. In the Cardinal sixth, with the score tied 1–1, St. Louis loaded the bases with two out. Bouton got Shannon to ground into a force play. The following inning, there was a runner at third with just one out, but Bouton again escaped without a run. Pitching with an exaggerated overhand motion, Bouton put such effort into each pitch that his cap often flew off during his follow through. Counting the de-cappings became a favorite media activity. Against the Cardinals, Bouton set a personal and World Series record by losing his cap 38 times in 123 pitches.*

The Yankees had two weaknesses, their bullpen and their defense. With Bouton still on the mound, relief pitching had not come into play, but in the ninth, the defense faltered, as Linz booted McCarver's easy grounder. McCarver was sacrificed to second, but died there as Bouton got Bob Skinner and Curt Flood on fly balls. Skinner had batted for Simmons, who had retired the Yanks in order in the seventh and eighth and had surrendered only four hits all afternoon. But with a chance to win the game, Keane sent Skinner up to bat for him and Simmons' magnificent day was over.

Schultz, the 38-year-old knuckleballer, came in to pitch the ninth inning. He had yielded just one regular season home run in 49 innings after joining the Cardinals in August, but his performance in the first two games had been a little shaky. He saved Game One with a three inning stint, but was short of invincible, surrendering a run on four hits and a walk. In the second game, Schultz gave up a home run to Linz and a single to Maris before being removed. Mantle had been the next batter, and Gordon Richardson had surmised that Keane didn't want Mantle batting left-handed with the short right field fence. Yankee Stadium also had a short fence in right, and Mantle, leading off the ninth, was batting left-handed against Schultz.

"I'm going to stay right by the runway," Berra told Mantle before he went to the plate, "so I can go quick because you're going to hit one." Schultz wound up and delivered his first pitch. "Did it get a good piece of the plate?" a reporter asked Keane after the game. "It sure got a good piece of the bat," the manager replied. "It just lay there," Mantle said. Mickey swung, and the ball took off like a rocket for the right field stands. There was no doubt from the moment it left the bat, and the ball landed in the upper deck. It was Mantle's 16th World Series homer, breaking a tie with Babe Ruth for the all-time record. More important, it gave the Yankees a lead of two games to one.

Like the third game, the fourth was decided by a single pitch. Ford was originally scheduled to start, but the Yankees announced that he had aggravated a heel injury while sliding in Game One. Ford's availability was the great mystery of the Series. On Friday, he'd said he would pitch Sunday. Ford wasn't ready on Sunday, but said he thought he would be ready for Game Five on Monday. Finally on October 15, Dick Young broke the story. "If you're wondering," wrote Young, "why Ford hasn't taken a novocaine shot for the allegedly sore heel that has idled him since the first game of the World Series.... Medical science hasn't yet come up with the miracle drug that can be shot into the right heel and numb the pain in the left arm." Actually, numbness was Ford's problem. During the first game of the series, Whitey's arm became weak and later, when he was in a restaurant with his wife, he lost the feeling completely. Ford had a circulatory problem that would require post-season surgery.

With Ford disabled, Downing had to start, which further weakened the depleted bullpen. Game Four was in some respects like Game Four of the 1960 Series. The Yanks had a two to one game lead and began as if they were going to make it a three to one advantage in short order. In the first inning, Linz doubled, Richardson doubled, and Maris and Mantle followed with singles. The Yankees had two runs in with no one out when Mantle foolishly tried to stretch his hit into a double. The powerful arm of Shannon gunned him down for the first out of the inning.

While Mantle was picking himself off the ground and heading back to the dugout, Keane

*Sports Illustrated *reported 47 cap losings.*

was walking to the mound with the hook for Sadecki. In from the bullpen came Craig, who immediately surrendered a single to Howard, which scored Maris for a 3–0 Yankee lead.

Downing, unlike his brief, ineffective appearance in Game One, looked terrific. Through five innings, he gave up just one hit and a walk, and it appeared as though neither Ford nor the bullpen would be needed. Craig, however, after Howard's single, had yielded nothing. He struck out the side in the second and fanned two more in the fourth. His curve was breaking so sharply that hitters were ducking away as it approached the plate. In the third, Craig gave up consecutive walks with two out but Mantle, who was on second, strayed too far off the bag. Craig, with one of the best pickoff moves in baseball, wheeled and fired to Groat, who tagged Mantle out. For the second time in three innings, Mickey, yesterday's hero, had committed a base running blunder.

In the sixth inning, Craig left for a pinch hitter. In 4⅔ innings, he had allowed no runs, just two hits and had eight strikeouts. The pinch hitter was Warwick, who had pinch hit in each game of the Series, singling in the first and second games, and walking on Saturday. On Sunday, he delivered for the fourth consecutive time, lining a single to left field. Flood followed with another single, but Downing got Brock to fly to Maris in center. Then came one of the key plays of the series. Groat, a slow runner, hit a grounder to Richardson. It looked like an easy double play, just like Virdon's grounder to Kubek in 1960. This time the ball took a true hop and lodged in Richardson's glove — lodged very firmly in Richardson's glove. He grabbed twice at it, and by the time he was able to flip it with his gloved hand to Linz, the shortstop had already crossed the bag. Linz, the ball and Flood arrived in the vicinity of second base simultaneously, and the ball fell harmlessly to the ground. The bases were loaded with one out.

Ken Boyer was the next batter. Thus far in the Series, Boyer had just one hit in fourteen times up and been struck out by Downing in the first inning. The Series had been billed as a battle of the Boyer brothers, and the town of Alba, Missouri closed down for the week as Mayor Vern Boyer and his wife, the city clerk, traveled to St. Louis and New York to watch their sons in action. Thus far, it had not been much of a battle. Ken had just one hit. Clete had three but made an error to let in three unearned runs in the first game.

Boyer took Downing's first pitch for a ball. Howard then signaled for a fastball, but Downing shook him off. He wanted to throw Boyer a changeup, thinking that, in such a key situation, Boyer might be anxious and out in front of an off speed pitch. The Cardinal third baseman was a little ahead of the pitch and pulled a high fly to left, near the foul pole. The wind kept it fair, and it dropped into the stands for the ninth grand slam home run in World Series history.

The Cardinals had a 4–3 lead, but the Yankees still had four turns at bat. Rather than bring in Schultz, who had been hit hard in each of the first three games, Keane called for Ron Taylor, a tall Canadian with a degree in electrical engineering. Prior to Schultz's arrival in late summer, the Cardinal bullpen had struggled as mightily as had the Yankees'. Taylor was part of the problem, having posted a 4.63 ERA in 61 games. The last time he'd faced the Yankees was 1962, when he was pitching for the Indians. The Yankees hit him so hard that Taylor was sent back to the minor leagues after the game.

On this day, however, Taylor was nearly flawless. "I was really focused," he said. "I was just ready to pitch that day. I was pitching to one hitter at a time. McCarver and I worked well together and I was really hitting my spots." When Taylor walked past Ken Boyer on his way in from the bullpen, Boyer told him it was very difficult to see the ball against the white shirts in the center field bleachers. "Just keep the ball down as low as you can," Boyer said, "and make them look for it. You can hardly see it."

Taylor retired the Yankees in order in the sixth and seventh. With two out in the eighth, he walked Mantle, but ended the inning by striking out Howard. In the ninth, the Yankees couldn't get the ball out of the infield, the Cardinals had tied the Series at two games each. Craig and Taylor combined for 8⅔ innings and gave up just two hits and struck out ten. "I talked with a few of the players," said Gordon Richardson recently, "and we all seemed to think that the pitching of Roger Craig and Ron Taylor turned the series around. I think that was the turning point."

Ford's "heel" injury was no better on Monday, Columbus Day, so Stottlemyre, with three days rest, opposed Gibson for the second time. For the third day in a row, the contest was decided on a single swing of the bat. Again, the twin Yankee nemeses, defense and the bullpen, combined to bring them down.

After a spell of wildness in the first inning, Stottlemyre settled down. In the fifth, with one out and Gibson at first, Flood hit a sharp ground ball to second, a great opportunity for an inning-ending double play. Richardson took his eye off the ball, booted it, and for the second consecutive game, the normally sure-handed second baseman had committed a crucial error. After Brock singled in the game's first run, White hit another grounder to Richardson. This time he fielded it cleanly and threw to Linz for the force play. Linz's relay to first was in the dirt, but Pepitone made a fine scoop for the inning ending double play; or so he thought. First base umpire Al Smith called White safe, bringing Berra from the dugout on the run, to dispute the call and to keep the irate Pepitone away from Smith. The argument followed the course of nearly all baseball disputes, and the Cardinals had a 2–0 lead.

Meanwhile, Gibson, who had been fighting the flu for three days, was overpowering the Yankees. He had eleven strikeouts in the first seven innings, and yielded just four harmless singles. Stottlemyre left for a pinch hitter in the seventh, and the Yankees entered the bottom of the ninth still facing a 2–0 deficit.

The Yankee half of the ninth inning contained a number of twists and turns, any one of which could have re-directed the Series to a different outcome. Mantle led off the inning by hitting a ground ball to Groat. While the Yankees had been fumbling the ball with regularity, the Cardinals, to that point, had made just a single error. Groat made the second, allowing Mantle to reach safely.

After Gibson made Howard his twelfth strikeout victim, Pepitone came to the plate. Joe was having a rough time, with just three hits in seventeen times up. The highlight of his Series had been the controversial nick on the thigh in the second game. Pepitone lashed a vicious line drive back at Gibson. The pitcher, whose every delivery was a concentrated burst of ferocious energy, ended his follow through by falling off to the right side of the mound, nearly facing first base. The ball hit Gibson on the backside and bounced toward the third base foul line, as Pepitone streaked for first. Gibson, an exceptional athlete who had once played basketball with the Harlem Globetrotters, sprinted over, picked up the ball and made a desperate, off-balance throw to first. Keane said that no other pitcher in the National League could have made the play. The ball hit Bill White's glove just about the time that Pepitone's lunging stride hit first base. Umpire Smith raised his hand in the out sign and, for a second time, brought Berra leaping from the dugout. Still pictures appear to show that Pepitone was safe, but Smith's decision had to be instantaneous, and he ruled that Joe was out.

There were now two outs. Mantle moved to second on the play and Tresh came to the plate as the last Yankee hope. Keane signaled for Gibson to take his full windup, since Mantle's run was meaningless. Gibson decided to pitch from the stretch, however, and his first pitch was a fastball right down the middle of the plate. Tresh hit it into the right field stands to tie the game. "I was just trying to get it over the outside of the plate with something on it," Gibson said afterward. "It was the one bad pitch I made all day." Had Pepitone been ruled safe, the game would have been over and the Yankees would have been one win from the championship.

Mikkelsen had relieved Hal Reniff in the eighth, and was still on the mound when the tenth began. He started the inning by walking White. "We thought we had him struck out," said

Mikkelsen recently, "but he called it a ball. Elston got all upset. We both did. But that's the game." Boyer, the next batter, had orders to sacrifice, something he had not done since 1958. He laid down a good bunt to the right of the mound. "I'm not a good fielder," Mikkelsen said after the game. "I've got to make up my mind which way I'll go to field it. He bunted it pretty hard and I couldn't change my direction to get to it." The ball got past Mikkelsen and rolled toward second base. By the time Richardson picked it up, White was at second and Boyer was crossing first.

With Groat at the plate, the Yankees were wary of another bunt and White, also anticipating a sacrifice attempt, was looking to get a good jump off second. He strayed too far and Howard threw behind him. White, caught well off the bag, took off for third. Linz's throw was in the dirt, and White slid in safely. The Cardinals now had runners on first and third, with none out. Groat hit a bouncer to third. Pedro Gonzalez, who went in after Boyer departed for a pinch hitter, checked White at third and threw to second for the force, keeping the possibility of a double play alive.

In the spring, Yogi kept Mikkelsen over Metcalf because he was a sinkerball pitcher who could get the double play. Here was his chance. A twin killing would get the Yankees out of the inning and give them an opportunity to win the game in the bottom of the tenth. Gibson was tiring. If Mikkelsen could get McCarver to hit the ball on the ground, Yogi's judgment would be vindicated, that is, if the Yankee infield could turn a double play. They never got the chance.

McCarver was a Cardinal bonus boy, who had received $80,000 when he graduated from high school. He took over the regular catching job in 1963, and at the age of just 22, was handling the veteran St. Louis staff with confidence. McCarver had hit Yankee pitching hard, and was 7 for 16, including a double and triple. He'd also drawn four walks. Berra later said that if Gonzalez had thrown to first and the base had been open, he would have walked McCarver. He didn't mention the possibility of bringing in Hamilton, his big lefty.

At first, Keane thought of having McCarver bunt. When the Cardinal manager saw Howard staring at him, however, he thought the Yankee catcher was on to him and ordered McCarver to swing away. The young catcher knew Mikkelsen threw a sinker and his only goal was to get the ball in the air to the outfield to drive in the lead run. Mikkelsen's sole aim was to get him to hit it on the ground. A sinker came in too high and McCarver, like Tresh a few minutes earlier, hit it into the right field seats, for a three run homer and a 5–2 St. Louis lead. "I didn't think it was a home run at first," McCarver said. He was happy because he thought he'd hit the ball far enough to score White from third. "I couldn't understand why Mickey Mantle kept running back after the ball," he said. "I saw the ball go into the stands as I neared first but I couldn't believe it. By the time I got to third, I was laughing out loud. I'm always laughing, you know, even when I'm sad. The way I feel now, I'll never be sad again."

After the Yankees went down meekly in the bottom of the tenth, Berra was sad, and he wasn't laughing. Above all, he was irate about Al Smith's two calls, which he said had cost his club the game. Had either one gone in their favor, it is likely the Yanks would have won. But they didn't, and Yogi prepared to go to St. Louis needing to win the final two games. He reminded everyone that his club was missing Ford and Kubek and hadn't gotten any breaks. He didn't mention the big home runs his staff had given up and how his infield had failed to execute some rather routine plays. If Richardson and Linz had been able to turn a couple of double plays, the bad umpiring calls would have gone for naught.

Neither of the final two games was decided by a single swing of the bat. The sixth game featured Bouton versus Simmons once more, and, through five innings, it was a replay of Game Three, with the two teams tied 1–1. In the sixth, the Yankee power, which had, other than Mantle's game winning homer, been held in check, exploded. Maris broke the tie with a homer, and Mantle followed with another on the next pitch. In the eighth, the Yanks broke the game open.

Again, Schultz was hit hard. He was removed with a run in and the bases loaded, when Keane decided to bring in the left-handed Richardson to pitch to Pepitone. The Cardinal pitcher had faced Pepitone in the minors and knew him well. "He wasn't a big guy," Richardson said. "He was a skinny guy. I pitched against him before and never had any real trouble with him. But some days you get 'em and some days you don't. That was one of the days I didn't." Pepitone hit a hanging curve ball for a grand slam home run, which gave the Yankees an 8–1 lead. Bouton tired in the ninth, and Hamilton came in to get the final two outs. The Series would be decided in a seventh game.

Who would pitch for the Yankees? Ford was definitely out. Bouton had pitched the day before. Downing could have pitched with three days' rest, but Yogi had lost confidence in Downing. After Pepitone's grand slam the previous day, Yogi approached Stottlemyre in the dugout and told him he was starting the final game, with just two days rest. Gibson, also on short rest, would oppose him for the Cardinals, if his arm could bounce back. If it couldn't, Sadecki would pitch. Gibson, who had a sore hip from Pepitone's drive and a sore ankle from a foul ball, said he would pitch unless he got hit by a truck overnight.

In the seventh game of the World Series, the Yankees were starting a rookie. Stottlemyre was no ordinary rookie, of course. He went out and pitched the seventh game like a seasoned veteran. Despite starting his third game in seven days, Stottlemyre held the Cardinals scoreless through the third. In the fourth, his defense did him in. Stottlemyre had outpitched Gibson in the second game. He'd pitched him to a standstill in the fifth game, and had the Yankee defense played as it had a few years earlier, he, not Gibson, might have been the most valuable player of the series.

The Yankee defense was not what it once was, however. Linz made a wild throw trying to complete a double play to let in the first St. Louis run. One hit later, the Cards attempted a hit and run play, which turned into a double steal attempt when Maxvill missed the ball. Howard's peg to second was wide of the bag and Richardson's return throw was not even close to catching McCarver. Maxvill singled, and Mantle, with a chance to nail Shannon at the plate, made a terrible throw.

Stottlemyre left for a pinch hitter and Downing came in to start the fifth. Lou Brock hit the left hander's first pitch 400 feet onto the right field pavilion. White hit his next pitch for a single, and Boyer hit his fourth off the right center field wall. Yogi called Sheldon in from the bullpen.

With the Yanks down 6–0 in the sixth, Mantle hit a three run homer, his third of the Series and 18th and last of his World Series career. Keane went to the mound to talk to Gibson, who thought he was going to be taken out. After the way Schultz, his bullpen ace, had been battered by the Yankees, however, Keane believed that his best chance lie with the strong right hander. Gibson repaid Keane's faith by shutting down the Yankees. In the eighth, he fanned Howard for his 29th strikeout of the Series, breaking the record set by Boston's Bill Dineen in 1903.

Meanwhile, the Cardinals got another run to boost their lead to 7–3 entering the ninth. Gibson, like Stottlemyre, had pitched three games in seven days, and was barely hanging on. Tresh, leading off the ninth, became strikeout victim #30, but Boyer homered into the left field seats to cut the lead to 7–4. Brother Ken had homered earlier, and it was the first time in Series history that brothers had hit home runs in the same game.

Blanchard, hitting for Hamilton, was strikeout victim #31, but Linz followed with his second homer of the Series. The lead was now 7–5 and Bobby Richardson, who already had 13 hits, (including seven against Gibson) an all time Series mark, was up. Sadecki was warming up in the bullpen, and Keane said later that if Richardson had gotten on base he would have taken Gibson out, for that would have brought Maris to the plate representing the potential tying run. Sadecki wasn't needed, however, as Gibson got Richardson to hit a pop fly to short center field. Second baseman Maxvill drifted back, made the catch and the Series was over.

For the second straight year, the Yankees had been defeated by the National League champions. In 1963, the explanation had been simple. Dodger pitchers had simply overpowered the Yankee hitters. In 1964, however, the Yankees were as much to blame for their defeat as were their opponents. Without Ramos, the bullpen had been atrocious. In 13⅓ innings, Yankee relievers gave up 11 runs. The only wins had been complete games by Stottlemyre and Bouton and a third game in which Bouton pitched into the ninth.

The Yankees made nine errors, just one short of the all-time mark for a seven game series. Even the 1919 Black Sox, who were trying to lose, made just eleven errors in the first seven games of their series. Failure to make a double play and two Mantle baserunning blunders had cost them Game Four, and Games Five and Seven featured a host of misplays and errors. After having only three passed balls all year, Howard had three more in the first two games of the Series. Mantle made a number of poor throws from right field. In the ninth inning of the final game, the Yanks botched a rundown play and, although they finally got the runner out, the sequence was a series of bad throws and poor execution. "There was a suspicion," wrote Bob Addie, "that a ghastly practical joke had been perpetrated and that the Mets, not the Yankees, were on the field."

"Nobody ever laughed at the old Yankees in the field," wrote Dick Young after the final game. "These Yankees don't make the play. These Yankees made nine Series errors, and a few other goofs that escape the box score.... The whole truth is that the old Yankees knew how to stop the other guy from scoring, too, and these Yankees don't." He commented on the play of Mantle in particular. "They run on Mantle now, because they know the arm has gone along with the legs, so they take liberties they wouldn't have dared a few years ago, when Mantle was a whole ballplayer, and great."

The Yankees had struggled, but won their 29th pennant. They had struggled and lost the World Series. With a few breaks, as Berra claimed, they might have won. If Ford hadn't been injured, if Pepitone had been safe at first. But even with the bad breaks, they could have won with tight fielding and strong relief pitching, two traits of former Yankee champions. They had neither, which boded poorly for 1965.

· 15 ·

Yogi and Johnny

The September pennant drives of the Yankees and Cardinals had taken many people by surprise, including the general manager of the Yankees and the owner of the Cardinals. In mid–August, with the Yankees wallowing in third place and seemingly coming apart at the seams, Ralph Houk came to the conclusion that it had been a mistake to give the managing job to Yogi Berra. Houk had assumed the Yankees were so good, and the rest of the American League so bad, that even Yogi could lead the team to a pennant, while boosting the Yankees' dwindling attendance in the process. By the middle of August, it didn't look like Berra was going to do either.

Houk shouldn't have been surprised by Yogi's performance. "Whatever shortcomings [Berra] possessed," wrote Leonard Koppett, "they were certainly well-known and predictable when Dan Topping and Ralph Houk decided to make him the manager.... And it was true that Berra did not possess Houk's unusual talents; the mystery was why anyone would expect him to."

Berra had been engaged to compete with Casey Stengel and divert attention from the Mets to the Yankees, but Yogi Berra was not Casey Stengel. Stengel's persona was legitimate and self-generated, while Berra's was largely the creation of the press and his pal Joe Garagiola. Stengel was a highly intelligent man while Yogi, who dropped out of school at 15, was not. "[P]itting him against Casey Stengel ... was the worst mismatch in history," wrote Bill Veeck. "No boxing commission would have allowed it.... Yogi is a completely manufactured product ... Yogi had originally become a figure of fun because with his corrugated face and his squat body he looked as if he should be funny."

Berra was also at a severe disadvantage in his competition with the ghost of manager Houk, whose earthly presence occupied the general manager's chair. Every time Yogi made a decision, the players asked, "What would Ralph have done?" Most thought Houk would have done better. By mid–August, Houk himself thought he could have done better, and laid the groundwork to jettison Yogi at the end of the season.

While Yogi's fate was being decided, another drama was taking place in St. Louis, where the Cardinals languished in the middle of the National League pack. In the Fall of 1962, after the Cardinals had finished sixth, owner Gussie Busch visited an old friend of his named Bob Cobb. Cobb had owned the Hollywood Stars of the Pacific Coast League when the Stars were a farm club of the Pirates, then operated by Branch Rickey. Cobb told Busch that Rickey, who'd built championship teams in St. Louis, Brooklyn and Pittsburgh, was the man he needed to return the Cardinals to glory. Busch agreed and hired the 82-year-old legend as a special advisor. This created a ticklish situation. Bing Devine was the Cardinal general manager, but Rickey, even though he was a consultant, could not imagine himself answering to Devine. He expected to report directly to the owner, circumventing Devine and threatening his position.

Devine foiled Rickey's ambition by producing a winning team. He and Manager Keane brought the Cards home second in 1963, giving the Dodgers a healthy scare before falling off the pace in September. In August, Busch rehired Devine and Keane, praising both for the job they'd done in building the Cardinal team. "Bing's trades and general leadership, and Keane's field managing," Busch said, "have, I believe, got the most out of the material available." At the end of the year, Devine was named *The Sporting News* Executive of the Year.

A year later, with the Cardinals seemingly out of contention, Busch was of a different opinion. Rickey, in his advisory role, advised Busch to get rid of Devine and Art Routzong, the business manager, and give Rickey additional authority. Busch therefore forced Devine's resignation in August. Bing, a Cardinal employee since 1939, and general manager since 1957, was replaced by Bob Howsam.

Devine's friendship with, and backing of, Keane, who was also disliked by Rickey, played a role in his dismissal. Keane and Devine had grown up together in the Cardinal organization, and each had a fierce loyalty to the other. When a number of Cardinal players, most notably Dick Groat, had complained about Keane, Devine intervened and insisted that Groat apologize for his comments. When his patron Devine left, it was only a matter of time before Keane followed. At the time Busch disposed of Devine, he thought about giving Keane the axe as well, but Rickey told him it would look bad to fire both the manager and general manager in mid-season. They decided to wait until October to dismiss Keane.

At about the time Devine was cut loose, Busch initiated discussions with Leo Durocher, then a Dodger coach, about managing the team in 1965. Busch loved the way Durocher managed, and was undeterred by the fact that he had hired two Durocher protégés, Eddie Stanky and Solly Hemus, and both had failed miserably, failing to win and leaving a trail of dissension in their wake.

On the Dodgers' last trip to St. Louis, Cardinal broadcaster Harry Caray interviewed Durocher on the air. After they finished, Caray asked Leo if he would be interested in a manager's job if one became available. Durocher had not managed since leaving the Giants in 1955. He'd been a broadcaster for NBC, second guessing managers and players and courting controversy at every step. There were plenty of rumors about where he might manage, and if there was a shortage of gossip, Durocher started a few rumors himself. Mostly, however, Leo lived like his friends Frank Sinatra, Dean Martin, Spencer Tracy and Jack Benny. He dressed expensively and exquisitely, and owned many more tailored suits than Johnny Keane. Keane, however, was wearing the one suit that Durocher coveted, that of Cardinal manager.

During his years out of baseball, Durocher discussed a few manager's jobs, but his requirements were such that he could never come to terms. "Suppose I can get $100,000," Leo once said. "Who needs it...? The income bracket Larraine and I are in, why, I'd finish with ten cents a month off one hundred thousand bucks a year."

Leo wanted a large salary and an ownership interest in the team. He claimed to have gotten a fabulous offer from Cleveland, which included the opportunity to profit handsomely from some sweetheart financial transactions. They weren't sweet enough for Leo, however, who declined. "Tradition was saved," wrote Bob Addie. "A season wouldn't be a season without Leo turning down at least one managerial job."

Durocher wanted the Giant job when Bill Rigney was fired in 1960. He thought he was going to be the Angels' manager when Gene Autry got a team in 1961, and was shocked when Rigney, one of his former players, was hired. Durocher said Charley Finley offered him the Athletics job in 1961, but Leo was not the Kansas City type. He was a candidate for the Met job, but lost out when Stengel's buddy Weiss was hired as President. As job after job went to someone else, Durocher went around telling people he was blackballed from baseball.

In 1961, Durocher was back in uniform as a Dodger coach, looking over the shoulder of

Walter Alston and fueling continual rumors that he was going to get Alston's job. Sometimes he tried to tell Alston how to manage, told the players what they should do, or told others how he would do Alston's job. Nobody told Walter Alston how to manage his team, a point he made abundantly clear to Durocher. He, not his third base coach, would tell players what they'd done wrong. After the 1962 Dodger collapse, general manager Buzzie Bavasi called Durocher disloyal for comments he made about would have happened if he rather than Alston had been managing.

Dodger owner Walter O'Malley was not about to replace the steady, competent Alston, who had won four pennants and three World Series titles in ten years, with the volatile Durocher, and the latter grew impatient. He was not a man to play second fiddle. After four years of coaching, Leo was ready to lower his demands. He told Caray he was interested.

That night, Caray called Durocher at his hotel and told him that Busch would like to speak with him. Caray drove Durocher to Busch's farm and waited in the car while the two men talked. Busch asked if Leo would take the Cardinal job if it was available. As Durocher and virtually every baseball insider knew, the job would be available. According to Durocher, as he and Busch parted, the owner said, "You're the manager of the ball club. Don't worry about the salary."

While Keane wasn't directly aware of the discussions with Durocher, he heard the rumors and knew he was on thin ice. "Leo being Leo," wrote Bill Veeck, "the word soon went out along all communications media, including Radio Free Europe, that he was all set to become the next Cardinal manager." Without his ally Devine, Keane felt he was left alone in the lion's den, with a very aged lion, but one who was still dangerous. In late August, Keane decided to leave the Cardinals, win or lose. On September 28, with his club 1½ games out of first place, Keane dictated a letter of resignation to his wife Lela, who typed it and gave it to her husband to hold until the end of the season.

Keane kept the letter and his thoughts to himself as his Cardinals swept to the world championship. On the final weekend of the season, with the Cards poised to clinch the pennant, Busch said he wanted to talk to Keane about a contract for 1965. Keane said he preferred to wait until after the season. On the morning following the Cardinals' Game Seven victory over the Yankees, Busch called a news conference, at which he intended to announce that Keane was to be rehired with a healthy raise. Thirty minutes before the conference was scheduled to begin, Keane handed Busch the letter he had been holding for nearly three weeks.

Busch was stunned. "I have no idea whatsoever as to what caused him to make this decision," he told the press somewhat disingenuously a few minutes later. Veeck wrote, "Johnny Keane displayed a most laudable sense for the dramatic and a sure instinct for the jugular. He and Bing Devine had been treated shabbily by Busch, and now Keane was paying him back. He knew very well Busch would be sitting there with a blank contract and a roomful of reporters in attendance. Don't tell me he couldn't have got word to Gussie somewhere along the line that he wasn't coming back. But he didn't." A few weeks later, Busch received a second slap in the face when his peers voted Devine Executive of the Year for 1964.

The day Keane resigned, Yogi Berra was asked to come to the Yankees' offices in downtown Manhattan, and assumed he was being summoned to discuss a contract for 1965. Like Gussie Busch, Berra was in for a big surprise. Just a few hours after the shocking announcement in St. Louis, Houk held his own press conference to inform the world that Berra would not return as the Yankee manager. "Is Johnny Keane a candidate for the position?" Houk was asked. "He's not available, is he?" Houk asked. When told that Keane had resigned earlier in the day, Houk expressed surprise and said that certainly Keane would be a candidate for the job.

Houk had managed against Keane in the American Association and had great respect for his ability. Supposedly, he sent Yankee employee Bill Bergesch to meet with Keane in early September to see if he would be interested in the soon-to-be-vacant Yankee job.*

Three days after Keane's departure, Rickey resigned his position as a consultant and longtime St. Louis favorite Red Schoendienst was named manager of the Cardinals. It was a good choice, for in St. Louis, only Stan Musial was more popular than Red Schoendienst. After the bad publicity generated from Keane's resignation, Busch needed to hire a local hero to pacify the fans. Hiring Durocher, whose secret agreement was bound to become public, would only make the situation worse. Busch called Durocher and told him he knew he would understand he could not follow through on his handshake agreement. Durocher, according to his own account, accepted the news graciously.

It was a busy week, for the day after Schoenedienst became the Cardinal skipper, Keane was named manager of the New York Yankees. Managing the Yankees would be a tremendous change in the life of Johnny Keane. A short, wiry man of 52, Keane had been with the Cardinal organization longer than anyone except clubhouse man Butch Yatkeman. He started his career as an infielder, but his hopes of reaching the major leagues ended when he was seriously beaned on two occasions. The second time came after he had hit an inside the park homer. As Keane was rounding the bases, the pitcher snarled, "I'll get you for that." He got Keane the next day, slamming a fastball into his temple and rendering him unconscious for a week.

His dreams of playing in the majors ended, Keane worked his way up through the extensive Cardinal system as a manager, starting in 1938, at the age of 26. He was considered for the St. Louis managing job in 1950, but lost out to Marty Marion. Keane didn't have major league experience, the Cardinals told him. He continued to manage in the minors, turning down offers to coach in St. Louis. When he went to the major leagues, Keane said, he wanted to go as a manager. Eventually, he realized that it was better to be seen in St. Louis than to continue to win in the minor leagues. When Keane was again offered a coaching job in 1959, he accepted. Two years later, when Solly Hemus was fired, Keane was named manager of the Cardinals. He was named AP manager of the year in 1963, and won the World Series the following season. Now he was about to assume the top managing job in baseball.

Reaction to Berra's firing was almost uniformly negative. Yogi was still very popular and, after all, he had won the pennant and taken the Series to seven games. He was named a "special field consultant" for the Yankees, with the right to terminate his contract if he received a better job offer. Offers were not long in coming. Sargent Shriver, newly named director of the government's war on poverty, offered Yogi a position in the bureau's youth program. Yogi turned it down, for a second proposition was more in his line of work.

At the 1961 World Series, just after Stengel had been named manager of the Mets, Berra asked him how long he intended to stay. "Stick around," Yogi told him. "When I get through here, I'll come over and give you a lift." George Weiss had been pulling off one public relations coup after the other ever since he joined the Mets. He'd hired Casey, he'd purchased Duke Snider, he even engaged former Yankee trainer Gus Mauch. In early November, Weiss offered Berra a two year contract to serve as a Met coach, with the option of returning to the active roster. For three weeks, Yogi played it coyly. Finally, on November 17, Yogi, a Yankee since 1943, accepted. He would work out with the club during spring training and decide whether he wanted to play or just coach.

Weiss had done it again. While the two pennant winners were desperately pursuing damage control strategies, the worst team in baseball had the best publicity in the major leagues. Public response to Berra's hiring was immediately favorable. Abraham and Strauss, a New York

---

*Durocher claimed that Keane made a deal with Houk a couple of weeks after Durocher agreed to take the Cardinal job.

clothing store, took out a large ad in The *New York Times* which featured a six inch picture of Berra's face and the caption: Yankees, no–Mets, si. Welcome Yogi.

The Yankees' attempt to become kinder and gentler had backfired, but they were still the American League champions. They might be cold, but at least they were winners. That would soon change.

· 16 ·

The End of an Era
The 1965 Season

In March, 1965, Johnny Keane took over what he believed to be the best team he had ever managed. This was his 35th spring training, but running a New York club was a novel experience for a man who'd spent his career in places like Omaha, Houston and St. Louis. For the first time, Keane was manager of a major league team that was expected to win the pennant.

Many things were different that spring in Fort Lauderdale. CBS was the owner of the Yankees and, for the first time, Ralph Houk had a manager of his own choosing. "Rarely in the history of a baseball club," said *The New York Times*, "is the beginning of a new era so clearly defined. This year, for the first time, there will be a new internal ownership, a new field manager and a completely new system of player procurement (the free agent draft), all simultaneously."

Both Keane and Houk felt the pressure. The Yankees had the highest payroll in baseball, and CBS expected a good return on its investment. "Houk ... must win," the *Times* continued, "and must keep winning. Even second place would constitute failure, and one more pennant isn't enough. Houk must convince his new owners that the traditional Yankee methods of operation work, and work over a period of time; his first stumble is likely to be the beginning of the end, and all the past Yankee victories don't mean a thing to him now."

If Houk was under pressure, Keane felt the heat even more directly. Houk had proven himself with the Yankees, with three pennants in as many years as manager, and when teams fail, it is generally the manager, not the general manager, who gets the axe. "In all [Keane's] other 34 years," wrote Leonard Koppett, "victory was a hope and a desire, and, rarely, an achievement. With the Yankees, it was normality, a demand and a right; anything less than first place at the end of the season would represent total failure."

There was no reason to think that 1965 would be different from recent Yankee seasons. IBM computers picked the Yankees and Phillies to meet in the World Series. Both Koppett and Durso of the *Times* picked the Yanks to win the pennant, and dismissed the Twins, who would win the flag, with, "Minnesota is the Milwaukee of the American League: awesome strength at bat, both for home runs and average, and some pretty good starting pitchers, but no bullpen and even less fielding ability." Durso picked the Twins for fourth and Koppett slated them sixth. Another *Times* reporter, Joseph Sheehan, wrote, "On paper, at least, the Bombers are far and away the best team in the American League. It's hard to fault them on any major account ... they should benefit from having the experienced Johnny Keane as manager." "I hope they win the pennant," said new Met coach Yogi Berra.

Sports Illustrated was more prescient. "The Yankees look weaker than they have in recent memory," read its pre-season prediction. "Their hitting is not strong, their pitching not as solid, their fielding not as sure-handed ... Yankee haters, take heart. This looks like the year!"

During the spring, Keane learned about his players, and the players learned about their new manager. "When I took over as Cardinal manager [in 1961]," Keane said, "I had been a coach and therefore was not only familiar with the entire organization, but was finally free to put in operation some theories I long had kept bottled up within me." Becoming the manager of the Yankees was altogether different. "The only difference I feel," Keane said a few days after camp began, "is a sense of newness and freshness. More action seems to evolve around the Yankees than any club in either league, plus the bigness of New York and the bigness of everything." He wasn't going to change anything, Keane said repeatedly. The question was: Did he mean he wasn't going to change anything he did or he wasn't going to change anything the Yankees did?

"They have a great tradition over there and I want to keep them winning," Keane said. "I think it would be rather foolish of me to make any radical changes. No, I figure to manage the Yankees just about the way I managed the Cardinals." Managing the Yankees the way he managed the Cardinals, however, would result in some rather drastic changes in the way the Yankees were managed. "I'm a man who likes to take chances," Keane said during the winter, "And I intend to use the hit and run and the stolen base as much as possible."

Keane did change things. Yankee camps had typically been leisurely affairs. The new manager, a firm believer in the value of exercise, brought in former Giant football star Andy Robustelli to lead calisthenics, and the fitness program was far more rigorous than in previous years. There was more practicing of fundamental baseball than ever before. The new manager decreed that rather than having each player take five swings in batting practice and rotate, each would hit for four minutes at a time. In 1966, Keane ordered the Yankees to take bunting practice, 50 to 100 bunts per player.

Not only did Keane change little things like exercise and practice routines; it seemed to some of the players that he wanted to alter the entire philosophy of the club. "The Cardinals had always been a team that played run-to-run," said Rollie Sheldon. "They didn't play for the big inning like the Yankees did. We just knew that if we were patient, worked the pitcher and got on base, and another guy got a hit, somebody was going to follow with a home run. I think we felt that the philosophy of the game was going to change."

"Johnny played a little different kind of baseball than we were used to in New York," said Tom Tresh. "We were used to having somebody get on and having somebody else hit one. When Johnny got there, he wanted to play more hit and run, stealing — that kind of baseball." "You didn't steal with the Yankees," said Jack Reed. "They had so much power. Why steal when the next guy might hit it out? Unless you absolutely needed a stolen base, you didn't do it."

Keane loved speed, which was fine when managing the Cardinal flyers like Lou Brock, Curt Flood and Bill White. Even Ken Boyer and Tim McCarver could run. But with a powerful ballclub and a couple of fragile superstars, moving to a speed-oriented attack may not have been the wisest strategy. Even if it was, Keane would have a difficult time convincing his team, which had been so successful doing things their way, that he was right. "Keane didn't know us," said Phil Linz, "and we didn't know him. We were pretty disappointed with him and he was pretty disappointed with us."

Keane had another problem: the memory of Houk. The players had generally liked Berra, although they felt he was over his head as a manager. On the other hand, they worshiped Houk, who made sure he wasn't forgotten. Houk had told Metcalf in 1964 that if he were manager, he wouldn't have demoted him to the minor leagues; it was Yogi's decision. The next year, Houk told seldom-used rookie pitcher Gil Blanco that he would have pitched him more often if he were managing; it was Keane's decision not to use him. "Ralph was always calling Kubek and

Richardson," said Linz, "to ask them how Yogi was doing. Houk didn't really want to be GM. He wanted to be down on the field."

Keane and Houk had nearly opposite personalities. Houk was the backslapping, gregarious, charismatic leader. Keane, as described by Koppett, was "an immensely moral, disciplined, polite, quiet, inward-turned person. Before turning to professional baseball, he had studied for the priesthood. His sense of humor is subdued, conversation does not come easily and the normal banter of clubhouse and dugout — a compound of insulting wisecracks, lurid language and gallows humor — is foreign to him."

Mantle, who'd loved Houk, was prepared not to like Keane, and the new manager helped fuel the emotion. One day in spring training, when Mantle showed up hung over, Keane sent him to the outfield and hit one fly ball after another to him. Mantle knew Keane was punishing him and didn't like it.

The manager was new in '65, but the playing personnel was essentially unchanged. The starters would be the same, and for the most part, so would the bench. The only newcomer who seemed certain to win a job was first baseman/outfielder Duke Carmel, drafted from the Mets' Buffalo farm club. Duke had been a hot prospect for several years but now, at nearly 28 years of age, was content to play a backup role for the Yanks.

Carmel was a New York native, who got his nickname from his boyhood idol Duke Snider. He nearly signed with the Dodgers, his favorite team, but decided he would have more opportunity in the Cardinal organization. In 1955, Carmel signed a St. Louis contract calling for a $2,000 bonus, and was sent to Albany, Georgia, a severe culture shock for the youngster who had rarely ventured outside of the five boroughs. "You learn a lot of different things when you get out of New York City," he said. "I was born and raised in Little Italy. The only salad dressing I knew was oil and vinegar. Thousand Island sounded weird."

Sometimes Carmel seemed a little weird. "Duke would probably be on Prozac if he played today," said Tracy Stallard. "He was from New York," recalled Don Rowe, "and he wore his hair long. He was a typical greaser guy. When we were playing for Buffalo, we were in Toronto the same time the Beatles were there. We were staying on the fifteenth floor of the King George Hotel, the same place as the Beatles, and people were all around the building. The Mounties were trying to hold them back. Duke stuck his head out the window and started rubbing his hands through his hair. Everybody thought he was one of the Beatles and they started charging the door. That's the kind of stuff Duke would do."

That kind of stuff was what had landed Duke in Buffalo in the first place. The Mets had acquired Carmel from the Cardinals in mid–1963. He was very excited about the prospect of performing in his home town, alongside Snider, his boyhood idol. After Carmel's arrival, one Polo Grounds patron hoisted a banner which read, "Casey, put up your Dukes." The younger Duke played decently but unspectacularly for the rest of the season, batting .235 with three home runs in 47 games. The following spring, he appeared to have the team made until the last week of spring training. "They had a party for the team," he recalled, "and I'm sitting around, talking to guys. I had a couple of beers. Casey got up to speak and I said something to somebody next to me. It had nothing to do with Casey, but he thought I was talking about him. From then on, it seemed like it was him or me, and I guess it was me."

A teammate had a different perspective. "He had a run-in with Stengel at Mrs. Payson's dinner. I think Duke had a couple too many and was mimicking Casey. I don't think he realized Casey was taking it all in. The next day he was sent down." In Buffalo, Carmel took aim at the short fence in right and had a terrific year, hitting 35 home runs. During the stretch run, there were rumors that the Yankees, engaged in a desperate fight for the pennant, wanted him as a pinch hitter. Duke injured his back and the Yankees lost interest. When the Mets made Carmel available in the minor league draft, however, the Yankees grabbed him. He had played for Keane in the minors, as well as in St. Louis, and Keane liked him. Carmel had good left-handed power, always a prime commodity in Yankee Stadium, but his 35 homers in 1964 were to some degree a function of the short right field porch at Buffalo's War Memorial Stadium. After the 1962 season, the Phillies terminated their affiliation with the Buffalo club, claiming that the fence fouled up their hitters by causing them to pull the ball and try for home runs. Still, the right field fence at Yankee Stadium was pretty close, and Duke might do as well as he had in Buffalo.

Carmel played winter ball in Puerto Rico and came to camp in good shape. Once again, he was excited about returning to his home town. "Do you realize," Carmel said during the spring, "that I'm the only ballplayer in the major leagues from New York?" What about Whitey Ford and Ed Kranepool, he was asked. Ford was from Queens, Carmel replied and Kranepool from the Bronx. When he said New York, Duke explained, he meant Manhattan, to which his birthplace of East Harlem belonged.

Carmel looked good in batting practice. When the exhibition games started, however, he couldn't buy a hit. "When you're in spring training and you've played as many years as I played," said Carmel, "you're just looking to get yourself in good shape and hit the ball well. I hit the ball well down there."

There were no base hits, however, and, when Duke committed a couple of misplays in the field, the certainty of his making the team became less certain. In late March, when Carmel was 0–12, Mike Hegan, who'd been ticketed for Toledo, was mentioned as a potential backup first baseman. On March 27, Duke played first base, went 0–4 and made another error. On the 29th, he struck out as a pinch hitter, making him 0–19. On the 3rd of April, Duke hit a foul sacrifice fly, causing Joe Durso to write, "Carmel still was without a hit in 20 times at bat as a Yankee, but it was one of the most effective foul balls he had hit since the Yankees drafted him from the Mets."

By the end of the exhibition season, despite the fact that Duke was hitless in 29 at bats, Keane brought him north as a member of the Yankee varsity. When the regular season began, Duke still couldn't get a hit. He was 0–8 in early May, with five strikeouts, making 37 hitless at bats in all, when the Yankees finally gave up on the Duke and waived him. "I was a little pissed off about that," Carmel said recently.

The Yankees' final exhibition games took place in the Astrodome, the first major league games ever played indoors. The newly-christened Astros were glad to have a new ballpark. Old Houston Stadium, which the Colt 45s had occupied during their first three years, was small, unbearably hot, and infested with mosquitoes the size of flying cows. "They'd come around the ballpark before the game," recalled Colt pitcher Skinny Brown, "and spray insecticide from a truck." Before one game with the Mets, Stengel walked into the dugout with a can of insect repellent and made a big show of spraying the entire area. In the Met broadcast booth, Ralph Kiner complimented Bob Murphy on his fly-swatting ability and suggested he might be ready to take on Kiner's tennis champion wife. The Astrodome wouldn't need to be sprayed, unless the mosquitoes bought tickets and came through the turnstiles.

Built at a cost of about $37 million, the new facility was officially called the Harris County Domed Stadium. Everyone, however, referred to it as the Astrodome. The structure was the brainchild of Judge Roy Hofheinz, the Astros' principal owner, a man who bore every trait of the stereotypical Texan. The bigger the better was the theme of the Astrodome, and if something could be big and glitzy, that was even better than merely big. The grounds crew wore spacesuits, and were referred to as "earthmen." The dugouts were the longest in the major leagues, for as Hofheinz noted, everyone wanted to sit behind the dugout. The Astrodome also contained a nightclub which was, amazingly for 1965, segregated.

Hofheinz was the first to conceive of the luxury suite, and the Astrodome had 53 of them, which could be rented for $14,784 per season and up. Each suite had a living room, bathroom, refrigerator, closed circuit television and its own engraved golden spatula, for serving the gourmet treats available from the catering service. Writer Roger Angell called the suites "sad, soft caves for indoor sportsmen." While the men might be sad and soft, the women would look terrific. Astro personnel spent a week around the box area determining which form of lighting would show women's makeup and clothing to best advantage.

Hofheinz's personal suite consisted of two rooms, a kitchenette and bath, and was furnished with a mixture of tasteful antiques and garish modern art, such as a marble lamp in the shape of Joan of Arc, complete with armor and a modern shade. The suite was a suitable abode for the man who claimed to have brought gentility to baseball. "We don't have any of those rowdies or semi-delinquents," he said, "who follow the Mets." No less an authority than Billy Graham proclaimed the Astrodome the eighth wonder of the world.

One of the most remarkable features of the Astrodome was its scoreboard. An Astro home run (which was not that frequent; only 65 homers were hit in Houston in1965) brought forth an electronic display featuring cowboys, steer, bullets and a plethora of pyrotechnics.

A problem arose when the Astros began playing in their new park. The roof consisted of 4,596 clear Lucite skylights, which posed 4,596 immediate problems. No one could see a fly ball. When the Astros held their first practice, balls were landing 30 feet from the fielders. "It wasn't something we had counted on," complained Houston GM Paul Richards. He suggested using lights for day games or placing a giant tarpaulin over the roof.

On April 9, with President Lyndon Johnson in attendance, the Yankees and Astros christened the new park. No one was sure how the players would adapt to indoor conditions. If the game proved a farce, Hofheinz was prepared to offer refunds to his ticket holders.

The game was a success in that it went off without any major hitches. In the first inning, Mantle got the first indoor hit in major league history. Five innings later, he hit the first homer. The Yankees eventually lost 2–1 in twelve innings.

Like Candlestick's wind, the Astrodome roof was the main topic of conversation. "It was terrible," said Carmel. "The worst place I ever played in my life. You couldn't see the ball. You had to wear a helmet in the outfield because you were afraid of getting hit in the head." At night, the lights helped, but during the day, fielding was a brutal experience. "On a pop fly," said former Met Bobby Klaus, "sometimes you have to turn around, run to a spot and then look up. You couldn't do that in the Astrodome." During the first weekend, the Astros experimented with orange balls and yellow balls, hoping they would be more visible.

The park may have had its artistic problems, but it was an immediate commercial success. By the first of June, Houston surpassed its 1964 total attendance. The full season's attendance of 2,151,470 was three times as many people who had come to Colt Stadium in 1964.

The Yankees opened the regular season in Minnesota, and lost when Arturo Lopez, a rookie left fielder, dropped a fly ball in the eleventh inning. Lopez, a 27-year-old rookie, had replaced Mantle for defensive purposes, a strategy which clearly had not worked. Lopez had an interesting background, having spent four years in the Navy, gotten married, sired four children, sold insurance and worked as a bank teller ... all prior to beginning his professional baseball career. The Yankees were no longer bringing up Tony Kubeks, Bobby Richardsons and Tom Treshes. Lopez, the top hitter on the 1964 Richmond team, was the best they had. The stinginess of the 1950s was coming back to haunt the club.

The Yankees could have had Carl Yastrzemski, rather than Arturo Lopez, in left field. Yaz, a Long Island boy, wanted to play in Yankee Stadium, and worked out for the Yankees, who offered him $40,000. The youngster was ready to sign, but his father was stubborn and insisted on at least $100,000. The senior Yastrzemski had been a pretty good ballplayer himself in his youth, and had been offered $75 a month to sign with the Dodgers in 1939, but that was the year young Carl was born and his father couldn't support him on $75 a month. Now he wanted his son to capitalize on his ability in a big way. Lee MacPhail, handling the negotiations for the Yankees, talked about the commercial opportunities available in New York, and the probability of winning a World Series share almost every year. Carl, Jr. begged his father to let him sign, but Carl, Sr. was unmoved and his son went off to Notre Dame. Following his freshman year, he signed with the Red Sox for the $100,000 his father wanted.

The Yankees might have had Tommy Davis in left field instead of Arturo Lopez. Davis was ready to sign with the Yankees in 1956, before Dodger scout Al Campanis convinced him that he should play in Brooklyn. "Boy did he talk," Davis recalled later of Campanis, "about the opportunities for a colored boy with the Dodgers, and this and that. He really sold you, and we signed."

The Yankees' opening day loss began a string of poor play which propelled Keane into panic mode. On May 15, the Yankees were 11–16, in eighth place. Their record was identical to that of the Mets. The biggest problem was that the bombers weren't bombing. In fact, they couldn't even hit singles. Boyer got off to a terrible start and was having trouble getting over the .150 mark. Pepitone was slumping, and in a terrible mental state. His first marriage had broken up, and he no longer saw his two children. He was reportedly $40,000 in debt, and often played when hung over from his nights at the Copa. Pepitone spent most of the season pursuing women and bill collectors spent most the season pursuing him.

Tresh and Richardson were the only Yankees who were both hitting and in good health. By mid–May, five starters had averages of less than .200. On bat day at the Stadium later in the season, one headline read, "Give the Yanks a Bat."

The club had started out sluggishly the previous season, mostly due to the fact that Berra could not field his regular lineup. The pattern continued in 1965. In late April, Maris severely pulled a hamstring muscle chasing a fly ball, and was sidelined for nearly a month. Mantle was as fragile as ever and subject to frequent leg problems. His damaged knee still made it difficult for him to hit left handed. Since there were many more right handed pitchers than left handed, that presented a serious difficulty.

Kubek was destined for a second season of nagging injuries. Perhaps the most serious blow of all, however, was a floating bone chip in the elbow of Elston Howard. In 1964, Howard had been one of the few stable elements on an unstable team. In a 1965 exhibition game in San Juan, he made an off-balance throw and felt pain in his right elbow. On opening day, he aggravated the injury, and was soon unable to throw at all. Ellie couldn't even straighten his elbow. Howard played a little at first base, and did some pinch hitting, but there was no improvement. Eventually, he could no longer swing the bat.

After x-ray treatments failed, Howard decided to have surgery, and was out for several weeks. He returned in June, carrying his two bone chips, one the size of a pea, the other even smaller, in a small plastic container. His elbow gradually improved, but Howard hit just .233, 80 points below his 1964 average. In the first few weeks after he returned, enemy base stealers took liberties on his weakened arm.

During a May broadcast, Red Barber noted that Washington GM George Selkirk said that if Mantle was hurt, the Yankees couldn't win. Oriole manager Hank Bauer said that if Howard was out, they couldn't win and Cleveland GM Gabe Paul said that if Maris were sidelined, the Yanks wouldn't win. Well, Barber noted, all three were injured. In Maris's absence, Keane platooned the Lopez's, right handed Hector and left handed Arturo. With Howard out, Keane went to another platoon, Johnny Blanchard and Bob Schmidt, a journeyman receiver who'd played with the Giants and Senators.

In past years, the Yankees had been loaded with catchers. In the '50s, they were supplying other teams with starting catchers such as Sherm Lollar, Cal Neeman, Clint Courtney, Hal Smith and Gus Triandos. Just four years earlier, Berra, Howard and Blanchard had combined for over 70 home runs. Now the farm system was bare, and the Yanks had only Schmidt, who had lost his Washington job to journeyman Ken Retzer and Blanchard, who had never caught regularly in the major leagues. "I didn't have real good ability behind the plate," said Blanchard. "I could handle the game alright for maybe two or three days in a row, but I don't know if I had the ability to catch every day. I don't know if I had major league defensive ability."

Houk and Keane didn't think either Blanchard or Schmidt could catch every day, and decided they needed to find a strong defensive catcher who could fill in until Howard returned. On May 3, they traded Blanchard and pitcher Rollie Sheldon to Kansas City for catcher Howard (Doc) Edwards.

Sheldon was surprised by the trade, which he thought was dictated by panic. He believed the club would have been better served by getting along with Blanchard and Schmidt for the relatively short time Howard was incapacitated. To give up their best bench player and a serviceable pitcher for someone to catch for a few weeks seemed unwise. "I still can't believe that Houk made that deal," Sheldon said. Finally, after so many one-sided trades between the Athletics and Yankees, Kansas City got the better end of a deal.

For Blanchard, a member of the Yankee organization for 13 years, the trade was a shattering event. "I didn't want to leave," he said. "These guys were my buddies, the guys I'd been with for so many years." "He was just devastated," said Sheldon. "He got to his cubicle and started crying." "A lot of guys could just laugh it off," Blanchard said, "go to their locker, clean it out and catch the airplane. I wasn't that way. I was too close to Mickey, Roger, Whitey and all the guys." Blanchard had played for Houk since the Major managed at Denver. He couldn't believe Houk would trade him, and asked to see him. Houk promised to come to the clubhouse to talk to him, but never showed up.

Blanchard debated quitting baseball, but decided to report to Kansas City. He missed a month with an injury, and batted .200 with just two home runs. "He and I started rooming together in Kansas City," said Sheldon, "and I just couldn't put up with his late hours. John was a pretty heavy drinker at that time. He'd come busting in at two or three in the morning."

Blanchard's stay in Kansas City was an experience he would rather forget. He played poorly, drank heavily, and in September, his wife was seriously injured in an automobile accident. Late in the season, Blanchard was sold to the Milwaukee Braves, and in spring training of 1966, was cut and decided to retire. "I don't think I ever recovered after that trade," he said recently. "I just wasn't the same person. I didn't have the same feeling about the game."

Blanchard announced that he might return to baseball if he could play with the hometown Twins. Twins owner Calvin Griffith said he would not trade for Blanchard, but would be interested if the Braves released him. The Braves wouldn't release him, and in 1967, Blanchard said he was going to attempt a comeback. Before reporting to spring training, however, he changed his mind and decided to remain retired.

The following year, Blanchard, then 35, announced he was going to try again. He had stopped drinking, he declared, and was ready to dedicate himself to getting in shape. Although he was on the Richmond roster, Blanchard was invited to the Braves camp and given an opportunity to make the club. Two years away from the game were too much and, teetotaler or not, Blanchard was unable to make the squad. His baseball career was officially over. It had been over, for all intents and purposes, when he left the Yankees and his desire for baseball left Blanchard.

Sheldon had never realized the promise he'd shown during his rookie year. During the winter of 1961, the Yankees had decided to change his motion. Sheldon kept his back too stiff, they said, and was tipping off his pitches. Even the clubhouse boy in Boston had been able to read them. The Yankees also thought Sheldon would be more effective if he threw from a three quarters motion, rather than using his natural overhand delivery.

While the hitters may not have known what was coming in 1962, the pitches were arriving with less velocity and less control. Sheldon couldn't keep the ball down, and was hit hard. He finished the season with a 7–8 record and an astronomical 5.49 ERA. "He was the biggest disappointment on the club," Johnny Sain said, "It got so we couldn't use him at all." Sain said that losing for the first time in his life had so unnerved the youngster that he became completely confused.

In the spring of '63, at the age of 26 (or was it 23?), Sheldon was sent to Richmond. It was the first time in Sheldon's life that he had been cut from a team, and he had another poor season. "It was very, very disappointing to get cut," he said. "I went down there, didn't have a lot of good focus and didn't get off to a good start. It just multiplied into a bad year." Sheldon buckled down in 1964, made it back to the majors and pitched in two World Series games.

Sheldon was disappointed but, unlike Blanchard, not devastated by the trade. He went to Kansas City and received an opportunity to pitch regularly for the first time in the major leagues. "I think maybe my best ball was pitched there," he said. Sheldon, working well under pitching coach Eddie Lopat, was 10–8 for the A's in 1965, and always saved his best efforts for the Yankees.

Sheldon pitched a complete game victory over the Yankees in June, and shut them out in August. On May 1, 1966, he started the first game of a Sunday afternoon doubleheader at Yankee Stadium against Whitey Ford. The game was scoreless in the fifth inning when Kansas City's Ossie Chiavarria bounced a ground rule double into the right field stands with two outs. The next hitter was rookie catcher Ken Suarez, who had batted .163 in the Southern League in 1965. Sheldon was on deck, expecting that Suarez would be walked intentionally to bring him to the plate. Much to his surprise, Ford chose to pitch to Suarez. "They threw him a low fastball and that's the only thing he could hit," Sheldon recalled. Suarez singled over shortstop Clete Boyer's head and Chiavarria scored the only run of the game. It was one of two runs that Suarez drove in all year. Sheldon finished with a three hitter and a much-savored 1–0 win over Ford and the Yankees. It was his third win in four decisions against New York since the trade, and his second straight shutout over the Bombers. Although the game matched teams that would finish seventh and tenth that year, it was far from a meaningless contest for Rollie Sheldon.

In mid–May of 1966, Sheldon had an ERA of 1.85. He and a youngster named Catfish Hunter were the top two Athletic starters. In mid-season, however, he was traded to the Red Sox and tailed off badly, finishing with a 5–13 record and a 4.11 ERA in what turned out to be his final major league campaign. Sheldon played in the minor leagues for a few seasons, reuniting with former Yankee teammate Jim Bouton in the Seattle Pilots' spring camp of 1969, and later at Vancouver. Although Bouton mentioned Rollie in the infamous *Ball Four*, there were no scandalous references. Sheldon's one moment of controversy remained appearing in the 1961 Yankee camp as a 21-year-old phenom.

Doc Edwards, the new Yankee catcher, was as surprised as everyone else by the trade. "They felt they needed somebody who could catch and throw," he said. "They had plenty of bats and thought they could afford to give up Blanchard. Little did they know that Maris would come up with a bad hammate bone. They could have used John's bat. But you never know those things when you make a trade."

The new catcher was eager to join the Yankees. "I was excited because they'd won five pennants in a row," he said. "I thought I'd go over, play until Ellie got well, then warm the bench and make sure Ellie doesn't get frostbite and sit back and maybe have a chance to get a World Series ring."

Edwards was an excellent defensive catcher. "I had a reputation as a seasoned handler of pitchers," he said. "I like to think that most pitchers I caught didn't have a problem with me." The Yankees needed more than just defense, however, because no one else was hitting.

Edwards didn't hit either. He'd done well in the minors, but couldn't duplicate his efforts in the major leagues. "Usually everyone hit well when they came to the Yankees," he said, 'but I wasn't one of those guys. I pressed so hard to prove I could do the job. I'm not talking about hitting .320. I just wanted to hit .250 or .260 and play decent defense. The harder I pressed, the worse I got. It was just too big a load for the rest of us guys to carry. Some guys are good in utility roles, but when they get in the lineup every day, people find their holes and live in them. When they're in and out of the lineup they get a chance to play a few days and get back on the bench before anybody figures them out."

Keane was also starting to press a little. "I remember the first meeting we had," said Linz. "It was about three weeks into the season and we were just under .500. We never worried about that because we figured we'd get hot and we would be alright. We'd won five pennants in a row and the first thing out of his mouth was, 'New York Yankees, my ass!' We were looking at each other, thinking, 'What is he talking about?' Then he proceeded to criticize each one of us, which never would have happened in public when Yogi or Ralph was there. They would take you off to the side or into their office. They would never criticize you in front of your teammates. We couldn't believe this. We were more or less used to managing ourselves."

If the Yankees were not accustomed to public criticism, Keane was not used to the freedom the Yankees expected. There were far more social opportunities in New York than in St. Louis, and many Yankee players took full advantage of them. For the most part, they kept things under wraps, but occasionally Yankee night life became public business. The most celebrated incident, of course, was the scene at the Copacabana which led to Billy Martin's departure from New York in 1957. In the spring of '65, an incident occurred in Florida.

Shortly after midnight on April 2, Maris, Boyer, Reniff and Joe Dimaggio were at Nick's Cocktail Lounge in Fort Lauderdale. Jerome Modzelewski, a 25-year-old professional model who had appeared in a number of television commercials, was leaving the bar with a 21-year-old Canadian redhead with the lyrical name of Angela Dellavedove. In his complaint, Modzelewski alleged that a member of the Yankee party (later identified as Boyer) shouted an obscenity at him. Modzelewski took his date outside, then went back into the bar and demanded an apology. Instead, he got a second reading of the same word, in case he hadn't understood it the first time. Then, Modzelewski alleged, the "man in the hat" [Boyer] and Maris jumped him and began punching him, inflicting cuts that eventually required eleven stitches. "It seemed Mr. Boyer went crazy," Modzelewski testified.

Maris, who was arrested on Modzelewski's complaint, claimed he was an innocent bystander who had not hit anyone. He nearly tripped over Modzelewski, he said, when the latter fell to the floor after being hit by someone else. He didn't identify Boyer, however, as the man who hit him. Maris threatened to sue Modzelewski. Keane supported Maris and the Yankee players responded in the usual fashion. Pepitone offered his services as defense attorney, "in case Perry Mason isn't available." Someone else suggested a defense of amnesia, since Maris had been hit in the neck by a pitch that afternoon.

Maris was released on a $200 bond and, eschewing Pepitone's offer, retained William F. Leonard to represent him. The day after the incident, after discovering the identity of the "man in the hat," a warrant was issued for the arrest of Boyer. Justice in Fort Lauderdale was swift, and Maris went on trial just five days after the incident. Testimony was vague, murky and conflicting, and tended to show that Maris was more of a peacemaker than an aggressor, who had tried to get between Boyer and Modzelewski. When Maris testified strongly in his own defense, he was acquitted.

At the time of Maris's acquittal, Leonard, who represented both players, said he had an equally strong case in Boyer's defense. Apparently, it was not quite as strong, for when Boyer finally went to trial in November, he was fined $175 and given a 30-day suspended jail sentence.

Two months later, there was a second incident. On Sunday night, June 6, after sweeping a doubleheader from the White Sox, the Yankees went to Newark Airport to board a flight to Kansas City. When they arrived at the airport, they learned there were mechanical problems with their plane, which would result in a delay of more than two hours. Richardson and Kubek repaired to the snack bar for sandwiches and Cokes. Al Downing worked on a crossword puzzle. A number of other players decided to kill time in the bar. No male models were punched, nor was anyone harmed, but the players clearly had quite a bit to drink and began acting silly. A couple of waitresses received appreciative whistles.

The situation created two problems. First, Keane was sitting nearby with his wife and observed the entire episode. A second problem was the fact that airports are busy on Sunday nights, and many travelers who walked by saw several of the great New York Yankees intoxicated. It was one thing to drink in a Fort Lauderdale bar at midnight, and quite another to be loud and boisterous in a public place filled with families who didn't frequent Nick's Cocktail Lounge.

With the Yankees' record at 22–27, Keane was in no mood for celebrating, and didn't think a three game winning streak was reason for such a scene. Houk backed him up. "Everyone gets one too many sometimes," the general manager said, "but there's a time and a place for it, and the place is not the airport terminal." Three Yankees (reportedly Mantle, Reniff and Ramos) were fined $250 each and others (supposedly Mikkelsen and Maris) were reprimanded but not fined. Keane blasted the team and, when a fourth straight win followed, the Yanks' seventh in ten games, visions of the harmonica incident danced in the writers' heads. Would the Newark affair jolt the Yankees like Mary had a Little Lamb had done a year earlier?*

With so many of the front line players injured, Keane and Houk reached out for reinforcements. Infielder Horace Clarke, who was hitting .361 at Toledo, was called up. First baseman Ray Barker was obtained from the Indians for infielder Pedro Gonzalez. Barker was a 29-year-old minor league veteran who spent ten years in the Baltimore and Cleveland organizations, and had played at the Triple A level for the past several years. He hit consistently for power in the minors, but had been able to accumulate only 11 major league at bats. "I was a step out of the big leagues for eight or nine years," he recalled. "I just kept hoping that I'd get a break and get up there. I knew it wouldn't be a long career, but I hoped I could get enough time in for my pension. [He didn't.] I thought maybe sometime I'd be in the right spot at the right time. Somebody might need a power hitting left handed hitter for the stretch run or the Series."

What separates the last man on a major league roster from the top players in the minor leagues? Why do some players have one good year after another in the minors without getting more than a token shot at a major league job? "I believe that about ten percent of the players are 'no-brainers,'" said ex–Met and long time minor leaguer Shaun Fitzmaurice, "and the other ninety percent could go either way." "There's a lot of politics involved," theorized John Miller, another who struggled to reach the majors. "It's no different than in the regular business world. The people who signed for the big bonuses generally got pushed up the organization quicker than the guys who didn't." "They pay closer attention to anybody they've given some money to," said former Yankee Andy Kosco, who received a sizable bonus, "both then and now." "The main thing," said outfielder Bobby Gene Smith, "is that it takes a lot of stamina to stay with it until you get your break." "The manager's got to believe in you," said Phil Linz.

There was a noticeable difference between Triple A ball and the major leagues. "The pitchers in the big leagues are around the plate a lot more," said Larry Burright. "In Triple A, you've got guys who can throw hard, but they don't have that control. In the big leagues, they knew

---

*Linz, the star of the harmonica incident, was a bit player this time. A UPI release the day after the events at Newark stated that Linz had been "noisy and abusive." In August, he filed a $200,000 suit against UPI for defamation.

exactly where they wanted to put the ball." "Major league pitchers back then didn't make as many mistakes as the minor league pitchers did," opined former Yankee Jim Lyttle. "You don't hit pitchers' pitches as rule. Hitters make their living on mistakes."

"In the majors," said pitcher Larry Miller, "pitchers can get their pitches over in any situation. Most good hitters are guess hitters. Most of them guess pitch rather than location. They figure you're going to throw a couple of balls, so they're going to have about five pitches to guess right once." If a pitcher only has one or two pitches they can get over the plate, the chance of guessing correctly is much higher.

"The biggest difference between the major leagues and Triple A is fastballs," said Bobby Klaus." I was a dead fastball hitter and on three and two in Triple A you know you're going to get a fastball. In the majors you don't know what you're going to get. That's what killed me. I was a dead fastball hitter. You put a spin on it and I'm screwed."

"In the minors," said Jim Pisoni, "each team has one or two good pitchers. In the majors, they've got four or five, plus the relief pitchers. They're all good. You don't get any slack at all. In the minors, you could just show up a couple of days and go crazy and a couple of days you'd have a hard time. That makes the batting average, home runs and RBIs go up, because you have two days you can whale away." "In the major leagues," added Lou Klimchock, "you're going to see a good starter every day. In Triple A you might see one and a half out of four. Plus, the fielding is one hundred per cent better in the majors. If you hit a hard ground ball up the middle in the minor leagues, you know it's a base hit. You do that in the big leagues and somebody's rolling around in front of it, throwing you out. They make all the plays." "You definitely have better defensive players in the majors," said former Met Bobby Pfeil. "In the minor leagues, you have guys that can swing the bat, but they're a liability defensively. Up in the majors, they make the plays."

Minor league hitters had many of the same traits as the pitchers. "In Triple A, you have three or four good hitters," said former Met pitcher Jerry Hinsley. "You get to the big leagues and they're all good hitters, one through eight." "In the minors," added Hinsley's teammate Darrell Sutherland, "there are three or four guys you can count on getting out just about all the time." "Major league hitters don't swing at bad pitches," said former Met Les Rohr. "They're more controlled. In Double A and Triple A, they like that high fast ball."

Klimchock was a Kansas City bonus player in 1958, who spent all or part of twelve seasons in the major leagues. He shuttled almost constantly between the majors and minors, and from position to position. It was not until 1969, when he was 29, that Klimchock appeared in more than 60 major league games in a year. He's thought a lot about what it took to get to the big leagues and what was required to stay there. "I think it's just a matter of positioning," he said, "and what they need up there. The pitching staff dictates that. How strong are the starters? How strong are the relievers? If you have a good pitching staff, you're going to carry a couple of extra hitters. A couple of times I got sent out because they needed pitching."

Versatility was another key to a big league job. "The guys who always amazed me," said Met pitcher Jim McAndrew, "were those good, stable middle infielders who would hit .220 but play for ten or fifteen years. They knew what their roles were and they were mature enough and disciplined enough to accept that and play within themselves. Look at Ducky Schofield and Al Weis." Bob Heise was a utility infielder who played with the Mets, Giants, Brewers, Cardinals, Angels, Red Sox and Royals from 1967–77. He was never in as many as 100 games in a season and his career average was .247. "I got the most out of my career," Heise said. "I could play three different positions, I had a strong arm, I could field well and I could do the little things, like bunt. Everybody can't be a starter. I realized that early in my career and made the best of it."

"I learned early on," said Bob Johnson, a utility man who played eleven seasons in the big leagues, "that if I could play more than one position, I might extend my career." "I could pinch run," said Tom Shopay, "I could pinch hit, I could go in for defense. I could catch."

Learning to catch was an excellent way for a fringe player to stay in the majors. Being able to catch in an emergency made one an extremely valuable performer, for it allowed a club to carry just two regular catchers, and use one of them as a pinch hitter if necessary. When Shopay was with the Orioles, Earl Weaver saw him fooling around with a catcher's mitt in the outfield. The Orioles were down to two catchers and needed a third. "He asked me if I could catch," Shopay said. "The only time I'd ever put on catching equipment was in college when two catchers got hurt and they asked for a volunteer. I caught about two innings. But I said, 'Heck, yeah.' I knew it was just another tool I'd have in my arsenal."

Shopay caught batting practice, worked with coach Cal Ripken, Sr., a former catcher, and was declared ready for action. At the end of the 1975 season, he got his chance. "It was the last game of the year in Yankee Stadium" Shopay recalled, "and the Yankees were pitching Larry Gura, a lefthander. I thought, 'I'll never play against a lefthander.' But I look at the lineup on the clubhouse door and I'm hitting second and there's a '2' [for catcher] after my name."

Shopay didn't do badly in his debut. "One guy stole on me," he recalled, "but I threw out two. I fielded a bunt in front of the plate and threw a guy out." All in all, he did pretty well for an outfielder—with one exception. Elston Howard, who Shopay knew from his days with the Yankees, was coaching first for New York. "After about the second inning," Shopay recalled, "Ellie hollers to me, 'Tom, Tom, come here.'" Shopay walked over. "Close your legs," Howard said. "I can see every sign you're giving."

Shopay caught only one more game in the big leagues. "Both times," he said, "Mike Flanagan was the pitcher and Nestor Chylak was the home plate umpire." Chylak had been a buddy of Shopay's father. "How's your dad doing," he asked Shopay, and told him how they used to have a drink together at a bar in Pennsylvania.

The second game Shopay caught was at Fenway Park, and went into extra innings. After ten innings, Weaver wanted to take him out, since it was the first time he had caught all year. "I looked at Weaver and said, 'As long as Fisk stays I there, I'm staying in there.' He stayed in all 15 innings and so did I." Harry Bright, Ray Barker and Klimchock were other utility players who learned how to catch after reaching the big leagues.

Klimchock's story is similar to that of Shopay. Al Dark, manager of the Indians, asked him if he could catch. "When you're the 25th man on a 25 man squad," Klimchock said, "you say, 'Yeah, I can catch.' Whatever it takes, you're going to do it. One night I pinch hit and was heading for the clubhouse to have my beer, when Dark said, 'Where are you going?' I'd pinch hit for the catcher and had to catch the last inning. Yastrzemski was the first batter and he hit a high popup on the third base line. I was just pointing to [third baseman] Max Alvis, saying, 'You got it. You got it. You got it.' Fortunately, it was an easy inning."

Sometimes the difference between a major leaguer and a Triple A player was a patron. Coaches or managers, when they came to a new team, often brought their favorite role players with them. "I give Whitey Herzog credit for the fact that I got eight full years in the big leagues," said Heise. "He was always a backer of mine." Herzog first got to know Heise in the Mets' minor league system, followed him throughout his career, and eventually brought him to the Royals in 1977. "When Whitey released me after the '77 season," Heise said, "I knew my career was over." He didn't even try to hook up with a new team. "If Whitey released me, I knew I just didn't have the skills to compete anymore."

An influential scout might help a player get to the big leagues. "When I was traded to the Mets," said pitcher Gordon Richardson, "I knew that I had lost my scout and was on my own. If I did not do real well, I'd be gone, because the Met scouts were pushing their own signees. I had nobody speaking up for me and nobody pushing for me."

Personality often played a role. Sometimes a pushy player might get a chance before a quiet sort. Ron Hunt, who turned out to be an excellent player, got his initial chance with the Mets through his brashness. "It seems like the sports world likes the flashy person," said pitcher Dennis Musgraves, a $100,000 bonus player who reached the major leagues, hurt his arm, and never made it back. "I wish I had been a little more forward. I'd never be one to make a fool of myself, but I'd be a little more aggressive in talking to management, just to know what they were thinking. I just went out there, put on my uniform, did the best I could and let things take care of themselves, but it would've been nice to know what they were thinking. I was just more naïve."

Nice guys didn't always finish last, however, for no one wanted a troublemaker as the 25th man on a club. "I moved around to quite a few teams," said Andy Kosco, "because managers thought they had an opportunity to get a player who wasn't a bad person, who would not cause any trouble among the players, and was able to fill in where he needed me and do the job."

Sometimes it was plain luck that brought a player to the majors. "You just need a break," said former Met pitcher Dave Eilers. "Somebody might even be having a bad year in the minors, but somebody else gets hurt and they get called up and take off from there, maybe doing better than they did in Triple A. I think it's all a matter of getting the breaks at the right time."

Getting a chance was the first part. Taking advantage of it and staying in the big leagues was the second. "Sparky Anderson once told me," Kosco related, "'If we start playing bad, they're not going to let me go. We're going to look at the 23rd, 24th, and 25th men on the roster. Those are the changes that are going to be made.'" "For me," said Shopay, "in spring training, every at bat, every ball hit to me, everything I did was a key situation in my eyes. I had to do well because I was always the 23rd, 24th or 25th player." Nick Willhite, a pitcher with great potential but a tender arm, shuttled between the Dodgers and the minors for several years. "I felt pressure every time I stepped on that mound," he said. "Boy, when you got to the big leagues, you had to win. I never felt comfortable. I had to do it right then and if I didn't do it right then I was going to be sent out. So I forced my way through the pain. I remember a couple of times I was hurting so bad that I had to go back to the clubhouse and puke. But I didn't want to say anything because I was afraid I was going to be pegged as having a bad arm so I just gutted myself up pretty good. It's very tough, because your rhythm is off and your concentration is off. You're trying to throw harder than you can. You're trying to do stuff your body won't let you do."

All top minor league players play every day, and everyone who ever picked up a bat or ball wants to play every day, but one of the keys to staying in the big leagues as a reserve is accepting the role. Billy Cowan came up to the Cubs in 1964 as the 1963 Pacific Coast League Player of the Year, and expected to be a regular. By the late '60s, after stints with the Cubs, Mets, Braves, Phillies and Yankees, he landed a job as a spare outfielder with the Angels. "I was more mature," he said. "I had three kids and I wanted to try to get my pension time in and just do a job someplace. I realized that nobody was going to give me a chance to be a starter again. At that point in time, you just change your outlook if you want to stay in baseball. I loved the game and wanted to stay in it."

By the time he reached the Yankees at the age of 29, Ray Barker was happy to fill whatever role he was given. His major league debut had taken place five years earlier, when the Orioles called him up in September, 1960. Barker had a couple of unsuccessful pinch hit appearances before the Orioles came into New York for the big series against the Yankees. In the second game of the Sunday doubleheader, he was on the bench watching a great pitching duel between Ralph Terry and Milt Pappas. "I'm sitting over there, having a chew, enjoying the hell out of myself," he said, "and all of a sudden, I hear Paul Richards say, 'Barker, get a bat!' I said, 'Oh, my god!,' never thinking I'd be in a clutch situation." The initial shock wore off and Barker started thinking. "Nobody knew who I was and they wouldn't know how to pitch me. When I started walking up to the plate, I saw Blanchard turn to the umpire and say, 'Who the hell is this guy?' I realized that was why Paul sent me up. Nobody knew me. I worked the count to 3–2 and fouled off about five pitches. Then Terry threw me a high outside fastball and I swung and missed."

Barker didn't get a hit for the rest of the season, and with sluggers Jim Gentile and Walt Dropo ahead of him, was back in the minors the following spring. In the four years that followed, Barker played in Vancouver, Rochester, Portland and Jacksonville, where he set a franchise record with 25 homers in 1962.

In the spring of 1965, Barker decided that, if he didn't make it to the big leagues, he would retire after the season. He had a good training camp and made the Cleveland squad as a pinch hitter and backup first baseman. Until 1968, each team was allowed a 28 man roster for the first 30 days of the season, after which they had to cut to 25. Cutdown day was always a nervous time for the fringe players. On May 12, 1965, Barker knew he was on the border line and suspected he might end up back in the minors. "We knew it was cutdown day and somebody was going," Barker said. "I figured it always happened to me and I'd be going back to Triple A again. So we went to a James Bond double feature in the afternoon." Perhaps if they couldn't find him, Barker reasoned, they'd cut someone else. Around four o'clock, he returned to his hotel room and found a message from the Indians' traveling secretary. "Where the hell have you been?" he asked Barker. "Get your ass up to Birdie [Tebbetts]'s suite." "I went up there," said Barker, "thinking, 'Well, back to the minors again.' But Birdie said, 'I don't think you'll be disappointed at where you're going." Barker was going to the Yankees, and he was not disappointed. "Just being up there with the Yankees when they had all those superstars," Barker said, "was worth all the years I spent in the minor leagues."

Barker left immediately to join the Yankees in Boston, arriving in the middle of a game. He went to the players' entrance and announced his presence. "I said, 'I just got traded to the Yankees,'" Barker recalled. "They said, 'Who are you?' I said, 'Ray Barker.' They said, 'Who's Ray Barker?'"

Barker finally got into the clubhouse and was told to get into uniform right away, because he might be needed as a pinch hitter. "All I had was a red Indians' sweatshirt," he said, "so I had to go out there without a sweatshirt." Barker was so happy at his reprieve from the minors that he probably would have gone out without his pants. He didn't play that night, but was welcomed to the club the next morning when he came downstairs to have breakfast at the hotel. "There was Mickey Mantle and Whitey Ford and Tom Tresh," he said. "Of course I knew who they were because I'd been watching them for years. As soon as I walked in, one of them waved me over. I went and sat down at their table. They said, 'Who the hell is Ray Barker?' They said the sports page was full of the trade of Pedro Gonzalez for Ray Barker, who'll be playing first base and hitting third today. I said, 'What!' By god, you talk about a thrill. I'm sitting there with three superstars and they're telling me I'm hitting third tonight."

Sure enough, Barker started and batted third in the order, in front of Mantle, getting a double (his first major league hit) and a single. He started the next night and got another hit. Barker hadn't even been able to make a second division club as a pinch hitter, and now he was batting in the heart of the order for a team that had won five straight pennants. It said something about Barker's perseverance, but it said more about the state of the '65 Yankees.

The following week, Barker hit his first major league home run, off Earl Wilson of the Red Sox. "The next time up," he recalled, "down I went." He hit a home run off Denny McLain. In June, Barker hit two pinch home runs in three days, and became the Yankees' best pinch hitter. "That's something I had never done until I got to the big leagues," Barker said. "I pinch hit against righties and Lu Clinton hit against lefties.* We did it almost every night, because we were always behind. I'd go into the clubhouse to loosen up. Johnny Keane would say, 'Get your

*Clinton joined the Yankees in 1966.

ass out here, you know when I'm going to need you.' I usually hit with somebody on base, and I was always a pretty good clutch hitter. I loved hitting with the bases loaded or two men on, or in the ninth inning with the winning run on base. I enjoyed that."

The Yankees were desperately looking for a hero, and Barker's early splurge produced hope that he would be the rabbit the Yankees always seemed to pull out of the hat, the journeyman who discovered magic in the pinstripes. Barker was not a miracle worker, however, merely a steady reserve and a good pinch hitter. When the season was over, he had a .254 average in 98 Yankee games, with seven home runs. Like the airport incident, Barker was a false harbinger of hope.

Houk, the eternal optimist, died hard. On May 23, with the Yankees in eighth place, he said, "I still think we're going to win the pennant. In fact, I'm confident we will. This club doesn't know how to lose. Before this season is over, the Yankee fans will have something to cheer about — and the Yankee haters will still have to hate us." "I don't see how they can write us off," he added a few days later.

Others saw Yankees losses, but Houk saw close games that would become wins when the injured Yankee stars returned. He saw three potentially outstanding young pitchers in Stottlemyre, Downing and Bouton. Others saw the replacements the Yankees summoned from the minors as "unknowns." Houk pointed out that everyone who came up from the minors had been unknown, including Pepitone and Tresh.

Two years earlier, Downing had been a sensation, arriving with a string of low hit games and a flurry of strikeouts. Howard said he threw harder than Koufax. Arthur Daley called him the heir apparent to Ford. In 1964, Downing led the league in strikeouts, posting the highest total for a Yankee since Jack Chesbro in 1904, but he was inconsistent, blowing several leads in the late innings. He'd pitched poorly in the World Series.

In the spring of 1965, Downing just couldn't seem to get going. He was wild in exhibition games, consistently missing high with his pitches. Downing didn't pitch badly when the regular season started, but he wasn't pitching like Sandy Koufax either. His record hovered around .500, he walked too many, and finished the year with a disappointing 12–14 record.

After Bouton won 21 games in '63 and 18 the following year, he seemed set as a solid starter for years to come. Just 26, he had a good fastball and a great curveball, according to many, the best in the league after Twins' veteran Camilo Pascual. Bouton was the Yankees' opening day starter in 1965, and pitched fairly well in April. Then his arm started hurting. "It was a dull pain," he reported the following winter, "like a toothache. They told me it was some sort of an inflamed muscle under my biceps." When he had five days rest or more, Bouton had a little jump on his fastball, but with three or four days, it was dead. In 1963 and '64, when Bouton was a big winner, people counted the number of times his cap fell off. Now they were afraid it was his arm that might come flying off.

Even though his arm hurt, Bouton continued to pitch, but his lack of velocity was apparent in the results. In his first ten starts, Bouton gave up 13 home runs in just 64 innings, and was 3–5 with a 5.03 ERA. Sometimes Bouton pitched well but the Yankees didn't score. Other times the Yankees scored and he pitched poorly. Bouton won just one game after May, losing 13 of his last 14 decisions, finishing 4–15, fourteen less wins than he had the previous year.

Although he was only 25 years old when the 1965 season started, Stafford was never able to regain his form of 1961 and 1962. After his poor 1963 season, he lost a considerable amount of weight, and claimed he would bounce back in 1964. His 5–0 record was deceptive, and *The New York Times* called him "one of the most unsuccessful undefeated pitchers in history." Tendinitis and a lack of stamina had hampered Stafford in '64, and during the off season he had an operation to remove excess cartilage from his nose. That would help his breathing, he believed, and allow him to be a nine inning pitcher again. In '65, however, Stafford was again plagued by injury, and wound up on the disabled list once again with tendinitis in his shoulder. He pitched a few good games, but was only 3–8 in 111 innings.

Houk said the Yankees didn't know how to lose, but they learned. Koppett, a much more objective observer, laid bare the weakness of Keane's troupe repeatedly throughout the season. On June 1, he pointed out, the club had the worst record of any Yankee team since 1925. The '25 club, which finished seventh with a 69–85 record in the year of Babe Ruth's infamous "belly-ache," became the standard of comparison as the dismal season wore on. It was the last season in which New York had finished out of the first division.

In late June, Koppett chronicled the Yankees' many problems. Mantle wasn't hitting. Downing was struggling. Kubek's shoulder was bothering him. Ford was not the pitcher he'd been a couple of years earlier. During the winter, Whitey had undergone surgery to correct the circulatory problem in his arm. Rehabilitation was not what it is today, and Ford spent the winter throwing a tennis ball against his basement wall trying to regain his strength. When he got to Fort Lauderdale, he could throw pretty well, but had limited feeling in the arm, and did not sweat on his left side. Whitey also had no pulse in his left hand.

Ford could pitch effectively only in warm weather. "When it's cold," he said, "I can't even warm up before the game." Whitey had always like to pitch in cool weather, for the heat fatigued him, but with his limited circulation, he couldn't get a good grip on ball when the weather was cold. Seventy degrees seemed to be the magic number. "If it's below 65 degrees," Ford said, "I can't start, and if it's above 75 I can't finish. The solution is obvious ... I should be sold to Houston."

Where were the replacements for the Yankees' fading and injured stars? "When I was in the minor leagues," said Pete Mikkelsen, "and the Yankees needed a player, they went and got him. If he was hitting .260 at Richmond, he hit .360 in New York. I don't know why that would happen, but it did. The players they traded for were doing alright where they were, but when they came to New York, they had career years. That didn't happen in 1965. Nobody had a career year."

For years, the Yankees had stayed out of the bonus game, believing it to be a waste of money to pay out huge sums to untested youngsters. In 1961, commencing with the signing of Jake Gibbs for $100,000, they got in the game, but it was too late. Still, there had been no indication in 1961 that the flow of prospects would dry up, for there seemed to be a number of talented youngsters in the Yankee farm system. One by one, however, they fell by the wayside. Deron Johnson, Don Lock and Lee Thomas were traded. Charley Keller, Jr. hurt his back and never made it. Hal Stowe, 14–1 at Amarillo in '61, made it to the Yankees for one game. Other top prospects like Bob Lasko, Frank Carpin and Bob Meyer failed to become big league stars. In 1956, seven of the American Association All Stars had been Yankee farmhands. In 1963, the entire Yankee farm system produced only one minor league all star, pitcher Gil Downs, who made the Class A Florida State League team.

Yet, tradition dies hard, and everyone thought the Yankees would continue to produce star players. In 1962, when the Richmond team was loaded with minor league journeymen, and the Yankee minor league affiliates posted the worst record of any major league farm system, Dan Daniel wrote, "The dope says the Yankees do not have another Tresh coming up. But somehow, somewhere, Houk will discover the help he needs. It's an old Yankee custom." Dan Topping excused the losing records by insisting that winning in the minors wasn't important, and that the Yankees were developing talent, not winning games. In fact, they were doing neither.

"The Yankees always had a great supply of talent coming up," said Gordon White, "and they had a great knack for buying great players late in the season. They got Johnny Mize, Enos Slaughter, and Johnny Sain. The Yankees fed off the Newark Bears and the Kansas City Blues for years. I went to see the Newark Bears as a kid. The players were unbelievable. The only major league team they couldn't beat was the Yankees."

There were no Newark Bears in 1965, but Houk continued to look at the bright side. "Suppose we win 65 [more] games," he said, "which isn't so hard to do. That would give us 93 victories, wouldn't it? That might do it." "Mickey is running better than at many other times you and I have seen him," Houk told Koppett. "but he's simply not hitting. I think he's pressing too hard trying to snap a slump." The players felt the same way. Sheldon, who had departed for Kansas City in May, said recently, "I could not see the Yankees falling apart at that particular time. I could not foresee the Yankees going downhill that rapidly."

Koppett was unconvinced. At the All Star break, he conceded that the Yankees still had a formidable array of talent, but cautioned, "[T]he Yankees must at last face the fact that Mickey Mantle has to be discounted.... Anything he gives the Yankees from now on will be gravy. They must make their plans as if he were no longer available." With Mantle's battered legs, Koppett pointed out, he could not condition himself to avoid injury, and would thus be continually susceptible to leg miseries.

Berra, who had been pilloried as a strategist, was looking better in hindsight. Koppett analyzed the criticisms that had been leveled in 1964. Yogi had prematurely given up, they said, on Stan Williams. Keane released Williams before the season started, and Cleveland sent him to the minors in May. Reniff and Boyer claimed Yogi lacked faith in them. By the middle of 1965, Reniff had no wins or saves and Boyer was hitting .158. Keane didn't have a lot of faith in them, either, and benched Boyer in favor of rookie Horace Clarke. Berra had babied Mantle too much, they said, but Yogi had gotten 143 games out of him. Keane worked Mantle like a plow horse, and after playing both games of a doubleheader on May 2, Mickey was out of action for a week.

Despite their record, people refused to believe the Yankees were as bad as they appeared. A June *Sports Illustrated* story on the team's decline elicited a stream of letters. "Methinks you speak too soon," wrote Michael Jay Kalter. "The Mick is mighty and shall prevail ... this Yankee lover will have the last laugh when the Yanks beat the Braves in the 1965 World Series." "The Yanks are far from through," added F. Jules Lund, Jr., "and when Mantle leads them back you'll have to eat that eighth cover with his picture on it." "Now that Howard is back," said Jim Nowakowski, "watch the Yanks rise."

The Yankees faced a last stand in Minneapolis in July, just before the All Star break. The Twins were doing what Keane wanted to do with the Yankees. After years of waiting for one of their sluggers to hit the ball over the fence, Minnesota had become a daring, exciting club. New third base coach Billy Martin instilled fire in moody shortstop Zoilo Versalles, and got the Twins running and taking chances on the basepaths.

The Yankees were 40–43, 12½ games behind Minnesota, with a four game series that represented their final chance to get back in the race. If the Yanks could sweep the series, they'd be 8½ back with half a season to go. If they took three of four, they'd still be 10½ behind, but would have delivered a message to the Twins and the rest of the American League that they were not dead yet. The Yankees had been winning for so long, that even when they fell far behind, no one was willing to declare them finished. If they were pounding on someone's heels, the sound would be louder than if it were coming from the Orioles or Tigers. All the Yanks needed was to get back in the race, and the pretenders would fall.

In the first game of the series, on Friday night, July 9, the Twins got four runs off Bouton in the first inning and went on to an easy 8–3 win. The Yanks also lost the second game of the series, the first of a day-night doubleheader. They were losing the night game 5–4 in the eighth inning, when Boyer's grand slam gave them an 8–6 win. If the Yanks could win the final game on Sunday, they would have salvaged a split and gained a little momentum going into the break. If they lost, they would be 14½ games behind and reeling.

Mantle, making his first start in 19 games, singled in the first inning, one of four singles the Yanks' first five batters got off Twin starter Jim Kaat. Somehow, the Yankees managed to get just one run. Downing, the Yankee starter, was hit hard, and by the ninth inning, both he and Kaat had long since departed for the showers.

When the Yanks batted in the top of the ninth, the score was tied 4–4. New York had runners on first and third with two out when Roger Repoz chopped a high bouncer near first base. Twin pitcher Jerry Fosnow grabbed the ball just as Repoz was passing him. Repoz knocked the ball loose and crossed first base as Howard scored the lead run. Home plate umpire Ed Hurley called Repoz out for interference, bringing Keane from the dugout on the gallop. The Yankee manager convinced Hurley to ask first base umpire Red Flaherty for a second opinion, and Flaherty reversed the call, allowing the Yankee run which gave them a 5–4 lead. This brought Twin manager Sam Mele charging out, but he was less persuasive than Keane and the second call stood. It was just what the old Yankees had always done — get a key break at the opportune moment to pull a seemingly lost game out of the fire.

This was 1965, however, and the Yankee magic was gone. In the bottom of the ninth, Mikkelsen had a runner on first and two out, with just Harmon Killebrew standing between him and a Yankee comeback win. Mikkelsen couldn't finish it off. Killebrew hit a long home run over the left field fence, giving the Twins a 6–5 victory and saddling the Yanks with a 14½ game deficit. "The blow," reported *Sports Illustrated*, "opened a five game lead [over the Indians and Orioles] but, more than that, it told the Twins, the rest of the league and the whole world, for that matter, that the Yankees were indeed dead." Even Houk was beginning to lose faith.

The distraught Keane began losing his health. He'd bottled up his anger all season, and now the inner turmoil surfaced. "He never hollered, ranted or raved," said Doc Edwards. "You could tell when he was displeased, but he was very professional about it." During the final game in Minnesota, Keane became ill on the bench, and had to be given oxygen. Afterwards, a doctor examined him, diagnosed an attack of nervous exhaustion and told Keane to rest during the All Star break.

Two days after Killebrew's home run drove the final nail into the Yankee coffin, the All Star Game was played in Minnesota. For the first time in 20 years, no Yankee was in the starting lineup. Just four years earlier, Mantle started in center field, Maris in right, Kubek at shortstop and Ford on the mound. During the past two years Richardson, Howard and Pepitone had all been starters. Only Richardson had any hope of selection in '65, and he lost out to former Met Felix Mantilla, who was having a stellar season with the Red Sox.

The superiority of the National League was evident in the all star rosters. The starting American League catcher, Detroit's Bill Freehan, had a .194 batting average. Howard, his backup, was hitting .221. One of the pitchers, Kansas City's John O'Donoghue (immortalized by the Orioles kangaroo court in 1969 by the awarding of the "John O'Donoghue Line Drive Award" to the pitcher who had taken the greatest beating) had a 4–11 record. As they had the past two years, the National League won the game.

Not only was the National League dominating the American League in all star play, the Met stars were outplaying their Yankee counterparts. At the break, Ron Swoboda and Ed Kranepool had a combined average of .275, with 22 home runs and 73 RBI. Mantle and Maris were batting a combined .241, with 19 homers and 52 RBI. Who would have made that bet prior to the season?

Even had he been selected, there was no way Maris could have played in the All Star game. On June 20th, while sliding into home plate, he injured his hand when it hit the umpire's shoe. It didn't appear to be anything serious. About a week later, Maris was swinging at a pitch when he felt something snap. His wrist became swollen and he couldn't even grip a bat, let alone swing one. What seemed at first to be a minor nick stubbornly refused to heal. Week after week went by and Maris stayed on the sideline. He didn't return until August 18, when he struck out as a pinch hitter, letting go of the bat with his right hand after every swing.

Maris pinch hit a few more times during the final weeks of the season, but was essentially finished for the year at the end of June. Since the injury seemed so minor at the time, the media questioned Maris's fortitude, which is the last thing anyone who knew him would have done. Like the controversies of '61, the suggestion that he was malingering infuriated the Yankee outfielder. He told Jake Gibbs, "The next time I get hurt, I hope there's a bone broken through the skin and blood is gushing out so people will believe me." After Dr. Gaynor and two other orthopedic surgeons found nothing seriously wrong, Maris went to his own doctor, who discovered that his hand had indeed been broken, and surgery was performed in October. Between the broken hand and the early season hamstring injury, Roger appeared in just 46 games.

The second half of the 1965 season was a quest to reach the .500 mark. The Yanks made it on August 14, and again on September 3, but each time they fell back. In September, with the pennant long gone and many of the regulars injured, the Yankees brought up the kids. Roy White, a young second baseman, shortstop Bobby Murcer, and Rich Beck, a pitcher, arrived from Columbus. Jack Cullen, 14–5 at Toledo, joined the starting rotation and pitched well. Maybe there were some future stars in the Yankee system after all.

On the 8th of September, the Yanks lost their seventh straight game, the team's longest losing streak in 12 years. The same day, the Yankees were eliminated from the pennant race, their earliest exit in many a year, and announced that Keane was rehired for 1966. "You cannot blame our present position on the manager," Houk said. With the Yanks officially eliminated, Houk had finally given up on 1965, but he was ready for 1966. "Johnny and I are not concerned with this ball club," he said. "We think we can win the pennant next year."

The Yankees finished the campaign in lackluster fashion, losing 24 of their last 38 games and ending the season in sixth place with a 77–85 record, their worst mark since 1925. The Cardinals, who had beaten the Yankees the previous October, also crashed in 1965, finishing seventh. It was the first time both World Series teams finished with sub-.500 records the next year. The only bright spots in the Yankee season were Stottlemyre, who won 20 games in his first full major league season and Ford, who went from a question mark in the spring to a 16 game winner. Steve Hamilton had a 1.40 ERA in relief, allowing just three earned runs in his last 29 appearances.

With many of the Yankee stars injured, Tresh was the best Yankee hitter. He led the club in hits, doubles, home runs (26), runs scored and runs batted in, while hitting .279, but didn't get much help. Keane attributed the Yankee failures in 1965 to an inability to deliver the key hit. The team wasn't getting many non-key hits either, as their .235 batting average was ninth in the league, 18 points lower than their 1964 mark. The home run total continued to decline, dropping from 162 in 1964 to 149. The Yankees were sixth in fielding average. "We ought to be the best fielding team in baseball," Clete Boyer said to Oriole coach Billy Hunter one day. Why, Hunter asked. "Because we spend so much time out here," Boyer replied. The Yankees finished the season without Pepitone, who missed the last four games and, at the insistence of Houk, checked into Lenox Hill Hospital to be treated by a psychologist.

Keane said in September that he was disappointed in the pitching, particularly that of Downing, Reniff, Stafford and Mikkelsen. The Yankee ERA was sixth in the league. Ramos wasn't the bullpen stopper he had been in September, 1964, and only the Red Sox posted fewer saves than the Yankees.

Houk expressed unbridled optimism for 1966, and attributed the poor season to injuries. "I don't think there's any mystery about it," he said after the season. "In the first place, we were hit by the worst streak of injuries I can ever remember hitting a ball club. You just can't operate as a pennant contender with players like Mickey Mantle, Roger Maris, Elston Howard and

Tony Kubek out of the lineup." "We just lost too many thoroughbreds," said Doc Edwards recently. "You just don't replace them with people who aren't everyday players and win. The people who had the ability to do it — there just weren't enough of them. The rest of us had to use every ounce of our talent and that still wasn't quite enough."

Houk's high hopes were predicated on the return to full capacity of his stars. That was unlikely, for Mantle was a battered 34, Howard a 37-year old catcher with a surgically repaired elbow, and Kubek was being examined at the Mayo Clinic to see if he could continue to play with his damaged neck. Maris, at 31, was the only injured star who still might be considered to be in his prime. The return to the top was not a one year proposition.

The Yankees were not only bad, they were boring. Only Mantle brought a reaction from the fans. Stottlemyre and Tresh were very good players, but neither was charismatic. In an age of revolution, Stottlemyre was a clean-cut, conservative, respectful young man. He spent his time on the road watching baseball games on television, and getting in early to talk baseball with Gibbs, his roommate. He was highly competent rather than spectacular, and totally non-controversial. "A Joe Namath he ain't," wrote Jim Ogle. Mantle got more reaction for a strike-out than Tresh got for a home run. If the Yankees were going to prosper, they believed, they desperately needed another Mickey Mantle.

· 17 ·

The Search for
the Next Mantle

When the 1965 season began, Mickey Mantle was 33 years old, chronological middle age for a star baseball player. Stan Musial and Ted Williams had played into their early forties. In 1965, thirty-four-year-old Willie Mays hit 52 home runs. But Mantle was an old 33. His legs were at least 83. Mickey was having increasing difficulty covering Yankee Stadium's vast center field, and during the latter stages of the 1964 season, Maris or Tresh had played center, while Mantle was shifted between left and right, depending on the park. He played right field at the Stadium and whichever field had the smallest amount of territory on the road. During the World Series, Maris often ranged far into right field to take fly balls that Mantle couldn't reach.

In the spring of 1965, with winter supposedly having given Mantle's aching legs time to heal, Johnny Keane returned Mickey to his old position in center. The long rest had not brought back the old Mantle, however. After a mid–March exhibition, Leonard Koppett wrote, "The most significant feature of the game was Mantle's evident difficulty in center field. For the first time this season, balls were hit into his territory that required a quick start, and Mickey looked bad half a dozen times as hits fell in front of him and beyond him. Once he fell down." In another spring game, Mantle was charged with two errors.

Although Mickey could move straight ahead once he got going, he could not start or stop quickly, and was incapable of pivoting and turning. Each outfield position presented some difficulty. There was a great expanse of ground to cover in center field, especially in Yankee Stadium. Right field was smaller and probably the best position for Mickey, but Roger Maris was perhaps the best defensive right fielder in the American League. In addition, Mantle's once powerful arm no longer had the strength required in right, a weakness the Cardinals had exploited to great advantage in the World Series. Left field at Yankee Stadium was almost as big as center.

Mickey wanted to play center, saying there were fewer quick starts and stops. He also felt uncomfortable with the backgrounds in left and right field, particularly in Yankee Stadium. Caroms off the low, curved walls gave him trouble. When Mantle struggled in center, however, Keane decided to put him in left and move Tresh, who had good speed and a strong arm, to center. "I've been pitching 14 years for this club," said Ford, "trying to keep guys from hitting the ball to Mantle in center field. Now I'm gonna have to keep them from hitting it to left."

Perhaps in Yankee Stadium, Keane said, with its endless left field, Tresh would move back to left and Mickey would play center. None of these solutions was ideal, but Mantle had batted .303 with 35 home runs in '64, was still the Yankees' star, and Keane had to find someplace to play him. "First base, often mentioned," wrote Koppett, "is out of the question for Mantle." The quick movements required of an infielder, he said, would be too much for Mickey.

No matter where he played, it was obvious that Mantle would not be playing much longer. In the spring of '65, he said he hoped to squeeze another three years out of his aching body, but Keane, Houk and all of the Yankees knew that his career could be over with one violent twist of a knee. Soon the Yankees would need to learn to get along without Mickey Mantle. Who would replace him?

Pepitone had long been the leading candidate, but Joe followed a promising '63 season with a decent but unspectacular 1964 and a disappointing 1965. More ominously, he continued to display the irresponsible behavior that would keep him from realizing his great potential. Tresh was another possibility. He was a switch hitter, which invited comparison to Mantle, but after four strong, steady seasons, he looked more like Tommy Henrich than Mickey Mantle.

Maybe there wasn't going to be another Mantle. "There's a lot of pressure," Tresh said, "when somebody says you're supposed to be the next Mantle. The Yankees were pretty lucky when Mickey became the next Dimaggio. They just assumed it was that easy to find somebody who could do that kind of job. Bernie Williams is probably the next best center fielder the Yankees have had, but there were an awful lot of years between Mickey and Bernie." Tresh was right, but the Yankees weren't willing to accept anything less than a superstar like Mickey Mantle.

The new superstar was elusive, but the Yankees kept hoping. "We've got no one down on the farm teams like Mantle," Houk said in 1963. "We need to direct all our efforts to coming up with a kid who can hit the long ball." On the last day of June, 1965, with the team languishing around the middle of the league, and Mantle and Maris injured, the Yanks recalled a muscular, slugging outfielder with a blond crew cut from their Triple A farm club at Toledo. In 75 International League games, Roger Repoz hit 14 home runs and, as Joe Durso wrote, was "rated the nearest thing to Mickey Mantle and Roger Maris that the Yankees owned in the minor leagues." "Roger even kind of resembled Mickey," said Tresh, "with the short, blond haircut."

In their desire to anoint a new slugger, the Yankees overlooked the fact that, from 1960 through 1964, Repoz struck out 483 times in 542 games, compiled an average of only .243 and averaged 11 homers per season. In 1963, he led the Sally League in strikeouts with 166, and had been among the league leaders wherever he played. From 1962 through 1964, Repoz never batted higher than .235. Such statistics did not suggest another Mantle, nor did a blond crew foretell the second coming, but there was no one else, so Repoz would have to carry the torch.

Repoz grew up in Bellingham, Washington, and attended Western Washington State College. He played well his freshman year, pitching and playing the outfield, and was named the MVP of the NAIA tournament. The Baltimore Orioles offered him $6,000 to sign, but he turned it down, figuring that with a strong second year he could improve his negotiating position. Repoz had a good second year in 1960 but, to his great dismay, received no offers. Baltimore, which had seen him at the tournament the prior year, didn't scout the State of Washington.

Yankee scout Eddie Taylor, the man who would sign Mel Stottlemyre a year later, approached Repoz. "Are you ready to sign?" he asked. Roger said yes. "OK," said Taylor, "we'll give you $4,000." "Wait a minute," Repoz said, "I turned down $6,000 from Baltimore." That was last year, Taylor reminded him, but agreed to see what he could do. He made a phone call to New York, and gave the impression to Repoz, hearing one end of the conversation, that serious doubts were being expressed and that he was fighting a difficult battle. Finally, Taylor hung up and said the Yankees had agreed to a bonus of $6,000. Six thousand dollars was an impressive sum to get from Taylor, for Stottlemyre, who became one of the Yankees' all time great pitchers, and Rich Beck, who also made it to the major leagues, received no signing bonuses at all. "We used to tease Roger," said Beck, "telling him that there was nothing left for Mel and I because he got all the money."

After toiling in the Yankee farm system for nearly five years, Repoz was recalled in September of 1964, serving as a defensive replacement for the gimpy-legged Mantle in the late innings and appearing in 11 games. When he was called up in '65, Repoz arrived in Baltimore on June 30th, and pinch hit on his first day in uniform. The following night, he started against Steve Barber, the Orioles' flame throwing lefthander who'd won 20 games in 1963. In the ninth inning, with the Yankees trailing 4–1 and a runner on base, Repoz hit his first major league home run into the right field bullpen. The following night in Boston, he hit a three run homer as the Yankees walloped the Red Sox 16–2, the team's highest run total since 1962. Their 21 hits had not been exceeded since 1958. Had the Yankees found the young phenom who would lead them back to glory?

Three days later, Repoz hit another homer, this one in Detroit. On July 9, in Minnesota, he hit an inside the park home run. The next day, in a doubleheader, he had two singles, a triple and yet another homer, giving him five home runs in 13 games and a team-leading .302 aver-

Roger Repoz was called up to the Yankees in 1965, with high expectations. A quick start raised hopes that Repoz would be the next Mickey Mantle. In mid–1966, he was traded to Kansas City, and didn't reach his potential until he played in Japan in the 1970s.

age. Five homers in 13 games equated to exactly 62 in 162 games, one ahead of Maris's record. "That's when they said, 'Ooh, this must be the next Mickey Mantle,'" Repoz recalled. "I remember an interview on the Game of the Week with Merle Harmon. The first thing he asked was, 'Well, how does it feel to be the next Mickey Mantle?' I just said, 'Uh, I don't know.'"

The fans in New York, eager to see the young phenom, were disappointed when the Yankees returned home after the All Star break. Repoz went into an 0 for 29 tailspin which dropped his average below .200. "I was still tearing the cover off the ball," Repoz said, "but all of a sudden I was hitting the ball right at somebody." Soon, Repoz went into a legitimate slump. "The pitchers found out pretty quickly," he said, "that they could throw me off-speed stuff and I would swing at anything." Repoz began to strike out with alarming frequency, the affliction which had plagued him in the minor leagues. But didn't Mantle strike out a lot?

Repoz was no Mantle, but he was a promising player with great potential. "Roger had great tools," said Tresh. "He was about 6'2". He could run like a deer. He covered a lot of ground and hit the ball with power." "I remember talking to one of my teammates [in the minor leagues]," said Archie Moore, "and he said he never really appreciated Roger until the next year, when he was playing someplace else and balls that Roger had caught, this center fielder couldn't get to."

The Yankees and their fans, however, didn't want a steady ballplayer and a good defensive outfielder. They wanted a superstar, which Repoz wasn't. "I just wanted to play my game," he said. It would be difficult for him to do that in New York.

As the dismal 1965 season dragged on, two things became apparent. The Yankees were not going to win the pennant and Roger Repoz was not going to become the next Yankee superstar. By the end of the year, he had 12 home runs and a .228 average in 79 games. He struck out 57 times in just 218 at bats. The seven homers he hit in his last 66 games equated to 17 in a 162 game season.

In the early months of 1966, Repoz appeared principally as a defensive replacement for Mantle, who had shoulder surgery in the off-season and couldn't throw. When Maris was injured, he got a chance to play regularly for a couple of weeks and was hitting .349 in 43 at bats. On June 10th, while the Yankees were in Detroit, Houk called Repoz into his office. He had considered Repoz the Yankee centerfielder of the future, Houk told him, but Whitey Ford was injured and he desperately needed a starting pitcher. Despite the fact that the club was in seventh place, Houk still believed they could win the pennant with a little pitching help. He wanted Fred Talbot of the Kansas City A's, and the only way the Athletics would part with Talbot, Houk said, was if Repoz were involved in the trade. Less than a year after he arrived with such fanfare, Repoz was gone. In the 1950s, the Kansas City shuttle had brought New York one prospect after another. Now the Yankees were sending their prospects to the Athletics.

After one season in Kansas City, during which he led the punchless As with 11 home runs, Repoz was traded to the Angels. In 1968, it appeared that Roger was about to achieve the stardom predicted for him in New York. After 22 games, he led the major leagues with eight home runs and 19 runs batted in, and had more than half of the Angels' home runs and a third of their RBIs. "Some guys come late," said California hitting instructor Joe Gordon, "I genuinely believe that this will be the year Roger will find himself. He has enormous talent." Unfortunately, the National Guard intervened and, in late May, Repoz had to spend two weeks on active duty. He lost his groove and never regained it, finishing the year with 13 homers and 54 RBIs.

It was not until Repoz left the United States that he realized his potential. He played in Japan from 1973–77 and hit 122 home runs, including 36 in one year. "Between the time I was released in the United States and I went to Japan," Repoz said, "I got a book: *The Science of Hitting*, by Ted Williams. I wish I had that book when I was 20 years old. It became my bible. The main premise behind his book is to always get a good pitch to hit. The pitcher can never throw the ball where he wants to all the time, and if you have the patience to wait, you'll get a good pitch. I'd always been an aggressive hitter and I had no patience. I learned it about ten or twelve years too late."

A little more than two months after Repoz was traded to Kansas City, the Yankees recalled outfielder Steve Whitaker from Toledo. Again, Ford was the catalyst, as his placement on the disabled list opened up a roster spot. Whitaker was a handsome 23-year-old from Tacoma, Washington, six feet tall and 180 pounds. He'd had a rough life in Tacoma, and stayed out of trouble by playing baseball. Like Repoz, Whitaker was signed by Eddie Taylor. "We lived in a house that had plaster falling from the ceiling," Whitaker said. "I'm from a big family and all the kids were sitting in the living room. Eddie drove up in a big white Cadillac, wearing a Panama hat and carrying a typewriter that looked like it was as old as he was. He told my father, 'The New York Yankees want to sign your son.' There was no bargaining. What were we going to do? We didn't have any money." Whitaker signed for a $5500 bonus. It didn't seem like much, but in this case, it was Taylor, the shrewd bargainer, who had been taken in by Whitaker.

"I'd hurt my arm," said Whitaker, "and I'd been hiding it. I'd go to the tryouts and hit well, and they'd want me to take infield. I didn't listen. I acted like I didn't hear them and I'd go in and change into my civilian clothes. I'd come back out and they'd say, 'We wanted to see you throw.' 'Oh,' I'd say, 'I didn't know that.' I faked the hell out of it."

Whitaker had tremendous physical talent. "That kid can't miss," Joe Dimaggio told Houk after seeing him as an 18-year-old in the Yankees' preliminary spring camp. Jack Reed, the former

Outfielder Steve Whitaker had a world of ability, but put so much pressure on himself to be a super-star that he lasted only a short time in New York. He was another potential Mickey Mantle who had a brief and unhappy Yankee career.

outfielder who managed in the Yankee farm system, was asked about the best player he ever managed. Reed didn't hesitate. "Steve Whitaker," he replied. There was a qualification, however. "Steve could have been a super ballplayer," Reed said, "if he had his head on right. He was an All-American kid off the field, but on the field he was a Jekyll and Hyde. If he got a hit the first time up, he'd be super the rest of the game. If he popped up, there's no telling what he might do. He might throw his helmet, throw his bat, or not run the ball out. He couldn't control his emotions on the field."

When I interviewed Whitaker in 2003, he was 60 years old. His voice, however, sounded much younger and was filled with animation and energy. From the perspective of middle age, Whitaker agreed wholeheartedly with Reed and everyone else who said he was his own worst enemy. "I really beat myself up," he said recently. "There was no room for failure in my game. I expected too much of myself in every at bat. If I went two for four, I beat myself up over the two outs. I used to beat myself up terribly. I was off the wall. I needed to be locked up." "He would self-destruct," said Tresh. "He was awfully hard on himself."

Whitaker missed the early part of the '64 season with a broken hand. "I said I fell over some bats," he said, "but I really got into a fight at the Valhalla Bar in Hollywood, Florida," he said. "I went back to the hotel and thought everything was fine. I'd gotten a couple of good punches in. But after a while, my wrist was killing me. My hand was fine, but my wrist was swelling up and getting real bad. After an hour, I couldn't even close my hand, so I made up a story about falling over some bats I kept under my bed." The wrist was placed in a cast and Whitaker spent the first six weeks of the season sitting in the stands watching his Greensboro teammates. When he finally got to play, he hit .303 with 27 home runs and 100 RBI.

Loren Babe was the Greensboro manager. Whitaker had played for Babe in Idaho Falls and had not gotten along with him particularly well, but a few home runs in Greensboro improved the relationship immensely. "He loved me now," said Whitaker. "All of a sudden I'm one of his best players." In 1965, Babe was promoted to Columbus in the Double A Southern League, and Whitaker went with him. There the relationship soured. As always, Whitaker sulked whenever he made an out. "I had 10 home runs," he said, "but I thought I should have had 20." Babe warned him many times about not running out grounders and eventually Whitaker exhausted his patience.

One day Whitaker hit a fly ball, became disgusted and peeled off toward the dugout. "Sure enough," he said, "I'm just about sitting in the dugout and the guy misses the ball. Babe told me to go to the clubhouse and a lot of 'fuck-yous' were thrown around." After the game, Babe told Whitaker he was being sent down to Fort Lauderdale of the Class A Florida State League and that he would never play for him again.

At Fort Lauderdale, Whitaker came under the patient handling of Jack Reed. Reed had been a marginal major leaguer, and understood the difficulties faced by young ballplayers. The game had not come easily to him and he had had to work very hard to make it to the majors. Reed knew that many of his players were plagued by insecurity and self-doubt. He tried to instill confidence in them, and attempted to convince Whitaker that he couldn't get a hit every at bat. "He just put things in the right perspective for me," Whitaker said. "He didn't mention the bad things that had happened and made me feel like I was better than I was." Fort Lauderdale won the championship of the Florida State League, and in the post game clubhouse celebration, Whitaker learned that he would go to spring training with the Yankees in 1966. "That was awesome," he said. "I went home on top of the world."

After appearing in one exhibition game with the Yankees, Whitaker was sent to the minors and began the season in Columbus, where he hit .311 with 20 home runs and 68 RBI in 86 games. In mid–July, he was promoted to Toledo, whose manager was Loren Babe. Again, a few home runs caused Babe to forget prior transgressions. Whitaker quickly hit five homers in the International League, and earned a promotion to New York.

When he arrived in the Yankee clubhouse, Whitaker was greeted by Roger Maris. "What took you so long?" Maris asked. "We've been waiting for you to come up for a couple of years, you red-ass. If you didn't have such a red-ass, you would have been here." Maris, who was planning to retire after the season, was somewhat of an authority on being a red-ass. He took Whitaker under his wing. "Roger took me out on the field the very first day," Whitaker remembered, "before everyone else got there. He said, 'Hey, you're playing. I'm out of here. Now here's what you've got to do.' He showed me the ropes. He was my mentor for the first couple of months I was there."

The Yankees were in seventh place and, with nothing to lose, Houk put Whitaker in the lineup immediately. In his first major league game, the opposing pitcher was California's Dean Chance, who had won the Cy Young Award just two years earlier. Whitaker struck out his first time at bat, and got his first major league hit, a single, in the eighth inning. Then came a week of unprecedented success. "That first week in the big leagues was my career," Whitaker recalled. "If it would've stopped right there, I'd have been in the Hall of Fame."

On August 26, Whitaker had three hits against the Tigers, including a triple and his first major league home run. The next day, he had two doubles and hit an inside the park home run, just as Repoz had done during his first week in the big leagues. The *New York Times* raved about Whitaker's potential, citing his fluid left-handed swing, which was ideal for the short right field porch in Yankee Stadium. It was no coincidence that nearly all of the Yankees' potential superstars swung from the left side. "Pull, pull, pull, pull. That was the whole minor league mantra of the Yankees," Whitaker said. "You've got to pull the ball if you're a left handed hitter. If you hit anything to the left of second base, shame on you. The Yankees wanted all of us to yank it down that line, goddamn it. But what happens when they start throwing you slop on the outside corner and you're still trying to turn on the ball? You roll it to second or hit stupid little lazy fly balls to center field."

In late August of '66, however, American League pitchers hadn't figured that out. On the day following his inside the park homer, Whitaker hit a grand slam off Detroit's Mickey Lolich, giving him three homers, a triple, two doubles and three singles in his first 22 times at bat. As writer Joe Durso noted, it was the most impressive Yankee debut since that of Roger Repoz. "It was like a storybook." Whitaker recalled. "They couldn't get me out. I was really just glad to be there and was in awe of everything, so I just relaxed. There was no pressure. I felt I could fail because I wasn't supposed to be there. I'm playing with Mickey Mantle and Roger Maris. Christ, how can you not feel comfortable having those guys around you?"

The pitchers' grapevine is an effective one, however, and Whitaker's spectacular debut had gotten everyone's attention. "All of a sudden," he said, "they realized that all they had to do was get me mad. 'If you get him mad,' they discovered, 'you can get him out throwing stuff right down the middle.'" Whitaker worried a lot, and got angry at himself, but was never a real student of the game. "I just went out and played," he said. "I think I could have been a hell of a lot better player if I had analyzed the game to see what the good ballplayers do on a daily basis— how they prepare — how they adjust. In the big leagues it's all about adjustment. Every kid who gets called up is a good player, but the biggest thing in the big leagues is not so much getting there. It's being able to make adjustments and stay there. When they starting adjusting to me, I did not make the same adjustments back to them."

Whitaker failed to adjust to the pitchers and his average sank as the season moved toward its close. He wound up hitting .243, with seven home runs. Whitaker had tailed off after his spectacular start, but seven home runs in six weeks, and 32 altogether, along with 103 RBI, during the '66 season, were enough to get attention on a last place team. Whitaker received a big buildup over the winter. Mike Burke, the Yankee's new president, was a former movie maker, and thought Whitaker had what the sagging franchise needed. "Steve Whitaker," he said, "has all the equipment. And he has the chemistry that could give him star quality. A lot of virility, full of fire, an attractive personality."

When Whitaker reported to Fort Lauderdale the following spring, he was issued Number 9, now unused following the trade of Maris to St. Louis. "Jesus Christ," said Whitaker, "now you're stepping into a whole different deal. Not only was he somebody I idolized, he was Roger Maris. You're the next Mickey Mantle and you're wearing Roger Maris's number." Whitaker was also given Maris's old locker.

The pressure overwhelmed Whitaker. He hit several home runs during the exhibition schedule, and when the season began, was platooned with Bill Robinson, another projected superstar.

Whitaker was hitting for a high average, one of the best on the club, but he was not hitting home runs. Houk kept telling everyone how pleased he was with Whitaker's performance, but, as usual, Whitaker wasn't pleased with himself. "It wasn't happening," he said. "I was missing balls, hitting long fly balls and popping up." One day in Baltimore, he went 0 for 4 and sat in his locker after the game, sulking. "I was sitting in my locker — not on the chair in front of my locker — but in my locker. Houk came over and said, 'Goddamn it, get your fucking ass out of that locker. What the fuck is wrong with you. Grow up!'"

It would be many years before Whitaker took Houk's advice, and he continued to put unbearable pressure on himself. He took out his frustration on umpires, and was ejected several times. Whitaker finished the 1967 season with a .243 average, 11 home runs and 50 RBI in 122 games. It was a decent season, but Whitaker was completely frustrated. He had hit seven home runs in just over 100 at bats in 1966 and figured that in 500 at bats he should have hit 35 homers.

If 1967 was disappointing, the following year was an unmitigated disaster. Like Pepitone, who made an annual vow to get serious, Whitaker pledged each year that he would learn to curb his temper. He said 1968 would be the year in which he would control himself. Like Pepitone, Whitaker was unable to keep his pledges of good behavior. When he got off to a slow start, Whitaker was relegated to pinch hitting duty. His play was further disrupted by the fact that he had to commute to Fort Drummond, New York, to serve in the Army Reserve. Under such circumstances, it was impossible for Whitaker to keep his timing, and he batted poorly. He didn't field well and at times his baserunning was atrocious. Finally, while on duty at Fort Drummond, Whitaker received a telegram instructing him to report to Syracuse, the Yankees' Triple A farm club, when he finished his tour. He thought it was his buddies Stan Bahnsen and Frank Fernandez playing a joke on him. "It wasn't a joke," Whitaker recalled. "It was real."

After his hitch ended, rather than report to Syracuse, Whitaker drove to Atlantic City and hid for about ten days. Finally, he agreed to report to the minor leagues. Frank Verdi, the Syracuse manager, tried to motivate Whitaker by telling him he wanted him to be a team leader and show the young players how hard a former major leaguer would work to get back to New York. Whitaker had enough trouble looking after himself, let alone an entire team. "I wasn't prepared for that," he said. After only 11 games in Syracuse, Verdi benched Whitaker for lackadaisical play and the Yankees transferred his option to Hawaii. He had a good final month in Hawaii, and was recalled to New York to spend the final weeks of the season on the Yankee bench. In a disjointed season, Whitaker had only seven hits in 60 major league at bats.

"My days with the Yankees were over," he said. "I'd burned my bridges. In those days, you didn't jump a club. It was unheard of." The Yankees made Whitaker available in the expansion draft, and he was chosen by the Kansas City Royals, where he looked forward to a fresh start. "It was a new life," he said. "I thought, 'New York hates me. I did some bad things up there.' But now somebody else likes me, so I was feeling pretty good about myself."

Before spring training even started, Whitaker found himself in trouble again, this time not of his own making. In the spring of 1969, the players staged their first strike, which lasted from the beginning of spring training until late February. "I got a call from Moe Drabowsky," Whitaker recalled, "who was the player rep for the Royals. He said, 'Don't report to spring training.' Being a trooper, and being a free spirit, I said 'OK, if that's what you want, I will not report.' So I'm staying at my future wife's home in Hollywood, Florida. I turn on the tube and find out that everybody reported for Kansas City. Only three or four of us didn't."

When Whitaker finally arrived at camp, he was greeted by Royal General Manager Cedric Tallis. "He said, 'What the fuck are you doing?'" Whitaker remembered. "You should have been here a week before you were supposed to report!'" Whitaker was in the doghouse again. He rarely played in spring training, and on April 1 was traded to the Seattle Pilots for Lou Piniella, another marginal player who had chosen not to report. Piniella's cockiness had irritated people in Seattle as much as Whitaker's had offended those in Kansas City, and the two teams decided to exchange a left handed troublemaker for a right handed one.

When Whitaker arrived in Tempe, Arizona, the Pilots' training site, he was met by Pilot GM Marvin Milkes. "On the ride from the airport to the hotel," he recalled, "Milkes told me, 'If you ever pull any of that shit here, you are gone. You won't even have a uniform to think of putting on.' That was my introduction to the Seattle Pilots, so needless to say, I'm carrying the piano on my back from one club to another."

Splitting the '69 season between Seattle and Vancouver of the Pacific Coast League, Whitaker appeared in 69 Pilot games and batted .250 with six home runs. When the Pilots tried to send him to Vancouver, Whitaker went AWOL again, this time for two weeks, before deciding to report. "What was I going to do," he said, "be a bartender?"

The following spring, Whitaker was with the San Francisco Giants, and beat out former All Star Jim Ray Hart for the final position on the roster. After a few pinch hit appearances, he went off to fulfill his reserve duty. When he returned, he joined the Giants in Houston, going straight to the ballpark from the airport, arriving two hours before game time. "I was shaking hands with everybody," he said, "and feeling good about being back in a major league uniform when about five minutes before game time we find out that Willie [Mays] can't play. [Manager] Clyde King comes up to me and says, 'Whit, can you play?' What was I going to say? So I said, 'Sure, I can play. Are you kidding? Put me in there.'"

Swinging a bat for the first time in a month, Whitaker had the worst game of his life. He went 0 for 5, striking out all five times. "I don't even think I hit a loud foul ball," he recalled. "You couldn't have had a worse game." Although he hung on with the Giants a while longer, that was for all practical purposes the end of Whitaker's major league career. He was sent to Phoenix, where he set a club record for home runs, but had a run-in with manager Hank Sauer. Near the end of the season, the two nearly came to blows on the bench. Whitaker was now persona non grata in New York, Kansas City, Seattle and San Francisco, and was rapidly running out of major league venues.

Steve went on to play two seasons in Hawaii, a Pacific Coast League club that signed former big leaguers and made money selling them to major league clubs. Whitaker was not one of those who returned to the majors, but he enjoyed his time in the islands immensely. He played with fun-loving veterans like Bo Belinsky, Ray Oyler, George Brunet and Clete Boyer and made more money than he had in the big leagues. "I used to surf until two in the afternoon," he said, "ride to the park with sand still in my shorts, shower, eat some pineapple and play the game."

Whitaker retired in 1973 and moved to Fort Lauderdale, where he sells high end residential waterfront real estate. He began his real estate career during his playing days and has been a broker for 33 years. "I can't work for anybody," he said. "That's why I've got my own business." Whitaker's partner is his son Chad, a former minor league ballplayer who was drafted by the Cleveland Indians in 1995, but whose career was cut short by a series of hand injuries. "He didn't get mad when he struck out," Steve said. "He ran everything out. He was totally different than I was."

At sixty years of age, Whitaker is a much different person than the red-ass ballplayer of the 1960s. Jake Gibbs was surprised when he ran into him recently at a Yankee fantasy camp. "He's an entirely different guy," said Gibbs. "He's been a different guy for the six years that he's come to the camp." Whitaker is fully aware of what could have been but, unlike some athletes who were disappointed by their careers, holds no lasting bitterness. "I was able to go on," he said, "and drop the why me?—I should have—I could have been. I stopped that a long time ago. I never really looked back and felt sorry for myself. To make it to the big leagues, you had to have something. I can be proud of that."

With Repoz in Kansas City and Whitaker in the doghouse, the search for the next Mickey Mantle continued, a quest that was to be as futile as the Yankees search to reclaim past glory.

• 18 •

Sinking to the Depths
The 1966 Season

The Yankees simply could not believe they had finished sixth in 1965. "No matter where we went," said Elston Howard after his winter vacation, "somebody or other was bound to ask, 'What's wrong with the Yankees?' I told them that the Yankees weren't dead yet. Just watch us in '66." "We'll come back," said Ford. "The past year was disappointing," said Johnny Keane, "but not disillusioning. At full strength, we would have stayed in contention all year and I am sure the other American League clubs know it, too.... [I]t is inconceivable to me that what happened to the Yankees last year can be repeated in 1966."

The 1959 Yankees, as plagued by injury as the '65 crew, had bounced back from a subpar season to win the pennant in 1960. Joe Dimaggio said the Yankees would surprise a lot of people in 1966. He said the Yankees would win the pennant and Maris was the player to watch. Keane said the Yankees would win the pennant, but needed to run more, rather than wait for the three run homer. Pitching, not power, would be the Yankees' strength in 1966. Keane and Houk weren't too interested in trading to improve the club, since the value of most of their players had been diminished by their poor 1965 seasons. Surely they would do better in 1966. "Self-deception played a key role in the demise of the Yankee empire," wrote Leonard Koppett. "The years of victory created a belief in their own excellence that outlived that excellence."

Houk, at least outwardly, was one of the most deceived. "We'll be on top when the season ends," he confidently proclaimed," and compared the lineups of the Yankees and Twins, the '65 pennant winners, position by position. Houk declared that the Yanks were better at five, two were even, and grudgingly admitted that MVP Zoilo Versalles was better than anybody the Yankees could put at shortstop. In the outfield, he said he'd take Tresh over Harmon Killebrew, who'd averaged 47 home runs during the past three full seasons, and declared a healthy Maris the equal of two time batting champ Tony Oliva. The Yankees' pitching was better than that of the Twins, Houk declared.

The injury jinx that hit the Yankees in 1965 didn't figure to subside in '66, because the Yankees had become an old team, and older players are much more susceptible to injury than young players. Moreover, they generally require a longer period of recuperation.

Kubek, who was bedeviled by injuries in 1965, was lost before the 1966 season began. While in the Army in 1962, Kubek sustained a neck injury playing touch football. It had bothered him ever since, and more than ever in 1965. During the winter, Tony entered the Mayo Clinic for a series of tests. The doctors told him he risked permanent paralysis if he continued to play. A fusion operation was necessary, and a fusion operation would mean the end of Kubek's base-ball career. In late January, the 29-year-old shortstop announced his retirement.

Kubek's departure prolonged the career of his long time double play partner, Bobby Richardson. Richardson, a religious family man, had pondered retirement for the past couple of years, but he and Kubek agreed that they would not quit in the same year and leave the Yankees shorthanded at two infield positions. Richardson had made up his mind to quit after the 1964 season, when he reportedly didn't see eye to eye with Berra, but Houk had persuaded him to return in 1965. When Kubek announced his retirement, Richardson agreed to play at least one more season.

During the winter, it appeared as though Mantle might join Kubek in retirement. The 1965 season was his worst ever. "His blazing speed has been reduced to a low fire," wrote Arthur Daley. "He no longer can throw. His fielding has become uncertain and his hitting hampered by the aches, pains and restrictions of a reluctant body. Only his spirit is unquenchable." "I haven't made up my mind that I'm going to play next summer," Mantle said in December. "Last season was really an embarrassing one. I'm not going to continue to embarrass myself."

Surprisingly, the biggest problem was not Mantle's legs, but his right shoulder. In the 1957 World Series, Mantle was sliding back into second base when Braves' second baseman Red Schoendienst fell on his shoulder, injuring him to the extent that he missed the sixth game. The shoulder had bothered him ever since, and the pain became almost unbearable, even for Mantle, in 1965. After the 1964 season, Mickey had been playing football in his backyard with his sons and brothers. His brother Ray hit him hard on his blind side and aggravated the damage in his shoulder. By the end of the 1965 season, Mantle could barely swing from the left side, and was throwing sidearm from the outfield because it hurt too much to throw a ball with his normal motion. Opposing base runners took liberties and ran on Mantle as they never would have done a few years earlier. Although he appeared in 122 games, Mickey played only 36 full contests.

After three months of rest, the shoulder still hurt so much that Mantle decided to quit. Mickey went to New York to tell Houk of his decision, and the general manager talked him out of it. He said Mantle would be a valuable player even if he could play only 60 or 70 games, and didn't want to see him go out after a bad season. What Houk didn't say was that the Yankees needed Mantle at the box office. When the club played two exhibition games at Atlanta's new park prior to the 1966 season, the first game, in which Mantle wasn't expected to play, drew less than 14,000. When his presence was announced for the second game, the crowd exceeded 21,000. Mickey was the only drawing card the Yankees had left.

"When I came to New York a few days ago," Mantle said after his meeting with Houk, "I was seriously thinking of quitting. My shoulder hurt so much that I couldn't even throw a ball, my legs will never be any better, and I was pretty discouraged. But Ralph Houk talked things over with me and told me what the people and the team expect, and now I feel better about it and I'm willing to try." Houk urged Mantle to go to the Mayo Clinic to see if the doctors could help him. Mickey agreed to go, but withheld a decision on whether to play in 1966.

The doctors found a bone chip and inflamed tendons in Mantle's shoulder and operated on January 25th. They removed the bone chip, cut the tendons and re-attached them to a key-hole drilled in Mantle's upper arm. The doctors predicted a full recovery, but doubted that Mickey would be ready to play by opening day. When he did return, where would Mantle play? First base? Probably not, said Houk, and Keane agreed. Mantle had never played first, and the sudden starts and stops might be more difficult on his legs than the longer but straight-ahead bursts required in the outfield. He might be bunted to death. Leonard Koppett offered a novel suggestion. Mantle could pinch hit in every game, 162 times in the course of the season.

Mantle reported to Fort Lauderdale on March 1, after signing another $100,000 contract, sporting a six inch scar on his upper right arm. He was ahead of schedule all spring, taking batting practice much earlier than expected, although hitting only right handed against easy tosses. Although he hadn't attempted to throw yet, Mickey said he wanted to play the last six exhibition games and then start the season opener. By March 19, he was able to hit left-handed, although he still couldn't throw. On the 24th, he tried to throw but had to quit because of the pain. The season opener was just 19 days away. On the 25th, two weeks ahead of his original schedule, he made his first appearance as a pinch hitter and struck out.

Finally, on April 8, just four days before the opener, Mantle made his first start, playing six innings against the Braves in Atlanta. About ninety minutes before the game, he had gone to Keane and told him he wanted to play. Mantle got a single, and flipped the ball in underhanded from the outfield when it was hit to him. On April 12, when the Yankees opened the season against the Tigers, Mickey Mantle, true to his word, was in center field, and got a double and single in three at bats.

The other half of the M&M duo was in only slightly better health. Still recovering from his hand surgery, Maris took his time rounding into shape. His hand and wrist still bothered him during the first few days of camp and prevented him from taking batting practice. Maris improved gradually, played in his first game March 18, and, like Mantle, was ready for the start of the season.

While Maris and Mantle were able to play, no one, other than perhaps Houk, claimed they were anywhere near the players they were in 1960–62. Neither were the other Yankees. "I remember running into Dick Hall," said Bob Friend, who joined the Yankees in the spring of 1966. "I played with Dick at Pittsburgh, and I said to him, 'We're looking pretty good.' He said, 'Bob, you haven't seen these guys. They're not the same team they were three or four years ago.' I told him I hadn't seen that yet, and he said, 'You'll see it.'"

Ford, whose condition was so uncertain in the spring of 1965, was coming off a 16–13 record and said he hoped to have four more good years before he retired. That would give him 20 years in the big leagues, and a nice fat pension. Whitey often had arm trouble in spring training, but in the spring of 1966, he pitched and felt better than he had in many years. Of course, Florida weather in March was much more to Ford's liking than April in New York.

Ford looked good on opening day, although he lost 2–1 to the Tigers. To counteract the effect of the cold on Whitey's arm, one of the New York trainers took an empty plastic deodorant bottle and filled it with hot water, a device Ford used frequently in 1965. He put the bottle in his back pocket, and used it between pitches to warm his fingers. After Whitey retired the opening Tiger batter in the first inning, Detroit manager Charley Dressen popped out of the dugout and complained to the umpires that Ford was using a foreign substance, which was illegal. The umpires agreed and made Ford discard the bottle. A few days later, a hot water bottle arrived in Dressen's hotel room, accompanied by a card signed "Whitey Ford." Ford, long known as a practical joker, disavowed any knowledge of the prank. The Rules Committee, which had little sense of humor, issued an edict stating that the bottle was forbidden.

For the first month of the season, Whitey pitched magnificently, although he did not win a game. In his first 39 innings, he was 0–3 but had a 2.08 ERA. One loss was by a 1–0 score and another the opening day 2–1 defeat. On May 13, after pitching two scoreless innings against the Athletics, Ford had to come out of the game because of soreness in his elbow. He rested a couple of weeks and tried to come back, but could pitch only one inning before the pain returned. When Whitey didn't respond to treatment and rest, he was placed on the disabled list in early June.

During the winter, when the Yanks were unsure whether Kubek would return, they acquired shortstop Ruben Amaro from the Phillies for Phil Linz. Linz, the Yankees felt, was no better than a utility player, who lacked sufficient range to play shortstop regularly. His best position was second base. "It was so much easier to play than shortstop," Linz said. "I had no problem turning the double play. I had good, quick hands and no fear of the runner." But the Yankees needed a shortstop and didn't think Linz was their man. Linz had loved Houk when he managed the Yankees, but when Houk was promoted to general manager, the relationship changed. Instead of telling his players how great they were, Houk had to tell them about all their shortcomings at salary time. When Linz held out prior to the 1964 season, Houk referred to his salary "demand" as "rather fantastic." "[W]hen you consider that in 186 at bats he drove in just 12 runs," Houk said, "I don't think that should call for any fabulous increase." How could Houk, who had always told Linz what a valuable player he was, tell him now that he didn't deserve much of a raise?

Amaro was a slick fielding 30-year-old who had been in the major leagues since 1958. His father, Santos, was in the Cuban Hall of Fame, and his mother had been a noted softball player. If Kubek couldn't return, Houk and Keane believed Amaro could play shortstop every day. He was not much of a hitter, but he had shown he could do the job defensively, having won a Gold Glove in 1964. Amaro, however, was not quite as quick as he had been and a scouting report filed in 1965 read, "He's getting a little lardy around the rear, and he doesn't have the range he did, but it's still better than the average." Amaro had played little shortstop in 1965, spending most of his time at first base for late inning defense.

Amaro opened the season at short, but his tenure was short-lived. In the fifth game of the season, he sprinted into short left field in pursuit of a popup. Tresh came in from left and, to avoid a collision, tried to slide under Amaro as the latter made the catch. Tresh's hit Amaro's leg, bent it backwards and tore ligaments in the shortstop's right knee. Ruben was placed on the disabled list and missed virtually the entire season. Kubek was gone and, now, so was his replacement. At Houk's insistence, Bobby Murcer, a 19-year-old rookie with less than two years of professional experience, replaced Amaro at short.

"In those years," said Tresh, "the Yankees signed a lot of shortstops. There's usually a lot of action at shortstop so most high schools and colleges put one of their best players there. The Yankees found they could sign shortstops and then move them around. Mantle was a shortstop. I was a shortstop. So were Kubek, Richardson, Horace Clarke and Roy White. Jake Gibbs was a third baseman. They got a lot of those kinds of guys and then, wherever the openings were, they moved them into them."

In 1966, the open position was shortstop, and the Yankees hoped that Murcer would be the one to fill it. During the spring, many hopeful comparisons had been drawn. Murcer was a young, raw shortstop from Oklahoma, like Mantle, who was also the last 19-year-old Yankee starter. He had a scatter arm like Mantle displayed when he played shortstop. He was just one year younger than Kubek when Tony was Rookie of the Year in 1957. He was signed by Tom Greenwade, the same scout who procured Mantle. Murcer, who grew up in Oklahoma City, not in a small town like Mantle, was much more mature and relaxed than Mickey had been at the same age,

Murcer, who batted .365 for Johnson City in 1964 and .322 for Greensboro in '65, made five errors in eleven games after being called up in September, 1965. He hit very well in exhibition games the following spring, but his fielding was reminiscent of the young Mantle. In the minors, his wild throws were legendary. "You couldn't sit women and children behind first base," recalled John Miller. "Bobby would field the ball," said Jack Cullen, "and throw it right into the stands. He had a strong arm, but it wasn't accurate." "Murcer was a shortstop," recalled Ray Barker, "and I said, 'god, what do you have that boy out there for?' He was a terrible shortstop." Even at 19, however, Murcer was a good hitter, and earned a place on the Yankee squad with his bat.

In his first game after taking over for Amaro, Murcer committed three errors, one of which led to the winning run. His tenure as the starting shortstop lasted less than a week. He had one hit in 14 at bats, and clearly needed seasoning in the field. "If we were going better," said Keane, "I might have left Murcer in. We could have helped him by helping ourselves. But the pressure has been on the youngster." Murcer was sent to Toledo in early May.

With Amaro and Murcer, the two top shortstops, out of the picture, who would start? In 1962, Tresh had been the All Star shortstop, but he hadn't played the infield since August of that year. When Boyer first came to the major leagues, he was considered one of the slickest fielding young shortstops in the game. In 1962, when Kubek went into the Army, one of the options had been to move Boyer to short, but Houk didn't want to do it. If Boyer made the move now, who would play third? Keane decided to do what he had wanted to do all along, move Tresh back to the infield, at third base, and shift Boyer to short. Rookie Roy White, who had gotten off to a hot start, took over Tresh's position in left field. "This is not a desperation move," Keane said. "I think it will produce."

Tresh, who had adapted so well to the outfield, was not enthusiastic about his new position. "As it turned out," he said recently, "it wasn't a very good move. I believe the thinking was that since I hadn't played short in quite a while, we'd have a better combination by moving Boyer to short and me to third. I'd never played third before. Clete was a great third baseman and had the tools and reflexes to play third, but wasn't fast. I think my tools were better for playing short and in hindsight, it might have been better to bring me back to short and leave him at third."

Tresh, in 64 games at third, didn't play that badly, despite his lack of experience. He made just nine errors, but couldn't come close to matching the brilliance of Boyer. The throws from third base hurt his arm, which affected his batting. Boyer fielded adequately at short, but not as well as he did at third. White fell into a deep slump and found himself on the bench. In July, the Yankees moved Boyer back to third and Tresh to left, putting an end to the experiment. Veteran Dick Schofield, obtained as a utility man from the Giants in May, took over at short.

Schofield, whose main claim to fame was owning perhaps the largest and most diverse wardrobe in the major leagues, was damaged goods. "I'd hurt my arm early in the season," he recalled, "and I couldn't throw. I couldn't play when I got to the Yankees and thought, 'Why am I going there?'" Not only couldn't Schofield throw, he couldn't hit. After batting just .155, and making nine errors in 19 games at short, he was sold to the Dodgers.

For the last two months of the season Horace Clarke, who began the season as Toledo's second baseman, was the Yankee shortstop. By the time the year was over, Amaro had played 14 games at short, Murcer 18, Boyer 59, Schofield 19, and Clarke 63. With Tresh and Boyer each playing third at various times, the left side of the infield was unsettled all year.

The catching was handled by a platoon of Howard and Jake Gibbs. Howard claimed his arm was sound, but other teams were running on him like they never had before. He was also hitting well below .200. Howard swore he wasn't about to quit, but it was clear that Houk needed to find a replacement soon.

Gibbs, the Yanks' first big bonus signee, was the most likely candidate. He had been an All American third baseman at the University of Mississippi, but was much better known as the All-American quarterback who led Ole Miss to victory in the 1961 Sugar Bowl, scoring both of his team's touchdowns. Gibbs was a good runner, as were most college quarterbacks in 1960, but he also threw 12 touchdown passes his senior year. While that total pales with current records, one must remember that Gibbs threw just 109 passes all season.

When he signed with the Yankees in '61, Gibbs spent a few days in New York to work out with the team and to allow Houk and his coaches see what they had spent $100,000 on. Gibbs likewise learned a lot about life in the major leagues. "We lost some games in Chicago," he recalled, "and I remember Ralph Houk getting upset with the pitchers, having a clubhouse meeting and really getting on their ass. He said he'd send their ass down to Triple A. I said, 'Holy shit, I've been up here eleven days and I've seen everything."

Gibbs made his major league debut late in the '62 season, as a pinch runner. "I looked up at the Stadium," he said, "and there was 50,000 people [actually 22,014] looking down at me. I was used to playing in front of three or four thousand. I got real nervous. I kept telling myself, 'Don't get picked off.'" Gibbs got to third, and tagged up on a fly ball to right. "Crosetti said, 'Tag up,'" he recalled, "'I think you can make it.' I tag up and I started running and sayin,' 'If you ever run fast, this is the time to run fast.'" Gibbs ran fast and scored his first major league run to tie the game.

After the season, Gibbs reported to Fort Gordon to fulfill his reserve obligations. One Saturday morning, he was walking around the base when a captain noticed his name tag and asked, "Are you the Gibbs that belongs to the Yankees?" He was, Gibbs replied. "You're going to be a catcher when you go to spring training," the captain informed him. The officer knew the general manager of the Yankees' Augusta farm club, who had told him of the planned switch before anyone told Gibbs. "That shocked the hell out of me," Gibbs said recently. "I thought I had a pretty good year at shortstop."

At first, Gibbs resisted the change. The Yankees had no one behind Howard, Houk told him. What about Alan Hall and Bill Madden, who had received large bonuses? They weren't going to make it, Houk said. Gibbs wasn't enthused, but told Houk he would try it. During the spring of '63, Gibbs worked with Jim Hegan to learn the rudiments of catching. Houk told Gibbs that if he didn't like it, he could return to the infield.

For three days, Gibbs warmed up pitchers in the bullpen. Then he caught batting practice. Houk asked him how he liked it. "I don't like it," Gibbs replied. "Let's give it one more week," Houk said. "That's how it all started," Gibbs said. "After a week I didn't feel too bad."

"I had pretty good hands," said Gibbs, "and I had good feet. I could catch the ball, but I didn't know anything about pitching. When you play third base, you don't really study the pitching like you should. Mentally, I just wasn't there at all."

Gibbs caught his first game in late March, and Houk was effusive in his praise. Was he worried about broken fingers, Gibbs was asked after the game. He tapped his knuckles on a wooden bench and replied, "I'm not worried." Gibbs agreed to go to Richmond and, by catching every day, learn the trade. "I was catching pitchers who were trying to get to the big leagues," he said, "and pitchers who'd been to the big leagues and were trying to get back, and here they are throwing to a catcher that had five weeks experience in spring training. I'd watch the other catchers to see how they did things. I learned a lot by watching people."

Gibbs's biggest problem was getting his hand out of the way of foul tips. As an infielder in 1962, he'd suffered a broken thumb. In the third game of the 1963 season, Gibb's first as a catcher, Buffalo's Pumpsie Green fouled a ball which hit Gibbs on the third finger of his exposed right hand. "It just shattered the joint," Gibbs recalled. "The finger was killing me, but I stayed in the game. Pumpsie hit the ball to the second baseman, and goddamned if he didn't make an error, so I've got to stay out there for another batter with the finger just throbbing." At the end of the inning, Gibbs went to the bench and, when Manager Preston Gomez saw his finger, to the hospital. The finger was broken.

The bone was set in Buffalo, and Gibbs flew to New York to be examined by Dr. Gaynor, the Yankees' physician. "I went to his office," said Gibbs, "and he takes off that l'il ol' cast they'd put on there. He just mashed my finger and I threw up in his garbage can. That's how it all started as a catcher." Gibbs was sidelined for seven weeks and sat home with his wife, chafing at the inactivity. "We were watching TV," he recalled, "baking a cake a week and I was getting fat and out of shape. Finally I started playing again and damned if three weeks later I didn't break another finger. My wife and I were laying in bed one night, and I said, 'Trish, this ain't workin' out. I just want to throw these damn shin guards in the river out there. I think I'll call Blanton Collier.'" After graduating from Ole Miss, Gibbs had been drafted by both the Cleveland Browns of the NFL and the Houston Oilers of the AFL. Gibbs had known Collier, the Browns' coach, when Collier was at the University of Kentucky. He told his wife he was going to call Collier in the morning and see if he needed a quarterback.

"I never called him," Gibbs said, "because I ain't that type of person. Once I've made a decision I'm gonna stay with it and make the best of it." Gibbs came back and finished the season at Richmond, and was called up by the Yankees in September. He spent the entire '64 season at Richmond, again troubled by injuries, and was called up for the final month of the season. When Kubek was injured, Gibbs was told that he would be activated for the Series. "I felt bad for Tony," Gibbs said, "but I felt good that I was on the list. Everybody looks forward to being in a World Series." On the final Sunday of the season, the day after the Yanks clinched the pennant, Gibbs caught against the Cleveland Indians. The game went into extra innings, and in the 13th, another foul tip caught him on the index finger, broke it, and chipped a bone in his middle finger. Gibbs was off the Series roster.

Gibbs was called up during the 1965 season, but appeared in just 37 games, frequently as a pinch hitter. He was becoming a good defensive catcher, but he wasn't hitting that well, and showed little power. For $100,000, the Yankees expected a slugger, but Gibbs never hit more than eight home runs in a minor league season. His offense suffered when he became a catcher, due to the tremendous concentration required to study the hitters, call the pitches and manage the game. Gibbs also felt the pressure of having received the largest bonus in Yankee history. "I was playing third base in Buffalo," he recalled, "and somebody in the stands yelled out, 'Have you got your money belt tied around your waist?' You could hear them talking about it. There is a certain amount of pressure on any young guy going to New York. I wanted to do as good as I possibly could, knowing that the Yankees were rich in catching history, from Bill Dickey to Yogi to Howard. You want to do as good as they did, but you know you probably ain't going to be as good as they were. But at least you want to be respected as a catcher. I think I put too much pressure on myself when I started catching."

In 1966, with Howard aging and sometimes ailing, the Yankees decided to find out whether Gibbs could catch in the big leagues. He got off to a good start, and was hitting over .300 in limited action. Gibbs caught more and more as the summer went on, and wound up hitting .258 in 62 games before his season was again ended by injury. This time, rather than breaking a finger, Gibbs broke his entire arm, which put him on the shelf in August.

With Ford's status questionable, and Bouton injured, the Yankees had acquired veteran pitcher Bob Friend from the Pirates. Friend was a 35-year-old right hander who had spent his entire big league career, spanning 15 seasons, with Pittsburgh. Thrown into a major league rotation at the age of 20 with a terrible Pirate team, Friend persevered and learned how to pitch. "A lot of us were there as prospects," he recalled. "We weren't solid major league players. We learned how to play in the big leagues."

Friend had to pitch under the dual handicaps of having a last place team behind him and the irascible Branch Rickey looking over his shoulder from the front office. After the 1954 season, Rickey said that if Friend didn't pitch better, he'd be sent to the minor leagues. Rickey shook the young pitcher's confidence on many occasions and once told manager Fred Haney not to use Friend as a starter. Haney 'hid' Friend by starting him only on the road, or on Sundays, when the religious Rickey didn't come to the park, until Friend experienced enough success to assuage Rickey.

In the late '50s, the Pirates got better and so did Friend. In 1955, he became the first pitcher to lead the league in ERA while pitching for a last place team. Friend won 22 games in 1958 and, by the time he arrived in New York, had 191 major league victories. He was a reliable starter who went to the post every four days. Each year since 1955, he'd pitched at least 200 innings.

Expansion had given many players an opportunity to play in the big leagues. It had given Friend a chance to prosper. During the first two and a half years of the expanded National League, he was 40–36. Against the Mets and Colts he was 16–3, while he was just 24–33 against the seven other clubs. In 1965, despite a fine 3.24 ERA, Friend was 8–12, only the second time since 1955 that he failed to win at least ten games.

Friend was a well-respected, educated man, who earned a business degree from Purdue in eight years by taking classes every winter. He was the player representative for the National League and served during the winter as assistant to the president of Commercial Bank and Trust Company and as a director of his own investment company. "What a prince he was," said former teammate Jack Lamabe. "What a gentleman. He was a first class gentleman."

During the winter of 1965–66, the Yankees acquired Friend from Pittsburgh for Mikkelsen, who had spent part of the 1965 season in the minors and fallen out of favor in New York. In Florida, Friend spent most of his time with pitching coach Jim Turner trying to get his curve ball to break. "That was the shock of my life," he said. "I couldn't get that curve ball to break. That's the first thing that goes. I know you lose a little steam off your fastball, but I just couldn't get that damn curve to break."

Friend never found the break on his curve ball, and couldn't get going once the season started. He made eight starts and four relief appearances and managed just one win. Sometimes he started out strong, but always seemed to fade. On June 15, the trade deadline, he was sold to the Mets. "I just didn't produce up there in New York," Friend said. "I pitched about one good game for the Yankees. I think maybe I tried too hard."

With Friend gone and Ford disabled, the Yankees had lost two fifths of their starting rotation. Another two fifths wasn't exactly setting the world on fire. Downing was inconsistent and Bouton, despite pitching well on occasion, wasn't winning. Stafford, only 27, reached the end of his Yankee career. He was sent to the minor leagues at the end of spring training, recalled in June, and immediately traded to Kansas City.

Fortunately, Keane discovered a rookie left hander with good stuff and remarkable control. Fred (Fritz) Peterson started the 1965 season in A ball at Greensboro but, after posting an 11–1 record and a 1.50 ERA, was promoted to Double A Columbus, where he won five more games. Given only an outside shot to make the club in spring training, Peterson opened Keane's eyes with some fine pitching. In his first 23 innings of exhibition work, he surrendered just three walks. For any pitcher, that was pinpoint control. For a rookie lefthander, it was downright remarkable. When the regular season started, Peterson was even better, giving up just one walk in his first 29 innings. He was so intent on not walking anyone, in fact, that sometimes his control was too good. He had to learn that there were times when it was better to give up a walk than a big hit. Peterson beat out Bouton for the fifth starting position, and when Friend and Ford faltered, became a regular starter.

Early in the year, Stottlemyre was the anchor of an unstable rotation. Mel got off to a terrific start and appeared poised to duplicate his 20 win season of 1965. By the end of May, despite having just a 5–4 record, he had a 2.17 ERA, and was the only starter Houk could rely on to produce a solid performance whenever he got the ball. Stottlemyre made the All Star team, where he became the first Yankee pitcher since Ralph Terry to face Willie McCovey. Mel did what many thought Terry should have done. He gave McCovey an intentional walk.

The biggest surprises on the pitching staff were Peterson and Dooley Womack, a 26-year-old right hander who had been in the Yankee farm system since 1958. Womack, like so many minor leaguers, was never given a long look by the Yankees because he wasn't big and didn't throw hard. Early in his career, people told Womack he needed to learn another pitch. He developed a sinker, won ten games with a 2.32 ERA in 1964 and had a fine 10–4 record with a league-leading 2.17 ERA for Toledo in 1965. "After the 1965 season," Womack recalled, "I heard that there were four ballclubs after me. My father-in-law came to visit us one morning and said he read in the paper — we couldn't afford a paper — he read in the paper that the Yankees had added me to the 40 man roster. My wife and I were shocked — or should I say pleasantly surprised. That day, in the middle of winter, I started running.

"When we reported to Fort Lauderdale, the first people we went to see were Jake Gibbs and his wife. Jake had been my catcher at Toledo the year before, and he told me, 'Dooley, you can make this ballclub. But you have to bust your buns. It's not going to be easy. Jake gave me an incentive. He had a new glove. Remember, in those days, when you played in the minor leagues, you bought your own equipment. I'd been using these old gloves that I'd buy and they'd wear out, but I'd keep using them because I couldn't afford a new glove. I was married, and didn't have much money, so I'd say, 'This glove's still in good shape, I can use it.' Well, Jake told me, 'If you make this ballclub, this MacGregor glove is yours.' That was my incentive."

Womack worked as hard as he could that spring. He ran, and ran, and ran. "I ran my way to the big leagues," he said. "My locker was located right at the door of the clubhouse. All they had to do was push my bag out the door and I was gone." Womack pitched well enough to make sure that no one had any reason to push his bag out the door. "This has been a make-or-break spring for [Womack] after a good year at Toledo," Leonard Koppett wrote. "Either he's ready now or not likely ever to be." Just before the Yankees left Florida, they optioned Stafford, a major leaguer since 1960, to Toledo, opening up a roster spot for Womack. Finally, in his ninth season of professional baseball, he was in the major leagues.

Womack was not out of the woods yet. By cutdown day, when the Yanks had to reduce the roster to 25, Womack had pitched just six innings and was a candidate to be sent to Toledo. He had options remaining and others who might be sent out did not. One of those was Bouton, trying to come back from his arm problems of 1965. After his 4–15 season, Bouton was the subject of trade discussions during the winter, signed for a $3,000 pay cut, and nearly lost his spot on the staff after a terrible spring. He gave up six home runs in his first 10 exhibition innings, a sure sign that his arm was not healthy. Bouton made the team, but pitched only one inning in the first seven weeks of the season. Houk wanted to send him to the minors, but couldn't get waivers, and had to keep him or lose him. Just two years earlier, Bouton won 18 games, and Houk was not about to give away a 27-year-old pitcher with that kind of ability. Bouton stayed.

Jack Cullen, who had pitched well in 1965, and sparingly in '66, was the one to go. "I wanted to see more of Dooley Womack," Houk said. "[Cullen] wasn't bad, and he wasn't great, but I'm sure he has a major league future." "We'd only won four games and I had one win and one save," Cullen said. Just a few days earlier he pitched the best game of his big league career, seven shutout relief innings, during which he allowed just three hits and got the win. "We were in Minnesota," he recalled. "It was a cold day, and Houk called me up and told me to come to his room because he had to talk to me. He said he had ten pitchers and I was the only one he could get waivers on. Houk told me that if I went down, he'd bring me back in a month. That just kind of took the heart out of me. I'd had a great year in '65 [14–5 at Toledo and 3–4 with the Yankees] and I thought, 'What have I got to do to make this team?' I got kind of disheartened. I went down to breakfast in the morning and I was beside myself. Lu Clinton sat next to me and said, 'What's the matter?' I told him they sent me out. He said, 'You've got to be kidding me! How could they send you out?' I told him they said I was the only guy they could get waivers on."

Contrary to Houk's assurances, Cullen didn't come back in a month. He didn't come back at all that year — or ever. "I didn't have my heart in it after that," he said. "I'd always wanted to be with the Yankees and when I got sent down, I just kind of went through the motions." Cullen went to Toledo, then was traded to the Dodger organization and finished his career in the Pacific Coast League, never pitching in the majors again. Like John Blanchard, Cullen left baseball emotionally the day he left the Yankees.

Womack, the survivor, saw increasing activity as the season wore on. There was ample opportunity in the 1966 Yankee bullpen. Ramos was not as effective as he had been in 1965, nor was Reniff, and Hamilton was used mainly in long relief and against left handed hitters. Womack pitched in 42 games and was 7–3 with four saves. He had a 2.64 ERA and a new glove, courtesy of Jake Gibbs. During one stretch late in the summer, Dooley strung together 26 consecutive scoreless innings. By the end of the year, Womack was Houk's most reliable bullpen operative.

Houk? What happened to Keane? Poor Johnny's misfortunes of the 1965 season had continued into the winter months. At Christmas, he was playing with his grandchildren and their toys when he was hit by a piece of metal, which led to surgery for a detached retina. Despite his travails, however, Keane, at least outwardly, exuded confidence in the spring. "Now we start a second season," he said, "and I just can't believe it will be like the last one."

It wasn't like the last one. It was worse — and much shorter. With Mantle and Maris below par, the shortstop position a gaping hole, Ford hurt and Friend ineffective, the Yankees got off to a horrible start. By losing 10 of their first 11 games, the Yankees produced the poorest beginning in the 64 year history of the franchise. Even the infamous last place team of 1912 had done better.

The 1966 Yankees couldn't score. The defense was porous. The bullpen was weak, as Ramos was the losing pitcher three times in the Yankees' first eight games. Keane, beginning to show signs of desperation, used eight different lineups in those eight games. Maris and Mantle combined for just two RBI in their first 76 at bats.

Koppett wrote in late April, "Hitting, pitching and fielding have all failed in the clutch and mental mistakes have been piled upon mechanical errors. The team has been disorganized, depressed and self-defeating." The 1966 Yankees even had trouble with college teams. In the annual exhibition game against Army on April 29, the woeful Yankees won 1–0, but managed just four hits off Cadet pitchers. Other signs of the Yankees' fall from grace were more subtle. In the old days, other clubs saved their best pitchers for the Yankees. In early May, when the Indians were in New York, Cleveland manager Birdie Tebbetts pulled his ace, Sam McDowell, out of rotation so he could skip pitching against the Yankees and be ready for a big series against Baltimore.

In early May, when the Yankees traveled to Anaheim, strong rumors were circulating that Keane would be fired. On May 7, Koppett wrote a story to that effect in the *Times*. The Yankees (then 4–16) couldn't get better players, he theorized, and their only hope was to get better performances from the ones they had. A new manager, especially if his name was Ralph Houk, might be able to achieve that. "If anyone at all can help," Koppett wrote, "Houk has the best chance.... The faith of the older Yankee players in him, justified or not, is all but mystical." Keane was a decent man, but he was a manager from the old school. He didn't relate to the players as Houk did, and didn't pump them up when they were going badly, as they were in 1965 and 1966. The players wanted Houk back.

The same day Koppett's article appeared, the change was announced. Dan Topping, recovering from pneumonia in Miami, called Houk and followed with a telegram which read: "Have decided we simply must make change, despite our efforts and hope to snap out of this. As discussed, Johnny Keane will be relieved immediately and you will be appointed manager on a four year contract." Dan Topping, Jr. was named acting general manager, although Houk would be responsible for player trades. It was rumored that Roy Hamey would emerge from retirement to put the successful Hamey-Houk team back together again.

Keane was the baseball equivalent of Herbert Hoover — a decent man in the wrong place at the wrong time. "Houk went on that road trip to California with us," said Jake Gibbs, "and the first day we were there, there was a big meeting and the next thing we knew, Johnny Keane had been relieved of his duties. I believe every player in that locker room went into Keane's office and told him they were sorry to hear about it. I did. That was just showing the guy respect. I didn't play that much for him, but I went in and told him I was sorry to see him go."

"He really showed me some guts," said Elston Howard, "the way he stood up there and told us. You had to feel for him." "It's good that it's over," added Richardson. "It's even better for Keane to be out of this tense situation, the way things developed. He's a fine man." "It's a shame," said Ford. "We never did anything for him. Last year everybody was hurt and this year nobody hit. It's not his fault." "All the guys wished him well," said Cullen. "He said, 'Don't worry about me. Take care of yourself.'" Pepitone, who'd been dating Keane's daughter Pat, an attractive 26-year-old divorcee, wondered if he'd have to find a new girlfriend.

"I was touched by the way the players reacted," Keane said. " I didn't expect it and, because they didn't have to do it, it was pretty big of them. It made me feel mighty good." He left immediately for New York to retrieve his belongings and think about what he wanted to do next.

Houk appeared in the dugout the next day wearing Maris's sweatshirt, Mantle's shoes and Pete Mikkelsen's old number 51 rather than his customary 35. He won his first game as manager, and took to the job with his usual enthusiasm. Houk had never really liked being out of the dugout, and his two year hiatus had made him eager to get back. "I didn't realize how good it felt to be back in uniform," he said shortly after assuming command, "and I've gotten the biggest kick out of things I hadn't even been conscious of before-the look of happy satisfaction on the face of a player when he does good. And then there is the realization that you are a part of it. It's a nice feeling.

"I think something can shake this club up," Houk said. "I still believe it can win a pennant — that may shock a lot of people — but if I didn't believe it, I wouldn't go back to managing. We still have 142 games to play-right?" Many of the players felt the same way. "You felt like, the Major is back and things are going to get back to normal," said Gibbs. "It was great," said Ray Barker. "All the guys felt, well, now we're back in the groove. We've got the man here who has led us to the World Series before. They all liked Johnny Keane, but he just wasn't the horse they needed to lead them. Ralph Houk was. When he came back as manager, everybody was happy. We said, 'This is it.' We jumped in there and the clutch hits started coming. Everybody started playing a little bit better. The defense was right and all of a sudden we fell back into the old groove."

"I think they thought, 'This guy is going to help us,'" said Friend. "I don't know if it was real. I don't know if they thought we had the stuff to bounce back. It might have been false, but there was real enthusiasm there for Ralph Houk, no question about it."

Arthur Daley reviewed the situation from a more objective posture. "Now it's Houk who's stuck with a disintegrated ballclub," he wrote. "From a short term viewpoint, everything is in his favor. Things can't get worse and every notch his team advances will be to his credit…. But from a long term viewpoint, the outlook is different. The old heroes are wearing out and no successors are in sight. Inferior performance by name stars have destroyed their attractiveness in trades…. What once was baseball's proudest and most successful dynasty is in trouble." Daley might have added that, despite the euphoria which accompanied Houk's return to the dugout, no team had ever won a pennant after changing managers in mid-season, and none had ever come from as far back as the 12 games the Yankees were behind when Houk assumed command.

The Yankees won the first three games Houk managed, and many of the players began to believe there was indeed magic in the Major's presence. Houk planned to junk the running game and win with power, which is what had worked before and was the strategy the players wanted. The clubhouse was looser and the players were happier. Tony Kubek, in his first season as an NBC announcer, visited the team in Minnesota and said, "[I]t was amazing. They were ten games or so out of first place, but they're all talking about winning the pennant now."

By May 28, the team had won 13 of 17 games under Houk, pulling them up to 17–20. Ramos, who'd been hit hard early, and chewed out by Keane for his poor play, saved eight straight games. Richardson, who'd been contemplating retirement, regained his enthusiasm. Pepitone and Maris started hitting. The Yanks committed only six errors in their first 17 games under Houk, after 23 in 20 games for Keane. The club moved from tenth to sixth place and believed it was only a matter of time before they would be in fifth, then fourth and then ... who knew?

The euphoria was short-lived. Houk could not conjure up miracles without talent, and the Yankees soon reverted to form. Maris, Boyer and Howard were injured, and Ford was unable to return to the rotation. Even Stottlemyre joined the slumpers. His earned run average climbed as the season progressed, and by the end of the year he had a 12–20 record with a 3.80 ERA. Stottlemyre was the first Yankee to lose 20 games since Sad Sam Jones lost 21 in 1925.

Despite all the problems, Houk insisted he could win the pennant with just a little luck and a bit more pitching. Just before the trading deadline, in the first trade the Yankees made after the change in management, Houk acquired pitcher Fred Talbot from Kansas City for Repoz, Stafford and young pitcher Gil Blanco. Talbot was "the man everyone's been after," according to Houk, a rugged 24-year-old, 200-pounder, who was 4–4 with a 4.79 ERA for Kansas City. Houk called the deal a "major coup." Perhaps the magic of the Yankee pinstripes would transform Talbot into another Stottlemyre. They didn't, and Talbot pitched in New York much as he had pitched in Kansas City, winning seven and losing seven.

By July, the early optimism of the Houk era was gone, replaced by the dull realization that the Major had a tough job on his hands. No one was talking about a pennant; the best anyone hoped for was a first division finish. "It is too apparent," wrote Washington columnist Shirley Povich, "that the main thing wrong with the Yankees is their day-to-day lineup. There aren't enough good ballplayers in it, and the best ones are either too old or too brittle." "We had a tired club," said Steve Whitaker.

The sorry state of the Yankees was emphasized, Koppett noted, not just by the fact that they were losing, but by who was victimizing them. From 1920 through 1964, the Yankees had won two thirds of their games from second division clubs. Now the Yanks had just been beaten by the pitching of Boston rookie Darrell Brandon and the hitting of Red Sox second baseman George Smith. In nine games against the Yankees, Smith was batting .371 with three home runs and 13 RBI. Against the rest of the league, in 58 games, he was hitting .209, with three homers and 13 RBI. Light-hitting Ken Berry of the White Sox hit three home runs against the Yankees in a single series. Would such mediocre players have bothered the Yankee championship teams?

The player who tormented the Yankees the most during their difficult years was first baseman Fred Whitfield of the Indians, a big, left hand hitter who had been acquired from the Cardinals after the 1962 season. In 1963, during a beanball battle precipitated by Pepitone, Whitfield was punched by the Yankee first baseman. That was the last time any Yankee got the better of Fred Whitfield. "You'd hear comments like, 'Whitfield's average is going up. The Yankees are coming to town,'" recalled Al Luplow. Whitfield had his best season in 1965, hitting 26 home runs. Ten of them, plus 26 RBI, were against the Yankees.

In 1966, Whitfield picked up where he left off, beating Stottlemyre with a three run homer the first time the two clubs met. The following night, he hit a game winning two run shot off Ramos, giving him 12 homers in 20 games against the Yanks. On May 4, Whitfield hit a game winning home run off Hamilton, and in rapid succession delivered game winning hits off Friend, Stottlemyre and Peterson. In August he hit two more homers off Stottlemyre, giving him 79 career home runs, 21 against the Yankees. Whitfield did more damage to the Yankees in 1967 before, fortunately, he was traded out of the American League.

At the All Star break, the Yankees were 36–48, in ninth place, 20½ games behind the first place Orioles, who were running away with the American League pennant. After the same number of games in 1965, the year the Yankees had insisted had been a drastic aberration, they had been 40–44, in sixth place, 13½ games behind.

Stottlemyre, despite his 7–10 record, and Richardson were the only Yankees named to the All Star team. For the second year in a row, there was no Yankee in the starting lineup. Mantle, who had pulled a hamstring muscle just before the break, was not a member of the squad, although he had a very good first half of the season, batting .281 with 18 home runs and 41 RBI. In late June, he tied a major league record with seven home runs in five games. If Mickey could do equally as well during the second half, and finish with 36 homers, it would be quite a comeback season.

For a while, that seemed very possible. On July 29, Mantle hit his 21st home run of the season, his 14th in his last 24 games. Between June 23 and July 30, in 27 starts, he batted .369, with 15 home runs. A homer on the 30th, the 494th of his career, moved him past Lou Gehrig for sixth place on the all time list.

Maris, who had also been injured, returned to the lineup late in July, and the Yankees began to win again. They ripped off a six game streak, their longest in two years, and moved up to seventh place. From May 7, when Houk managed his first game, through July 25, the Yankees had the second best record in the league (41–35), trailing only the Orioles, managed by Houk's old buddy Hank Bauer. "Even if not a contender," wrote Koppett, "the Yankees should be one of the stronger teams in the league."

For the remainder of 1966, the Yankees were not one of the strongest teams in the league. As in 1965, Mantle faded in August and September. He hit only two home runs and, while his final average was .288, Mickey wound up playing only 108 games. Bedeviled by pulled hamstrings and an injured toe, he spent most of the last two months of the season on the bench. Mantle was third in the voting for Comeback Player of the Year, but the three time Most Valuable Player didn't get a single vote for MVP.

Maris and Ford likewise contributed little in the latter stages of the season. Maris played more than Mantle, appearing in 133 games, but hit only .233, with 13 homers and 43 RBI. He ran into the outfield wall in May and had to be carried off the field on a stretcher with injuries to both knees. The injuries were not as severe as they appeared, but Maris aggravated the condition on several occasions. Sometimes the fans booed him, and sometimes they ignored him. At the end of the year, he said he would retire rather than return for another season with the Yankees. "Maris has achieved what he inflexibly pursued when the spotlight shone brightest," Koppett wrote, "comparative, and presumably comfortable, obscurity."

When Ford returned from the disabled list, he was bombed in his first start, giving up 15 hits and 10 runs in six innings. Houk sent him to the bullpen, believing that limited work would reduce the strain on his arm. As in the case of Murcer, the media looked for positive precedents, pointing to past instances where the conversion of a fabled starting pitcher to relief late in his career had worked magic for the Yankees. Johnny Sain became a Yankee bullpen ace, as did Jim Turner, after winning 20 games earlier in their careers. Ford didn't become a bullpen ace, but he did pitch well in 13 relief appearances. For the year, he was in 22 games, with a 2–5 record and a 2.47 ERA. In late August, he wound up in the hospital with a recurrence of his circulatory problems and had a second operation on his arm.

On September 5, one day after the Mets had been eliminated from the National League pennant race, the Yankees were eliminated from the American League chase. It was the latest date on which the Mets had ever been disqualified and the Yankees' earliest exit since the infamous year of 1925.

The Yankee lowlights continued to accumulate during the latter half of September. On the

15th, they lost to the Senators for the tenth time, guaranteeing they would lose a season series to a Washington team for the first time since 1933. On the 19th, they dropped their 44th game at the Stadium, the most they had ever lost in a season. Only one more ignominious mark remained. The Yankees had finished last once before, in 1912, before the major leagues expanded. Never had they finished tenth.

The last weekend of the 1949 season and that of 1964 had decided American League pennants. The only drama looming during the final three days of 1966 was the battle of the Yankees to avoid the embarrassment of finishing in the American League basement. During the previous week, all three games of a scheduled series in Washington had been rained out, leaving the Yankees with three games against the White Sox to finish the season. Due to an unusual schedule, both the eighth place Senators and ninth place Red Sox had already finished their seasons. New York needed to win all three games to overtake the Red Sox for ninth place.

The drama ended early, when the Yankees lost the Friday night game in the eleventh inning. Stottlemyre, pitching in relief, absorbed his 20th loss. Maris hit his final home run as a Yankee. When the ledgers were closed, there were the once-invincible Yankees in 10th place with a 70–89 mark, one half game behind Boston. It was little solace, but the 1966 Yankees may have been the best last place team of all time. Never before in the history of the American League had a tailender posted a higher winning percentage than the Yankees' .440. Moreover, the team lost 38 games by one run, tying a league mark, while winning only 15 one run contests. Over the entire season, the Yankees gave up just one more run than they scored. While the old Yankees had always found a way to win the close games, the new Yankees found a way to lose them.

Jim Ogle, Yankee beat writer and cheerleader, refused to admit that his beloved team could be that bad. Ogle couldn't bring himself to concede that the Yankee talent was gone, and reported that the Yankee problem was a lack of desire. How else could a club that was fifth in pitching and seventh in batting finish tenth? Elston Howard, who'd said before the season that the Yankees wouldn't finish sixth again, added at the end of the year, "I can't believe we're a tenth place club. There's no way this club can stay in the cellar, no way."

Amidst the overall misery, there were some good performances. Pepitone hit a career-high 31 home runs, and Tresh hit 27. Peterson won 12 games in his rookie season, tying Stottlemyre for the team lead, and led the club with 11 complete games. By the end of the season, he was the Yankees' best pitcher. Hamilton was 8–3 with a 3.00 ERA.

Bouton, despite a 3–8 record, had a fine ERA of 2.69. On May 31, after having pitched just a single inning all season, Bouton made his first start, and threw seven strong innings. In his next start, he earned his first win in nearly a year. In late August, Bouton got his first win at Yankee Stadium since 1964. During the last month of the season, he was one of the Yankees' best pitchers, and gave indications that the old Bulldog might be back. He didn't throw as hard as he did in 1963, but during the second half of the year, Bouton's ERA was 1.66, and he didn't allow a run in his last 19 innings. In mid–September, he pitched a two hitter, retiring the first 22 men in order, but lost. The game was typical of Bouton's season.

The left side of the infield, with Boyer and the endless wave of shortstops, was virtually punchless. On June 1, Boyer was hitting .150, although he rallied during the second half to end up at .240. As in 1962, his resurgence led to the conclusion that Boyer had finally learned to hit. Howard was in good health for most of the season, but was only a shadow of the man who had been the American League's Most Valuable Player in 1963. He batted .256 in 126 games with just six home runs and 35 RBI.

In September, Houk said there would be a massive overhaul during the winter, the biggest in the history of the team, and predicted that a third of the roster would be gone. In the final weeks of the season, he decided to play the youngsters. Steve Whitaker played right field in place of Maris, Mike Hegan played first, Mike Ferraro played third and John Miller played first base and the outfield. Miller, who hit over .300 with Columbus in the Southern League, was promoted to Toledo for a few games and arrived in New York when the roster limits expanded to 40 men on September 1. He almost made his major league debut on September 6. Miller was on deck to pinch hit for the pitcher with two out in the ninth, but Richardson made the final out of the ballgame.

Five days later, in Boston, Miller finally saw action. He started the game in left field and came to bat for the first time against Red Sox righty Lee Stange in the second inning. "I was just a dumb kid who got called up and was swinging at everything," Miller said. "He threw a slider that was almost in the dirt and I golfed it into the left field screen." New York had an American League franchise since 1903, but never, until September 11, 1966, had a Yankee hit a home run in his first major league at bat. "It was just a huge thrill," said Miller. "It still is."

Miller added a single later in the game, but the two hits were the only ones he ever got as a Yankee. The following spring, he decided to hold out. "I didn't have an agent, and I didn't get a lot of guidance from my parents," he said. "Sometimes you make stupid decisions and that was one of them. In those days they sent you a contract and you either signed it or you went out and carried a lunch pail and got a job." Miller eventually signed, after incurring Houk's enmity, and then had a terrible spring. In early April, he was sold to Spokane.

In 1969, Miller spent most of the season with the Dodgers, but appeared in just 26 games, hitting one more home run, on September 23. It was Miller's final time at bat in the major leagues. He had just two major league round trippers, one in his first at bat, the other in his last. When the Dodgers decided to send him to the minor leagues, Miller didn't take it well. "I had a pretty good temper," he said. "Al Campanis asked me when he sent me down, whether I thought I could run the team better than he could. I said yes. That was my demise." Miller remained the only Yankee to hit a home run in his first major league at bat until his record was matched by Marcus Thames in 2002.

In early September, Richardson, a 12-year veteran at the age of 31, announced he would retire at the end of the season. He had, as promised, given the Yankees one more year after his pal Kubek retired, and now wanted to go back home to South Carolina to coach, work with his church and spend more time with his family. Womack, a fellow South Carolinian, tried to talk him out of it. "You spend ten years away from your family in South Carolina," Richardson told him, "and then come see me." There was no talking Richardson out of his retirement plans. Despite the fact that Houk, his favorite manager, was back at the helm, he stood firm.

On September 17, the Yankees honored Richardson with a day at the Stadium. Like the club had with other stars, they showered him with gifts. Richardson, however, was the only one to receive one thousand copies of the New Testament. The club also presented him with a bitter pill, as a loss to the Twins on Bobby Richardson Day dropped the club into a tie for last place.

Richardson was a consummate professional whose presence would be missed dearly. Womack recalled the final game of the season, the last game Richardson played. Womack was pitching in the ninth inning with Don Buford of the White Sox on second base. Richardson came to the mound and told Womack he thought they could pick Buford off because he was just one stolen base behind Bert Campaneris for the league lead and would probably try to steal. Womack was astonished. The Yankees were in the final meaningless game of a last place season and Richardson was in the last game of his career, yet he was as aware of the situation as if it were the seventh game of a World Series.

With Richardson's departure, another member of the Yankee dynasty was gone. The exodus continued after the season, as Maris and Boyer were traded. Maris went to the Cardinals for former Met third baseman Charley Smith. "I knew Charley Smith and I'm not saying anything personally against him," said Johnny Blanchard, "but good lord, I think I can get more for Roger Maris than Charley Smith. CBS owned the club at the time and I think Jackie Gleason and Art Carney made that trade." "[Maris] was disdainfully dealt away," wrote Arthur Daley, "for the equivalent of a couple of broken bats and a scuffed baseball."

Actually, Maris had backed the Yankees into a corner by making it clear that he would not return to New York, and would retire unless he was traded to a team near his home. That limited the takers to Kansas City and St. Louis. Maris's salary was estimated at $72,000, which under baseball rules could not be cut more than 25 percent. Not many teams were willing to spend $54,000 a year or more on a 32-year-old with a history of injury and two poor seasons behind him. In his last two years, Maris had hit a total of 21 home runs, the same number he hit between May 30th and July 2, 1961. The Yankees were lucky to get anything for him.

Yet Maris had to go, for his own sake as well as the team's. The Yankees were in a rebuilding mode, and Maris clearly wasn't going to be around when and if they came out the other side of the tunnel. Further, he and the Yankees had many irreconcilable differences, and it was time for a divorce. In 1961 and 1962, the writers and fans had been the bane of Maris's existence, while the players stood by him. Now, many of Maris's teammates, most of whom hadn't been with him in the glory years, didn't care for him. Even Houk hinted that it took Maris a very long time to recover from his numerous injuries. New York was tired of Maris and he was tired of New York. "I had seven years in New York," Maris said in the spring of 1967. "Seven long years." He referred to the 1961 season as "that mess." A change of scenery would be good for everyone.

The change was certainly good for Maris. His two seasons in St. Louis were no more than adequate, but they were probably the happiest two years of Roger's major league career. He got more affection for hitting five home runs in his final season than he received while hitting 61. In his last regular season at bat in St. Louis, Maris received a standing ovation.

Maris's post-season performances with the Yankees had been disappointing, but he was one of the heroes of the St. Louis victory over the Red Sox in 1967. Maris played in all seven games, batted .385 and drove in seven runs, playing better than he had in any of his Yankee Series appearances.*

Boyer went to the Braves for young outfield prospect Bill Robinson. From the starters who had won the Yankees' last World Championship in 1962, only Tresh and the aging Howard and Mantle remained. In October, Ford, one of only two pitchers (Bouton was the other) remaining from the 1962 champions, was released in order to free a spot on the roster for the youngsters the Yankees desperately needed to protect. Ford was invited to spring training with the understanding that he would be signed to a contract if his arm was sound and he could pitch.

The guard was clearly changing, and Jim Ogle was pleased. He wrote that Boyer, Maris and Ramos, who was traded to Philadelphia, had been lacking in effort, and their departure would impart more hustle to the Yankee club. The newcomers, even though they didn't have much natural talent, would add verve and zest.

Ramos was traded to the Phillies for pitcher Joe Verbanic, but lasted less than half a season in Philadelphia. He went back to the minor leagues, pitching for Columbus in 1968 and 1969. During the winter, Ramos managed in the Venezuelan League, where he shocked his players with an extensive set of rules. He had hurt his own career, he said, with his lax habits, and was not going to let the same thing happen to them.

Ramos's last major league appearance came in 1970 with the Washington Senators, the club with which he had made his debut fifteen seasons earlier. After a brief comeback attempt with

---

*Maris did not play as well in the 1968 Series. In Game Five, with the Cardinals leading the Tigers three games to one, he pinch hit in the bottom of the ninth inning. The Tigers led 5–3 and there were two Cardinals on base. Had Maris hit a home run, he would have ended his career with a series-winning three run homer. Unfortunately, he struck out.

the Mets in 1972, Ramos left baseball and fell upon difficult times. In 1965, when he was with the Yankees, Ramos had been arrested for interfering with the arrest of another man on a charge of drunkenness. He claimed he was only trying to help by acting as an interpreter, and avoided serious trouble. The next year, he was attacked by a knife-wielding man outside a Bronx bar, but escaped with minor wounds. "The exact nature of the altercation remained unexplained," reported *The New York Times*.

On September 3, 1978, Ramos was not so lucky. He was arrested for possessing a gun and a small amount of marijuana. Ramos was not prosecuted on the condition that he enter a drug treatment program. Less than a year later, he was arrested while allegedly making a large delivery of cocaine. The Cuban Cowboy was referred to in the newspapers as the Cocaine Cowboy. Ramos claimed he was framed, and was eventually exonerated. In 1980, however, he was arrested for threatening a bar owner with a Colt revolver and placed on probation. On August 24, 1981, Ramos violated his probation by being arrested for speeding, drunken driving and carrying a concealed weapon. He was sentenced to three years in prison. After serving his time at the Hendry Correctional Institute in Florida, Ramos served as a college pitching coach in Florida.

The old guard was leaving the Yankees, but the performance of the new guard in September didn't bode well for the future. Hegan hit .205, Ferraro .179, and Miller .087. Whitaker faded after his spectacular start and Murcer was erratic at shortstop.

Not only were the Yankees an artistic failure, they were losing ground financially. They had been outdrawn by the Mets when they were winning, and now that they were losing, the gap widened. Attendance at Yankee Stadium suffered its fifth consecutive year of decline, reaching a 21-year low of 1,124,648. The Mets, finishing ninth, drew 1,932,693 to Shea Stadium. On September 22, only 413 fans showed up to watch the Yankees lose to the White Sox. The Yankees had hit bottom.

· 19 ·

The Good Old Days

"I've been out of baseball 34 years," said former pitcher Don Nottebart, "and I still get fan mail. People tell me how they miss the '50s, '60s and '70s." "It used to be," said Dick Schofield, "that when you were on a team, you were pretty much tied in with that team. Now, with free agency, you have a hard time keeping up with who's going where. It's great for the players, but I don't think it leads to the team atmosphere we once had."

Tracy Stallard offered a dissenting view. "I really believe it was more of an individual deal when we were playing," he said. "They seem to pull for each other more now than we did back then. I don't think money's a problem for them so they've got nothing else to do but be a team player and pull for everybody. Back then, I think there was too much individualism."

Undeniably, one of the biggest differences in today's game is economic. "I got called up to the Yankees in 1969," recalled Tom Shopay, "and I had to find a place to live. I wound up paying $500 a month for a one bedroom apartment in Hackensack, and then had to buy furniture and pay for utilities. I was making the minimum salary of $10,000, and that was gone."

"My first year [1960]," said Bob Johnson, "I got six thousand, and another thousand for staying with the team past June 15. My final contract in 1970 was for $26,500, which was pretty good money in those days. I don't blame today's ballplayers. The increases in salary and all the money they give away aren't the ballplayers' fault. It's the guy who signs the check and that's the owner. I think the thing that's hurt the game is the agents, but the owners cry wolf for so long and when it comes down to the nuts and bolts, they give in. So I don't have a lot of compassion for the owners."

"It's ridiculous today," said Nottebart. "The problem is that they're getting greedy. If I was playing today and made a million dollars a year, I wouldn't have any financial worries because I would save and invest. But now these guys make one million and then they've got to make two million, and they've got to make more than the next guy and bing, bing, bing. It's a vicious cycle."

"I don't blame the players," said Bobby Klaus. "If my boss came to me today and said, 'Bob, I want to sign you to a contract for $100,000 a year for ten years,' I'm going to turn it down? It's wonderful, but it's not the same. It's not the same clubhouse. It's not the same road trips. Now, everybody's got a laptop and an agent with them. I remember the contracts we used to get. There's an X, sign it. If not, get your lunch pail out." Roger Repoz recalled such a conversation with Dick Walsh, general manager of the Angels. "He told me," Repoz said, "'I'll offer you a $500 raise. Take it or leave it. If you don't like it, go get a lunch pail.' That was the end of the conversation."

"The minimum salary when I played," said Ken Johnson, "was $7,000 and the top guys like Mays, Aaron, Musial and Mantle made $100,000. We thought that was too much money for a baseball player. Now it's priced out of sight. If they find a cure for cancer they deserve that kind of money, but for playing baseball, uh-uh."

Jim McAndrew retired after the 1974 season due to a bad knee injury. "I was 30," he said, "with two children and expecting a third and making $40–45 thousand a year." "I thought I could get that much in the corporate world in a year or two. I didn't realize that free agency was going to take place and a year later I could be making $150–200 thousand in baseball. I had perfect timing. I signed in '65, the first year of the draft, so I couldn't negotiate a signing bonus, and my last year was '74, two years before free agency. As far as economics were concerned, I probably picked the worst ten year window."

Some players joke about wanting to make the salaries that are paid today, but, for the most part, there is little resentment. "You ask anyone who played the game in that era," said Yankee pitcher Tom Metcalf, "and they'll tell you it would be nice to get the money today's players get, but the one thing they valued more than the money was their ability to play and perform. That was why you did it. You wanted to be on that field and you wanted to be a winner."

"It's like an education," said Rich Beck. "They can't take it away from you. I didn't make any money out of baseball. To be truthful, I'm a little envious of the money that's being made now. If a person goes up for a month now, they make $35,000. I made $1200."

"I'm not envious of the money they make," said Shopay. "The best to them on that. I'm happy with what I made. It was enough to make a living at that time. Now I make four times as much as I ever made as a player. It's like the old saying, 'Baseball has been very good to me.' I got a chance to play. It's a childhood dream of about 98 percent of all kids to be a professional athlete, whether it be baseball, football or basketball. I had that opportunity and I cherish it. I made a lot of good friends, friends I still have today. And I love the game."

Today's higher paid players hit many more home runs than those of the 1960s. Maris's record of 61 home runs has not only been broken, but shattered convincingly. There are a number of theories regarding the dramatic increase in power. "We'd love to walk up to the plate and know that the ball is going to be from the middle of the plate out," said catcher Joe Ginsberg. "They never throw the ball from the middle of the plate in. They never throw at you anymore. I talked to some real good hitters and they said, 'Wouldn't it be nice to go up there, look out there and know that's where the ball is going to be.'"

"The strike zone is only about a foot square," said former pitcher Fred Kipp. "I think it's a number of things," said Met pitcher Bill Wakefield. "The parks are different, the ball might be a little different, and the equipment's better. I think the biggest single thing is weight training and the fact that players are bigger and stronger. Pitchers can't pitch inside as much and hitters lean over the plate. There were very few opposite field home runs when I was playing. When players hit home runs, they pulled them. Now you see shortstops who've hit the weights hitting home runs to the opposite field."

"We pitched to take the power away from the batter," said Joe Grzenda. "If he could pull it 700 feet down the left field line, don't let him hit it there. Throw it outside. Set it up for him and let him hit it. Today, if you make the same kind of pitches, it's going to be a 500 foot shot the other way." "They tell me they're using a Titlist these days instead of a baseball," said Pete Mikkelsen, while echoing the comments about the proliferation of opposite field home runs. "It's got to be the ball. They say they're bigger and stronger, but there were big, strong guys when I played. They didn't hit the ball like they do now."

In addition to money and home runs, a third area in which players of the '60s see a major difference is the dilution of talent created by continuing expansion. "You have guys who would be in Triple A ball in our day playing in the major leagues," said Jack Lamabe. "The good hitters just got better, because they were feasting on pitchers who shouldn't be there. The good pitchers got better because they were facing hitters who shouldn't be there."

"I think when we played," said former Met Al Moran, "we were more serious, because in Triple A ball and Double A ball, there were great ballplayers. If you didn't do your job, boom, you were gone. Now it's so diluted that if you make the major leagues and you're not doing the job, you just get traded to somebody else. You know you're going to play. You've got your superstars now, but back then I think there were a lot more." "I think 60 percent of the pitchers out there today couldn't have pitched in the 1960s," added former pitcher Dennis Bennett. "Back then, there were a lot of good ballplayers playing in Double A and Triple A."

"This is just my opinion," said catcher Johnny Ellis, "but I can't imagine that there were teams better than the Oakland As with Reggie Jackson and Sal Bando and the Baltimore Orioles with Brooks Robinson, Mark Belanger, Davey Johnson and Boog Powell. Their pitching staffs were tremendous, both the starters and relievers. It's hard for me to imagine that there are teams today, as great as the Yankees have been and as great as the Red Sox have been, that are as good as those teams. During the decade that I played [the '70s], I believe that those teams and those pitching staffs were as good as any teams that ever played the game. "

"A lot of players who are in the major leagues shouldn't be in the major leagues," said former Met Joe Christopher. "When I was coming up, there were guys like Steve Bilko in the Pacific Coast League, and Joe Taylor, and Rocky Nelson. All these guys were good major league ballplayers, but there was no place to put them."

"There were only eight or ten teams in the league then," said Klaus, "and they were all loaded. I batted against Bob Friend, Bob Gibson and Fergie Jenkins. I hit against Drysdale and Koufax-well, I swung against Koufax. No wonder I hit .210. [Klaus exaggerated. His career average was actually only .208.] Guys like me hoped for a four game series, because maybe in the last game I could go one for four if they brought up somebody from Triple A to fill in."

"I think the owners had a certain mind-set back then," said Ed Bressoud. "If a player got to be 33 or 34, they'd think about unloading him and bringing up a new player. Each club had 15, 16 or 17 minor league teams and there was always somebody in the wings waiting to take your place. Now they have four of five minor league teams and the supply isn't there anymore. You see a lot of players now who are 37 or 38 years old. You didn't have that years ago."

"When you started a game in the National League," said Nottebart, "you didn't know how far you could get. You'd look down the lineup and the first seven hitters were good hitters. The two out men were at the bottom. Nowadays I watch these ballgames, and there are five good hitters in the lineup. Maybe five."

"You'd go into Cleveland in the '50s," said Joe Ginsberg, "and you'd bat against Feller, Wynn, Garcia and Lemon. Now you might go into a town and see two real good starting pitchers and two others who might not be of major league caliber." "When I played," said Bob Hendley, "when you went to the major leagues, you were ready to be a major leaguer. Today, I think a lot of guys are coming up and learning how to be a major league pitcher. I think the arms are just as good, but I'm not sure they're ready to do the things you need to do to win. We worked on our bunting, which I think today might be a lost art. And today, they have all the opportunity in the world to practice. They have batting cages set up under the stands. They can work on it any time they want."

With no long term contracts, and the minor leagues packed with talent, no one wanted to come out of the lineup. "I look at the number of players on the disabled list today," said Hendley, "versus the number who were on the disabled list when I played. There are an awful lot of people on the DL today. We played hurt."

"The older players played through injury," said former Met Don Bosch. "They couldn't walk in the morning, but they'd figure out a way to get on the field at night. Today if you have an ingrown toenail, you're out for a week, because they've got such a grand investment in you." "In today's market," said Tex Clevenger, "everybody's got a sore finger, or a pulled groin, or something. We didn't have those problems, and I think the cause of it is all the bodybuilding they do today."

"My old roommate Bobby Knoop was coaching with the Angels," said Met Rick Herrscher, "and he told me all you have to do is go to the trainer and tell him you've got an ingrown toenail [ingrown toenails seems to be a particular bane of the modern player] or whatever and can't play. The trainer has to put your name on a list and give it to the manager and the manager can't play them!"

"I look in the paper today," said Bressoud, "and read about a rotator cuff or the famous groin pull. Nobody ever heard of a rotator cuff 35 years ago. You had a sore arm. As far as groin pulls, they just strapped you up and you played. It's so different today. My wife died in he spring of 1958. She died on a Tuesday. We buried her on Thursday. I was back at the ballpark Friday and played Saturday."

Hendley is a classic example of playing through pain. In 1961, he spent the winter in the Army, tried to throw hard too soon the following spring and suffered an elbow injury that plagued him for the rest of his career. "I was never the same," he said. "I had to learn how to pitch, change speeds and hit spots better. I came up with a slip pitch. When I went to the Mets, they knew I had serious problems. I had bone chips that had broken loose and were floating around. The last few years I pitched, I really struggled with my arm. Sometimes if I had enough rest, I'd pitch well, but with the arm problems, I just couldn't do it consistently. When you get to the point where you know you don't have good stuff and you're facing guys who are better, it's time to say that it's over.

"I pitched a game in Pittsburgh once when the chips broke loose. I threw a pitch and the elbow locked up. The chip had gotten down between the bones in the elbow and locked the joint up. I had to turn around, take my glove off, and push the chip back up through the slot above the elbow. Then I turned around and pitched. It was pure pain."

When the Mets acquired Hendley, they intended to have him undergo surgery immediately. He pitched a couple of good games, however, and he and the club decided he would pitch as long as he could stand the pain and was effective. Hendley kept pitching through that 1967 season before having surgery in September. "The crazy thing about it is that I ended up crippled but had a won lost record [5–3] that was probably the best I ever had."

Hendley was only 28 at the time of his operation, and the Mets expected him to come back and help the club in 1968. By that time, however, the Mets had Seaver, Koosman, and Ryan, with more prospects on the way. There was no room for a middle-aged, soft-throwing lefty with a history of arm trouble, and Hendley was released after the 1969 season. "I think of what they can do arthroscopically today," he said. "If they could have done that back then, I probably would have pitched until I was 40 or 45 years old. I've had people ask me if I had any regrets because I was released at 30. I say no, I have none because I knew I did everything I could to get myself back and it just wasn't meant to be. I feel very fortunate to have played nine years with a bad elbow."

"For pitchers," said Bill Denehy, "surgery was the last, last, last resort. If you were a power pitcher and went under the knife, you came out a finesse pitcher. If they had to go into your shoulder, they didn't have arthroscopic surgery. They had to go in and do some heavy cutting into the muscles."

Denehy, whose career was derailed by arm trouble, found a non-surgical solution to his problem, a drug called dimethyl sulfoxide (DMSO). DMSO was applied topically (Denehy put it on his arm with a toothbrush) and gave a burning sensation to the arm. There were rumors of a number of potential side effects, including blindness, but the prospect of a cure without cutting into those precious muscles was worth the risk. "I had reached a point," Denehy said, "that if my companion had been a Haitian voodoo doctor instructing me to kill three chickens and rub the blood on my arm and shoulder while kneeling naked in a pigpen, I would have done it if it would have saved my baseball career."

Ron Taylor, after retiring from baseball, attended medical school and is now the team physician for the Toronto Blue Jays. "It's not so much the treatment that's changed," he said. "It's the diagnostic skills that people in medicine have now. I can recall that if a pitcher tore his rotator cuff, he was finished. That was it. Now they can repair it. The pitcher's out for a year, but he comes back. The same thing with the elbow and the 'Tommy John' operation that Frank Jobe pioneered. Some guys are coming back and I think they're throwing harder after the operation." It might become elective surgery, I suggested. Taylor laughed. "They'll be lined up," he said.

The 1960s must have been the unquestioned Golden Age of Baseball, one concludes after more than a hundred interviews. Players were more talented, more team-oriented, and tougher. They didn't make much money, and played for the love of the game. At the time, however, old timers saw that era much as the players of the 1960s see the baseball of today. In the mid–'60s, *Sports Illustrated* asked a number of veteran players and coaches what they thought about the game and the players of that time. "The whole standard is lower," said pitching coach Harvey Haddix. "and I mean the pitchers, too. They win 12 games and think they did a hell of a job." A skeptic might have pointed out that Haddix himself won more than 12 games only three times in 14 big league seasons, but he continued on to hitters. "Almost nobody practices anymore," Haddix added. "Anyway, they're bigger, stronger kids now, and the way the ball jumps, why should they learn to hit?"

"I think the caliber of the baseball player just isn't there," Joe Garagiola said in 1969, "and I sound like an old man, but I know guys that were in the [St. Louis] Muny League that probably could be on an expansion club right now." "We don't have the quality of player we used to have," lamented Yankee farm director Johnny Johnson, "because it just isn't there anymore."

Gabe Paul, a sagacious baseball executive whose career spanned several decades, thought otherwise. "I keep hearing some people tell about the 'good old days,'" Paul said in 1966, "and I'm beginning to wonder what they're talking about. I go back to the good old days myself and it wasn't as rosy as everyone seems to think. " He pointed out that the Gashouse Gang Cardinals of 1934 drew slightly more than 300,000 spectators the entire season.

"Some college teams of today," Paul continued, "are as good as many of the professional teams of 20 or 30 years ago.... This is a natural improvement, a natural evolution that comes with the changing times. Players are certainly in better physical shape today than ever before."

Paul was a lone voice in the wilderness, however, for the common wisdom among the old timers was that the players of the '60s just weren't what their predecessors had been. Much earlier in the decade, Stanley Frank wrote an article in *SI* titled "What Ever Happened to Baseball?" "The trouble," Frank wrote, "is that all the fun has been diluted out of baseball. Once an asylum for amiable eccentrics, it has become a lifeless charade by actors who look as impersonal as motorcycle cops." The problem, Frank said, was that not only had the average salary increased to $17,000 per year; the players now had a pension plan. A five year man could collect $112.50 per month commencing at age 50. The opportunity to earn such riches had made the players fearful of offending ownership. "Everybody is security conscious," said Pirate general manager Joe Brown. "Five years in the big leagues and you can get a pension, so that's all they try to do: last five years and get the pension."

Rabbit Maranville, a Hall of Fame shortstop who played from 1912–1935, chimed in. "Guys in my time played for the love of the game," Maranville told Frank. "Nobody gets a kick out of baseball anymore, because big salaries and the pension fund have made it a more serious business than running a bank.... Sometimes it seems they're just using baseball as a front for the restaurants, bowling alleys and other sidelines they buy as soon as they get a bonus for signing."

Other old timers lamented the fact that the quality of play on the field had deteriorated. "As everyone knows," Frankie Frisch said in 1962, "I don't think major league baseball players today can be compared to the old timers. I think the slider is a nickel curve and I detest hearing the modern sissies moan about how it has ruined batting averages."

George Sisler, the Hall of Fame first baseman, wrote an article for *The Sporting News* stating that Gil Hodges was the only major league first baseman who played the position with the same level of skill demonstrated in Sisler's era. When Hodges, who was near the end of the line, retired, said Sisler, there would be no first baseman in either league who was an accomplished fielder. Players were bigger and stronger, and fielding averages were much higher than they were 40 years earlier, but one must remember that Sisler was a coach for the Pirates and spent much of his time watching bumbling Dick Stuart. He recalled himself and Lou Gehrig, and conveniently forgot about lummoxes like Zeke Bonura and Dale Alexander, who led the American League in hitting in 1929, yet found himself out of the majors after just six seasons because his fielding at first was so dreadful. In the following week's edition, Rogers Hornsby, the irascible Hall of Fame second baseman, echoed Sisler's opinions in his article on the decline of second base play.

Modern pitchers, said the old timers, were too timid. "Pitchers forget that the best batter hits only a little better than .300," said retired catcher Spud Davis in 1951. "That means he'll get three hits out of ten. The seven other times the pitcher will get the batter out. Yet the pitchers will try to cut the corners of the plate, find themselves behind the batter and give up walks. The best way to get a batter out is to make him hit the ball." Does that sound familiar?

The ballplayers of the 1960s were not only inferior, said the old timers, they were coddled. "Everything possible has been done to make it easier to do a ballplayer's job," said Frisch. "We used to have leather pancakes for gloves. We had to make stops with our bare hands. Now they have snaring nets they call baseball gloves. The first baseman's glove is like a basketball hoop with a net in it.... Baseball players today do not have the same urge, the old fighting spirit that characterized the ballplayers of what I call the old-timers' era. Everything is made easy for them. Training camps are country clubs without dues. We used to be housed in one hotel and our life was regimented." The regression of values wasn't a recent development, according to Frisch. In 1954, he wrote an article in *The Saturday Evening Post* titled "Is Baseball Getting Sissy?" "Unfortunately," said broadcaster Red Barber in 1966, "the idea today is not to be humble, but to be big and strong and virile and to hit home runs to prove it ... I say society is to blame."

Old Timers Day at Yankee Stadium in 1968 gave the retired stars an opportunity to fire a few more barbs at their successors. "One thing wrong with baseball now," said one, "is the pension.... Now all these guys think about is getting their five years in to be eligible for the pension. Once they do, they lose all interest and couldn't care less whether they continue playing or not. Today's players take the collar or leave a winning run on base and forget all about it a few minutes later."

The more things change, they say, the more they remain the same. Bill Hepler, former Met lefthander, was at a Devil Ray game recently, watching Tampa play the Yankees. "Derek Jeter came up," Hepler said. "He stood there and dug his feet in, and dug his feet in, then put his arm up to ask the umpire for time, as if to say, 'Wait 'til I get situated.' I said to my wife, 'If he did that back when I pitched, they would have knocked him down right away. You didn't do things like that."

Hepler played for the Mets in 1966, a year before Yankee announcer Joe Garagiola lamented the fact that hitters spent far too much time smoothing out dirt in the batters' box. "In the old days," Garagiola said, "pitchers would upend you." "Don't they have knockdown signs in baseball anymore," Frisch had lamented a few years earlier. "Do you see what those hitters do now? They rake the batter's box with their bats. They pat down the dirt, and fix it. They look like they're planting petunias. I'd like to see some of these guys planting petunias in the batter's box if Pat Malone was pitching."

Virtually everyone other than television sponsors and concessionaires agrees that today's games are simply too long. "My youngest daughter has a boyfriend who plays for Cal State–Fullerton," said former Met Rod Gaspar, "and we go out and watch him. They have four hour games! It's terrible! After every pitch, the catcher looks in the dugout and gets the sign. How can you learn the game if you're going to have somebody else think for you? Especially a catcher, my goodness. He's probably the smartest guy on the field. I last about three innings at those types of games. It's just not the same and they don't play it the same way. But I guess that's just how it is nowadays. It's a lot different than when we played."

One of the biggest problems with the games of the 1960s, everyone agreed at the time, was that they were too long. In 1905, the average major league game lasted just one hour and forty nine minutes. By 1962, it had dragged out to two hours and forty one minutes. The causes of delay, according to George Sisler, were too many 3–2 counts, too many pitching changes and too much time taken between pitches by both hitters and pitchers. The pitchers were afraid, he said, to challenge the hitters. There were also too many mound conferences. Old Cincinnati manager Bill McKechnie said he couldn't remember his catcher, Ernie Lombardi, ever going out to talk to a pitcher.

During the good old days of the 1960s, players were dignified and showed respect for the veterans. "I see some of these jocks today," said Johnny Blanchard, "and I laugh and say, 'He wouldn't be in a pinstriped uniform two days. You see guys that are popping off now. There's no discipline. We had one hundred percent discipline from the word go. Nobody ran off at the jaws."

"When we played," said Phil Linz, "we never talked to the opposing players. Now they're buddy-buddy. It's an important game with everything riding on it and they're laughing." Laughing after a big loss, of course, is what Linz had done to upset Yogi Berra on the bus in Chicago 40 years ago. "I think it has a lot to do with the money. That winning World Series share was very important to us. We were playing season to season, without long term contracts. Our batting average and everything we did determined where we would be next year. We were fighting for our lives every year."

"In those days," added Roger Repoz, "you treated the old pros with respect. You couldn't even get in the training room until they were done. If you were in there, somebody like Blanchard would come in and say, 'What the heck are you doing in here, let the big guys come in first.' They'd run us off. It wasn't like it is today. These guys don't have any respect for the older players."

Back in 1953, farm director Joe Reardon of the Phillies had voiced a similar sentiment. "The 'good old days' when rookies came to camp with cap in hand," he said, "and said 'yes, sir' to the groundskeeper, were over." "Now," Reardon said, "they perch their caps on the back of their heads, stick their tongues out, and don't even say 'good morning' to the manager. Many want transportation for their wives, permission to bring their pet dogs and promise of a day off to go home."

In the '60s, the manager was king, or so the players said. "Billy Martin was great," said Joe Grzenda. "He knew his guys and he had big balls. When Billy said something, he meant it. He was the boss. How can they manage these guys who are making a million dollars? I called a manager who's a friend of mine and asked him how he was getting along. He said, 'Hey, I love 'em all.' He's not going to make enemies with any of these ballplayers because they're making a lot more money than he is." "They're liked spoiled kids now," added Tom Shopay.

Yet, in the mid–'60s, Red Sox coach Sal Maglie said, "Today, you handle the players with kid gloves." "Today you can't threaten a player," Yogi Berra said when he managed the Yankees in 1964. "You got to pat him on the back or he won't play for you. They're all college men today. If they don't like what's happening, they'll pack up and go home.... It was a lot better in the old days when you had to play or someone else got your job. Today there's nobody around to give them that push." Were Yogi, Maglie, Grzenda and Shopay speaking of the same era?

Old timers have always lamented the decline of the ability of pitchers to throw a complete game. The following quote is illustrative. "There has never been any objection to the relief of a pitcher, if his delivery were not baffling the batters, but the new school of managers rushes relief pitchers to the front whenever there is a slightest indication of wavering." Those sentiments could have been written today, but they appeared in 1910, when, for example, Philadelphia Athletic hurlers completed 123 of 150 starts.

In 1960, former Yankee pitcher Eddie Lopat said, "The youngster is indoctrinated to throw as hard as he can for as long as he can. The idea that he cannot pitch nine innings is false; he is neither taught nor expected to do so." There wouldn't be many 20 game winners in the future, Lopat predicted.

Lopat's comments notwithstanding, in the 1960s the starting pitcher was expected to pitch a complete game and, if he failed, the short man was supposed to close it out. Some managers, such as Paul Richards and Charley Dressen, loved to change pitchers and make the famed lefty-righty switch, but they were in the minority. Not today. "I saw a game the other night," said Linz, "and a left hander came in to relieve. He was pitching great, throwing strikes, and you could see he had great stuff. Tell me he couldn't pitch the next inning. But here comes a right hand batter so you've got to take him out and bring in the right hander. I think the managers are afraid to use their gut instincts anymore. I guess the criticism makes a difference. If they do something a little unorthodox, boy do they get criticized if it doesn't work out."

"I think the managers love to use the bullpen," laughed Chuck Estrada. "It gives them something to do. The game has changed so much since I played. I think teams spend more time building their bullpens now than they do starters. They make a lot of appearance, but they don't pitch a lot of innings. Dick Radatz and those guys always pitched two or three innings. If I was a bullpenner and I only pitched one inning, god almighty, I'd pitch for twenty years."

Some retired players are fans of today's game. "The 2003 postseason was baseball at it's best," said Bill Monbouquette. Some aren't. "The game on the field is different," said Grzenda, "and it makes me not watch the game I loved and the one that was my life. As far as the millions they're making, more power to 'em. I don't begrudge nobody nothin.' But the game on the field is different." "I don't watch a lot of baseball," said Mikkelsen. "If the kids put it on, I'll watch a little bit of it. I don't go to any games or anything. It's just kind of like part of your life that's history."

Lindy McDaniel is a casual fan. "I don't relate to the modern game," he said, "because it differs, in terms of salary and so many other ways, from baseball as I knew it. I watch some games, and I guess I'm like most fans in that I get interested during the playoffs and World Series. I really enjoyed the [2003] World Series, but to say I follow a team day-by-day during the season, I don't do that."

The attitude of many former players is soured by the fact that, despite the phenomenal wealth being accumulated by today's players, they have done little to aid those who came before them and made their lofty salaries possible. The major bone of contention is the pension plan. Today, any player who appears on a big league roster is vested almost immediately. In 1969, a player needed four full years of service to be vested and, prior to that, he needed five years. Achieving full vesting was a cherished goal of nearly every player. "All of us," said Chuck Hiller, "not the stars like Mays, but the rest of us, were just trying to get the five years in. Man, it was a hell of a relief when you got it." "I was there before the rules changed," said Grzenda, "and I needed five years to qualify for a pension. If you went out and got beat around a little bit, you'd say, 'Oh, god, am I going to get it?' And buddy, does that turn into pressure. Finally, the day came and Ted Williams, who was my manager, came over and said, 'How do you feel today?' I wanted to give him a big hug. I'd qualified for my pension and I felt he helped me get it."

"In 1966," said Galen Cisco, "I had a real good year for Dick Williams in Toronto. He got the Red Sox job in '67. I needed 60 more days to qualify for a pension. Dick told me that if things worked out right, he would try to get me my 60 days, because I'd had such a good year for him in '66. I made the team out of spring training, and I think I got in 57 days before they had to make a move." Cisco went down, and asked Williams if he planned to bring him back. "I've only got three or four more days to qualify for the pension," he told Williams, "and I'd sure like to get it." Williams said he would try, and brought Cisco back to get his time in. For others, the ending was not as happy, and many left baseball with nothing more than their final paycheck.

In 2003, former Met shortstop Al Moran and former Houston and Kansas City infielder Ernie Fazio organized the old players and attempted to raise money for a suit designed to gain benefits for players with less than five years of major league service, who had no pension rights under the current plan. "If there's anything you can do to help these guys," Rick Herrscher told me, "I'd appreciate it if you'd write about it." Herrscher went to dental school after retiring from baseball and, as a successful orthodontist, doesn't need the extra money. "There are a lot of players out there," he said, "who could use a few of those dollars from the rich pension plan the players have."

"I don't know why the modern day players won't vote to go back and pick up some of the old timers on the pension plan," said Tracy Stallard. "That's a mystery to me." "It's disturbing," added Ray Barker, "when so many say that we take care of our own."

"Lately," said Yankee pitcher Bill Burbach, "I've been a little less enamored of the game because of the pension issue. There were 1,033 of us at last count, and more of us are dying every day. There's so much money available, but they don't see fit to take care of the people who enabled them to make that kind of money."

"Nowadays," said Bill Hepler, "ballplayers have to spend one day in the big leagues and they get medical coverage for the rest of their lives. They spend 43 days and they get a pension. I think that everybody who ever played in the big leagues should get a pension, because if you take the number of people all over the world who wanted to play major league baseball, see how few of them did. I think the thousand or so of us who played but didn't qualify should be recognized for the fact that we did make the major leagues." "If you look at the players union," said Bob Meyer, "you could embrace those thousand guys and barely touch the money that's coming in. It's so incredible today. They just don't have any feeling for the players who are older. But in fairness to them, when I was 22 or 23, I didn't either."

Meyer is absolutely correct in all respects, but particularly in his final point. In the late 1950s, former Red Sox third baseman Larry Gardner tried to organize a small pension plan for needy former ballplayers. He suggested playing old timers' games in major league parks to raise money, but got nowhere.

On December 15, 1966, former Yankee pitcher Allie Reynolds filed a suit in federal court attempting to block a revision to the pension plan that would substantially increase pensions for all players who were active after 1957. Like Gardner, Reynolds was unsuccessful.

A sentiment frequently expressed by retired players is that they played not for money, but for the love of the game. "When I played ball," said Jim Lyttle, "I think the players played because they loved the game. The players today undoubtedly love the game, but they play for the money, too."

"We didn't make much money," said former Yankee Len Boehmer, "we just had a love of the game. I would've played for nothing if I could afford to do that and think most of the guys were that way. They loved the game." "We played because we loved baseball," added Chuck Hiller. "We didn't play for the money 'cause we didn't make any." "I would have paid the Yankees $7,000 to let me play," said Dooley Womack. "They pay $3,500 for a few days at a fantasy camp. To play a whole season would be worth at least $7,000."

Had players always played for the "love of the game?" At an old timers' event in 1961, Hall of Fame first baseman Bill Terry, a Giant star in the 1920s and '30s, said, "Let's get it straight. I swung the bat for base hits and money." In 1956, Roger Kahn wrote an article with Duke Snider titled "I Play Baseball for Money — Not Fun." In 1963, after signing his first $100,000 contract, Mickey Mantle said, "Well, it's a big thrill. It's about what everybody tries to do in baseball, to make as much money as he can."

Whatever criticism one finds of modern players, chances are it was leveled at an earlier generation of athletes by their predecessors. On the same day in 1961 that Terry talked about hitting for money, Leo Durocher complained that pitchers no longer went the distance like they used to. "You hear them warning the manager to have somebody ready," he said, "when they have pitched a good game for six or seven innings." There wouldn't be any more 300 game winners, said Early Wynn, who achieved the milestone in 1963. Too few pitchers went the route and relievers would get the wins. Players didn't have to fight for positions, said former Giant pitcher Rube Marquard, and didn't have the intense competitive spirit of players from his era. There was no fun in the game anymore, said Met VP Johnny Murphy. In his day (the '30s and '40s) there had been more camaraderie in the clubhouse, whereas in the '60s, the players were too businesslike and just showed up to play the games.

In March, 1962, the front page of *The Sporting News* proclaimed, "Era of Great Players May Be Near End." "Is the day of the super star of baseball disappearing?" was the question under discussion. With Williams, Dimaggio and Feller retired, and Musial and Spahn near the end of the line, were there any other superstars on the horizon, or would baseball be condemned to a world of players who were merely good? Mickey Mantle and Willie Mays, *TSN* admitted, were pretty good ballplayers, but they weren't Dimaggio and Williams.

I recall, in the late 1960s, watching an All Star Game with my father, who made the same point. When players like Mays, Mantle, Aaron, Clemente and Killebrew retired, he claimed, there would be no more superstars in baseball. All the aforementioned moved on, and in their place came Reggie Jackson, Rod Carew, Nolan Ryan and Mike Schmidt, who gave way to Alex Rodriguez, Roger Clemens and Barry Bonds. Each generation thinks it has seen the last of a good thing, but down the road, another good thing replaces it, though the prophets are loath to admit it.

Baseball today isn't the same as it was in the good old days. It never was. Today, one can hear television analysts like Rick Sutcliffe and Tony Gwynn talk about how the players of today aren't like they were in the 1980s and 1990s. The players are never as good, never as tough, and earn far too much money. That's been true since baseball began a century and a half ago, and it will be true as long as baseball is played. Nothing will be like it was in the good old days.

Appendix:
In Their Own Words

Of all the young boys who dream of a career in major league baseball, only a handful are able to realize their ambition. Most careers end on the sandlot, or on high school or college diamonds. Even for those who sign professional contracts, most see their dreams end in Johnson City, Tennessee, or Kearney, Nebraska, due to a sore elbow, a damaged shoulder, or simply the realization they don't have what it takes. They go back home and build careers as teachers, accountants, or tradesmen and think about what might have been. Of those who persevere and make it to the major leagues, few achieve stardom. Most play a few games, or a few seasons, return to the minor leagues and eventually find themselves back in civilian life.

The Yogi Berras, Bill Skowrons and Bobby Richardsons have endless memories of their baseball careers. What about those who didn't achieve the stardom they dreamed of on the schoolyards? Are they bitter? A few are. Do they feel that others robbed them of their dream? Some do. The passage of time, however, adds a perspective that is often missing in the moment. Former pitcher Bob Meyer explained. "This stuff is really quite interesting," he said, "when you peel it away and start looking at why some guys were great and others weren't. I think players have the feeling that they got screwed in the first ten years after they're out of the game. Then, as you age, you look at things a little more philosophically. Millions of people would have given their right arm to be where I was for a few years. You see that when you're 65, but when you're released at 32 and think you got screwed at 27, it's a lot more numbing because it's so close to the experience. But over time, you say, 'You know what, it was a hell of a deal.'

"I thoroughly enjoyed my time in the Yankee organization. It's a tremendous organization with a lot of pride, all the way down through the farm system. Everybody involved was first class. I have nothing but good, warm feelings toward the Yankees and everybody I came in contact with.

"I remember the very first major league game I went to. I went to Detroit when they were playing Cleveland. It's almost as if the frame is frozen. I remember Herb Score hitting fungoes to the outfielders and Bob Lemon hitting fungoes to the infielders. I can't describe the feeling. It was a magic moment. Once you get into pro ball it loses some of the magic it had as a fan. I don't know if it has the same magic for the kids today, but I imagine it does. Everybody's got an imagination. You see yourself doing it. I used to go to sleep at night and see myself pitching in the big leagues."

Archie Moore spent the entire 1964 season with the Yankees as a protected first year player, rarely leaving the bench and batting only 23 times all year. He was called up at the end of the 1965 season for a few games, but never again played in the major leagues. "I'm really kind of sorry that I didn't have a better career or a longer career," he said. "Maybe it just wasn't meant to be. But I was grateful. I had some great experiences and it's something I look back on with a measure of fondness. I certainly don't feel that I was denied anything. I felt I was given an opportunity. I never thought that baseball was going to be my life."

Billy Short opened the 1960 season in the Yankee starting rotation, before an elbow injury resulted in his demotion to Richmond. For the rest of his career, he struggled with his injury, and never fulfilled the prediction that he would be another Whitey Ford. Short pitched in six major league seasons between 1960 and 1969, and ended his career with a 5-11 record in 73 games. "I don't think I would have changed a whole lot," Short said. "It was a great, great time in my life. I enjoyed baseball so much. I never made any money and really didn't care. I just enjoyed the game."

Several Hall of Famers played for the Yankees during the 1960s. As Andy Warhol pointed out, however, everyone has their fifteen minutes of fame, and many New York players who did not have the stature of Mantle, Ford, or Berra achieved notoriety for a lesser known, but equally precious achievement.

- *Jim Pisoni*: "I saw the last ball ever hit out of the park in St. Louis against the Browns. Jungle Jim Rivera hit it in the ninth inning and beat us. The ball went right over my head."

- *Tom Metcalf*: "Dick Gephardt was my roommate at Northwestern. He was at law school at the University of Michigan while I was playing with the Yankees. When we played the Tigers at Detroit he called me and wanted to come to the ballgame. I hadn't seen Gephardt in about two years. I got him the tickets and after the game he came back to the hotel with me. He was an avid Cardinal fan and a great admirer of Red Schoendienst. We used to kid him because he looked a lot like Schoendienst.

  "I didn't hang out with Mantle and Ford and those guys. They were ten years older than me and besides, there was a little disparity in accomplishments. I was standing in front of the hotel talking to Gephardt, when Mantle and Ford walked out the door and asked me what we were doing. We didn't have any plans. They said, 'C'mon, we're going down the street to celebrate Whitey's 20th win.' We went to a real blue collar place. There was an elbow in the bar. I was sitting on the end, Gephardt was next to me at the elbow and then there was Mantle and Ford. Ford and Mantle were talking, and once in a while they'd say something to me. During the entire time, I never had a conversation with Gephardt because he had his back turned to me watching those guys talk. When we were walking back to the hotel, he said, 'God, I feel awful. I know I ignored you, but I can't tell you how thrilled I was just sitting there listening to those two guys talk.'

  "When Dick ran for President in 1988, he asked me to help him raise money. I told him I was a Republican and didn't know any Democrats. Then I said, 'When you become President, I expect an invitation to the White House, and when we're having dinner, I want to be seated right next to Gorbachov. I hope you won't mind if I don't pay much attention to you during dinner because I learned that trick from you.'"

- *Dick Schofield* was a bonus player who, under the prevailing rules, was required to spend two years on the Cardinals' roster. Fresh out of high school, he joined the Cardinals in 1953. On June 25, he threw a towel from the bench and was given the thumb by umpire Augie Donatelli, being ejected from a major league game before he ever played in one.

- *Bobby Shantz* was the first major league pitcher ever to suffer a defeat at the hands of a Japanese team.

- *Danny McDevitt* pitched a five hit shutout and beat the Pirates 2–0 in the last game ever played in Ebbets Field.

• While pitching for the Kansas City Athletics in 1964, *Bob Meyer* hurled a one hitter against the Baltimore Orioles, but lost the game 1–0. He also established a major league record when the Orioles had only 19 official at bats in a full game. How can there be just 19 official at bats in a game when there must be 27 outs? The game was played in Baltimore, and with the Orioles leading, they didn't bat in he bottom of the ninth, reducing the total number of outs to 24. Three outs were recorded on sacrifice bunts, which don't count as official at bats, and one more on a sacrifice fly. Meyer walked six, and one was erased on a double play, which reduced the Orioles to nineteen official at bats in a nine inning game, besting the mark set by the Detroit Tigers on April 27, 1915.

The past always seems sweeter with the passage of time. Good times are remembered while the bad tends to be consigned to oblivion. Many thanks are due these old Yankees for sharing the good times.

Bibliography

Allen, Maury. *Roger Maris: A Man for All Seasons.* New York: Donald I. Fine, 1986.
_____. *You Could Look It Up: The Life of Casey Stengel.* New York: Times Books, 1979.
Angell, Roger. *The Summer Game.* New York: Viking, 1972.
Basche, Phillip. *Dog Days: The New York Yankees' Fall from Grace and Return to Glory, 1964–1976.* New York: Random House, 1994.
Brosnan, Jim. *The Long Season.* New York: Harper and Row, 1960.
Clendenon, Donn. *Miracle in New York.* Sioux Falls, SD: Pennmarch, 1999.
Durocher, Leo, with Ed Linn. *Nice Guys Finish Last.* New York: Simon and Schuster, 1975.
Golenbock, Peter. *Dynasty.* Englewood Cliffs, NJ: Prentice Hall, 1975.
Houk, Ralph, with Robert Creamer. *Season of Glory.* New York: Pocket, 1988.
Houk, Ralph, with Charles Dexter. *Ballplayers are Human, Too.* New York: Putnam, 1962.
Kahn, Roger. *The Boys of Summer.* New York: Harper and Row, 1971.
Keene, Kerry. *1960, The Last Pure Season.* Champaign, IL: Sports Publishing, 2000.
Kelley, Brent P. *They Too Wore Pinstripes.* Jefferson, NC: McFarland, 1998.
Kiersh, Edward. *Where Have You Gone, Vince Dimaggio?* New York: Bantam, 1983.
Kuenster, John. *Heartbreakers.* Chicago: Ivan R. Dee, 2001.
Mann, Jack. *The Decline and Fall of the New York Yankees.* New York: Simon and Schuster, 1967.
Mantle, Mickey, with Herb Gluck. *The Mick.* Garden City, NY: Doubleday, 1985.
Pepitone, Joe, with Berry Stainback. *Joe, You Coulda Made Us Proud.* Chicago: Playboy Press, 1975.
Schecter, Leonard. *Once Upon the Polo Grounds.* New York: Dial, 1970.

Newspapers

Meriden Record Journal 1965
New York Daily News, 1960–1969
New York Newsday, 1960–1969
New York Post, 1960–1969
New York Times, 1959–1969
Richmond Virginian 1964

Periodicals

The Sporting News
Sports Illustrated

Many of the details in the sad tale of Joe Pepitone, the subject of Chapter One, are discussed at greater length in Pepitone's autobiography, *Joe, You Coulda Made Us Proud.* My primary source of information about Mel Stottlemyre's exploits in the International League in 1964 was the *Richmond Virginian.* Maury Allen's biography of Roger Maris was very helpful for background information on the Yankee slugger, and Mickey Mantle's autobiography yielded the information on Mickey's salary history. The brief excerpts from Bill Veeck's *The Hustler's Handbook,* regarding the tale of intrigue in St. Louis in 1964, were first printed in *Sports Illustrated.*

Index

251